DATE DUE

JAN 3 1 2007	
NOV 1 0 2007	
APR 0 7 2008	
MAY 1 1 2013	

Grasping the Nettle

Grasping the Nettle

Analyzing Cases of Intractable Conflict

Chester A. Crocker,
Fen Osler Hampson,
and Pamela Aall

UNITED STATES INSTITUTE OF PEACE PRESS
Washington, D.C.

The views expressed in this book are those of the authors alone. They do not necessarily reflect views of the United States Institute of Peace.

UNITED STATES INSTITUTE OF PEACE
1200 17th Street NW, Suite 200
Washington, DC 20036-3011

First published 2005

Printed in the United States of America

The paper used in this publication meets the minimum requirements of American National Standards for Information Science—Permanence of Paper for Printed Library Materials, ANSI Z39.48-1984.

Library of Congress Cataloging-in-Publication Data

Crocker, Chester A.
    Grasping the nettle : analyzing cases of intractable conflict / Chester A. Crocker, Fen Osler Hampson, and Pamela Aall.
       p. cm.
    Includes bibliographical references and index.
    ISBN 1-929223-61-7 (alk. paper) — ISBN 1-929223-60-9 (pbk. : alk. paper)
       1. War. 2. War—Case studies. 3. Mediation, International. 4. International relations. I. Hampson, Fen Osler. II. Aall, Pamela R. III. Title.

    JZ6385.C76 2005
    327.1'6—dc22

                      2004054915

Contents

Foreword   ix
Richard H. Solomon

Preface   xiii

Contributors   xvii

The Intractable Conflicts Experts Group   xxiii

1. Introduction: Mapping the Nettle Field   3
   Chester A. Crocker, Fen Osler Hampson, Pamela Aall

Understanding Intractability

2. Comparative Studies of Long Wars   33
   Roy Licklider

3. Analyzing Intractability   47
   I. William Zartman

4. Nature, Dynamics, and Phases of Intractability   65
   Louis Kriesberg

5. Mediation in the Most Resistant Cases   99
   Jacob Bercovitch

6. Negotiating Intractable Conflicts:
   The Contributions of Unofficial Intermediaries   123
   Diana Chigas

Cases of Intractable Conflict

7. Can Sudan Escape Its Intractability?   161
   J. Stephen Morrison and Alex de Waal

8. Intractability and Third-Party Mediation in the Balkans 183
   Steven L. Burg

9. Angola: The End of an Intractable Conflict   209
   Paul Hare

10. Third Parties and Intractable Conflicts:
    The Case of Colombia   231
    Cynthia J. Arnson and Teresa Whitfield

11. The Uses of Deadlock: Intractability in Eurasia   269
    Charles King

12. Kashmir: Fifty Years of Running in Place   295
    Howard B. Schaffer and Teresita C. Schaffer

13. "Intractable" Confrontation on the Korean Peninsula:
    A Contribution to Regional Stability?   319
    Scott Snyder

14. Intractability and the Israeli-Palestinian Conflict   343
    Stephen Cohen

15. Beyond Resolution? The Palestinian-Israeli Conflict   357
    Shibley Telhami

When Endless Conflicts End

16. Conclusion: From Intractable to Tractable—
    the Outlook and Implications for Third Parties   375
    Chester A. Crocker, Fen Osler Hampson, and Pamela Aall

    Index   387

Foreword

SHORTLY AFTER THE DISASTROUS EVENTS of September 11, 2001, the United States Institute of Peace convened a meeting of scholars and practitioners to focus on the special challenge of ending intractable conflicts. The participants were individuals with deep knowledge of international conflicts and a driving interest in promoting ways to manage and resolve them. Collectively, these specialists had studied or been directly involved in efforts to deal with many—indeed, probably the majority—of the most obstinate conflicts of the past thirty years: Angola, Cambodia, Central America, Colombia, Cyprus, Iraq, the Balkans, Indonesia, Kashmir, Korea, the Middle East, Nigeria, the Philippines, Somalia, Southern Africa, Sri Lanka, and Sudan. Over the next two years, this group grappled with the complexities of mediation in intractable conflicts. Along the way they developed important insights about when and why third-party interventions can help—or hinder—the movement toward peace in such cases.

Grasping the Nettle: Analyzing Cases of Intractable Conflict gathers the thoughtful and significant lessons that emerged from the deliberations of the experts group. As we examined cases, we saw intractable conflicts trapped—or embedded—in larger geopolitical circumstances. The conflict between the two Koreas, for instance, was reinforced by the clash between East and West during the Cold War. But we also saw that the end of the Cold War did not bring peace to Northeast Asia. The long-running conflict had hardened identities and made reconciliation politically or economically unpalatable or—in the case of the North—a self-destructive option for the leadership.

It became clear that the source of a conflict's intractability was often quite different from the original source of the conflict. We found that the local culture of a conflict could play an important role in sustaining the

confrontation. In the Middle East, for example, antagonists are locked
into conflict by virtue of a "culture of revenge" or a "culture of no compromise," which produces an unending cycle of clash and counterclash. In
certain circumstances, the international community and the conflicting parties themselves prefer to manage the confrontation rather than resolve it.
In the case of separatist strife in Eurasia since the collapse of the Soviet
Union, for instance, self-determination conflicts have brought benefits to
the major contestants, and the international community has not mustered
sufficient political will and resources to force a resolution of the disputes.
Moreover, since 9/11 we have seen a clear link between these intractable
conflicts and the global security threat of terrorism. Many of these conflicts
have occurred in states such as Sudan, Pakistan, and Colombia that have
either failed as effective political systems or are in danger of doing so. These
regions of dispute provide safe havens and an army of recruits for terrorists and transnational criminals. 9/11 highlighted for the world the daunt-
ing fact that intractable conflicts—even those that take place in remote
places—can provide grave threats to the national security of distant states
and international order.

It was, however, the relationship between third-party interventions
and intractable conflicts that focused the experts group's deliberations.
Given that the members of the group, together with the United States
Institute of Peace, are strong proponents of the value of negotiating as a
vehicle for conflict management, the topic of how third-party peacemakers
might transform a conflict's intractability was a critical issue. The group
thought it was important to recognize the serious damage that could be
caused by promoting a peacemaking effort that fails. Mediated accords
that are not implemented may lead to cynicism, mistrust, and resistance
to future efforts. Such was the case in Angola, Columbia, and Sudan. Prolonged third-party pressure to reach a settlement may inadvertently create
resistance to mediation, harden public opinion, and result in the promotion
of mutually exclusive preconditions for negotiations. Such has been the
case in the Middle East. Poor planning and uncoordinated diplomacy may
polarize positions and diminish hopes for a future settlement, such as in
the Great Lakes crisis in Central Africa. Inevitably, such failures lead to
more bloodshed and human suffering.

While the dangers of exacerbating intractability through third-party
intervention are real, they are overshadowed by the dangers of inaction,

which can see a conflict fester in the absence of responsible third-party engagement—a point made by this book's companion volume, *Taming Intractable Conflicts: Mediation in the Hardest Cases.* The experience of the International Commission in Northern Ireland (led by former Senator George Mitchell) points out the invaluable role that mediators can play in helping hostile antagonists become negotiating partners, however reluctant. Equally, the efforts of the Norwegians in Sri Lanka in recent years, the United Nations in El Salvador and Guatemala in the 1980s and 1990s, the United States in Cambodia in the early 1990s, and the Community of Sant'Egidio in Mozambique from the 1970s into the 1990s support the argument that a helping hand offered by the right intermediary at the right time can change the course of a protracted conflict.

How do we determine when third-party interventions in intractable conflicts are likely to either facilitate a negotiation or create additional obstacles to peace? Only in recent years have diplomats, scholars, and policymakers begun developing robust theories and methodologies that attempt to deal with ancient hatreds and ongoing conflict. Given the relative infancy of the field of conflict resolution studies and despite advances in other areas of the field, no clear-cut answer yet exists to this strikingly salient question. But by examining this issue both theoretically and through practical case-based analyses, this volume's editors, Chester A. Crocker, Fen Osler Hampson, and Pamela Aall, and its highly respected cast of contributors have created a work that should have an immediate impact on the way third-party interventions in intractable conflicts are conceived, designed, and implemented.

The excellent essays and case studies in *Grasping the Nettle* provide a wealth of material on differing conceptual approaches to understanding intractability and the differing ways that intractability has manifested itself in specific conflicts. Together with *Taming Intractable Conflicts,* this book also provides useful insights into the tradecraft of third-party intervention in such conflicts. *Grasping the Nettle* joins other Institute publications—from tightly focused special reports to dozens of volumes with a broad-ranging, even panoramic, purview—in addressing the causes and dynamics of contemporary violent conflict and in exploring the ways in which such conflict can be prevented, managed, or resolved. For instance, the Institute has published a series of country-specific studies of negotiating behavior spotlighting the bargaining behavior of negotiators from China, Japan,

North Korea, Russia, Germany, and France. The Institute's book catalog also includes two volumes that, like *Grasping the Nettle*, have been piloted by the editorial trio of Crocker, Hampson, and Aall: *Turbulent Peace*, a comprehensive survey of the challenges of managing contemporary international conflict; and *Herding Cats*, which draws on firsthand accounts by eminent diplomats who explore the problems and opportunities presented by a multiplicity of mediators. *Grasping the Nettle* is a worthy addition to this record of rich experience and accomplishment, furthering our understanding of intractable conflicts while fueling the hope that even the most obstinate confrontation may yield to skillful intervention structured around a combination of invention, wisdom, and pragmatism.

RICHARD H. SOLOMON, PRESIDENT
UNITED STATES INSTITUTE OF PEACE

Preface

AMONG AESOP'S MANY FABLES is one about a young boy who encountered a stinging nettle, a wild perennial that grows in fields and woods in Europe and parts of Canada and the United States. Upon any contact, even of the lightest variety, these nettles can release an acid that irritates the skin and causes a rash. In the fable, the boy runs home to his mother and complains about the pain he feels from just touching the plant inadvertently. The mother answers that rather than brushing the plant, he should seize it firmly and "it will be soft as silk to your hand, and not in the least hurt you." In other words, he should grasp the nettle with all his might.

In reality, however, opinion seems to be divided on whether this is the optimum response. Many claim that the pain is just as bad—if not worse—if you grab and hold the nettle tightly. Others agree with the mother in the fable that a superficial engagement will hurt more than a powerful one. But in the end, most people would prefer not to test these hypotheses, opting instead to avoid the problem altogether.

We thought that this fable provided an apt metaphor for third-party interaction with intractable conflicts. Like nettles, intractable conflicts will cause pain to anyone who touches them. Most potential intervenors would prefer to avoid tangling with these conflicts. They may do this out of a sense that it is not in their national or institutional interest to become involved. Or they may believe that some conflicts cannot be settled politically until the parties are completely exhausted, and that the only way to handle these conflicts is to let them burn themselves out. If potential intervenors do become involved, they often react to the excruciating encounter by dropping the conflict and returning home to nurse the pain. Only a few mediators act with such determined commitment that they are in fact able to help the parties reach a negotiated agreement, or at least another stage in the journey. Despite the pain, they are willing to grasp the nettle with all their might in order to reach peace.

Grasping the nettle does not mean applying force as part of the peacemaking process. Some who have grasped the nettle have used a gentle approach, as Norway has done in Sri Lanka. Others, such as the United States on the Korean peninsula, have used force and the threat of force to bring order and quell conflict. And still others, such as the United Nations in Cyprus, have tried both approaches, using peacekeeping troops to freeze the conflict while engaging politically with the two parties in order to encourage them to settle their differences. Grasping the nettle does not guarantee success. In many cases, third-party intervention has failed to eradicate the conflict, in spite of the dedication and commitment of the outside party. And in some cases, it seems that the third parties, while trying to act as peacemakers, have in fact added to the conflict's intractability. In other cases, however, this determined engagement has worked. The 1978 Egyptian-Israeli accord brokered at Camp David, the 1992 peace agreement that ended the civil war in Mozambique, and the Good Friday Agreement that transformed the conflict in Northern Ireland, for instance, confirm that third parties can play a crucial role in helping conflicts come to a negotiated end.

In light of these different experiences, it seemed that a hard look at the interaction between outside peacemakers and intractable conflicts would yield some lessons about when third parties could help and when their interventions were likely to fail, become protracted, or even make things worse. To get to the heart of these issues, the United States Institute of Peace convened an intractable conflicts experts group that met periodically from October 2001 to April 2003 to consider the nature of intractability and to examine specific cases of third-party interaction in intractable conflicts. Through the experts group, we were able to gather together in one room a wealth of academic and practitioner expertise. Members included Morton Abramowitz, Pauline Baker, Jacob Bercovitch, Diana Chigas, Jan Eliasson, Melanie Greenberg, Paul Hare, Bruce Jentleson, Richard Kauzlarich, Louis Kriesberg, Samuel Lewis, Roy Licklider, William Nash, Charles Nelson, Joyce Neu, Meghan O'Sullivan, Marina Ottaway, Robert Pastor, Harold Saunders, Teresita Schaffer, Stephen Solarz, Richard Solomon, Paul Stares, Stephen Stedman, and William Zartman. Several members of the group—Jacob Bercovitch, Diana Chiagas, Paul Hare, Louis Kriesberg, Roy Licklider, Tezi Schaffer, and Bill Zartman—wrote chapters for this book, and all members of the group added to our understanding of the complexities of the topic. In order to gain a fuller sense of actual cases, we asked several outstanding experts—including Cynthia Arnson, Steven Burg, Stephen P. Cohen, Alex de Waal, Charles King, Stephen Morrison, Howard Schaffer, Scott Snyder, Shibley Telhami, and Teresa Whitfield—to reflect on the nature and dynamics of intractability in the specific cases of Angola, the Balkans, Colombia, Eurasia, Kashmir, Korea, the Middle East, and Sudan. The discussion of the experts group, whether centering on theory or on case studies, was always wide-ranging, creative, informed, and inspiring. The outcome of this discussion is reflected in all of the chapters of the book, most specifically in the introduction and conclusion.

Grasping the Nettle is a companion volume to *Taming Intractable Conflicts: Mediation in the Hardest Cases,* a book that also emerged from the experts group meetings. Whereas *Grasping the Nettle* attempts to marry theoretical approaches to intractability and the evidence emerging from specific cases, *Taming Intractable Conflicts* has a more practical focus, concentrating on third-party tradecraft in protracted conflicts. Both books add to a long list of United States Institute of Peace publications on third-party intervention.

Many people have helped make this effort a success. First and foremost is Richard Solomon, president of the United States Institute of Peace, whose leadership throughout the project supported and encouraged us, as did his contributions as a member of the experts group. Raina Kim made the meetings happen and handled all sorts of issues with her usual aplomb and grace. Naren Kumarakulasingam shared with us both enthusiasm for the project and wisdom gained from direct experience with the Sri Lankan conflict, helping us capture the essence of the discussions. Jon Alterman, Dipankar Banerjee, Judy Barsalou, Francis Deng, Bill Drennan, Ron Fisher, Roy Gutman, Jeff Helsing, Harriet Hentges, Farooq Kathwari, Nancy Lubin, Philip Mattar, Joe Montville, Martha Olcott, Robin Raphel, Steve Riskin, Daniel Serwer, David Smock, Marie Smyth, George Ward, and Tom Weston all offered valuable perspectives. The publications program, under the leadership of Dan Snodderly and Michael Graham, once again did an excellent job in the production of this book. And, as always, we owe a deep debt of gratitude to Nigel Quinney, gifted editor and wonderful colleague, for his creative and careful work in making this book come to life.

Contributors

Chester A. Crocker is the James R. Schlesinger Professor of Strategic Studies at Georgetown University and former chairman of the board of directors of the United States Institute of Peace. From 1981 to 1989 he was assistant secretary of state for African affairs; as such, he was the principal diplomatic architect and mediator in the prolonged negotiations among Angola, Cuba, and South Africa that led to Namibia's transition to democratic governance and independence, and to the withdrawal of Cuban forces from Angola. He is the author of *High Noon in Southern Africa: Making Peace in a Rough Neighborhood,* coauthor (with Fen Osler Hampson and Pamela Aall) of *Taming Intractable Conflicts: Mediation in the Hardest Cases,* and coeditor of *Turbulent Peace: The Challenges of Managing International Conflict; Managing Global Chaos: Sources of and Responses to International Conflict; African Conflict Resolution: The U.S. Role in Peacemaking;* and *Herding Cats: Multiparty Mediation in a Complex World.* He is also an adviser on strategy and negotiation to U.S. and European firms.

Fen Osler Hampson is professor of international affairs at and director of the Norman Paterson School of International Affairs, Carleton University, Ottawa, Canada. He is the author of five books, including *Nurturing Peace: Why Peace Settlements Succeed or Fail,* and coeditor or coauthor of twenty others, including *Turbulent Peace: The Challenges of Managing International Conflict; Managing Global Chaos: Sources of and Responses to International Conflict;* and *Herding Cats: Multiparty Mediation in a Complex World.* His recent books include *Madness in the Multitude: Human Security and World Disorder* and *Taming Intractable Conflicts: Mediation in the Hardest Cases* (with Chester A. Crocker and Pamela Aall). Hampson was a senior fellow at the United States Institute of Peace in 1993–94. He is chair of the

Human Security Track of the Helsinki Process on Globalization and Democracy, a joint initiative of the governments of Finland and Tanzania.

Pamela Aall is director of the Education Program at the United States Institute of Peace. Before joining the Institute, she worked for the President's Committee on the Arts and the Humanities, the Institute of International Education, the Rockefeller Foundation, the European Cultural Foundation, and the International Council for Educational Development. She is also president of Women in International Security. She is coeditor of *Turbulent Peace: The Challenges of Managing International Conflict; Managing Global Chaos: Sources of and Responses to International Conflict;* and *Herding Cats: Multiparty Mediation in a Complex World.* She is coauthor (with Daniel Miltenberger and Thomas G. Weiss) of *Guide to IGOs, NGOs, and the Military in Peace and Relief Operations* and (with Chester A. Crocker and Fen Osler Hampson) of *Taming Intractable Conflicts: Mediation in the Hardest Cases.*

❑   ❑   ❑

Cynthia J. Arnson is deputy director of the Latin American Program of the Woodrow Wilson International Center for Scholars. She is editor of *Comparative Peace Processes in Latin America* (1999) and author of *Crossroads: Congress, the President, and Central America, 1976–1993* (2d ed., 1993). Arnson is a member of the editorial advisory board of *Foreign Affairs en Español* and a member of the advisory board of Human Rights Watch/Americas, where she previously served as associate director.

Jacob Bercovitch is professor of international relations and head of the School of Political Science at the University of Canterbury in Christchurch, New Zealand. His main research interests are in the areas of international conflict resolution and mediation, areas in which he has published very widely. His most recent book is *Regional Guide to International Conflict* (with J. Fretter), published by Congressional Quarterly in 2004. He was a senior fellow at the United States Institute of Peace in 2002.

Steven L. Burg is Adlai E. Stevenson Professor of International Politics, Brandeis University. His most recent book, coauthored with Paul S. Shoup,

The War in Bosnia-Herzegovina: Ethnic Conflict and International Intervention (1999), was awarded the year 2000 Ralph J. Bunche Prize of the American Political Science Association for "the best scholarly work in political science which explores the phenomenon of ethnic and cultural pluralism." He is currently at work on a comparative analysis of ethnic conflict.

Diana Chigas is codirector of the Reflecting on Peace Practice project at CDA–Collaborative Learning Projects. She also teaches negotiation and conflict resolution at the Fletcher School of Law and Diplomacy. Before joining CDA, she served as vice president, regional director for Europe and the former Soviet Union, and director of research and evaluation at Conflict Management Group, where she facilitated dialogue and problem solving in Cyprus, Georgia and South Ossetia, El Salvador, and South Africa.

Stephen P. Cohen is a leader in the practice and theory of track-two diplomacy, in which he works behind the scenes in bringing Arabs and Israelis together. In 1979, he founded the Institute for Middle East Peace and Development to serve as facilitator and private intermediary in peacemaking and has served as its president ever since. He is a National Scholar of the Israel Policy Forum and has been a visiting professor at Princeton University and Lehigh University.

Alex de Waal is a writer and activist on African issues. In his twenty-year career, he has studied the social, political, and health dimensions of famine, war, genocide, and the HIV/AIDS epidemic, especially in the Horn of Africa and the Great Lakes region. He has been at the forefront of mobilizing African and international responses to these problems. He is the author of *Famine That Kills: Darfur, Sudan, 1984–5* (revised ed., 2004) and *Islamism and Its Enemies in the Horn* (2004).

Paul J. Hare was a senior fellow at the United States Institute of Peace in 1996–97 and is now executive director of the United States–Angola Chamber of Commerce. A career officer of the U.S. Foreign Service, he served as the U.S. special representative for the Angolan peace process from 1993 to 1998. He is the author of *Angola's Last Best Chance for Peace: An Insider's Account of the Peace Process* (1998).

Charles King is associate professor of foreign service and government at Georgetown University. His books include *The Black Sea: A History* (2004) and *The Moldovans: Romania, Russia, and the Politics of Culture* (2000).

Louis Kriesberg is Professor Emeritus of Sociology, Maxwell Professor Emeritus of Social Conflict Studies, and founding director of the Program on the Analysis and Resolution of Conflicts (1986–94) at Syracuse University. In addition to writing more than 150 book chapters and articles, he has authored *Constructive Conflicts* (2d ed., 2003) and *International Conflict Resolution* (1992) and has coedited *Intractable Conflicts and Their Transformation* (1989) and *Timing the De-escalation of International Conflicts* (1991).

Roy Licklider is professor of political science at Rutgers University, specializing in foreign policy and international relations. His books include *The Private Nuclear Strategists, Political Power and the Arab Oil Weapon,* and *Stopping the Killing: How Civil Wars End.* For the past several years his research has been on civil war termination, investigating how people who have been killing one another with considerable skill and enthusiasm can (sometimes) form working political communities.

J. Stephen Morrison directs the CSIS Africa Program and leads the CSIS Task Force on HIV/AIDS. He served in 2003–4 as executive secretary of the Africa Policy Advisory Board, authorized by Congress and appointed by Secretary of State Colin Powell. Its final report, *Rising U.S. Stakes in Africa: Seven Proposals to Strengthen U.S.-Africa Policy,* includes an analysis of the implementation challenges Sudan will face following the signature of a final negotiated peace accord.

Howard B. Schaffer is a retired U.S. Foreign Service officer. He served as ambassador to Bangladesh, political counselor in both India and Pakistan, and deputy assistant secretary of state for South Asia. He now teaches at Georgetown University, where he is deputy director of the Institute for the Study of Diplomacy. Schaffer has published two biographies of American statesmen, *Chester Bowles: New Dealer in the Cold War* and *Ellsworth Bunker, Global Troubleshooter, Vietnam Hawk.*

Teresita C. Schaffer heads a program of policy research and analysis on South Asia at the Center for Strategic and International Studies in Washington, D.C. Her thirty-year diplomatic career included postings at the U.S. embassies in Islamabad and New Delhi and as ambassador to Sri Lanka. Her writings include *Rising India and U.S. Policy Options in Asia* and *Pakistan's Future and U.S. Policy Options.*

Scott Snyder is a senior associate in the international relations program of the Asia Foundation and Pacific Forum CSIS. Previously, he was the Asia Foundation's representative in Korea, program officer in the Research and Studies Program of the United States Institute of Peace, and acting director of the Asia Society's Contemporary Affairs Program. He is co-editor, with L. Gordon Flake, of *Paved with Good Intentions: The NGO Experience in North Korea* (2003) and author of *Negotiating on the Edge: North Korean Negotiating Behavior* (1999).

Shibley Telhami is the Anwar Sadat Professor for Peace and Development at the University of Maryland, College Park, and nonresident senior fellow at the Saban Center at the Brookings Institution. His most recent book is *The Stakes: America in the Middle East.* He is a member of the Council on Foreign Relations and serves on the board of Human Rights Watch.

Teresa Whitfield is a visiting fellow at New York University's Center on International Cooperation, where she is researching a book on the United Nations and conflict resolution. She served from 1995 to 2000 in the United Nations' Department of Political Affairs and from 2001 to 2002 as acting director of the Conflict Prevention and Peace Forum. Her publications include *Paying the Price: Ignacio Ellacuría and the Murdered Jesuits of El Salvador* (1994).

I. William Zartman is Jacob Blaustein Distinguished Professor of International Organization and Conflict Resolution and director of the Conflict

Management Program at the Nitze School of Advanced International Studies (SAIS) of the Johns Hopkins University. He is author of a number of works on negotiation, including *The Practical Negotiator* (1982), *Ripe for Resolution* (1989), *Elusive Peace* (1995), *Preventive Negotiations* (2001), and *Cowardly Lions: Missed Opportunities to Prevent Deadly Conflict and State Collapse* (forthcoming).

The Intractable Conflicts Experts Group

The following individuals were members of the experts group convened by the United States Institute of Peace to examine intractable conflicts. The group met between October 2001 and April 2003.

Pamela Aall, Director, Education Program, United States Institute of Peace

Morton L. Abramowitz, Senior Fellow, The Century Foundation

Pauline H. Baker, President, Fund for Peace

Jacob Bercovitch, Professor of International Relations, University of Canterbury, Christchurch

Chester A. Crocker, James R. Schlesinger Professor of Strategic Studies, Georgetown University

Diana Chigas, Codirector, Reflecting on Peace Practice Project, Collaborative for Development Action

Jan Eliasson, Ambassador, Embassy of Sweden

Melanie Greenberg, Visiting Scholar, Nitze School of Advanced International Studies, The Johns Hopkins University

Paul J. Hare, Executive Director, U.S.-Angola Chamber of Commerce

Fen Osler Hampson, Director, Norman Paterson School of International Affairs, Carleton University

Bruce W. Jentleson, Director, Terry Sanford Institute of Public Policy, Duke University

Louis Kriesberg, Maxwell Professor Emeritus of Social Conflict Studies, Syracuse University

Samuel W. Lewis, Member, American Academy of Diplomacy

Roy Licklider, Professor of Political Science, Rutgers University

William L. Nash, Director, Center for Preventive Action, Council on Foreign Relations

Charles E. Nelson, Vice President, United States Institute of Peace

Joyce Neu, Executive Director, Joan B. Kroc Institute for Peace and Justice, University of San Diego

Meghan O'Sullivan, Member, Policy Planning Staff, Department of State

Marina S. Ottaway, Senior Associate, Carnegie Endowment for International Peace

Robert A. Pastor, Vice President of International Affairs, American University

Harold H. Saunders, Director, International Affairs, Kettering Foundation

Teresita C. Schaffer, Director, South Asia Program, Center for Strategic and International Studies

Stephen J. Solarz, President, Solarz Associates

Richard H. Solomon, President, United States Institute of Peace

Paul Stares, Director of Research and Studies, United States Institute of Peace

Stephen John Stedman, Senior Research Scholar, Center for International Security and Cooperation, Stanford University

I. William Zartman, Jacob Blaustein Distinguished Professor of International Organization and Conflict Resolution, Nitze School of Advanced International Studies, The Johns Hopkins University

Grasping the Nettle

1

Introduction

Mapping the Nettle Field

Chester A. Crocker,
Fen Osler Hampson,
and Pamela R. Aall

IN THE MINDS OF MANY the end of the Cold War was supposed to halt the torrent of conflict that characterized the twentieth century, the bloodiest century in history. Instead, it unleashed or unmasked a dozen conflicts in Africa, Asia, Europe, and Latin America. Although a number of these conflicts—Cambodia, El Salvador, Guatemala, Mozambique, and Namibia—were settled during the late 1980s and 1990s, others proved resistant to resolution. In the Middle East, in spite of almost five decades of peacemaking by the United States and other third parties, the conflict between Israelis and Palestinians continued, with recurring outbreaks of violence and terrorism hardening public opinion on both sides and threatening regional stability.

In Sri Lanka a civil war marked by ongoing violence and terrorism eluded efforts to negotiate a durable cease-fire between the Sinhalese-dominated government in the south and the insurgent Tamil guerrilla movement in the north. The territories of Jammu and Kashmir, which sit on the northern border between India and Pakistan, have also experienced an ongoing war of attrition since the mid-1960s, because of a seemingly irreconcilable border dispute between the two countries. Africa has seen ongoing conflict in Burundi, Côte d'Ivoire, the Democratic Republic of

Congo, Rwanda, Sierra Leone, Somalia, Sudan, Uganda, and—until recently—Liberia. In Latin America, which did reap a peace dividend with the end of authoritarian rule and the transition to democracy in the 1980s, some countries continue to experience major social and political upheaval and violence, most notably Colombia, where, since the 1960s, various guerrilla groups have waged war against the government. And Europe, too, has seen long-enduring conflicts, most notably in the Balkans and Northern Ireland.[1]

These and other long conflicts have been called intractable, protracted, self-sustaining, deep-rooted, the product of ancient hatreds. Much intellectual effort has been devoted to studying their origins, causes, and consequences. Many of these conflicts—though obviously not all—have also been the subject of prolonged and sustained international efforts to end them, including diplomacy, mediation, military intervention, peacekeeping, and humanitarian and development assistance. However, they continue to resist any kind of settlement or resolution.

The events of September 11, 2001, demonstrate that there are real risks in allowing these intractable conflicts to fester. Many of these hot zones are home to insurgent groups and other political movements that have powerful incentives and growing capacity to build global networks to project their power and influence. Some of these groups have purely local targets for their violence. Others, as evidenced by Osama bin Laden's activities, intend to cause global chaos in pursuit of their objectives. The combination of a struggle for power, disputed governance, a need for revenue, a demand for arms, and war-hardened ruthlessness creates fetid breeding grounds for all sorts of illicit phenomena: terrorism, illegal weapons proliferation, drug smuggling, forced labor, money laundering—a long list of hard-to-control activities that affect the world far beyond the boundaries of the conflict. To state this another way, it is not very helpful to rank conflicts in an A, B, and C list according to the importance of the countries in which they occur. As we have seen in the past few years, C-list countries can produce an A list of trouble.[2]

The Meaning of Intractability

Many scholars, analysts, and practitioners have tried to define the complex nature of intractability.[3] The experts group of academics and practitioners brought together by the United States Institute of Peace for periodic discussions between October 2001 and April 2003 recognized that the term "intractable" is often understood to refer to a conflict that is unresolvable rather than one that resists resolution. There was some concern among the group that even calling a conflict intractable introduced an element of inevitability, thereby affecting the attitudes and perceptions of the parties to the conflict and the third-party peacemakers. In the end, the group—and this book, which emerged from the group's meetings—settled on a very broad definition: intractable conflicts are conflicts that have persisted over time and refused to yield to efforts—through either direct negotiations by the parties or mediation with third-party assistance—to arrive at a political settlement.

Their resistance to a settlement may appear to derive from a single cause or principal ingredient, but closer examination usually points to multiple causes and many contributing factors. Whatever their source, intractable conflicts share a common characteristic: they defy settlement because leaders believe their objectives are fundamentally irreconcilable and parties have more interest in the hot war or cold stalemate than in any known alternative state of being. In other words, these local decision makers seek to resist or prevent the emergence of politics as the arena for settling their differences because they see their battle as a zero-sum game: what their opponent gains, they lose. In intractable conflicts armed parties enjoy relative autonomy to pursue their unilateral objectives. They are not accountable to anyone. Although intractable conflicts may share these characteristics, the actual level of violence and the potential for an escalation of military hostilities may vary from one setting to another. During its conflict, Angola experienced a high level of violence, while Northern Ireland had relatively few casualties in the long history of its sectarian strife. And the Middle East shows that levels of violence can escalate, de-escalate, and re-escalate over the lifetime of a conflict.

What Causes Intractability?

Understanding intractable conflicts starts with recognizing that sources of intractability are not the same as the original causes of the conflict, a point that Roy Licklider emphasizes in his chapter in this volume. No matter what issues formed the foundation for the initial conflict, a number of other elements will come into the mix to augment or even supplant the original disputes. Wars over time create new issues and agendas that were not present at the outset, including the way each side treats the other. For instance, the conflict in Kashmir is part of a larger set of bilateral conflict issues that have divided India and Pakistan since their joint emergence from the British Empire in the 1940s. Now, that agenda includes nuclear risk reduction and targeting/weaponization programs, trade/travel issues, other border issues, regional rivalries, and above all the identity dispute between Muslim homeland Pakistan and secular India. The bilateral issue agenda has ballooned with the passage of time, so that today Kashmir is much more deeply embedded in polarized issues than it was in the late 1940s.

Geography and geopolitics may also promote intractability, an observation that I. William Zartman makes in his chapter. Some states lie on the borderline between larger civilizations—Sudan between black and Arab Africa, and Kashmir between large Islamic and Hindu states. In other cases, neighboring wars may engulf a conflict, holding it captive to a resolution of the larger war, as Burundi's conflict was engulfed by the war in neighboring Congo. And many so-called internal patterns of enmity and amity are shaped by regional power distributions and specific factors such as border disputes, ethnic diasporas, ideological alignments, and neighboring states whose interests are served by continuing conflict.[4]

There are several schools of thought about the many causes of contemporary civil wars.[5] Intractable conflicts that take place within the borders of one country may be particularly resistant to settlement because of the nature of the conflict itself. These conflicts, manipulated as they may be by political agency entrepreneurs—or what Michael Brown calls "bad leaders" —often involve deep-seated identity and grievance issues as well as a considerable amount of war profiteering by representatives of one group or another.[6] Some analysts stress the role of poverty and the denial of basic human needs as key sources of conflict. The extent to which certain groups in society are systematically discriminated against and/or have their basic needs denied by those in power can lay the seeds for conflict, especially if there is no legitimate way to channel those grievances through the political process.[7]

In other cases, however, it is not internal instability that feeds intractability but rather a kind of stasis that develops around the fighting. For instance, a stable and tolerable stalemate makes it easy for sides to settle into comfortable accommodation with persistent warfare that sustains power bases. Continued war is a comfort zone that does not jeopardize either side's core constituency, even though those who suffer and pay the price for continued fighting—especially the civilian targets—are disenfranchised in every sense. For example, the fact that officials on both sides of the Eurasian cases—examined in Charles King's chapter—benefit from the conflict raises the question of whether there is such a thing as "happy" intractability, an untidy but possibly acceptable status quo. If there is, does this status quo provide a form of de facto conflict management that keeps the conflict at a low level? A variation on this theme occurs in some situations, illustrated well by the North Korean leadership regime. In North Korea, a culture of intractability has emerged in which elites seem comfortable only if they are in a steady state of conflict with a long-standing adversary, be it South Korea or the United States.

Intractability can also be the product of polarized, zero-sum notions of identity. Conflicts that continue over long periods lead to the accumulation of grievances incorporated into each party's version of history. Each side sees itself as a victim and creates or reinterprets key cultural and religious symbols that perpetuate both the sense of resentment and the conflict. In intractable conflicts, violence enters the everyday world of thousands of people and becomes a way of life. Conflict becomes institutionalized as vested interests rise in keeping the conflict going. Violence becomes the norm as parties become wedded to a logic and culture of violence and revenge. Young people who grow up in a conflict know no other way of life. As a population becomes inured to conflict, the hope that it will end recedes.

Domestic politics can also promote intractability. Lack of internal coherence in the parties can augment intractability, especially in democracies, as the conflict becomes part of campaign promises and political considerations create difficulties in making concessions. In his chapter on the Israeli-Palestinian conflict, Shibley Telhami suggests that violent reciprocity becomes normalized but cooperation does not because domestic politics blocks any move to cooperate. Among the general public, "there is an insidious belief on each side that not acting is worse than acting: that if one does not respond, the other side will interpret the lack of action as weakness and that the nonacting side will therefore be the target of more violence." In these situations, politicians often credibly claim that violence pays.

Another important factor in intractable conflict settings is the avarice of predatory warlords who profit from the political economy of violence through arms sales, smuggling, and other illicit commercial practices and transactions. As Paul Collier and others argue, it is clear that "conflict pays" in monetary as well as political terms.[8] And the dividends are such that those who are the chief beneficiaries of the war economy may have strong economic incentives to keep the conflict boiling. Nowhere is this more evident than in Angola and Sierra Leone, where civil wars have literally been paid for by the illicit sale of smuggled "blood" diamonds that have eventually found their way into regular commercial markets.

The failure of previous efforts can have a negative impact on possibilities for peacemaking. The discrediting of an "acceptable" agreement in an earlier phase of negotiation can force a solution off the table despite the fact that it may be the only "salient solution," as William Zartman argues in his chapter. A literature of accord becomes a weapon of political warfare, and agreements that are never implemented can lead to cynicism and resistance to peace initiatives. Several case studies in this book, including Angola, Colombia, and Sudan, give all-too-vivid illustrations of the deleterious result of missing opportunities and the price of failed peace agreements.

Changes in the way the parties to the conflict pursue their objectives through political channels can also serve to promote intractability. As parties gain experience in negotiation and in dealing with third parties, they develop a tendency to manipulate talks. A single party may simultaneously pursue very contradictory policies, sowing confusion among adversaries and third parties. Intentional misunderstandings between the parties may serve the purpose of papering over internal discord and factionalism. For this reason, parties may resist any outsider effort to make them clarify their goals. In some cases conflict parties become more purposeful and strategic in their behavior than the intervening third parties. In Bosnia the conflict parties viewed third-party mediation as an opportunity for a double game, seeking alliances with mediators to pursue their version of the mediator's stated norms and principles. In other cases negotiations become another means of conducting the conflict rather than a means for settling it.

Long exposure to the pressure to reach a settlement may paradoxically create increasing resistance to mediation by one side. The very question of whether to accept mediation becomes another point of real contention between the two parties. In the Kashmir conflict, Pakistan has actively sought international intervention as the key to upsetting an unsatisfactory status quo, while India has tended to assume that outside involvement would damage its interests. The Kashmir conflict illustrates the point that some conflicts become intractable because the stronger party is a status quo power that naturally resists or refuses external mediation and intervention.

Failures in earlier peacemaking efforts can also result in the promotion by the parties of mutually exclusive basic requirements and preconditions for negotiations. These basic requirements may mask a fundamental unwillingness to negotiate, as both parties know that you cannot satisfy the requirements of one side without contradicting the basic requirements of the other side. For instance, in many internal conflicts, the underdog insurgents keep the ability to continue the struggle as a primary card, while curbing insurgent violence and terrorism is a primary precondition or negotiating card in the hands of the government. This naturally leads to a procedural and substantive standoff as one side says that it needs a signed agreement in order to stop fighting, and the other refuses to talk until violence ceases. In fact, both sides may be posturing, because they view any movement to the negotiating table as a dangerously risky zero-sum game.

In most long-enduring conflicts, overlapping sources of intractability converge to build up a massive wall of resistance to settlement. The conflict in Cyprus, for instance, has at various points featured many sources of intractability: personalities, leadership factors, domestic politics in the Cypriot communities, the island's dependence on and linkage to two metropoles, the complexities of Cyprus's and Turkey's evolving relationships with the European Union, and the U.S. view that Cyprus is less important than other interests in the eastern Mediterranean. A similar pattern of multiple, overlapping layers of intractability can be seen in Colombia and Kashmir. In both cases even the basic conflict structure and identity of the parties are unclear. Who should sit at the table and who—if anyone—should mediate are still unsolved issues. It is also somewhat unclear in both cases what the issues are. In Kashmir they include borders, sovereignty, identity and self-determination, broader bilateral relationships, and terrorism. In Colombia the issues include ending guerrilla violence, getting paramilitaries under control, rural self-government, political reform, and socioeconomic change. As these cases show, even basic questions of defining the parties and defining the issues can contribute to a conflict's intractability.

Types of Intractable Conflicts

Interstate and Intrastate Conflicts

There are as many types of intractable conflicts as there are individual conflicts, as each arises out of a specific set of circumstances and involves specific actors and issues. But it is possible to establish some categories that can help to further our understanding of intractable conflicts. A basic structural difference exists between interstate wars and civil wars. Although most intractable conflicts do occur within states, it is important to recognize that some of the most durable intractables—Kashmir and Korea, for instance—are interstate conflicts with potentially devastating consequences for their immediate regions and the wider world if the conflicts were to erupt into full-fledged warfare. However, we also recognize that the distinction between interstate and intrastate conflicts starts to break down when contested sovereignty, or the refusal of one or more parties to recognize the sovereign claims of the other side, lies at the heart of the dispute. Further, many so-called intrastate, or civil, conflicts—Cyprus, for instance—will engage external actors, including regional neighbors, which not only try to manipulate the conflict for their own ends but also may be actively involved in the fighting itself. In examining long-standing wars, we see that the actual line between "civil" and "interstate" disputes is a blurry one.

Active Intractable Conflicts

Another distinction revolves around the level of violence and the persistence of fighting. Some intractable conflicts are hot conflict zones, such as Israel-Palestine and Sudan. Violence is a more or less permanent feature of these conflicts, even though the actual level of violence may be intermittent, sporadic, or even seasonal (dry seasons, for example, are good for launching conventional military offensives against insurgents). Such conflicts may be stalemated because they have not reached that plateau where the costs of a political settlement are appreciably lower (and recognized to be so) than the military and political costs of continued fighting.[9] They therefore elude the moment of "ripeness," that is, the moment when all of the parties are seriously interested in exploring their political options and finally commit themselves to resolving their differences through negotiation rather than force of arms.

In active intractable conflicts, parties also see themselves as fighting a war of attrition, or a "stamina war," in which the goal is not just to score points against the opponent but also to score points with one's own domestic constituents without alienating key allies and sources of international support. Active intractable conflicts are durable and usually recognized as such by the parties to the conflict themselves, even though they may underestimate the potential for escalation in violent acts of retribution.

The Israeli-Palestinian conflict is a classic example of an active intractable conflict: it has persisted—sometimes as an autonomous bilateral contest, sometimes linked to regional, interstate struggles involving Egypt, Jordan, Lebanon, and Syria—for almost five decades. Violence is episodic but recurrent, and the conflict has refused to yield to the persistent efforts of various third parties, including small countries such as Norway and a superpower such as the United States, to mediate a peaceful settlement to the conflict. Most important, though, the conflict falls into the active intractable category because the parties are not prepared to renounce completely the use of force and violence to achieve their political objectives. Conflicts in Colombia, Kashmir, Sri Lanka, and Sudan also fall into the active intractable category because the parties to these disputes have not completely renounced violence.

Abeyant Intractable Conflicts

Abeyant intractable conflicts share a common characteristic with active intractable conflicts: they are not ripe because the parties themselves have not experienced the full and direct costs of a mutually hurting stalemate. They differ, however, in crucial ways. In abeyant intractable conflicts violence is suspended, or "frozen" (i.e., they have gone into remission), usually because a third party is willing and able to guarantee the terms of a negotiated cease-fire—a cease-fire that may also include the broad outlines of a political settlement. When outsiders freeze a conflict by providing the means to check violence and keep peace, they save lives and manage the problem, preventing it from spreading and limiting damage, but they may also, perversely, sustain the underlying polarity and delay political solutions. In this situation outsiders become indispensable, and their eventual departure presents a security dilemma for local parties as there is real potential for escalation if those third-party security guarantees are withdrawn.

Abeyant intractable conflicts are characterized by an equilibrium that is relatively stable, because any attempt to escalate the conflict would inflict higher costs than does the existing cease-fire. At the same time, the political and security costs of moving to a new set of political arrangements, in which the third-party security guarantees could be withdrawn, are also higher than the costs of the status quo. A lasting peace therefore remains elusive.

Cyprus is a classic example of an intractable conflict that was frozen for decades. Here, the long-term inability (before the major progress achieved in 2003–4) of the United Nations, as well as other third parties, to bring about a negotiated settlement and a withdrawal of UN forces was testimony to the intractable nature of the dispute—a dispute involving not just competing communal interests on the island but also conflicting regional interests, namely, those of Greece and Turkey.

In table 1 we have categorized a number of intractable conflicts along four dimensions—interstate and intrastate, active and abeyant.

Categorizing by Principal Factors

In looking at the cases included in this book, however, we see that categorizing active and abeyant conflicts only starts the process of defining types of intractable conflicts. Table 1 presents a spectrum of intractability that ranges in prospect for resolution from hard to really hard, but some general clusters of different types of conflicts also start to appear. These clusters are defined by the principal agents or factors behind the intractability and may be characterized as follows:

❑ Conflicts in which there is a lack of accountability for the leadership, whether that leadership represents the ruling party and rebel elites in an intrastate conflict or the governments and other influentials in an interstate conflict. In these conflicts individuals or groups develop strong vested interests in the conflict as a means to gain or keep power, status, or wealth (whatever their public platforms may say about rights, grievances, and victimhood). In some of these conflicts there may be straightforward grabs for gain; in others the initial "cause" involved a fight over rights and needs that descended into a struggle for control of political power, goods, rents, and exports. This creates a winner-take-all pattern of behavior and presents

Table 1. Different Types of Intractable Conflicts

Level of Violence	Nature of Dispute	
	Intrastate conflict	*Interstate conflict*
Active intractable conflict	Abkhazia-Georgia Aceh-Indonesia Afghanistan Angola (pre-2002) Burma Burundi Colombia Democratic Republic of Congo East Timor (pre-1999) Georgia Liberia (pre-2003) Nepal Northern Ireland (pre-1998) Sierra Leone (pre-2000) Somalia South Ossetia–Georgia Sri Lanka Sudan	Israel-Palestine Kashmir Nagorno-Karabakh Western Sahara
Abeyant intractable conflict	Bosnia Chechnya Cyprus Kosovo	Israel-Syria North and South Korea People's Republic of China–Taiwan

specific obstacles to settlement that severely challenge the peace-makers. These conflicts may also be essentially rooted in a comfortable stasis for elites for years. In some conflicts the absence of continued violence may make the conflict tolerable for all sides, Cyprus again providing an example. In others the problem may be low levels of violence that are tolerable, as in Northern Ireland. In still others high levels of violence that do not adversely affect the interests of elites make the conflicts tolerable—here we look to Angola, Colombia, and Sudan.

❑ Conflicts that occur in societies where there are weak or divided decision-making structures. A principal factor behind intractability may be party fragility or fragmentation that makes it difficult to build (or sustain) durable coalitions for peace as negotiations move forward. Leaders whose basis for political support is weak and whose domestic coalitions are shaky have less freedom to maneuver and can make fewer concessions at the negotiating table than leaders who are in a strong political position with their own constituents. The corresponding bargaining "win-win" set—the negotiating range, or "zone of potential agreement" represented by the overlapping preferences of the parties—will shrink. Intractable conflicts in democracies—the Philippines, Sri Lanka—are particularly vulnerable to these problems, as the conflict becomes fodder for political debate and electioneering.

❑ Conflicts that are characterized by deep-rooted communal or ethnic cleavages. These conflicts are driven by ever-expanding and -deepening definitions of identity: (1) the parties refuse to recognize each other's identity, which essentially makes it difficult to lay the groundwork for negotiations, and (2) the parties (especially elites) have come to define themselves and the very core of their existence in terms of the conflict itself. This intermingling of identity and conflict severely limits the possibility of any peace process except one imposed from the outside to transform relationships and society.

❑ Conflicts that occur in "bad neighborhoods," becoming embedded in a wider set of issues and interests. These conflicts become impacted in surrounding regional geopolitics and stall for decades until a major shift of tectonic plates occurs, opening the way for real movement in the peace process. Conflicts can also be impacted because the third parties involved in the peacemaking think that solving the conflict is less important than maintaining good links with the neighboring states. And there are conflicts, such as in the former Yugoslavia and parts of Africa and the Caucasus, in which it is hard to know if an actor is internal or external to the conflict. Actors wear multiple hats, and their views of a neighboring conflict are defined by its potential impact as a precedent for their own.

❏ Conflicts that fail to generate serious, sustained, high-quality thir..
party intervention by key international actors. Some of these intractable conflicts involve parties that want to keep third parties out, as has
happened in Kashmir. Some are intractable in large part because no
high-quality external intervention is likely to happen—and these conflicts don't settle themselves. They are intractable, in a sense, because
they do not matter enough for concerted international reaction.

Table 2 divides conflict into two major categories. The left-hand
column shows primary factors affecting intractability—lack of accountability, weak decision-making structures, deep-rooted cleavages, bad neighborhoods, and the lack of outside help. The four right-hand columns
divide conflicts according to whether they are active or abeyant, interstate
or intrastate. The cells suggest where the conflicts discussed in this book,
as well as some other conflicts, might fall in terms of classification. The
fact that several conflicts appear in several cells serves only to reinforce
the point that intractable conflicts spring from many sources and may
move from one category to another over their lifetimes.

Negotiation Challenges in Intractable Conflicts

Since intractable conflicts typically have many causes, they require multifaceted responses and management strategies that address social problems
as well as political ones. However, the political problems may present the
most immediate challenge. Those doing the intervening must recognize
that in long-enduring conflict settings, not only have positions hardened,
but divisions run deep. This is because the parties have not given up on
their hopes for victory or their fear of defeat. The third-party challenge,
therefore, is not just to level the playing field but also to change the cost-
benefit calculations so the parties themselves become not only more interested in pursuing their political options but also firmly committed to a
political process for resolving their differences. The challenges that third
parties face in establishing a political dialogue and getting parties to the
table include the following.

Two-Level Games. The relationship between elites and their constituents
and the depth of political support they may (or may not) enjoy once they

Table 2. Typology of Conflicts

Primary Factors Affecting Intractability	Different Types of Intractable Conflicts				
	Active interstate	Active intrastate	Abeyant interstate	Abeyant intrastate
Lack of accountability of warring parties (bad leaders, warlordism, greed, fringe spoilers)	Balkans (pre-Dayton) Nagorno-Karabakh	Abkhazia Afghanistan Angola Burma Colombia Croatia Liberia Sierra Leone Somalia South Ossetia	North and South Korea	Cyprus Moldova
Weak or divided decision-making structures	Uganda-Sudan Western Sahara	Abkhazia Colombia Croatia Nepal Northern Ireland Philippines (Mindanao) South Ossetia	Kashmir	Kosovo

Deep-rooted communal or ethnic cleavages contributing to "winner-take-all" psychology	Kashmir	Afghanistan Balkans (post-Dayton) Sri Lanka Sudan	Israel-Palestine	Cyprus
Bad neighborhoods that embed conflict in wider set of issues and interests	Kashmir Nagorno-Karabakh Western Sahara	Afghanistan Burundi Cambodia Georgia Sierra Leone Sudan	Indochina (Cold War) Israel-Syria	
Lack of access to the conflict or lack of sustained third-party interest	Aceh-Indonesia Western Sahara Zaire/Democratic Republic of Congo Rwanda-Burundi	Colombia	Kashmir	Chechnya

decide to commit themselves to talking to the enemy are critical to the prospect of establishing negotiations. There is a two-level game aspect to most international negotiations, as Robert Putnam and others have convincingly argued.[10] Mediators in intractable conflict settings all too often run into the perverse and frustrating dynamics of this two-level game, not only in launching negotiations, but also when negotiations come down to the wire and the endgame is in sight. In intractable conflict settings the elite-constituency problem has special meaning and poses its own unique obstacles to any kind of *negotiated* attempt to bring about an end to conflict. Although two-level game considerations are not "causes" of intractability per se, they do influence the political environment and the strategic calculus of elites who may be interested in considering their political alternatives to a continuation of conflict.

Faction-Traction Problems. One result of the two-level games is that movements toward peace have difficulty gaining traction and the number of factions and shifting alliances increases. The large number of factions in any given conflict may, in turn, be a function of the large number of ethnic or communal groups that reside within the borders of a given country. As different groups vie for power and influence and seek to expand their political base, different coalitions and alliances will form. However, as the constellation of forces shifts in the jockeying for power, some coalitions will crumble while new ones rise to take their place. This is not to say that some factions may not want to pursue a negotiated solution to the conflict with the passage of time. However, their own basis of political support may be tenuous at best, and the balance of power may turn against them as the war unfolds, making it difficult for peace-oriented coalitions (or at the very least coalitions that are interested in pursuing negotiated political options) to form.

Nowhere are the problems of shifting coalitions of interest and power more readily apparent than in the twenty-year conflict in Sudan. Although the conflict has been portrayed as a religious war between Arabs governed by the highly repressive "fundamentalist" Islamic regime in the north and the largely Christian or animist African peoples who inhabit the south, this description captures only a partial picture of reality. Sudan comprises some five hundred ethnic groups, who speak more than a hundred different languages and profess adherence not just to Christianity and Islam but also to traditional African religions. The country's problems have been compounded by unequal socioeconomic development in different regions of the country and an economy that is highly dependent on exploitation of Sudan's natural resources, especially oil. Although Khartoum's intransigence presented a fundamental challenge to any kind of negotiated settlement, the shifting constellation of power among rival warring factions in the south also posed its own special obstacles. The highly factionalized nature of the Sudanese conflict made it difficult for third parties not only to gain entry into the conflict but also to gain any sufficient traction to move negotiations forward, a situation that changed only with the concerted effort of several determined intermediaries working together.

Delivery Dilemmas. A related problem in many intractable situations is the prevalence of weak or trapped leaders who are unable to deliver their own political constituency to the negotiating table as negotiating positions converge and a peace agreement appears to be within sight. Parties with a weak or eroding power base are more likely to be forced into strategies that treat successive bargaining encounters as conflictual rather than cooperative exercises.[11] Such pressures may well intensify the longer the parties are seated at the negotiating table. We refer to this negotiating conundrum in intractable conflict settings as the delivery dilemma.

The delivery dilemma of intractable conflicts is evident in efforts to negotiate an end to the Israeli-Palestinian conflict. After secret talks in Oslo, the Israelis and Palestinians signed a peace treaty at the White House in Washington in September 1993. Prime Minister Yitzhak Rabin, the leader of the Israeli Labor Party, was in a strong position domestically and was able to sell the terms of the Oslo settlement to Labor's coalition partners in the Knesset. Following Rabin's assassination at the hands of a political extremist and the subsequent defeat of Labor by the nationalist Likud party, U.S.-sponsored negotiations continued. However, as a result of electoral reforms that enhanced the power and influence of minority parties in the Knesset, the new prime minister, Benjamin Netanyahu, was in a relatively weak position politically within his own parliamentary coalition. Netanyahu (although himself no fan of the Oslo process) found that his own freedom of maneuver at the negotiating table was limited, and relations between Israel and its Arab neighbors worsened.

Netanyahu's defeat at the hands of Ehud Barak, leader of a Labor-led coalition, ushered in a new era of peacemaking and a series of intensive negotiations with PLO leader Yasir Arafat that culminated in a series of summit meetings, mediated by U.S. president Bill Clinton in 2000. Although Prime Minister Barak offered a series of dramatic and unprecedented concessions, negotiations collapsed over differences on the future of Palestinian refugees, the extent of territorial concessions, and the status of East Jerusalem. There are many reasons and differing interpretations as to why these talks collapsed. Even so, there is more or less general agreement that Arafat's intransigence and refusal to make concessions in the negotiations were linked to the shaky basis of his domestic political support, the growing challenge he faced from the extremist Hamas faction—which was (and is) carrying out its own terrorist attacks against Israel—and the fact that his own "divide-and-rule" approach to power had left his own people increasingly discontented and divided.

Discredited or Worn-Out Salient Solutions. Another negotiating dilemma in intractable conflict settings is the absence of a clearly identifiable resolving formula or, as William Zartman's chapter points out, the presence of a resolving formula that is already discredited or rejected by the parties. One school of thought argues that the negotiating challenge in intractable conflicts is to keep old ideas alive or on life support on the grounds that "[y]esterday's rejected or ignored proposal, document, or procedure may become tomorrow's accepted agreement, new adopted position, or process."[12] Another school of thought says that some negotiating formulas may simply be too worn out because they have already been tried and failed. As Paul Hare argues, one of the reasons for the demise of the Lusaka peace process in Angola in 1998 was that it failed to handle demobilization and reintegration issues before elections—a formula that had plagued the implementation of the Bicesse Accords in 1991–92 (see Hare's chapter in this book).

Insurmountable Risks. A further negotiating dilemma involves the inherent risks of settlement in an intractable conflict. In some intractable conflicts the risks of default in a negotiated settlement may seem to be insurmountable. That is, the risks associated with the possibility that a negotiating partner will not live up to his or her contractual obligations at the time that they fall due (or any time thereafter) are deemed to be unacceptably high because there is no judicial or political remedy for recovering the losses arising from a default.

These default risks may well have domestic as well as international consequences. A failed agreement may mean the fall of a coalition government, an irredeemable loss of confidence in the leader who negotiated the agreement, and/or a major escalation in violence if military action is required to restore the security situation and the political or territorial status quo ante. These risks also tend to affect parties' perceptions about the desirability of an accord. In those cases of high moral hazard—the risk that once an agreement is signed, one party to a contract will change its behavior to the detriment of the other party—a party may shy away from entering into negotiated commitments or look to third parties to underwrite its losses. If a party to an agreement defaults, third parties may also be called upon to restructure or reconceive the agreement. At various points in their tortured histories, the conflicts between Israelis and Palestinians; between Angolans, Cubans, and South Africans; between Turkish and Greek Cypriots; and within Angola, Mozambique, Sri Lanka, and Sudan have all demonstrated aspects of this existential dilemma.

Third Parties and the Intractable Conflict Phenomenon: Motives, Strategic Priorities, Tradecraft, and Geopolitics

Since 1990, third-party intervention in conflicts has increased significantly. This increase has come about for many reasons: the explosion of vicious civil and regional wars at the end of the Cold War; the willingness of a number of official institutions to intervene; the growing appreciation for the complexity and multidimensional nature of peacemaking; the evolution of nonofficial approaches to conflict resolution; and at times the interest in political settlements by the warring parties. It is now generally accepted that third parties can play widely differing roles in conflict resolution processes and that they have been helpful—if not vital—in resolving some conflicts. But in many intractable conflicts, the track record of third parties is not good. The question is why.

Bad Tradecraft

In some instances the answer lies with inappropriate ripening agents whose interventions end up making the problem worse. In other instances the absence of strategic and operational readiness by third parties means that negotiated interventions are needlessly delayed and take place well after the conflict has escalated and passed the all-too-elusive "ripe moment." Poor diplomatic tradecraft, inept policies, and a faulty settlement can also be blamed for making a conflict worse by polarizing positions and scuttling chances for future negotiations. The 1990s, for example, witnessed a remarkable flurry of mediated interventions by a large number of third parties in the Great Lakes crisis in Central Africa. In addition to the United Nations, the Organization of African Unity, the European Union, the Arusha Group, and the United States, a large number of nongovernmental organizations also jumped into the fray. Although the international community wanted peace, as each envoy crisscrossed the region promoting his or her own agenda, the level of confusion grew.[13] Many of these initiatives contributed to communications gridlock and endless "forum shopping" by the parties to the conflict. Because many of the negotiators focused on too narrow an agenda and failed to grasp the bigger humanitarian, development, and human rights picture, they also compounded the difficulty of reaching any kind of broader political settlement.

Orphaned Conflicts

The absence of third parties may also be a problem. Some conflicts fail to get the attention of powerful or effective peacemakers that could help the conflict parties through a peace process. They may be neglected or orphaned by the international community or suffer from sporadic attention.[14] Third parties seeking a peaceful resolution to a dispute may not be able to gain entry when faced with "denial" by a relatively powerful state, as illustrated in the Indian-Pakistani conflict over Jammu and Kashmir. In these cases international inattention may spring from a judgment that these conflicts are not important enough to matter, but it also springs from the respect for national sovereignty that has characterized the post-Westphalia international system. Until recently, both Afghanistan and Sri Lanka suffered from a lack of strategic attention and interest by great powers that could create leverage, offer guidance and strategic direction, and perhaps even change the calculus of the warring parties themselves.

Subsidiarity

Another factor may be a subsidiarity problem—the unwillingness of third parties to elevate a conflict to the number one priority in their relations with conflicting parties. Although the third party does not neglect a conflict, it sees resolution of the conflict as subsidiary to its principal interests in relationships with the conflict parties. A classic example of this is Cyprus. Although the absence of a hurting stalemate is one possible impediment to resolution for the reasons mentioned above, the United Nations' problems in reaching a negotiated settlement historically have been compounded by the "hands-off" attitude of the United States and other permanent members of the Security Council toward the self-determination and territorial claims of the parties.[15]

In addition, third parties with clout and capacity may have no interest in grasping the nettle, that is, getting involved in conflicts where the costs and risks of potential engagement are high and where others are willing or can be pressured to try their skill at conflict management. But delegation of authority can easily slide into buck-passing in risky ventures. Some of these problems are reflected in the hands-off position taken by the United States in the early years of the Balkan crisis. After it failed to prevent the breakup of Yugoslavia, the United States essentially left the crisis to its European allies. This pattern of disengagement was to continue for almost four years, with adverse consequences for the peace process.[16]

Strategic Impaction

In a more extreme case, conflicts may become impacted in the third party's strong geopolitical or strategic interests in the conflict region. A mediated settlement that entails engagement and negotiation with the enemy of a regional ally involves real risks—not least in terms of relations with the affected ally and other allies who could see a precedent in the attempt. In these cases the conflict may be set off-limits for mediation until the third party's interests shift. Third parties may perceive a higher interest—as well as lower risk—in managing the conflict than in attempts to resolve it. That is, they may prefer to freeze or suppress the conflict in order to contain its spread, deter an adversary or rogue power, and limit the potential regional damage of continued conflict. For instance, for many years the United States has stationed its troops in South Korea because deterrence is seen as the best conflict management strategy for the Korean peninsula. Other cases include Cuba's role in southern Africa until the late 1980s and the roles that Vietnam and China played in Cambodia until the early 1990s.[17]

Admittedly, there is a strong counterfactual element to our assessment of what would have happened had the mediator not gone "missing," had third-party strategic priorities been different, had third parties with clout and capacity become involved, or had third parties behaved differently. We suppose that in some instances the right kind of third party, operating under a different or clearer mandate and possessing the right kind of backup (including resources and leverage), could have altered the path of these seemingly intractable conflicts. In rendering this assessment —summarized in table 3—we are aware of not only the importance of third-party interventions in alleviating or managing conflict but also the many things that can (and do) go wrong even when third parties acting with the best of intentions and enjoying strong political and institutional support intervene in intractable conflicts. And we would underscore the point that third parties will make mediated solutions their top priority only when they perceive that such settlements are both available and preferable to other forms of conflict management.

Examining Intractability

Most lessons about mediation are drawn from cases of successful intervention. In contrast, this project draws lessons from mediation in unyielding conflicts. It examines the sources—internal and external—of intractability; the consequences for mediation of deep-rooted, long-term violence; the tools that mediators have developed and deployed in these circumstances; and the strategic options for staying engaged and disengaging in the most difficult circumstances. In examining intractable conflict, this book focuses on three themes: (1) What are the central characteristics of intractable conflicts? (2) Under what conditions do intractable conflicts become tractable? And (3) what is the relationship between intractability and mediator involvement—that is, when does third-party peacemaking reduce conflict and increase the prospects of a negotiated settlement, and when does it aggravate conflict, thereby adding to its "intractability"?

The book is divided into two principal parts. The first part examines general characteristics of intractability and the challenges of mediation in intractable conflicts. Some authors in this section—especially Roy Lick-lider and Jacob Bercovitch—look at evidence provided by quantitative studies of intractable conflicts and discuss the conclusions that these large-number studies draw about the nature of prolonged conflicts and general prospects for third-party intervention. Louis Kriesberg and William Zart-man look closely at the qualitative characteristics of intractable conflicts, including those that arise as a result of the sheer duration of the intense disputes, and offer specific suggestions for identifying moments when third-party intervention may be effective. Following suit, Diana Chigas reviews the special role that nonofficial institutions can play in encouraging peace in situations of deeply rooted social conflict.

In the second part of the book, twelve experts examine eight cases of intractable conflict—Sudan, the Balkans, Angola, Colombia, Eurasia, Kashmir, North and South Korea, and the Middle East. Each chapter focuses on a specific conflict, but in writing their chapters all authors addressed a common set of questions:

❑ What are the causes (internal and external) of the conflict and of its intractability?

❑ What are the main obstacles (internal and external) to settlement?

❑ What are the third parties' interests and objectives, and have they changed over time?

❑ How have these objectives been pursued? What tools have the third parties used? How serious have the intervention efforts been, and has this changed over time? Have they been the right third parties?

❑ In those cases in which there has been no consistent third-party involvement, why has this been so? Is it due to the conflict's inaccessibility, to third-party indifference, or to a lack of unified understanding of what the problems are?

❑ What lessons can be drawn from this case?

We felt that the Israeli-Palestinian conflict, an intractable conflict in a class of its own, deserved two chapters. These two chapters do not reflect the two parties' points of view; rather, they reflect a common understanding that any third-party attempt to help end the conflict will have to address intractability on many levels.

Table 3. Sources and Cases of Intractability

Primary Factors Affecting Intractability	Third-Party Contributions to Intractability			
	Poor tradecraft problems	*Orphan problem*	*Subsidiarity problems*	*Strategically impacted*
Lack of accountability of warring parties (bad leaders, warlordism, greed, fringe spoilers)	Angola (1991–92) Balkans (pre-Dayton)	Afghanistan Burma Georgia Liberia Nagorno-Karabakh Sierra Leone Somalia South Ossetia	Chechnya East Timor Nagorno-Karabakh	Abkhazia Israel-Palestine Nagorno-Karabakh North Korea South Ossetia
Weak or divided decision-making structures	Northern Ireland	Abkhazia Colombia Nepal Sri Lanka Sudan	Uganda-Sudan Western Sahara	Kashmir

Deep-rooted communal, ethnic cleavages contributing to "winner–take–all" psychology	Israel-Palestine Sudan	Afghanistan Kashmir Sri Lanka Sudan	Cyprus (pre-2003) Kashmir	Balkans (post-Dayton) Cyprus Israel-Palestine Kashmir
Bad neighborhoods that embed conflict in wider set of issues and interests	Western Sahara	Afghanistan Georgia Nagorno-Karabakh Sudan	Burundi Sierra Leone	Israel-Syria Kashmir

Note: The examples given in this table are illustrative of the multiple causes of intractability and are not intended to be definitive characterizations of each conflict.

The last chapter of the book reflects the insights provided both by the chapters in this book and by the discussion in the experts group meeting about specific recommendations for third-party intervention in intractable conflicts. Like nettles, intractable conflicts promise to inflict pain on anyone who tries to deal with them. However, the more that scholars and practitioners understand about why and where they grow, and what we can do about them, the greater the chances for successful peacemaking in these seemingly endless conflicts. The purpose of this book, and its companion volume, *Taming Intractable Conflicts: Mediation in the Hardest Cases,* is to provide potential peacemakers, be they government officials, UN special representatives, NGO workers, faculty, or students, with a better grasp of intractable conflicts and how third parties can help to make them tractable.

Notes

1. John de Chastelain, "The Good Friday Agreement in Northern Ireland," in *Herding Cats: Multiparty Mediation in a Complex World,* ed. Chester A. Crocker, Fen Osler Hampson, and Pamela Aall (Washington, D.C.: United States Institute of Peace Press, 1999), 431–468; and Richard Holbrooke, "The Road to Sarajevo," in *Turbulent Peace: The Challenges of Managing International Conflict,* ed. Chester A. Crocker, Fen Osler Hampson, and Pamela Aall (Washington, D.C.: United States Institute of Peace Press, 2001), 325–343.

2. Joseph S. Nye Jr., "Redefining the National Interest," *Foreign Affairs* 78, no. 4 (1999): 22–35; Chester A. Crocker, "A Poor Case for Quitting: Mistaking Incompetence for Interventionism," *Foreign Affairs* 79, no. 1 (2000): 183–186; and Chester A. Crocker, "Engaging Failing States," *Foreign Affairs* 82, no. 5 (2003): 32–45.

3. See, for example, Edward E. Azar, "Protracted International Conflicts: Ten Propositions," in *International Conflict Resolution: Theory and Practice,* ed. Edward E. Azar and John W. Burton (Brighton, U.K.: Wheatsheaf Books, 1986), 28–39; John Burton, *Resolving Deep-Rooted Conflict: A Handbook* (Lanham, Md.: University Press of America, 1987); Peter Coleman, "Intractable Conflict," in *The Handbook of Conflict Resolution: Theory and Practice,* ed. Morton Deutsch and Peter T. Coleman (San Francisco: Jossey-Bass, 2000), 428–450; Louis Kriesberg, *Constructive Conflicts: From Escalation to Resolution,* 2d ed. (Lanham, Md.: Rowman and Littlefield, 2003); Dean G. Pruitt and P. Olczak, "Beyond Hope: Approaches to Resolving Seemingly Intractable Conflict," in *Cooperation, Conflict, and Justice: Essays Inspired by the Work of Morton Deutsch,* ed. B. B. Bunker and Jeffrey Z. Rubin (New York: Sage, 1995), 59–62; and Jeffrey Z. Rubin, Dean G. Pruitt, and Sung Hee Kim, *Social Conflict: Escalation, Stalemate, Settlement* (New York: McGraw-Hill, 1994).

4. Although there are certain obvious structural differences, which have been much discussed in the expert literature, there are also important common features of intractability shared by interstate and intrastate conflicts. These include leadership variables, characteristics of domestic structure (such as the absence of accountability), potential contributions to the conflict of the surrounding region and the availability of security mechanisms, and the character of third-party interventions. In certain circumstances the identity and avarice dimensions of intractability can readily occur at the interstate level—one thinks of Kashmir and the Middle East cases as well as the internationalized African ones, such as the current conflict in the Democratic Republic of Congo or the conflict in Angola when Cuban troops were deployed in the region. See, for example, Stephen John Stedman, "Negotiation and Mediation in Internal Conflict," in *The International Dimensions of Internal Conflict*, ed. Michael Brown (Cambridge, Mass.: MIT Press, 1996), 341–376; and Jack Snyder and Robert Jervis, "Civil War and the Security Dilemma," in *Civil Wars, Insecurity, and Intervention*, ed. Barbara F. Walter and Jack Snyder (New York: Columbia University Press, 1999), 15–37.

5. Jack S. Levy, "Theories of Interstate and Intrastate War: A Levels-of-Analysis Approach," in *Turbulent Peace*, 3–28; and I. William Zartman, "Ethnic Conflicts: Mediating Conflicts of Need, Greed, and Creed," *Orbis 42*, no. 2 (2000): 255–266.

6. Michael E. Brown, "Ethnic and Internal Conflicts: Causes and Implications," in *Turbulent Peace*, 209–226.

7. An important strand in the literature suggests that there is a direct causal link between group-based, socioeconomic inequalities and political disorder. According to this view, "horizontal inequalities" in a society increase the potential for violent conflict. As Frances Stewart argues, poverty and civil conflict have a tendency to feed on each other: eight of the ten countries that scored lowest on the United Nations' Development Programme's human development index rating and eight out of ten countries with the lowest GNP per capita have experienced civil wars in recent decades. About half of low-income countries have also been subject to major political violence. Frances Stewart, "Crisis Prevention: Tackling Horizontal Inequalities," in *From Reaction to Conflict Prevention: Opportunities for the UN in the New Millennium* (Boulder, Colo.: Lynne Rienner, 2001), also published in *Oxford Development Studies* 28, no. 3 (October 2000); and Frances Stewart and E. K. V. FitzGerald, *War and Underdevelopment: The Economic and Social Consequences of Conflict* (Oxford: Oxford University Press, 2001).

8. Paul Collier, "Doing Well Out of War: An Economic Perspective," in *Greed and Grievance: Economic Agendas in Civil Wars*, ed. Mats Berdal and David M. Malone (Boulder, Colo.: Lynne Rienner, 2000), 91–113; Paul Collier, "Economic Causes of Civil Conflict and Their Implications for Policy," in *Turbulent Peace*, 143–162; and Paul Collier, *Breaking the Conflict Trap: Civil War and Development Policy* (Washington, D.C.: World Bank and Oxford University Press, 2003). See also the thoughtful critiques of this approach in Karen Ballentine and Jake Sherman, eds., *The Political Economy of Armed Conflict: Beyond Greed and Grievance* (Boulder, Colo.: Lynne Rienner, 2003).

9. I. William Zartman, *Ripe for Resolution: Conflict and Intervention in Africa* (New York: Oxford University Press, 1985).

10. Robert Putnam, "Diplomacy and Domestic Politics," *International Organization* 42, no. 3 (1988): 427–460; Fred Charles Ikle, *Every War Must End* (New York: Columbia University Press, 1971); Howard Lehman and Jennifer McCoy, "The Dynamics of the Two-Level Bargaining Game," *World Politics* 44, no. 4 (1992): 600–644; and Frederick Mayer, "Managing Domestic Differences in International Negotiation," *International Negotiation* 46, no. 4 (1992): 793–818.

11. P. Terrence Hopmann, "Two Paradigms of Negotiation Bargaining and Problem Solving," *Annals of the American Academy of Political and Social Science* 542 (November 1995): 24–47.

12. Kenneth W. Stein and Samuel W. Lewis, *Mediation in the Middle East*, Occasional Paper (Washington, D.C.: United States Institute of Peace Press, 1991).

13. Fabienne Hara, "Burundi: A Case Study of Parallel Diplomacy," in *Herding Cats*, 135–158.

14. See "Out of Sight, Out of Mind: The Fate of Forgotten Conflicts," in Chester A. Crocker, Fen Osler Hampson, and Pamela Aall, *Taming Intractable Conflict: Mediation in the Hardest Cases* (Washington, D.C. United States Institute of Peace Press, 2004), 45–72.

15. Karl Th. Birgisson, "United Nations Peacekeeping Force in Cyprus," in *The Evolution of United Nations Peacekeeping: Case Studies and Comparative Analysis*, ed. William J. Durch (New York: St. Martin's Press, 1993), 219–236; and Fen Osler Hampson, *Nurturing Peace: Why Peace Settlements Succeed or Fail* (Washington, D.C.: United States Institute of Peace Press, 1996), 27–52.

16. William J. Durch, "The UN Operation in the Congo," in *The Evolution of United Nations Peacekeeping*, 285–298. See also Steven Burg's chapter in this book.

17. Chester A. Crocker, "Peacemaking in Southern Africa: The Namibia-Angola Settlement of 1988," in *Herding Cats*, 207–244; and Richard H. Solomon, "Bringing Peace to Cambodia," in *Herding Cats*, 275–324.

Understanding Intractability

2

Comparative Studies of Long Wars

Roy Licklider

"INTRACTABLE CONFLICT" is a misleadingly simple term, and it is probably useful to start this discussion by making some distinctions.[1] A conflict is simply a disagreement among people on some issue. In this volume we use the term "intractable conflict" to refer to a particular type of conflict, one that divides large groups of people and is either accompanied by large-scale violence now or will be in the foreseeable future ("frozen" conflicts). I may have an intractable conflict with my students about my grading standards (at least my teaching evaluations regularly suggest that I do), but no one asked for a chapter on that conflict in this volume. It is telling that much of the literature on intractable conflicts is framed in terms of war, which in turn is defined in terms of substantial human casualties. The study of war has traditionally focused on interstate wars; the recent focus on "enduring rivalries" is particularly relevant here. The recent decrease in the number of interstate wars has brought more attention to civil wars. Interestingly enough, researchers in interstate and civil wars have not had much contact, although there is considerable overlap in their findings.

What, then, is meant by an "intractable conflict"? Our editors suggest that it is a conflict accompanied by large-scale violence that has lasted some considerable time and has resisted efforts at settlement, by either the parties themselves or outsiders. This concept seems straightforward (although the term might better be "intractable violence" or "intractable war"), but the boundaries of the concept are not specified (how large, how long), and it does beg the definition of a settlement. The term "settlement" usually means an agreement among the parties that makes further large-scale violence very unlikely. The expectation of future violence is a matter of judgment; it is always possible that the American Civil War will break out again, but most of us regard it as settled. Obviously, this judgment is harder to make for more recent events; thus the decision to include in this volume several conflicts that are not currently violent ("frozen" in the editors' language—see chapter 1) reflects such a judgment.

What do we mean when we say that a war "resists settlement"? Wars do not, of course, resist anything; people do. One interesting aspect of post–Cold War international affairs is a mini-industry of people and organizations dedicated to encouraging combatants to stop killing one another and reach a settlement of some sort; they in turn make up part of the rather disparate group we call the "international community." Their work is frustrating because it is very difficult to tell whether progress has been made toward a settlement until the settlement itself is reached and has held for some time. At almost any time before this, some outsiders will argue that progress is being made and others will disagree, saying that the conflict is intractable. In practice, the latter judgment means that the observers see little hope of reaching a settlement in the foreseeable future; often the observers also mean that scarce resources should not be expended on this conflict at this time. Intractability is thus a judgment that can be and often is contested.

There are degrees of intractability, and they also are matters of judgment; it depends on what we think would make a settlement possible. We can say that a war is intractable because of a particular obstacle to settlement (one particularly intransigent individual, the lack of a single essential resource such as money or a peacekeeping force, etc.); this presumably can change at some point in the future. We can say that other wars are intractable because of things that are unlikely to change, such as deep-seated animosities among combatants, incentives for elites to continue the war, or the lack of an obvious settlement strategy.

At least in civil wars, settlement has traditionally been reached by one side (usually the government) winning the war, dictating the terms of settlement to the losers, and using a combination of enforcement and enticements to persuade the losers to accept the terms. Negotiated settlements, agreements that either side could have rejected to continue the war, are unusual in civil wars, although not unheard of (Colombia in 1957 is a good example; I would argue that the American Civil War really ended with a negotiated settlement in 1876, but that is obviously a controversial judgment [Hartlyn 1993; Stedman 1993]). Since the end of the Cold War, outside pressures have encouraged more negotiated settlements to civil wars, but we do not yet have much historical experience with which to evaluate these settlements.

Neither a military victory nor a negotiated agreement necessarily involves "resolving" the conflict, that is, ending it. On the contrary, real conflict resolution is quite unlikely immediately after a prolonged period of violence. If the violence between two groups has been driven by economic inequalities between them, for example, war is unlikely to have decreased the inequalities; indeed, they may well be greater than before. If the violence has been caused by one group's grievances toward another, killing one another in large numbers has probably not made the groups more amicable. The same is true for any other "cause" of large-scale violence.

"Conflict resolution," then, is something of a misnomer; in practice we are usually talking about an agreement, not to end the conflict, but to continue it by nonviolent, political means, what is sometimes called conflict management. This sort of coexistence is hard enough if the two parties are independent states. Each presumably withdraws to its own territory, retains its own alliances and military forces, and operates as a sovereign state, maintaining control of its own population. Thus, the ability of states to shift from enmity to alliance (the United States and Germany or Japan after World War II are obvious examples) is perhaps understandable, although still a little startling.

If, on the other hand, the groups are still within the same state, a negotiated settlement means establishing a political system in which the violent conflict can be transformed into a political conflict. Indeed, the central purpose of government is precisely to prevent inevitable conflicts within its own population from erupting into large-scale violence. But this process means that one side or both sides must give up the ability to defend themselves and trust themselves and their children to a government made up in part or largely of their deadly enemies, which therefore may appear to be less than trustworthy (Walter 2002).

How does this happen? How do people who have been killing one another with considerable skill and enthusiasm come together to form a

common government? How can you work together with the people who
have killed your parents, your children, your friends or lovers? On the surface it seems impossible, even grotesque. But we know that it happens all
the time. England is not torn by war over York and Lancaster or King and
Parliament. The French no longer kill one another over the divine right of
kings. Americans seem agreed to be independent of English rule and that
the South should not secede. The ideologies of the Spanish Civil War now
seem irrelevant to Spaniards. More recently, since World War II civil wars
in countries as various as Azerbaijan, Bangladesh, Cambodia, Central
African Republic, Chad, Costa Rica, Croatia, Cyprus, Djibouti, Domini-
can Republic, El Salvador, Ethiopia, Georgia, Greece, Guatemala, Iran,
Jordan, Korea, Laos, Lebanon, Malaysia, Moldova, Mozambique, Namibia, Nicaragua, Nigeria, Papua New Guinea, Paraguay, Peru, Romania,
South Africa, Syria, Taiwan, Uganda, and Vietnam have ended and, in
the vast majority, seem unlikely to resume in the near future. We thus know
that this process occurs a lot, but we do not know much about when it is
more or less likely, much less how it works.

Following the pioneering lead of J. David Singer and his associates,
scholars have focused much of their statistical analysis of interstate wars
on the period from 1815 to the present. Within the literature of interstate
wars there is considerable discussion of "enduring rivalries," groups of states
that engage in repeated conflict acts with one another. States in rivalries
do not always go to war (the Cold War is a recent example), but research
shows that a relatively small number of such pairs account for roughly
half of the wars in the international system between 1815 and 1992
(Goertz and Diehl 2000b, 198–200).

There have been so many civil wars since 1945 that scholars have
studied them as a group, using statistical analysis to try to detect patterns.
Their results often differ, in part because of different definitions of terms
such as "civil war" and "settlement" and the poor quality of important statistics such as casualty rates in many countries. (Sambanis [2002] provides
an excellent comparison of several of the most important data sets.) Nonetheless, there is general agreement that between one hundred and two
hundred such events have occurred since 1945.

What, then, is an "intractable" war? This term is not used much in
quantitative studies, which instead focus on the length of the war, its
duration, and the length of time before it is resumed. The assumption is

that length itself is a proxy for other qualities that we might use to define "intractable," such as difficulty in reaching agreements, intensity of animosities, lack of trust, and so on.

These studies have produced or confirmed a few interesting possible explanations for why some violent conflicts last much longer than others. Of the roughly eleven hundred interstate rivalries between 1816 and 1992, most involved only one or two militarized disputes and ended within three years; only 5 percent lasted twenty years or longer (Diehl and Goertz 2000, 43, 50). Similarly, a number of different studies confirm that most civil wars end in a few years and are won by the government (Small and Singer 1982, 222; Stedman 1991; Licklider 1995, 683–684; Dixon 2001, 290–291).

This conclusion is particularly important because it is counterintuitive, perhaps because the mass media focus on stories of conflict and violence all over the world. Walter Lippmann once compared the media to a searchlight in the dark, illuminating one spot briefly, then leaping to another and another, leaving the viewers to draw their own conclusions. Given little foreign news other than of violence, it is not hard to assume that all the world is violent, rather like the doctor who assumes the whole world is sick because everyone he sees every day is sick. Because peace is not interesting to the media, it goes unreported. This in turn obscures the important point that intractable conflicts are exceptional, not common, and that they need to be explained, not assumed away under labels such as "ancient hatreds."

Enduring rivalries disproportionately involve states of roughly equal power, although there are exceptions (Diehl and Goertz 2000, 50–51); presumably, many rivalries between unequal opponents end with the weaker power losing. Civil wars are inherently less equal. Most civil wars are won by governments because they have major advantages in finance and organization (Wagner 1993, 253–260; Dixon 2001, 292). Financially, they can borrow money and get arms relatively easily. Other governments can extend technical assistance and training to them without violating international law and norms. Rebel groups usually have none of these advantages, and the end of the Cold War has meant that outside powers have had less interest in supporting such activities, with some obvious exceptions.

The organizational advantage may be less obvious but is even more important. A government by definition is already organized; it has an army, a police force, and a set of bureaucracies able to extract resources from its people and deliver services to them. A new rebel group has none of these; they must be created from scratch. The start-up costs of rebellion are high, which explains why most rebellions are snuffed out before they reach the level of civil war, and why most civil wars are won by the government within a year or so.

How do some rebels overcome these advantages and maintain resistance long enough to create intractable civil wars? A number of analysts associated with the World Bank have asked how rebels can afford to maintain a civil war and have concluded that in many cases the rebels gain control of some resource that can be used to purchase weapons and support armies (Collier, Hoeffler, and Söderbom 2004). Often this involves some sort of criminal activity, such as diamond, cocaine, or opium trafficking (Fearon 2004, 283–284). The notion of the "resource curse," prolonged civil war visited upon countries with such sources of wealth, has acquired some popularity.

Because of the poor quality of data, it is difficult to do persuasive statistical analysis of this issue. In a comparison of thirteen cases mentioned as possible examples of this resource curse, Michael Ross argues that resource looting did not contribute to the outbreak of wars but was important for their duration. Resources that could be "looted" by both sides lengthened the wars in six states, but when only the government had access to the resources, as in the Democratic Republic of Congo in 1997, the war was shortened. Cambodia is a particularly interesting case in this regard: the Khmer Rouge's control of resources lengthened the war until 1995, but the government was able to reverse the situation by giving control of resources to defecting Khmer Rouge leaders, thus helping to shorten the war (Ross 2004).

Rebels can also be sustained by external support, of course, but groups that control their own resources have some protection from the fickle decisions of other states and members of their diaspora. In any case, the question of how both sides are able to mobilize sufficient resources to continue the fighting for years is potentially important.

James Fearon (2004) explains duration and intractability with a different argument, suggesting that the type of civil war matters. In particular, he distinguishes between "coups and popular revolutions," which are struggles for control of the government centering around the capital city, and "peripheral wars," in which a dominant ethnic group attempts to extend effective control into rural areas inhabited by a different group. Fearon argues that urban wars tend to be short because they generally succeed or fail fairly quickly, and it is difficult for the losing side to regroup. Rural wars, in contrast, tend to be long since the government has trouble exerting force in such areas and resistance tends to be widespread and difficult to reduce. But even successful local resistance may not deter renewed efforts by a government that is motivated by a desire to control resources in the contested region or to encourage the migration of members of its own ethnic group into the area because of population pressures at the center. It is entirely possible for such conflicts to settle into a sort of stable stalemate in which the rebels hold effective control of the territory and the government remains in power in the capital (Zartman 1993), one particular type of intractable conflict. In such a situation, each side may feel that the status quo is better than any alternative that the other side would accept.

The international neighborhood also matters; wars in one country seem to encourage longer civil wars in neighboring countries. Several processes may well be involved. Large quantities of weapons and people skilled in their use may make it easier to maintain a war. Ethnic links often cross state boundaries, which may make a settlement in one country difficult. Civil war contagion seems evident in West and Central Africa, for example.

We have some evidence that long civil wars are disproportionately likely to be ended with negotiated settlements rather than military victories (Mason and Fett 1996, 563; Licklider 1995). This is plausible since a long civil war means that neither side has been able to achieve a military victory. Other studies have found that settlements of long civil wars are more likely to last than those of shorter wars, although not if the long civil wars have been particularly intense (Hartzell, Hoddie, and Rothchild 2001, 198; Doyle and Sambanis 2000, 787–789). Dubey (2002, 25) found that increased intensity made settlements less stable up to a point, after which it had the opposite effect.

Outside intervention is quite common in civil wars; Regan (2002) finds it in about two-thirds of his cases. However, despite a great deal of effort, no simple relationship has been found between outside intervention and civil war duration (Elbadawi and Sambanis 2000; Ayres 2000; Dixon 2001; Dubey 2002; Doyle and Sambanis 2000; Fortna 2004a). Some research on interstate wars suggests that rivalries are often strengthened by the actions of outside powers but that "external attempts to mitigate

. . . recurring conflict are largely ineffective, at least in the short term"
(Goertz and Diehl 2000b, 212).

Much of this work focuses on the length of particular civil wars.
However, another pattern to study would be a series of wars over many
years between the same parties in the state, each of which could be fairly
short. An example of such enduring rivalries (as they are called in a similar
literature on interstate war) would include the several Tibetan civil wars
in China. Thus, we must ask ourselves under what conditions a civil war
that has "ended" is likely to resume. There is some evidence that wars that
end in military victories are less likely to resume than those that end in
negotiated settlement, a depressing finding (Licklider 1995; Carment and
Harvey 2001; Toft 2003). Interestingly, similar findings appear with interstate wars as well (Maoz 1984 and Hensel 1994, cited in Goertz and
Diehl 2000b, 209–210).

Since recurring wars are the exception rather than the rule, it is
worth asking what kinds of settlements have a better chance of success
than others. Several scholars have borrowed the notion of a security
dilemma from international relations (Posen 1993; Walter 2002; Walter
and Snyder 1999; Fearon 2004). Ending a civil war, especially disarming
and demobilizing your forces, is very dangerous because of the risk that
your antagonist may renew the struggle once you are weak. Security
assurances from a third party seem useful in reassuring all sides that no
one group will be able to violate the agreement in secret. Despite a number of problems associated with such assurances, evidence suggests that
they do in fact make settlements more likely to hold in both civil war
(Walter 2002; Hartzell, Hoddie, and Rothchild 2001) and interstate war
(Fortna 2004a).

A broader application of this logic is for the settlement to include
postsettlement institutions that will serve the same purpose, particularly
democratic and power-sharing ones (Hartzell, Hoddie, and Rothchild
2001; Gurr 2000, 275–288). Several studies of interstate war have concluded that democratic governments are unlikely to be involved in enduring rivalries with one another (Bennett 1997; Hensel, Goertz, and Diehl
2000). The record in civil wars is more mixed. Two studies found that
democracy and political openness reduced the probability of civil war renewal (Dubey 2002, 23; Walter 2004, but another, admittedly incomplete,

study was unable to trace the predicted links between the two variables (Licklider 2001).

Most of these findings make sense intuitively. A much less obvious conclusion from the civil war literature, which remains controversial among scholars as well, is that the factors associated with a long war may be quite different from those associated with the outbreak of civil war. What does this mean? Let us take an example. Poor countries are more likely to have civil wars than rich countries, all things being equal. However, when only countries involved in civil wars are studied, some scholars find that poor countries are no more likely to have long civil wars than rich countries (Fearon 2004, 287). Thus, poverty may be a good predictor of the outbreak of civil war but not its duration.

Many other factors that help explain the outbreak of civil war do not seem related to its duration: prewar political and economic inequality, political repression, prewar democracy, military expenditures, ethnic fractionalization, level of violence, prewar population and population density, ethnic as opposed to nonethnic wars, and secessionist goals as opposed to control of the central government (Mason and Fett 1996, 563–564; Ayres 2001, 13–14; Collier, Hoeffler, and Söderbom 2001; Licklider 1995; Balch-Lindsay and Enterline 2000, 630–637; Fearon 2004).[2] This does not mean that one of these factors may not explain why a particular conflict is intractable, since we are talking about general patterns here, but if, say, poverty is seen as one reason why a particular war continued for a long time, we have to explain why this example is so different from other cases. We cannot simply cite poverty as a cause of duration if it is not in fact associated with duration in most cases.

Of these factors, secessionist goals may deserve special mention, since the interstate war literature suggests that the presence of territorial issues (the equivalent of secession in civil wars) made rivalries more likely to form, more likely to escalate to war, and less likely to end (Goertz and Diehl 2000a, 256; Vasquez and Leskiw 2001). The implication is that wars of secession should be more likely to become intractable than those involving changing the existing regime, but, as noted, the empirical evidence on this point is, at best, mixed.

One other interesting issue is whether outsiders can help end intractable conflicts, assuming this seems like a good idea. The evidence suggests that mediation is not likely to succeed, at least in the short run. For enduring rivalries in interstate wars, Bercovitch and Diehl (1997) concluded that mediation slightly increased the time between disputes but otherwise was not important either in ending the dispute or in preventing it from escalating to war. Similarly, Barbara Walter (2002, 82–83, 89) and Doyle and Sambanis (2000) found that external mediation had little, if any, impact on civil war settlements. However, most researchers agree that intervention involving military force, especially when it is multilateral, does reduce the likelihood of civil war resumption (Doyle and Sambanis 2000; Fortna 2004b; Enterline and Kang 2002; Balch-Lindsay and Enterline 2000). Dubey (2002) is a significant dissenter, as is Nilsson (2003).

Implications for the Cases in This Book

What difference does all this make? At least three conclusions would seem to follow.

1. The examples of intractable wars examined in this book are exceptions to the rule; precisely because they are intractable, they are not typical. Indeed, this is one reason why we need to examine them closely and in considerable detail; we need to find out what it was about a particular conflict that made it so difficult to resolve. We need to be especially concerned about these events, but we also need to avoid the problem of the doctor who believes the whole world is sick because everyone he sees is sick.

2. When we attempt to discover why each example wound up being intractable, we are also looking for patterns, for things that the wars may have in common that may explain their common outcome. This is a difficult process, both because it is hard to know what to look for and because without cases of tractable wars it is hard to know whether the factors we isolate are unique to this particular group of cases or not. That must wait for another kind of analysis. But the search for patterns, which is at the heart of social science, remains central to our enterprise.

3. In our search for the explanation of the course of these wars, it is important to remember that the factors that caused a war to begin are probably *not* the same ones that caused it to last so long. Sorting these

out in individual cases is obviously a delicate task, but the evidence that we have, tentative as it is, suggests that it is a requirement in our search for understanding these tragic events and devising appropriate responses to them.

Notes

1. In gathering material for this chapter, I started out looking strictly at large-N, quantitative studies of civil wars but then was tempted to look at both comparative case studies and interstate war analysis. However, most of the citations are from the quantitative literature on civil wars, reflecting my idiosyncratic reading habits. I use the terms "large-N" and "quantitative" interchangeably; they refer to studies in which the number of examples or cases is large enough for statistical techniques to be used to summarize the results. In practice this usually means the one hundred or so incidents since 1945 that many observers have called civil wars, or the substantially larger number of interstate wars over a longer time period. I acknowledge with gratitude the assistance of my colleagues on the War Termination Listserv in locating literature, particularly Robert Art, William Ayres, Karen Ballentine, Jeffrey Dixon, James Fearon, George Irani, T. David Mason, Curtis Meek, David Rapoport, Patrick Regan, Steve Saideman, and Elisabeth Wood, and my colleague Jack Levy for guiding me through the literature on enduring rivalries.

2. I have oversimplified a lot of complex and conflicting analysis here. Overall I have been most influenced by James Fearon's analysis, which found that some of these factors had influence until controls were added. There is no reason, however, to believe that this issue has now been resolved beyond doubt.

References

Ayres, R. William. 2000. "Separation or Inclusion: Testing Hypotheses on the End of Ethnic Conflict." *International Journal of Peace Studies* 5, no. 2 (autumn/winter): 1–25.

———. 2001. "Strategies, Capabilities, and Demands: Explaining Outcomes in Violent Intrastate Nationalist Conflicts." *International Interactions* 27, no. 1: 61–93.

Balch-Lindsay, Dylan, and Andrew Enterline. 2000. "Killing Time: The World Politics of Civil War Duration, 1820–1992." *International Studies Quarterly* 44, no. 4 (December): 615–642.

Bennett, D. Scott. 1997. "Democracy, Regime Change, and Rivalry Termination." *International Interactions* 22, no. 4: 369–397.

Bercovitch, Jacob, and Paul F. Diehl. 1997. "Conflict Management of Enduring Rivalries: Frequency, Timing, and Impact of Short-Term Mediation." *International Interactions* 22, no. 4: 299–320.

Carment, David, and Frank Harvey. 2001. *Using Force to Prevent Ethnic Violence: An Evaluation of Theory and Evidence.* Westport, Conn.: Praeger.

Collier, Paul, Anke Hoeffler, and Måns Söderbom. 2004. "On the Duration of Civil War." *Journal of Peace Research* 41, no. 3 (May): 253–273.

Diehl, Paul F., and Gary Goertz. 2000. *War and Peace in International Rivalry.* Ann Arbor: University of Michigan Press.

Dixon, Jeffrey Scott. 2001. "Intervention, Capabilities, Costs, and the Outcome of Civil Wars." Ph.D. diss., Political Science Department, Rice University, April, http://www.personal.psu.edu/jsd11/.

Doyle, Michael W., and Nicholas Sambanis. 2000. "International Peacebuilding: A Theoretical and Quantitative Analysis." *American Political Science Review* 94, no. 4 (December): 779–801.

Dubey, Amitabh. 2002. "Domestic Institutions and Duration of Civil War Settlements." New York: Political Science Department, Columbia University, May 6, ad258@columbia.edu.

Elbadawi, Ibrahim A., and Nicholas Sambanis. 2000. "External Interventions and the Duration of Civil Wars." World Bank Policy Research Working Paper 2433 (September).

Enterline, Andrew J., and Seonjou Kang. 2002. "Stopping the Killing Sooner: Assessing the Success of United Nations Peacekeeping in Civil Wars, 1946–1997." Paper presented at Peace Science Society [International], Tucson, Ariz., November 1–3.

Fearon, James. 2004. "Why Do Some Civil Wars Last So Much Longer Than Others?" *Journal of Peace Research* 41, no. 3 (May): 275–301.

Fortna, Virginia Page. 2004a. *Peace Time: Cease-fire Agreements and the Durability of Peace.* Princeton, N.J.: Princeton University Press.

———. 2004b. "Does Peacekeeping Keep Peace? International Intervention and the Duration of Peace after Civil War." *International Studies Quarterly* 48, no. 2: 269–292.

Goertz, Gary, and Paul F. Diehl. 2000a. "(Enduring) Rivalries." In *Handbook of War Studies II,* edited by Manus Midlarsky, 222–267. Ann Arbor: University of Michigan Press.

———. 2000b. "Rivalries: The Conflict Process." In *What Do We Know about War?* edited by John Vasquez, 197–217. Lanham, Md.: Rowman and Littlefield.

Gurr, Ted Robert. 2000. *People versus States: Minorities at Risk in the New Century.* Washington, D.C.: United States Institute of Peace Press.

Hartlyn, Jonathan. 1993. "Civil Violence and Conflict Resolution: The Case of Colombia." In *Stopping the Killing: How Civil Wars End,* edited by Roy Licklider, 37–62. New York: New York University Press.

Hartzell, Caroline, Matthew Hoddie, and Donald Rothchild. 2001. "Stabilizing the Peace after Civil War: An Investigation of Some Key Variables." *International Organization* 55, no. 1 (winter): 183–209.

Hensel, Paul R. 1994. "One Thing Leads to Another: Recurrent Militarized Disputes in Latin America, 1816–1986." *Journal of Peace Research* 31: 281–298.

Hensel, Paul R., Gary Goertz, and Paul F. Diehl. 2000. "The Democratic Peace and Rivalries." *Journal of Politics* 62, no. 4 (November): 1173–1188.

Licklider, Roy. 1995. "The Consequences of Negotiated Settlements in Civil Wars, 1945–1993." *American Political Science Review* 89, no. 3 (September): 681–690.

———. 2001. "False Hopes? Democracy and the Resumption of Civil War." Paper presented at the Economics and Politics of Civil War: Launching a Case Study Project, sponsored by the International Peace Research Institute, the World Bank, and the Norwegian Ministry of Foreign Affairs, Oslo, Norway, June 2001.

Maoz, Zeev. 1984. "Peace by Empire? Conflict Outcomes and International Stability, 1816–1976." *Journal of Peace Research* 21: 227–241.

Mason, T. David, and Patrick J. Fett. 1996. "How Civil Wars End: A Rational Choice Approach." *Journal of Conflict Resolution* 40, no. 4 (December): 546–568.

Nilsson, Desirée. 2003. "Who Returns to War and Why? Spoilers to Peace Agreements in Interstate Armed Conflicts in Africa, 1989–2001." Paper presented at the conference of the International Studies Association, Portland, Ore., February 26–March 1.

Posen, Barry. 1993. "The Security Dilemma and Ethnic Conflict." *Survival* 35 (spring): 27–47.

Regan, Patrick M. 2002. "Third-Party Interventions and the Duration of Intrastate Conflicts." *Journal of Conflict Resolution* 46, no. 1 (February): 55–73.

Ross, Michael. 2004. "How Do Natural Resources Influence Civil Wars?" *International Organization* 58 (winter): 35–67.

Sambanis, Nicholas. 2002. "A Review of Recent Advances and Future Directions in the Literature on Civil War." *Defense and Peace Economics* 13, no. 2 (June): 215–243.

Small, Melvin, and J. David Singer. 1982. *Resort to Arms: International and Civil Wars, 1816–1980.* 2d ed. Beverly Hills, Calif.: Sage.

Stedman, Stephen John. 1991. *Peacemaking in Civil Wars: International Mediation in Zimbabwe, 1974–1980.* Boulder, Colo.: Lynne Rienner.

———. 1993. "The End of the American Civil War." In *Stopping the Killing: How Civil Wars End,* edited by Roy Licklider, 164–188. New York: New York University Press.

Toft, Monica. 2003. "Peace through Victory?" Paper presented at the American Political Science Association, Philadelphia, August 2003.

Vasquez, John, and Christopher S. Leskiw. 2001. "The Origins and War Proneness of Interstate Rivalries." *Annual Review of Political Science* 4: 295–316.

Wagner, Robert Harrison. 1993. "The Causes of Peace." In *Stopping the Killing: How Civil Wars End,* edited by Roy Licklider, 235–268. New York: New York University Press.

Walter, Barbara. 2002. *Committing to Peace: The Successful Settlement of Civil Wars.* Princeton, N.J.: Princeton University Press.

———. 2004. "Does Conflict Beget Conflict? Explaining Recurring Civil War." *Journal of Peace Research* 41, no. 3 (May): 371–388.

Walter, Barbara, and Jack Snyder. 1999. *Civil Wars, Insecurity, and Intervention.* New York: Columbia University Press.

Zartman, I. William. 1993. "The Unfinished Agenda: Negotiating Internal Conflicts." In *Stopping the Killing: How Civil Wars End,* edited by Roy Licklider, 20–36. New York: New York University Press.

3

Analyzing Intractability

I. William Zartman

THE PRIOR QUESTION shadowing an analysis of intractability is whether it is a permanent condition of "true intractability" or whether it itself is conditional, dependent on some other characteristic that can be manipulated. In part, to pose the question is to answer it, since "true intractability" would mean that the subject area would always be in conflict, a condition that exists nowhere (despite some "primordial" claims). Nonetheless, some conditions of intractability may be longer-lasting and less manipulable than others. This chapter discusses a set of contextual characteristics associated with the mediation process plus a structural or geographic characteristic as well. None of these elements is absolute, but then neither is the characterization of intractability. There are a number of different kinds of intractability, and as long as a single airtight category is not established, a single airtight causal fit is unlikely. Since the first is improbable if not impossible, as the introductory chapter discusses, the absence of the second is pardonable in the present chapter.

The following discussion will proceed inductively from the cases examined in this book to establish two different types of characteristics that can be tested deductively in any other cases and, if sustained, can be used to help design appropriate policies to overcome intractability. First, five internal characteristics of intractability as a process will be discussed, and then three external characteristics of the context of intractability will be analyzed. The chapter will conclude by examining actions that can be taken to break intractability's hold on conflict.

Process

Five internal characteristics combine to identify intractable conflicts. They are protracted time, identity denigration, conflict profitability, absence of ripeness, and solution polarization. These are not causal elements for the conflict's initiation but rather processual features that evolve as the conflict continues and serve to develop and reinforce its intractability. They may be considered causal elements in the conflict's intractability, but they are more appropriately considered as definitional elements that help make understandable the challenge and complexity of intractability (Mandel and Clarke 1982). As such, it is important that they be seen as obstructing characteristics that any effort to overcome intractability must face and that make this particular type of conflict so difficult to overcome. In addition, the significant feature of all these characteristics is their evolving and self-reinforcing nature. Even as identified, they are not static; they grow, in both degree and nature, extending and defending themselves, so that efforts to overcome them must penetrate several layers and deal with their protective dynamics.

Protraction is a definitional characteristic of intractable conflict and it is self-reinforcing. Intractability feeds on intractability and grows with the feeding. As alluded to in the previous paragraphs, a skilled observer might point out ahead of time that a particular conflict has all the earmarks of something that will turn intractable over time, given a chance, but a conflict is not really intractable until it has gone on for a while and resisted attempts to render it tractable. It is impossible to give a fixed-time threshold to protraction, and even if one were possible, it would not help, since many of the cases examined in this book, while undeniably protracted, are not likely to attract agreement on how long they have actually lasted. All depends on when they were considered to have begun. But did the Sudanese conflict begin in 1983 (latest round) or 1956 (independence) or 1898 (colonization), the Balkan conflict in 1990 (Yugoslav collapse) or 1389 (battle of Kosovo), Angola in 1974 (independence) or 1960 (nationalist revolt) or 1484 (colonization), Colombia in 1964 (FARC) or 1958 (National Front), Eurasia in 1991 (end of the USSR) or 1917 (beginning of the USSR), Cyprus in 1974 (Turkish invasion) or 1960 (independence), Korea in 1953 (end of Korean War) or 1945 (partition), Palestine in 1947 (partition) or ca. 1800 BC (birth of Ishmael and Isaac)?

Only the Kashmir conflict seems to have an agreed-on starting point, with independence in 1947.

The importance of protraction, however, lies not in its numerical duration but in that duration's effect. Duration sets up an increasing number of hurdles in the course of the conflict that add to the problems of treating (etymologically, "tracting") them. Conflicts are folded into the history and mythology of the parties, an ideological explanation for national efforts and problems, and so parties become reliant on them and are loath to part with them (Rosoux 2000). They become institutionalized by the parties, as Louis Kriesberg notes in the following chapter, the subjects of perverse routines for carrying out the conflict economically, stretching from alliances and resolutions to hotlines and border regimes. They become the subjects of sunk costs, the vehicles of entrapment, which blind the parties to possible cooperation and solution (Meerts 2004). As a result, parties become insulated against the perception of stalemate and the costs attached to it. Instead, they look for opportunities to escalate the conflict to possible advantage (transitive escalation) and at the same time become vulnerable to internal and external dynamics of the conflict to escalate on its own, by accident or incident (intransitive escalation) (Smoke 1977; Zartman 2004). In so doing, they turn old scars into new wounds, reaffirming history with new proofs and transforming momentary incidents into primordial hostility. In turn, the conflict develops a reputation for intractability, so the mediators do not want to touch it.

Examples of this rolling degeneration can be found in all the conflicts treated here, as well as those not included. The Arab-Israeli conflict has become part of the justifying mythology of both sides, identifying the undifferentiated enemy and explaining delays in national economic development, as have the conflicts of the Balkans and Sudan. Routines for conducting daily affairs across the lines of conflict in these cases manage its permanence in the most efficient way possible and prevent the parties from feeling the pain of the deadlock that governs their daily lives; proposals in Cyprus, Korea, and Palestine for communication and interaction across the dividing lines seek to remove the inconveniences of the conflict without resolving the conflict itself or dissolving the parties to it. Instead, the conflicting parties in Angola, Colombia, Israel, and Sudan look for momentary changes in the conflict and its context to seize an offensive or initiative that will tip the balance of forces in their favor and thereby escalate the conflict to a new level of intractability. And so, as U.S. under-secretary of state Lawrence Eagleburger, an expert on Yugo-slavia, observed, "There is no rationality at all about ethnic conflict. It is gut; it is hatred; it's not for any common set of values or purposes; it just goes on. And that kind of warfare is most difficult to bring to a halt" (quoted in Bert 1997, 102)—and the United States avoided any positive role in the Yugoslav conflict for five wasted years. Similar gaps in poten-tial mediators' attentions have marked the other conflicts studied in this book, reinforcing their characteristic protraction.

Identities in intractable conflicts not only are polarized but are actually dependent on the denigration of the Other. Normally, there is nothing con-flictual about identity: I can be me without my troubling or being trou-bled by your being you (Deng et al. 1996). Conflict can arise when iden-tities become polarized, with no room for grayness or mixture in between: You are either one of us or against us. The polarized conflict moves toward intractability when identities become zero sum and one identity actually depends on demeaning and demonizing the other: Being myself requires me to put you down and deny your full identity as a human being.

The examples are many and varied in the cases studied. Northern Sudanese feel required by their Muslim calling to denigrate the kafirs of the South and to refer to them as *abid* (slaves); Northern Irish Protestants feel a need to parade in Catholic neighborhoods to recall centuries-old victo-ries over the Catholics, and vice versa; North and South Koreans justify their separate identities by the need to protect themselves against the aggressive inferiority of each other; the two lines of descendants from Abraham/Ibrahim, disputing all aspects of their common heritage down to the spelling of their common ancestor's name, proclaim their separate superiorities, hold each other in disdain, and justify their beleaguered existence through the threat from the Other. And so it goes.

Zero-sum identities are not the end of the problem, however. Because the identity of the party is threatened, the conflict takes on exis-tential dimensions: it is a fight for life, for the survival of the party itself. Existential conflict can command enormous commitment and sacrifice from the parties and thus justify any pain and cost that the conflict entails. The conflict plays back on the identity itself, turning it into a beleaguered self-awareness, and its object into an endangered species for which en-dangerment becomes part of the identity itself. Further ramifications include the formation of a grudge culture, in which people revel in being threatened, and the incorporation of conspiracy thinking, in which the enemy becomes the cause of all evil, often through fantastic machinations. Southern Sudanese, Bosniacs and Serbs, Chechens, Turkish Cypriots, Kashmiris, and Israelis and Palestinians often see their struggle as a fight for the continued existence of the nation, against an enemy bent on their elimination. As a result, compromise as a path to resolution becomes impossible, a half-step to suicide; the only position to take is to insist on total victory for one's own side, thus reinforcing the opponent's view of the conflict as existential.

Profitability is a commonplace—someone profits in any conflict—and so is an oft-forgotten characteristic of lasting conflict, as attention focuses much more on the costs and losses, the pain and suffering that unresolved conflict brings to the losers. Much research has been carried out lately attributing the feasibility—a synonym for duration—of conflict to "mobilizable" resources such as diamonds, drugs, and timber, as in Angola, Colombia, Serbia, and Chechnya. Initially sought by rebel groups to keep their struggle alive, resources give rise to a dependency that is habit forming and become the end rather than the means of the conflict (Collier 2000; Collier and Hoeffler 2002). On the other side of the conflict, governments value resources—especially oil—because they enable uncompromising pursuit of the conflict, as in Angola, Georgia, and Sudan among the present cases. Both sides' calculations are relevant to the sustainability of intractable conflicts and are little explored, counterintuitive, and obstructive of efforts at resolution. While the ability to bear the costs of conflict is basic to its duration, that ability is highly elastic, particularly under conditions of high commitment. States always have other ways to use fungible resources. But when the leaders of the conflict themselves get hooked on their resources, attention to initial grievances and underlying causes as a path to resolution becomes irrelevant.

In any kind of continuing situation, however, profit-taking and parasitic industries are bound to arise. Most direct are the arms suppliers, and also the military charged with conducting the conflict and thereby winning an important role in the home country's politics. But the military is not the only political actor to profit from conflict: political leaders come to power and make their reputations on their pursuit of the enemy and their defense of the homeland, leaving little room for doves (or even owls) in the hawks' nest. Jaafar Nimeiri, Omer al Bashir, and John Garang in Sudan, Slobodan Milosevic and Franjo Tudjman in Yugoslavia, Robert Kocharian in Armenia, Igor Smirnov in Transnistria, Jonas Savimbi and José Eduardo dos Santos in Angola, and Rauf Denktaş in Cyprus were only the more prominent politicians who made their careers on keeping their conflicts intractable, reaping from the venture profits that were not only political. Since war, like peace, makes money, profitability lurks somewhere in every intractable conflict, obscuring resolvable grievances for principal actors.

Ripeness as a pressure toward negotiation tends to be absent in intractable conflict. Instead of a mutually hurting stalemate pushing the parties into a search for solutions, there is only a stable, soft, self-serving (4-S) stalemate that is preferable to any attainable solutions and the uncertainties of a search for them (Zartman 1996). A 4-S stalemate is generally bearable to the parties, both in the absolute and relative to any likely solution on the table at the moment (except one's own, currently unattainable). It leaves each of the parties in control of some portion of the territory and population, able to claim that it has not been defeated, which is a victory of sorts. Because of other characteristics, such as zero-sum identity, the existential nature of the conflict, duration, and entrapment, a soft stalemate in a low-level conflict, even when punctuated by occasional blips of violence, avoids the worst, controls losses (gains are seen as impossible), and protects existence and identity—a prospect theorist's dream (Farnham 1994). If there is ever any pressure to look for alternatives to conflict, it is one-sided instead of operating on both parties, and so one of the parties has every interest in pursuing the conflict while the other suffers; frequently the situation is reversed in a future change of fortunes.

In many cases, a simultaneous sense of stalemate has not occurred to both parties, and in others even one-sided stalemate has not taken place. Sudan is a particularly good example of one-sided blockage that never hits both parties at the same time (Deng and Morrison 2000); Angola, Cyprus, and Kashmir are others. North Korea has manipulated crises to avoid and rationalize its own stalemates and throw the monkey on another party's back—South Korea, Japan, and the United States (Sigal 1998). A mutually hurting stalemate led to a cease-fire agreement in Karabakh in 1994 without resolving the basic issue (Mooradian and Druckman 1999); ripeness was also present and pressing for the Oslo negotiations, but the ensuing agreement failed in the implementation and each party's subsequent actions convinced the other that pain was a sign of commitment and a proof of the other's unreliability (Pruitt 1997).

The predominance of 4-S stalemates instead of ripe moments in intractable conflicts means that there is no pressure on the parties to come to a resolution of the conflict on their own or even to listen to mediators. At most, there may be motivation to manage the conflict, that is, to reduce the conflict to a less costly level without touching the basic issues and underlying causes, as in the Karabakh case. But reducing the cost also reduces the pressure for a settlement and so further contributes to intractability. Indeed, since conflict management measures tend to carry with them the promise of conflict resolution at a later moment, when that next step is not taken, the conflict flares up again, heightened by feelings of betrayal and faithlessness, hardening the parties against sensitivity to ripeness and again contributing to the conflict's intractability. Thus, like the other characteristics, the absence of ripeness in intractable conflicts contains a compounding element that reinforces and exacerbates its effects.

Solutions in intractable conflicts also tend to be polarized. (Solutions are related to the other characteristic of ripeness, a way out [Zartman 2000].) Whereas many conflicts are pulled toward one salient solution but experience difficulties in the process of getting there, intractables are generally characterized by the competing pulls of two salient solutions, posing an extreme Prisoner's Dilemma or collaboration problem, where noncooperation, though mutually hurtful, is the outcome logically preferred to unilateral attempts at cooperation (Hasenclever, Mayer, and Rittberger 1997, 46–48). Each side wants its solution in its entirety and can accept neither the Other's nor even a combination of or a compromise between the two solutions. The characteristic of existential, zero-sum identities hardens the parties' demands for their competing solutions. When faced with one salient solution, a mediator is useful in finding ways of getting to it, overcoming distrust, providing step-by-step pathways, formulating combinations and compromises, and working out details. The mediator's role is much more difficult and less clear, however, when confronted with a collaboration problem, in which there may in fact be no room and role for mediation at all.

The Balkans, Eurasia, Karabakh, and Kashmir are all cases of competing solutions: the territory and its people go to one side or the other, and solutions are unacceptable to the loser. There is, of course, a salient solution in Kashmir in the form of the Line of Control that divides the area, but it does not have the strong justifications that underlie the two competing claims. Perhaps autonomous status could be considered an intermediate solution for Karabakh, but it is such a weak solution that it cannot stand up against the two salient solutions in the conflict. The Balkans presented a cascading succession of competing salient solutions, beginning with federal versus republics' sovereignty and passing through various expressions of national versus state self-determination—the same polarized situation found in the Russian Near Abroad. Colombia may also be a case of two salient solutions, although it is not clear what the rebels' solution is.

In some cases there even was once a single salient solution, but it has been exhausted or delegitimized by previous misuse or failure. When a peace process focusing on a single salient solution breaks down, the people tend to feel betrayed and abused and cry out for blood, falling back on their own demands, convinced that the other party is simply incapable of making peace, as in Colombia, Israel, and Palestine in 2002–3. Angola, Palestine, and Sudan illustrate the situation in which a former single salient solution was removed by misuse. Elections in Angola were rejected by the loser, Jonas Savimbi; the Oslo process toward the obvious two-state solution was delegitimized by Israeli delays and Palestinian reticence; and federation in Sudan was undermined by both President Jaafar Nimeiri and the South. Korea alone appears to be a case of a single salient solution of unification and no way to get there, in which the parties prefer the status quo (Choi 2001).

It could be argued that any conflict begins with opposing solutions or notions of justice and that conflict resolution is merely a matter of finding a middle ground or an agreed-on sense of justice through the process of negotiation (Zartman 1999). What, then, distinguishes this situation from an intractable conflict? The answer returns to the distinction between nonexistent "true intractability" and conditional intractability. Although all conflicts tend to begin with a number of competing solutions, many soon move to an acceptable solution through a process of direct or mediated negotiation (or the outright victory of one side). When they do not, they take on a characteristic of intractability. If a single salient solution emerges and attracts the conflicting parties' attention, the condition of intractability recedes; if the parties cling to their competing solutions, it remains.

The Middle East conflict illustrates this condition. Until United Nations Security Council Resolution 242 establishing the conditions for a Middle East settlement was enunciated in 1967, the conflict was intractable. The identification of a single salient solution, embodied in the formula "Security for territory," and then its acceptance as the basis for Israeli withdrawals from Sinai and Golan in 1974–75 moved the conflict away from intractability, and the peace treaties with Egypt and later Jordan ensued. The Syrian problem remains intractable, despite the formula. The negotiation of a modified formula at Oslo in 1993 moved the core conflict between Israel and Palestine away from intractability, but the breakdown of the Oslo process restored its intractability. That there are benchmark dates and events in this process but no absolute thresholds should not trouble even orderly minds accustomed to dealing in human relations.

Together, these five characteristics—protraction, identity, profitability, ripeness, and solutions—are generally shared by intractable conflicts and go far to explain the difficulty of bringing them under control. While the characteristics are independent of one another, they also tend to reinforce one another, which in itself is an additional characteristic of intractability, making it hard to pry them apart and deal with them one by one. This interlocked, exacerbating dynamic is clearly expressed in the Cypriot reactions to the collapse of the European Union plan in March 2003: "I expected it to end like this, and I think things are going to be worse now in terms of cementing the final partition of the island [Greek Cypriot]. . . . I wish the Annan plan had never been introduced. It gave us hope, a hope which is obviously now a false one. As a Turkish Cypriot, I now wonder what our future will be, what my children's future will be. . . . Many younger people want change, and many younger people [Turkish Cypriots] are planning to leave the island" (*New York Times* 2003). As the characteristics show, intractability is a dynamic, self-reinforcing condition, digging an ever-deepening hole for itself and feeding itself like a vortex.

Geopolitics

One frequently mentioned characteristic has not been mentioned here— the contextual nature of intractability. It was long thought that lesser intractabilities were held in place by the biggest one of all, the East-West conflict of the Cold War. The end of the Great Intractable carried with it others as well—Cambodia, the Central American insurgencies, Mozambique, Germany, and Yemen, among others. Still others remained, intractable in their own right. Yet it would be hasty to dismiss the role of external actors and context. Whether in the global bipolar configuration or within some other geopolitical context, intractability is affected by its location. This characteristic is of a different nature than the preceding five because it is structural and external to the conflict rather than internal and process related. Three aspects of context are significant—embeddedness, bias, and buffering. None of them appear to be as universal as the internal characteristics, but they are still powerful influences in many cases.

Many of the intractable cases are prolonged and made more difficult to resolve because they are *embedded* in a multilayered set of relationships. Left to their own devices, the parties might be able to find a solution in their own interests, but they have been hindered by the need to resolve several layers of the same conflict at once. All of the characteristics already noted—long history, zero-sum identities, conflict profitability, 4-S stalemates, polarized solutions—are heightened by the fact that the parties engage patrons or supporters further away from the conflict as well. Parties are not puppets, and patrons are not just string pullers; the relationship runs in both directions, but that is what complicates the conflict and its management. Patrons have their own interests in addition to those covering their involvement in the conflict; these interests probably favor management of the conflict and may even favor its settlement, independent of the interests of the parties themselves, but patron interests may also favor conflict continuation when the parties directly involved are tired and would like to settle if left to their own devices (Zartman 1992).

Many of the examples are obvious. They begin with the Bosnian Serbs and Croats, shunted aside by Slobodan Milosevic and Franjo Tudjman under pressure from Charles Redman and Richard Holbrooke. They continue with Glafcos Clerides and especially Rauf Denktaş, players on the Greek and Turkish scenes as well as among Greek and Turkish Cypriots, with the conflict the key piece in Greek-Turkish relations. In Kashmir, the mujahideen are the tail that wags the Pakistani dog, whereas the ruling Abdullah family, father and sons, were rather Indian agents; in between,

Kashmiri nationalists are their own men, but the conflict is nonetheless the key piece in Pakistani-Indian relations, too.

The second external or contextual characteristic concerns the *biased* relations of potential conflict managers to the intractable conflicts. Mediators with policies and interests that favor one of the conflicting parties tend to be hampered, both operationally and ideologically, in their efforts to bring the conflict to an end. Instead of being able to help the parties out of the conflict, the potential mediator sees its national interest in supporting one side and in assuring its continuing security or even victory, rather than in finding compromises. In many intractable conflicts, bias, however justified, has tended to affect the leading mediator, who then blocks the way for others who play the same role, possibly more effectively. In such cases, the parties are not going to get any real help out of their conflict, even though the mediator's preferences may be very soundly grounded in interest and values.

The United States, as the principal mediator on the world scene, has had its friends in the conflicts in Afghanistan, Angola, Colombia, Kashmir, Korea, and the Middle East, and its enemies (if not its friends) in Bosnia and Sudan. Mediation is not thereby impossible, as efforts in some of these cases have shown, but it does become much more delicate and difficult. The mediator is not required to be unbiased, but if it does have favorites, it is expected to deliver their acceptance of the agreement (Touval and Zartman 2001), a requirement that can pose as much of an obstacle as evenhanded mediation itself.

Most of the cases examined in this book also share a special form of embedded relations—a *buffer* status between major blocs, powers, or civilizations. Ideally, a buffer state is a neutral area with its own personality, contested by each side but left alone as long as the other side does not claim it—the null possession status. The alternative is either partition between the two sides or domination by one of them. Some cases have long histories as buffers or contested areas; these include vestiges of a past rivalry or encroachments of one side on another that carry the buffer into foreign territory. In some cases the notion of the buffer is only one interpretation of the situation or even an element of the conflict itself, but in all cases it provides enough insight into the conflict to be sustainable.

Afghanistan, Kashmir, and Sudan are classical cases of buffer states between large civilizational areas—Afghanistan the site of the Great Game between Russia and (British) India (Kipling 1896; Ahari 1996), Kashmir between the Muslim and Hindu worlds, and Sudan between black and Arab Africa (Deng 1995). Korea is a double buffer, historically between China and Japan, synthesizing a vigorous civilization of its own out of elements from both neighbors and more recently being split between the free and communist worlds; like other split nations, such as Germany, Vietnam, and Yemen (Choi 2001), Korea remains the site of intractable conflict only as long as the split is maintained. Of these cases, Afghanistan is the only true buffer, a neutral territory with its own identity between large forces—no longer just Russia and British India but Turkey, Pakistan, and Iran, and behind them Russia and the United States, the British heir. Most other cases are buffers split between the forces they are supposed to buffer. Kashmir, Korea, and Cyprus (if an island can be a buffer) would also be examples of a true buffer if they were not divided into two parts. So would Sudan if John Garang's dream of a single Sudanese civilization were realized instead of two nations (still) in the same state. Bosnia, too, was historically conceived as a buffer and may again become one if its state unity finally overcomes its national divisions. But in both bistate nations and binational states, it is the effort to either divide the buffer or take it over by one side or the other that causes the conflict and makes it intractable.

The other cases are variations on the theme of differing magnitudes. Karabakh is a hostage in a smaller civilizational clash, between Christian Armenians and Muslim Azeris. Angola is an ethnically divided nation, between *assimilados* and indigenous peoples, as well as a victim of the Great Intractable and of a charismatic spoiler. Only Colombia represents a new and different type, not a buffer in any sense but simply a state dying of cancer, a chilling harbinger of catastrophes to come.

These three structural characteristics—embeddedness, bias, and buffering—tend to be less dynamic than the processual ones, and they lack the latter's self-reinforcing, exacerbating nature. In that sense, they may be easier to overcome or even turn into an advantage in managing intractable conflict.

Policy

There are answers to all of these eight characteristics; none is absolute. Answers may be more or less difficult to apply, but the advantage of identifying the characteristics is that they point to specific policies and tactics for resolving intractability. Thus, a special diplomacy is indeed required for intractables, not always distinct from normal diplomacy in all its details but special in its combination of policies and tactics. That combination is important, since optimally intractability needs to be countered on all its characteristics, lest one untended remain to revive the others. Dealing with intractability is not an incidental exercise; it requires sustained, coordinated effort. The other glaring lesson is the need for early action, before the exacerbating characteristics become operative. As in so many instances, vigilance, early awareness, and normal diplomacy need to be deployed if more costly, more encumbering, more difficult efforts to manage conflicts turned intractable are to be avoided (Zartman forthcoming).

Early efforts are the best answer to protraction, and efforts at any stage are always early in the course of a conflict untended. The best answer to entrapment is not to sink costs in yet another attempt to escalate out of the conflict that digs in deeper instead. The more fresh wounds and confirming incidents can be avoided, the more the self-reinforcing nature of protraction can be weakened, or at least prevented from further strengthening. The best time to interrupt protraction is a moment when the objective conditions of ripeness appear and can be used by interested third parties to cultivate the subjective perceptions of a mutually hurting stalemate and a way out, discussed later. This is what Chester Crocker did in 1987 after seven years of minding and ripening the Namibian-Angolan standoff, what Alvaro de Soto did in 1990 after tending the El Salvador civil war for four years and in 2002–3 after working in Cyprus for two years, and what Ibrahim Gambari was appointed by UN secretary-general Kofi Annan to do in 2002–3 after waiting out the period following the signing of the Lusaka Protocol in 1994 (Crocker, Hampson, and Aall 1999).

Ripeness is a matter of perception and thus of persuasion. As the theory indicates, subjective perception is helped by objective evidence, but it is the former that is crucial. Mediators have an important role to play in capitalizing on the parties' perception of ripeness, but they also have a crucial role to play in enhancing that perception if it does not appear on its own (Zartman 2000). Elements in such persuasion include convincing the parties that a mutually hurting stalemate exists in reality or looms in the future as the projection of the current course of conflict, or that a 4-S stalemate is neither soft nor stable nor satisfactory in comparison to the benefits that could be obtained from a settlement.

Zero-sum identity is perhaps the most difficult to deal with because it is a broad popular perception rather than an elite matter, and thus more difficult to manipulate. Zero-sum identity underwrites competing solutions and makes it hard for single salient solutions to emerge. It also clouds the parties' perceptions of a hurting stalemate, since it provides the righteous cause that thrives on pain. Thus, dealing with identity conflict requires enlightened leadership that is able to portray a better future for its people than dogged adherence to uncompromising notions of the self and finds greater satisfaction in material accomplishments and betterment. This is the basis for inducements from the mediator and the international community as part of a settlement, to divert attentions from identity fixations and turn them to the improvement of welfare (as fundamentalists fear).

The identification of a single salient solution is crucial to any effort at resolution. Unless the two opposing solutions are not mutually exclusive and can be combined to produce a positive-sum outcome, dual competing solutions provide a mutually blocking situation and often lead to simply projecting the preferred outcome, however unattainable now, into the infinite future. The combination of two competing solutions into one was seen in the Namibia-Angola negotiations, but the projection of the integral solution into the future when even half a loaf is not considered attainable is now seen in the Palestinians' reversion to total claims under Hamas after the failure of Oslo. Identifying and legitimizing the salience of a single solution are a matter of persuasion, like all diplomacy, but it is good to identify it as a prime target of focus. It can also be reinforced by repetition and legitimization by international organizations and nongovernmental fora. Buffer state status is one such salient solution, as discussed below.

The current focus on profitability, particularly through blood diamonds and drugs, has led to measures of control through the United Nations in regard to Angola and Sierra Leone, for example, or national measures of control, such as by the United States in regard to Colombian drugs and Sudanese oil. However, there is no possibility of eliminating the characteristic; the most important policy advice is to be aware of it and to try to control its relevant form in particular cases.

The structural characteristics by their nature lend themselves more directly to policy applications. Bias can be combined with effective mediation, but it requires an enlightened understanding by the mediator as a background to its skillful exercise of persuasion on the parties. There are times when keeping one's ally in the game is the most a third party can do, and so doing weakens any possibility of mediation. But there are other times in the same conflict when such support can be turned to the advantage of mediation, when helping the parties out of a costly conflict can be portrayed as the best way to protect one's ally's interests, and when the possibility of delivering one's ally to an agreement satisfactory to both sides is the key to protecting the mediator's relations and interests with both parties. The mediator may be able to formulate the terms of an agreement that protects the interests of the party it favors while providing enough benefits for the other side to gain its acceptance. Alternatively, the mediator may find its own interest in an evenhanded agreement, despite its own biases, in order to keep or restore good relations with both parties. Nonetheless, these ways out of the mediator's dilemma are not easy recipes for playing one side and the middle at the same time. But the mediator itself must be persuaded of this possibility before it can help the parties out of their conflict.

Historically, buffering has been a useful concept, and the elimination of a buffer state tends to have serious consequences, as moments in the histories of Cambodia, Moldova, Poland, and others have shown. The most successful buffer states are those that are allowed to develop their own culture and integrity and are left to perform their buffering functions undisturbed. The histories of Afghanistan, Cambodia, Chad, Cyprus, and Korea, among others, show that external meddling is deleterious to healthy buffering, but the histories of Mauritania, Nepal, and Sudan show that buffer states do not always perform well even when left alone. In general, as a policy recommendation, either splitting a buffer state between the two sides or taking it over by one of them tends to prolong conflict rather than reducing it, even if respecting buffer states does not always ensure that they will buffer well.

Embeddedness can constitute an opportunity as well as an obstacle to the resolution of intractables. One of Crocker's lessons, applied to the southwest African dispute, was to separate the external dimension from the internal dimension of the conflict (Crocker 1992), an insightful tactic that has been found pertinent elsewhere as well. Whatever the judgment one holds on the degree of concessions at Camp David in 1979, separation of the Israeli-Egyptian dimension from the larger Arab- (including Palestinian-) Israeli context made the Israeli-Egyptian peace treaty possible. Attempts have been made to deal with Cyprus directly, disconnected from Greek-Turkish relations, or to deal with Cyprus by first improving Greek-Turkish relations, although it was the accession of Cyprus, in part or in whole, to the European Union that put the greatest—but not in the end sufficient—pressure on both levels of the conflict for a solution. Separation of the Angolan conflict from its Cold War and even southern African context made the 1992 Bicesse and 1994 Lusaka agreements possible, even if the core conflict itself proved stronger than their implementation. Embedded conflicts face the challenge of double triangulation, whereby the host country of a neighbor's insurgency finds support for the insurgency in its interest in its relations with the home country, until the time when hosting begins to hurt it and then its interest turns to reconciliation with its neighbor at the expense of the insurgency, a challenge repeatedly faced by Sudan's neighbors, particularly Ethiopia and Uganda (Zartman 1996).

But embeddedness also may be construed as the key required for the solution of a conflict that is as complex and prolonged as to qualify as an intractable. The rejected mediation in Cyprus suggests the importance of using a larger project or relationship, such as would have been provided by European Union accession for only a united island, as the bait and guarantor of a stable, long-term solution in the same way that European unification formed the context for the elimination of the intractable Franco-German dispute (Rosoux 2000). Similarly, the Helsinki Final Act of 1975 and the Conference (now Organization) on Security and Cooperation in Europe (C/OSCE) provided the nest for the solution of the intractable Cold War. The multilateral arrangements provided in the Madrid peace process were designed to provide a network of relationships to enmesh the search for an Israeli-Palestinian solution. It is striking that none of the other intractables furnish any examples of such attempts. Conflicts as big as intractables require big solutions.

Short of a solution, the best approach to intractables may well be one of management rather than resolution, for all the traps that conflict management contains, already noted. Management preserves the conflict for resolution another day, at a more propitious time, and may be able to forestall the self-reinforcing effects of some of the characteristics. After all, freezing is better and less painful than boiling.

References

Ahari, M. E. 1996. *The New Great Game in Muslim Central Asia,* McNair Paper 47. Washington, D.C.: Institute for National Strategic Studies, National Defense University.

Bert, Wayne. 1997. *The Reluctant Superpower: United States' Policy in Bosnia, 1991–95.* New York: St Martin's.

Choi, Sukyong. 2001. "Divided States: Reunifying without Conquest." In *Preventive Negotiation,* edited by I. William Zartman. Lanham, Md.: Rowman and Littlefield.

Collier, Paul. 2000. "Rebellion as a Quasi-Criminal Activity." *Journal of Conflict Resolution* 44, no. 4: 839–853.

Collier, Paul, and Anke Hoeffler. 2002. "On the Edge of Civil War in Africa." *Journal of Conflict Resolution* 46, no. 1: 13–28.

Crocker, Chester A., 1992. *High Noon in Southern Africa.* New York: W. W. Norton.

Crocker, Chester A., Fen Osler Hampson, and Pamela Aall, eds. 1999. *Herding Cats: Multiparty Mediation in a Complex World.* Washington, D.C.: United States Institute of Peace Press.

Deng. Francis. 1995. *War of Visions.* Washington, D.C.: Brookings Institution.

Deng, Francis, and Stephen Morrison. 2000. *Task Force Report on Sudan.* Washington, D.C.: Center for Strategic and International Studies.

Deng, Francis, et al. 1996. *Sovereignty as Responsibility.* Washington, D.C.: Brookings Institution.

Farnham, Barbara, ed. 1994. *Avoiding Losses/Taking Risks.* Ann Arbor, Mich.: University of Michigan Press.

Hasenclever, Andreas, Peter Mayer, and Volker Rittberger. 1997. *Theories of International Regimes.* New York: Cambridge University Press.

Kipling, Rudyard. 1896. *Kim.*

Mandel, Robert, and Sarah Clarke. 1982. "Intractability and International Bargaining." Paper presented at the annual meeting of the International Studies Association.

Meerts, Paul. 2004. "Entrapment and Escalation." In *Escalation and Negotiation,* edited by I. William Zartman and Guy Olivier Faure. Lanham, Md.: Rowman and Littlefield.

Mooradian, Moorad, and Daniel Druckman. 1999. "Hurting Stalemate or Mediation? The Conflict over Nagorno-Karabakh, 1990–95." *Journal of Peace Research* 36, no. 6: 709–727.

New York Times. 2003. "Cypriots Unsurprised as 4th Peace Deal Fails." March 12, A8.

Pruitt, Dean G., ed. 1997. "Lessons Learned from the Middle East Peace Process." Special issue of *International Negotiation* 2, no. 2.

Rosoux, Valerie. 2000. *Les usages de la mémoire dans les relations internationals*. Brussels: Bruylant.

Sigal, Leon. 1998. *Disarming Strangers*. Princeton, N.J.: Princeton University Press.

Smoke, Richard. 1977. *War*. Cambridge, Mass.: Harvard University Press.

Touval, Saadia, and I. William Zartman. 2001. "International Mediation in the Post–Cold War Era." In *Turbulent Peace: The Challenges of Managing International Conflict*, edited by Chester A. Crocker, Fen Osler Hampson, and Pamela Aall, 427–443. Washington, D.C.: United States Institute of Peace Press.

Zartman, I. William. 1992. "Internationalization of Communal Strife." In *The Internationalization of Communal Strife*, edited by Manus Midlarsky. New York: Routledge.

———, ed. 1996. *Elusive Peace: Negotiating to End Civil War*. Washington, D.C.: Brookings Institution.

———. 1999. "Justice in Negotiation." In *International Negotiation: Actors, Structure/Process, Values*, edited by Peter Berton, Hiroshi Kimura, and I. William Zartman. New York: St. Martin's Press.

———. 2000. "Ripeness: The Hurting Stalemate and Beyond." In *International Conflict Resolution after the Cold War*, edited by Paul Stern and Daniel Druckman. Washington, D.C.: National Academy.

———, ed. 2001. "Negotiating Internal Conflict: Incentives and Intractability." Special issue of *International Negotiation* 6, no. 3.

———. 2004. "The Dynamics of Escalation." In *Escalation and Negotiation*, edited by I. William Zartman and Guy Olivier Faure. Laxenburg, Austria: International Institute of Applied Systems Analysis.

———. Forthcoming. *Cowardly Lions: Missed Opportunities to Prevent Deadly Conflict and State Collapse*.

4

Nature, Dynamics, and Phases of Intractability

Louis Kriesberg

ALL LARGE-SCALE SOCIAL CONFLICTS change over time, and
some become intractable with recurrent violent escalations. Nevertheless,
even intractable conflicts often have periods of subdued conflict and over
time become transformed and tractable or otherwise terminated. As conflicts become more intractable and then become less so, they go through
many phases. This chapter argues that particular strategies, pursued by
diverse actors, tend to be suitable for controlling intractable conflicts in
different phases.

Although conflict intractability is multidimensional and varies over
time, the concept incorporates certain core elements (Kriesberg, Northrup,
and Thorson 1989; Putnam and Wondolleck 2002). Essentially, intractable conflicts persist for a long time in a way that is objectionable to at
least some partisans or interveners and despite their efforts to end or transform what they view as objectionable. In this chapter, I focus on conflicts
between large-scale adversaries such as countries or entities identified in
ethnic, religious, language, or other communal terms. Furthermore, most
attention is on conflicts that entail direct physical violence or the threat of
such violence.

This chapter is divided into three sections. First, I discuss the complex
and dynamic nature of conflicts in general and then focus on conflicts
that become more intractable, mapping out the major phases through
which they generally move. Second, I examine the factors that shape the
degree and character of intractability as conflicts move from one phase to

another. This provides the analytic background for discerning appropriate moderating strategies at different phases. Finally, I discuss policies that antagonists and intermediaries may pursue to prevent a conflict from becoming intractable, to interrupt its increasing intractability, to transform the conflict into a more tractable one, and to consolidate a more peaceful relationship.

Nature of Conflicts and Intractability

Since intractability is a quality of particular social conflicts, clarity about the definition of social conflicts and the major ways they differ is needed. I adopt a broad meaning of social conflict here: it is a relationship in which at least one party manifests the belief that it has incompatible goals with another (Kriesberg 2003). So defined, many conflicts are not destructive but are conducted in accord with rules the adversaries regard as legitimate. This is true in most domestic conflicts, waged within the context of political and judicial institutions. Furthermore, such conflicts are widely viewed as serving the interests of the adversaries and the welfare of the society as a whole. Thus, citizens in democratic societies generally regard the regulated adversarial political and judicial systems of their countries as essential to their democracy.

Defining Intractable Conflicts

Intractability, like social conflict itself, is variously defined. For some observers, it is viewed as an analytic concept, but partisans and intermediaries may use the term to characterize a conflict and so try to affect its future course. In this chapter, the concept is treated analytically and three dimensions are stressed. First, intractable conflicts are protracted conflicts, persisting for a long time. Second, they are waged in ways that the adversaries or interested observers regard as destructive. Third, partisans and intermediaries attempt, but fail, to end or transform them. As viewed here, conflicts are more or less intractable, not wholly intractable.

Even duration can change and become shorter as well as longer and is not determined by a calendar. Some fights may be regarded as protracted if they persist for a year, when the issues in contention are usually resolved in a matter of days or weeks. Social expectations are important in judging a conflict's persistence. Analytically, however, it is useful to set some parameters, and for large-scale social conflicts, persistence beyond one social generation is appropriate. That indicates that the parties in the conflict are likely to have learned and internalized reasons to continue their fight with each other.

Conflicts certainly vary in their duration, but measurements of duration depend on the identification of the parties on each side of the conflict and their continuity. The identities and the duration therefore can change. Leaders of one side in a fight may evoke old battles with the adversary and try to characterize a new fight as part of a long-standing, perhaps decades- or centuries-old intractable conflict. The breakup of Yugoslavia was a scene for such conflicts among some Serbs, Croats, and Bosnian Muslims. As the conflict de-escalates or becomes transformed, the fight may come to be regarded as between nationalist political leaders and the supporters they mobilized, not the peoples they claimed to represent. The conflict then is only years long.

Characterizing a particular conflict as highly intractable may be disputed, since the characterization depends on the time perspective that is used as well as the qualities of the conflict that are stressed in defining intractability. A conflict's intractability depends upon who the adversaries are deemed to be, since a conflict may be intractable for some members of one or more sides but not for others.

As defined here, not all prolonged conflicts are highly intractable. Thus, conflicts between workers and managers and between people of the right and of the left may seem interminable, but in many circumstances the conflicts are well managed and therefore not regarded as intractable. When the persisting conflicts are or threaten to be conducted with extensive violence or otherwise destructive behavior, observers and partisans are prone to regard them as intractable. Conflicts certainly vary in their degree of intensity, in the imposition of injuries, and in the expressions of hatred and hostility.

In addition, if conflicts are long and destructive, efforts to end or transform them are likely to be made; but their failure contributes to the conflicts' being regarded as intractable. The de-escalating efforts may be undertaken by partisans of one or more sides in the conflict or by outside intermediaries. The magnitude of the efforts, in terms of parties engaged, the resources used, and the frequency of peacemaking attempts made, characterizes variations in this dimension.

These three dimensions jointly define intractability. None alone suffices. A conflict, manifested in economic or political strife, may endure for generations but at such a comfortable level of rivalry that it is not viewed as intractable. Or a conflict may explode in a terribly destructive outburst, which is swiftly and clearly terminated, perhaps by the destruction or dissolution of one of the parties. Finally, a conflict may be subjected to many attempts at its resolution but be regarded as below the level of severity or longevity necessary to be characterized as highly intractable.

These dimensions are not independent of one another. In many ways high levels in one dimension tend to produce high levels in other dimensions. Thus, a destructively conducted struggle tends to be prolonged and the target of many failed peacemaking efforts. Similarly, as a conflict goes on, it is likely to be waged increasingly destructively and with more unsuccessful efforts to end it. Finally, failed efforts at peacemaking often result in hardened antagonistic positions, thus increasing the difficulties in reaching a mutually acceptable accommodation. Despite all this, as I discuss later, transitions do occur and processes of de-escalation and transformation result in highly intractable conflicts becoming much less intractable.

Phases of Intractability

Intractable conflicts often fluctuate in magnitude during their course; indeed, they generally consist of a series of relatively intense conflict episodes linked by dormancy or low-intensity fighting. Nevertheless, major phases of intractable conflicts can be analytically distinguished, and distinguishing those shifts will facilitate explaining how conflicts become intractable, how they remain so, and how they are transformed so that they are conducted constructively or otherwise are terminated.

Six phases are particularly significant: (1) the eruption of conflict episodes with high potentiality of generating intractability, (2) escalation marked by destructive qualities, (3) failed peacemaking efforts, (4) institutionalization of destructive conflict, (5) de-escalation leading to transformation, and (6) termination and recovery from the intractable conflict. These six phases are only loosely sequential, since some may be occurring simultaneously for different actors, and regressions to an earlier phase often occur.

The character of a conflict changes as it becomes more or less intractable. The changing character may be seen in variations in the core components of every conflict. I stress four components of social conflicts: the identities or conceptions the adversaries have of themselves and of their adversaries, the grievances they hold against each other, the goals they set to change the other to reduce their grievance, and the means they use to achieve their goals. Some conceptions of self and others, certain grievances, various goals, and particular conflict methods are especially conducive to a conflict becoming and remaining intractable. Changes in each of these components contribute to the transition of a conflict from one phase of intractability to another.

First, how members of each side in a conflict view their collective self is shaped by their conception of other collectivities and by how those others view them. Thus, during the Cold War many Americans regarded being anticommunist as an important component of being American. In general, members of one or more sides often rank themselves as superior to the other side's members. Most extremely, one side may view another group as subhuman or as evil and therefore an appropriate target for destruction (Coy and Woehrle 2000; Northrup 1989); such conceptions foster highly destructive intractable conflicts (Thompson 1990). They may be aroused by and contribute to great spikes in genocidal actions and cycles of retaliation, as has been the case between Hutus and Tutsis in Rwanda.

Second, although members of one or more sides in every conflict have grievances, some kinds are likely to contribute to a conflict's intractability. This is the case when members of one side feel grossly wronged by the oppressiveness and injustices imposed by the other side or feel that their very existence is threatened. Changes in the level and character of the grievances felt by members of either side affect the movement from one phase to another of a conflict's intractability.

Third, members of one side may formulate goals that the opposing side's members regard as particularly damaging and costly, and that do not appear to be subject to compromise. Intractability increases as the goals are formulated in zero-sum terms, so that what is sought is at the expense of the other side; shared interests and objectives are minimized.

Finally, members of one or both sides may believe that the other side will yield only to force, and they have the capacity to inflict extreme violence that will coerce members of the opposing side to yield. When used, these methods tend to be reciprocated and thus contribute to the conflict's destructiveness and persistence.

Eruption Phase. We can now examine the important qualities of the core components of conflicts at six major phases of intractable conflicts. I begin with the occurrence of a contentious episode that may intensify and prolong a conflict. The episode may be a confrontation that erupts in the context of a campaign that is part of a protracted but dormant or low-level conflict. Thus, in Northern Ireland, the Catholic minority undertook a nonviolent civil rights campaign in 1968; the police of the Protestant-controlled government broke up nonviolent demonstrations, which were also attacked by Protestant vigilantes. The dormant Irish Republican Army began to organize to defend the Catholic community. Subsequently, the struggle between Catholics seeking to join the Republic of Ireland and Protestants wanting Northern Ireland to remain united with Great Britain was renewed violently.

Such episodes tend to raise the salience of identities that contribute to intractability. Threats to collective existence may be evoked and old traumas aroused, as was the case in Northern Ireland. Identities emphasizing victimization by another group frequently play crucial roles in the prolongation of destructive social conflicts. Past traumas often leave legacies of fear and hatred that can be aroused by political and intellectual figures (Volkan 1988). For example, Serb nationalism was aroused by accounts of past atrocities and defeats by Croats and Muslims and contributed to the violent breakup of Yugoslavia (Glenny 1992).

Long-standing grievances may be reshaped by new expectations and threats, as happened in Northern Ireland by the reframing of a civil rights struggle into a nationalist struggle over separation versus union. Prolonged oppression and injustice become starkly visible and unacceptable by new and brutal encounters with them. On the other hand, the privileged strata are likely to fear the loss of privilege and of their way of life as threats arise that their advantages will be taken from them.

Modest reformist goals may come to appear inadequate in the face of the revelations made visible by the new encounters with the dominant groups. The goals are then reformulated so that the adversaries are required to make more radical changes. The conflict increasingly is seen by the opponents to be zero sum, so that whatever one side gains is at the expense of the other. Consequently, the conflict will tend to erupt in a way that contributes to its intractability.

The methods used in the struggle and beliefs about their effectiveness also are part of the conflict's character and may contribute to its intractability. A conflict's intensification often seems to justify more radical methods, as the old methods seem inadequate. In South Africa in the 1950s, the struggle against apartheid used nonviolent means; one campaign included large demonstrations against laws requiring blacks to carry pass books. In March 1960 at a demonstration in Sharpeville, police fired on an unarmed crowd of protestors, killing sixty-nine Africans and wounding many more. Nonviolent resistance grew, the government banned the Pan African Congress and the African National Congress, and some form of armed struggle seemed necessary to Nelson Mandela and other African leaders (Mandela 1994). Preparations for armed resistance began, and Mandela and many of his colleagues were arrested, tried, and found guilty; he and many others were imprisoned for life in 1964. An intense and often violent struggle of suppression and resistance then continued for more than two decades, in a severe intractable conflict.

Escalation Phase. Once a conflict is in the phase of escalation, identities, grievances, goals, and methods often change in ways that perpetuate the conflict in increasingly destructive fashion (Kriesberg 2003). Thus, each side's collective identity is shaped in opposition to the enemy. Furthermore, group loyalty is often characterized as demonstrating antagonism toward the enemy. Additionally, good qualities are increasingly attributed to one's own group, while bad qualities are increasingly attributed to the enemy, with some groups sometimes going so far as to demonize the enemy.

The fighting itself generates new grievances among members of each side as the adversaries inflict injuries and pain on each other. In addition, old dissatisfactions and injustices are aroused, and responsibility for them is ascribed to the current enemy. Of course, many agents—political leaders, intellectuals, and religious leaders—play crucial roles in formulating grievances and identifying the injustices suffered and those responsible for them.

Goals tend to become firmer as a conflict escalates, since making concessions seems more difficult after sacrificing much in waging the struggle (Brockner and Rubin 1985). Goals also sometimes expand to include harming the adversary for the sake of retribution. Furthermore, old unsettled issues are often revived, further increasing the goals in contention.

Methods of fighting may lose their practical connection with the goals of each side as anger, hate, and revenge-seeking result in atrocities that further inflame the fight. This in many ways happened with the breakdown in Israeli-Palestinian peace negotiations and the second intifada that erupted in September 2000 (Khalidi 2002).

Failed-Peacemaking-Efforts Phase. Efforts to interrupt and transform intractable conflicts are likely as the conflict persists. They may take various forms—including vague exploratory overtures, broad peace proposals, and unilateral conciliatory gestures—and may be communicated either publicly through announcements or privately through deniable intermediaries. The initiators' intention may be to test the readiness of the other side to de-escalate the conflict or to convince the other side that de-escalation and a settlement are possible.

Peace moves, however, are often made with the expectation that the adversary will reject them. They are actually made to mobilize constituency support or to demonstrate to allies and observers that the other side is the obstacle to a peaceful resolution of the conflict.

Assessing the real intentions of the initiator is difficult in the midst of a prolonged destructive conflict. Indeed, the intentions are likely to be mixed and depend in part on the response of the other side. Some negotiations, indirect or direct, may begin to uncover the realistic possibilities of reaching an acceptable agreement. This is usually a necessary but difficult course as both sides proceed with care and mistrust. Consequently, peace overtures and negotiations often fail in intractable conflicts, and new destructive escalations ensue.

For example, shortly after Anwar el-Sadat succeeded Gamal Abdel Nasser as president of Egypt in 1970, he began to reduce reliance on the Soviet Union and sought to improve relations with the United States. In February 1971 he proposed that Israel withdraw from a portion of the occupied Sinai and that Egypt reopen the Suez Canal for shipping. The U.S. officials tried to broker such an interim agreement, but despite some negotiations, no agreement on the terms of the settlement was reached. Sadat believed that he had made great concessions, but the U.S. government failed to induce the Israeli government to change positions sufficiently to reach a settlement. "Frustrated and humiliated, Sadat decided to abandon the interim-settlement idea" (Quandt 1992, 128–129). In October 1973 Egypt and Syria made war on Israel.

Persons or groups who are not members of the leadership of either camp or who do not represent the leadership also may undertake peace initiatives. They may exert pressure on their own leadership to de-escalate or to end the fighting and to reach a negotiated settlement. This may embolden the adversary camp, however, to hold out for a better result as dissent increases within the opposing side. To minimize this risk, some non-official groups in both adversarial camps may try to join forces and gain more credibility and effectiveness. For example, in 1976 Betty Williams and Mairead Corrigan led in organizing Women for Peace and very quickly tens of thousands of Catholics and Protestants were participating in marches against the violence in Northern Ireland; but soon the organization membership declined.

External actors also may intervene to interrupt what appears to be an increasingly intractable conflict. This may take the form of imposing arms embargoes or economic sanctions, or of conducting quiet or forceful mediation of imposed cease-fires. Appropriate, well-timed interventions can be helpful, but interventions often fail to end or transform intractable conflicts. Some interventions freeze the conflict while ending violent efforts to change the status quo, as happened with the major UN peace-keeping deployment in Cyprus in 1974.

The repeated failure of one adversary to impose an ending, the failure of parties to negotiate an ending after trying to do so, and the failure of external intervention to stop or transform the intractable confirm the conflict's intractability. Failures often discourage new attempts and constitute a burden of mistrust to be overcome. Consequently, the struggle continues, even at a reduced level and even with no overt physical injurious conduct. Sometimes, the conflict persists with a low level of violence and occasional outbreaks of large-scale violence, as in the case of the Indian-Pakistani struggle about controlling Kashmir.

The failure to sustain agreements that were reached is a severe setback to the transformation of an intractable conflict. Supporters of an agreement who believe that the other side violated it feel deceived, even betrayed, and are less trusting about any future accord. Such failures in Sri Lanka, Sudan, and many other places attest to this experience. The consequences of the failures of the Israeli government and the Palestinian Authority to adhere to the agreements they made after the signing of the Declaration of Principles in September 1993 and the subsequent explosion of violence profoundly embittered nearly everyone associated with the peace process (Kriesberg 2002).

The failures affect each side's identity and the characterization of the enemy: members of each side tend to view themselves as virtuous and the enemy as duplicitous. New grievances are sometimes added to the old ones. Goals are also formulated to avoid such failures in the future. For some people the response is to emphasize even more coercive methods for imposing adherence to any future agreement.

Institutionalization Phase. Once a conflict is under way, many processes contribute to its institutionalization and self-perpetuation. As a conflict persists, many members of each side increasingly view members of the other side as enemies with many bad qualities, as cruel and untrustworthy. Such socialization contributes to a conflict's further intractability. Mutual fear increases and people on each side are concerned about their vulnerability if they should yield. One group may hear the call for justice by another group as a cry for revenge.

In addition to internalizing attitudes and beliefs about each other, people on each side develop guiding rules about how to wage their struggle. The rules make certain means of struggle legitimate, and as the authorities and others waging the struggle seem to support the rules and even punish dissenters, the rules increasingly constrain conduct. Alternative courses of action become ever more difficult to undertake.

Furthermore, as the fight persists, some people on each side develop vested interests in continuing the struggle. Some people gain prestige, income, and power by participating as warriors in the fight, and they may lack alternative careers promising equal gains. Others may profit by engaging in a variety of illegal activities associated with the struggle. The nature of their identities, their grievances, and their goals are changed in ways that make a mutual accommodation more difficult to reach. The ongoing methods of struggle may seem suitable for their new goals, and the fight with the enemy is tenaciously pursued in the same old manner.

De-escalation and Transformation Phase. Many intractable conflicts gradually wind down, becoming less destructive, and are transformed in some degree so that they begin to be regarded as tractable. An intractable conflict may persist in relatively dormant antagonism and be regarded as managed, as happened for some interludes during the Cold War between the Soviet Union and the United States. A well-managed conflict may be the prelude to a fundamental transformation of the conflict.

Collective identities often change concomitantly with the de-escalation of a conflict and contribute to its further transformation. For example, the meaning of being South African changed as the wrongness of apartheid was widely recognized, even by the whites of South Africa. Adversaries may come to emphasize shared identities, sometimes in response to threats from a common enemy.

Conflict de-escalation and transformation are often associated with reduced grievances, at least for members of one side. This occurs as relations between the adversaries change in the course of the struggle. Thus, some rights that one party sought may be at least partially won, and that party's goals are then accordingly softened.

Goals also change as they become seen as unattainable or as requiring unacceptable burdens and are recast so that they might be achieved with reasonable means. They may even be reformulated so as to provide mutual benefits for the opposing sides. For example, Frederik Willem de Klerk, as president of South Africa, led in modifying the goals of the National Party, of Afrikaners, and of whites in general.

The methods that adversaries believe they can use effectively in a conflict do not constantly become more destructive as a conflict persists. Those methods sometimes become too costly or ineffective after a while. Supporters cease to be supportive at some point, when norms are violated or costs become too burdensome. The methods may come to be seen as counterproductive for the goals sought, particularly if alternative methods promising more constructive outcomes seem feasible.

Termination and Recovery Phase. An intractable conflict can end in various ways, including one or both sides becoming internally transformed so that the conflict largely is resolved, the adversaries forging mutually agreed-upon settlements, or one side destroying or permanently suppressing the other. However arrived at, for a conflict ending to endure, and not simply be a period of dormancy until the intractable conflict erupts into renewed destructiveness, the adversaries must recover from past disasters and build satisfying relationships with each other.

Once an intractable conflict ends, the basic components of the conflict become different. Greatly changed or new collective identities become dominant. Thus, with the overthrow of Jim Crow laws in the American South and at the insistence of peoples with diverse cultural backgrounds, the multicultural character of American identity was heightened. Thus, too, the transformation of Franco-German enmity after World War II was aided by the increased salience of the European identity.

Grievances underlying the conflict are often reduced for one side, but for a conflict's intractability to be enduringly overcome, new grievances for the other side must be minimized. Thus, after World War II the United States and Western European governments tried to avoid the kinds of grievances among Germans that arose after World War I, which were attributed to the harsh terms of the Versailles treaty.

Goals, too, become different as intractable conflicts end. Thus, neither side's goals would include the destruction of its adversary; this might reflect a break between a few leaders of one side and their now transformed constituency. The members of a communal or ideological organization may repudiate the organization leaders upon their defeat, and the victorious other side accepts the genuineness of the repudiation.

Significantly, the methods of struggle also change as an intractable conflict comes to an end. Often a political process is established, providing legitimate, regulated procedures for settling disputes; the conflict then ceases to be regarded as destructive and hence intractable. Groups that had been excluded from effective participation in making decisions of central concern to them may gain access to effective engagement in such decision making.

General Observations. The sequences of these phases may very well differ for groups on each side of the conflict. Moderates, hard-liners, spoilers, and various other factions within each camp tend to be in different phases of intractability at any given time. Therefore, shifts in the relative size and influence of these factions will produce changes in the conflict's course.

Factors Shaping Phases of Intractability

Understanding the many factors that affect the emergence, persistence, and transformation of intractable conflicts is essential in developing effective policies that limit and end them. Partisans on each side usually blame members of the other side for the destructive course of their conflict; it is the adversaries' character, ideology, or leadership that is responsible. Outside observers more often see fault on both sides, with the way the adversaries relate to each other shaping a conflict's trajectory. Possible interveners may stress the role of outside actors who exacerbate a local fight. Academic analysts tend to emphasize long-term structural features of each side and the larger sociopolitical environment within which the adversaries contend with each other.

This section discusses three sets of factors: internal, relational, and external. For each set, I consider both structural factors, which are usually regarded as relatively impersonal forces constraining human conduct, and also agency factors, which are embodied by persons who choose to take specific actions and so have agency (Giddens 1979). Given the interest in policy in this volume, I give less attention to structural factors than to ones involving agency. However, the two kinds of factors are not wholly distinct from each other. What is structural and what is a matter of agency depends in part on the time perspective taken and the power of the agent being considered. What appears to be structural for an individual with few resources may appear subject to control by large powerful actors over time.

Finally, various factors are more or less important at different phases of intractable conflicts. As Roy Licklider notes in this volume, the starting factors are not necessarily the same as the factors that sustain an intractable conflict. In discussing each set of factors in this section, I give attention to their effects on the adversaries' identities, grievances, goals, and conflict methods as they shape the trajectory of a conflict's intractability.

Internal Factors

Structural factors of each conflict party set parameters within which individuals and groups may have agency in affecting the course of a conflict. These structural factors include, for example, the level of economic development, capacities for different ways of fighting, cultural patterns, and decision-making institutions. These factors influence self-conceptions and identities, how grievances are experienced and interpreted, what goals are formulated, and the methods used to attain them.

There is much literature about characteristics of societies that make them prone to engage in wars, and by extension these characteristics would increase the probability of waging intractable conflicts. These publications refer, for example, to the form of government, the prominence of a military-industrial complex, the lack of socialization and education promoting peacefulness, and the prevalence of aggressive personalities (Ross 1993).

I turn next to internal factors that entail a greater element of agency. The structure of the decision-making process can affect intractability, with a broader and more diverse participation providing more options and reducing the likelihood of a group persisting in conduct that perpetuates or escalates a difficult conflict. Sometimes high officials, such as presidents, seek to engage persons with different views in order to learn from the disagreements and better understand different options.

How leaders deal with rivals and opponents within their own camp has great implications for a conflict's intractability. In some cases, they are disregarded, and sometimes they are even suppressed. If the course of action is wholly dominated by the hard-liners, the conflict is likely to remain intractable. For example, this has been a problem in transforming the conflict between Sinhalese and Tamils in Sri Lanka, which erupted and escalated soon after Sri Lanka (then Ceylon) gained independence in 1948. After terrible acts of violence and devastation, major steps toward peacemaking were finally taken in 2002, with mediation help from the Norwegian government.

Official leaders are very important actors affecting the course of a conflict, but officials are not the only leaders, even when they claim to represent the collectivity as a whole. There are oppositional leaders and leaders at various levels of the collectivity and in different realms of activity. The leaders help define who is on each side of a fight and influence the sense of grievance. They also significantly contribute to formulating goals and beliefs about which methods their constituents can effectively use to gain their goals. Hence, if a conflict has become impacted with one set of leaders, a change of leadership opens new possibilities for transformation, as exemplified by Mikhail Gorbachev's selection as leader of the Soviet Union in 1985 and Frederik Willem de Klerk's election to the presidency of South Africa in 1989.

Other internal factors include social movement organizations, such as those within peace movements. In addition, many groups have vested interests in the conflict continuing at a highly antagonistic level, but there are also groups with vested interests in reducing the destructiveness of the conflict. For example, some people may be profiting from war or even sanctions, but others may see lost opportunities for profit as a result of the disruptions caused by the conflict's destructiveness. The shifting balance between such groups and their changing relations with the political leadership powerfully affect the course of a conflict.

Relational Factors

The paths of large-scale conflicts are profoundly shaped by the structure of the relations between the opposing collectivities and by how various agents interpret those structures. The structural character of the relationships importantly includes differences in population size, economic resources, coercive capabilities, and cultural patterns of conduct. It also includes the nature and degree of integration between adversaries in economic, social, and cultural domains.

Anticipated changes in the relative size of various communal groups within a society profoundly affect the course of a conflict among the communal groups. Thus, many white South Africans anticipating a decline in numbers relative to nonwhites thought they should reach an accommodation with blacks sooner rather than later. The nature of the effect, however, is not determined solely by the phenomenon but is also shaped by the interpretation of it. In the 1990s some Israeli Jews, anticipating an increasing proportion of Arab Palestinians in the area of the former British-mandated Palestine, strove for an independent Palestinian state to be established alongside Israel close to the 1967 armistice lines, to keep Israel both Jewish and democratic. However, other Israeli Jews thought that Israel should avert the growing threat Palestinians would pose by increasing the territory fully controlled by Israel and maintaining some control even in Palestinian territories.

Differences in economic resources, coercive power capabilities, organizational skills, and other resources affecting relative power have great impact on the terms of the accommodations that are reached. However, the degree that values and beliefs are shared and the degree that economic and social life are integrated profoundly affect whether a stable accommodation is reached and the extent to which it is mutually acceptable. Crosscutting identities (religious or ethnic) and interests (class or occupational) also tend to limit the destructiveness of a conflict. Thus, in the

United States during the civil rights struggle, many blacks and whites were affected by their shared Christian identity.

People shape and interpret their structural conditions and are shaped by them, and therefore agency and structure are not wholly independent of each other. Thus, when some people strive to change relationship structures, even those persons believing the structures to be proper and natural, God-given, and unchangeable often are compelled to see that the relationship structures were socially constructed and can be changed. Indeed, persons in each adversarial group act in ways that affect the interpretations made by persons on the opposing side. Leaders often act intentionally to influence people in the other camp, trying to intimidate them or to convince them not to feel threatened. Their actions, however, are very often directed at their own constituency, rallying the constituents to support their leadership; but those actions also may powerfully affect people in the other camp, resulting in misunderstandings and unintended interpretations.

A few persons from each camp may have direct communications with each other and the opportunity to explore contentious matters in detail. Such exchanges may take place with or without a mediator, facilitator, or other intermediary, and they take a variety of forms. They vary in duration and continuity, and they occur between officials of various ranks or between nonofficials with varying standing within their own camps. They can provide vehicles for reframing and de-escalating intractable conflicts.

Many other kinds of noncontentious interactions follow agreements for limited areas of cooperation, which tend to occur when an intractable conflict is in the process of transformation. These include confidence-building measures such as establishing procedures for informing each other about military exercises. They also include establishing organizations to coordinate activities regarding matters of common interest. Such arrangements can reduce the chances of conflicts escalating destructively or advance and solidify a conflict's transformation and resolution. For example, several of the countries along the Nile River have been engaged in severe protracted conflicts with one another. Nevertheless, in 1992 the Council of Ministers of Water Affairs of the Nile Basin States undertook an initiative to foster development and cooperation in the basin (see http://www. nilebasin.org). The ten riparian states are Burundi, the Democratic Republic of Congo, Egypt, Eritrea, Ethiopia, Kenya, Rwanda, Sudan, Tanzania, and Uganda. In 1999 these countries created the Nile Basin

Initiative to foster collaboration activities in matters such as crafting credible proposals for development projects that require sizable international financing (Murray 2002). Working together on various relatively technical matters has resulted in a network of relations among relevant government officials and experts in countries in the basin.

Finally, one particular aspect of the relations between adversaries in an intractable conflict, which has deservedly attracted much attention, must be noted here. Conflicts persist, even with mutual losses, when leaders of each of the opposing sides believe that yielding to the other is worse for them and their side than persisting with the prospect of the other side yielding. The conflict, therefore, is likely to de-escalate and reach some kind of end when the parties believe they are in an enduring stalemate that is hurting and believe that a better option for both sides is possible. This is discussed in I. William Zartman's chapter in this book.

External Factors and Actors

A conflict's trajectory is affected by a multitude of external factors, of varying scope and impact. I discuss both structural and agency factors as part of that social context.

A major structural factor is the set of other conflicts that are superimposed or impinge upon any particular conflict. Thus, the Cold War had immense effect on many other conflicts, often exacerbating their intractability. During the Cold War, many regional conflicts were sustained by military and other kinds of support each side received from the Soviet Union and its allies or from the United States and its allies. Each side in a local fight could believe that it would not be defeated, given the support it was getting.

The U.S. war on terrorism that began after the September 11, 2001, attacks on the United States affects the intractability of local conflicts around the world. In some instances, it seems to have dampened particular local conflicts, contributing to their transformation by reducing reliance on methods of struggle that might be branded as terrorist. For example, the almost universal condemnation of the suicidal mass murders contributed to a measure of progress in ending the Northern Ireland conflict by helping push the IRA holdouts to start decommissioning arms and comply with previously signed agreements. In another case, the government of Pakistan acted relatively strongly, for a time, to control militant Islamic groups that conducted terrorist acts against India as part of the campaign to change India's policy regarding the status of Kashmir. This helped avert a new escalation of the intractable Indian-Pakistani conflict. The widespread rejection of terrorism after September 11, 2001, also contributed to the cease-fire in Sri Lanka and the beginning of direct negotiations between the Tamil Tigers and the Sri Lankan government (Waldman 2002).

The war on terrorism, however, can also contribute to the intensification and prolongation of conflicts. One side in a conflict may escalate its efforts to suppress groups it can claim to be terrorists and therefore illegitimate. Thus, the Israeli government believed that it could act forcefully, without external constraints, against Palestinian groups that had committed terrorist acts. In another case, the Indian government believed that in the context of the war on terrorism it could be more insistent about the Pakistan government's handling of militant Islamic groups engaging in the fight against Indian authority in Kashmir.

This discussion also indicates that global norms can constrain how conflicts are waged and that affects the intractability of conflicts. The increasing strength of norms about genocide and human rights makes that evident. Such global norms spurred the intervention, belated as it may have been, in the wars in the former Yugoslavia.

Many other external structural factors might be discussed, but I mention only a few. They include a multitude of social institutions constituting the global economic market affecting trade, investment, and migration; the technological capabilities underlying communication, travel, and production; and the nonsocial environment of global climate, water and mineral resources, pollution, and land quality.

How these structural factors have an impact upon the intractability of a conflict depends in good measure on the way they are perceived and used by various persons and organizations. For example, the superimposition of some conflicts on others and the additional ways conflicts are interlocked makes possible changes in the salience of each conflict. Conflict interveners as well as partisans of a struggle often strive to assert that one conflict should be given higher priority than another. They thus try to reframe the conflict, to either escalate or de-escalate it.

External interveners can undertake many other actions that perpetuate a conflict's intractability or reduce it and transform it. They may provide or withhold military or other materials that one or more sides in a conflict would use to wage their struggle. That kind of assistance may help to create a hurting stalemate. The interveners may also help generate new options that offer acceptable escapes from the destructive stalemate in which the opposing sides are stuck. These include economic assistance for reconstruction, personal sanctuary for some leaders, or even resettlement of peoples.

Intervention may also be forceful, either to assist one side or to impose a cessation of violent struggle by the adversaries. These interventions may be combined and even be the prelude to mediation, as was the case in regard to the conflict in Bosnia (Holbrooke 1998).

Interveners engage in a broad range of mediating activities. At the relatively muscular end of the range, the mediators propose solutions and strive to construct a deal based on each side's concerns and then work to win the adversaries' acceptance of the proposed settlement. At the relatively facilitative and nonforceful end of the range, the mediators pass on communications between the adversaries as they explore possible de-escalating moves; they may also simply provide a safe and neutral setting in which adversaries can meet and talk with each other.

The parties carrying out these diverse kinds of interventions include a wide variety of governmental and nongovernmental actors, with varying capabilities of conducting the activities identified earlier. Among the governmental actors are the states of the world, including the globally powerful United States. Many other governments singly or in ad hoc combinations also carry out various significant interventions. Governments have also formed a variety of international organizations (IGOs), which themselves are international actors. These IGOs include the United Nations and its specialized agencies and a multitude of regional as well as global organizations.

Increasingly, nongovernmental organizations (NGOs) play major intervention roles, often helping to moderate or transform intractable conflicts, but also sometimes exacerbating and perpetuating them. They include multinational corporations, churches, ethnic organizations linking people in several countries, humanitarian service organizations, and human rights and other activist organizations.

Countering Intractability at Various Phases

This analysis should make it clear that conflicts are not inherently intractable. Furthermore, the many factors affecting the intractability of conflicts reveal the multitude of ways for conflict partisans and outsiders to act that help prevent, limit, or transform intractable conflicts. No one approach is good for all purposes; certain policies are effective in some circumstances but not in others.

Efforts to mitigate and transform an intractable conflict obviously are not always successful; indeed, they are risky and sometimes counterproductive. Therefore, attention needs to be given to those negative possibilities. Sometimes that leads to tentativeness in making the effort, and that itself may contribute to the effort's failure. Certainly, good judgment is required in executing any of the policies discussed here. Thus, mapping out many options can only suggest the most effective possible options and combinations of options that may be taken by different actors in different sequences. Much knowledge of the particularities of the case, wisdom, and good fortune are also needed to maximize the desired effects of any policy choice.

In this section, I discuss possible policies by members of each side who have primary responsibility for their conflict's course, as well as by interveners. I also discuss policies at each phase of conflict intractability, with the exception of the failed-intervention phase, since I examine intervention in relation to each of the other phases.

Preventive Policies

Some policies to counter intractable conflicts may be pursued before the eruption of major contentious actions that move adversaries toward intractability. Policies may also be conducted that help prevent a sharp escalation of a relatively low-intensity intractable conflict.

Partisan Policies. Members of each of the opposing sides in a conflict can do much to prevent it from becoming intractable. One fundamental approach especially relevant for domestic conflicts is to foster democratic institutions. Democracy, insofar as it provides a significant degree of political equality and of individual and group freedom, in itself tends to reduce many grievances. Moreover, it generally provides legitimate mechanisms to channel the inevitable conflicts of social relations so that they do not destructively escalate and become intractable.

Another general approach is to foster common identities and interests, sometimes by developing superordinate goals whose attainment would solve shared problems. Economic backwardness and environmental degradation could be such problems, as illustrated by the Nile Basin Initiative. Often, the broader identity or the superordinate goal is directed against a common enemy, as adversaries put aside their disagreements to confront an immediate grave threat. For example, the antagonism between the Soviet Union on one side and the United States, Great Britain, and France on the other was put aside to defeat Nazi Germany after it attacked the Soviet Union in 1941. Thus, too, national identity may be promoted while class, political, regional, or ethnic identities are subordinated to it, as leaders strive to rally support against an external enemy. Indeed, government leaders may undertake or escalate an external conflict as a way to sustain support for themselves.

Some efforts to promote a shared identity, however, may be experienced by subordinated groups as a form of domination imposed by the ruling ethnic or political group. That occurs if the identity is characterized in narrow terms giving primacy to one language, religion, or ethnicity. The insistence on ethno-nationalism or religious nationalism, as occurred in Sri Lanka, can generate an intractable conflict. Much depends, then, on the content of the identity that is being promoted.

Other preventive policies may help to manage particular contentious issues when they arise. Policies introduced early in response to emerging demands for greater political or economic rights may effectively prevent an intractable conflict from developing. This seems to have worked in Malaysia, where the Malays and the indigenous peoples, known as Bumiputra, tended to be poor, less educated, and more engaged in traditional occupations compared with the non-Bumiputra minorities, such as the Chinese (Mauzy 1993; Gurr 2000). In May 1969, large-scale ethnic riots erupted in Malaysia, which resulted in negotiations in which the leaders of the major ethnic communities instituted preferential ethnic policies of affirmative action.

Such efforts also have risks. The policies may raise expectations of the previously disadvantaged people that are not satisfied. Furthermore, having gained some concessions, they may believe that they can successfully obtain more from their adversary. On the other hand, some members of the side that has made concessions may come to feel that they are paying too high a price for the concessions, and a backlash results.

Intermediary Policies. Officials of governments or of IGOs can provide economic, social, and political assistance that is extremely helpful in averting the development of intractable conflicts. Thus, Max van der Stoel, the Organization of Security and Cooperation in Europe (OSCE) high commissioner on national minorities (HCNM), has contributed to many activities that helped reduce tensions and construct institutions that would provide solutions to potentially grave conflicts relating to minority groups (van der Stoel 1999). These include establishing round tables, councils, and other venues within which dialogue is conducted between majority and minority representatives. They also include helping to develop standards for minority participation in public life and recommendations about linguistic and educational rights for minorities. Such activities can help fashion agreements in particular circumstances, as they have in negotiating the Treaty between the Republic of Hungary and the Republic of Romania on Understanding, Co-operation and Good Neighborliness, concluded in 1996.

Governments may provide training, consultations, and other services to improve the capabilities of governments and their agencies in other countries. Thus, military, police, and other security forces may be trained to act in nonprovocative ways in managing crowds and demonstrations. Provision of weapons and some kinds of training, however, may lend support to diffuse repressive policies that escalate and perpetuate conflicts.

Nongovernmental organizations also can pursue a variety of policies that help prevent a conflict from becoming intractable (Aall 2001). At the local and national levels, NGOs provide networks of relationships that help prevent outbreaks of violence from escalating into large-scale riots. Transnational organizations provide a venue for the exchange of information between people in countries whose governments are in an adversarial relationship. Such information may avert or limit the escalation of intractable conflicts.

NGOs may also engage in activities that directly serve to prevent or limit conflict intractability (Moser-Puangsuwan and Weber 2000). Some provide training in nonviolent action and in conflict resolution methods, and others obtain information and publicize the early signs of gross human rights violations that may instigate conflict escalations. Still others provide protection to dissenters by accompanying them in settings that otherwise would be extremely dangerous for them, as exemplified by the work of Peace Brigades International (Mahony and Eguren 1997).

Interrupting Intractability Processes

Even when actions are taken that tend to send a conflict down the road to intractability, the movement may be interrupted. The processes making for intractability are not irreversible. I will discuss some of the ways adversaries and intermediaries may stop and even turn back a conflict's course of increasing intractability.

Partisan Policies. Both sides in a conflict usually enter into a confrontation with the expectation that it will be short-lived. They may act in ways they think will bring them a quick victory or at least a negotiated agreement that yields them much of what they seek. But often they are mistaken, and the course of action they choose results in a series of interactions that generate a protracted destructive struggle. Some policies can be pursued that may avoid such destructive interactions or at least interrupt them as they begin and before they badly deteriorate.

The use of violence often provokes reprisals of violence that enhance a conflict's intractability. Each side can act, however, to minimize that tendency, even if some violence is committed. This was the case even after the startling armed uprising of the Zapatista National Liberation Army (EZLN), in Chiapas, Mexico, on January 1, 1994 (Ronfeldt et al. 1998). The Mexican government's immediate response was to militarily suppress the uprising. After shots were exchanged with the troops, the Zapatistas disappeared into the jungle and the army pursued them. However, on January 12, the president of Mexico, Carlos Salinas de Gortari, declared a unilateral cease-fire and called on the EZLN to put down its arms and negotiate. Peace talks began on February 21.

The Zapatistas framed their use of violence so that negotiations were possible, and the Mexican government took that route. Aspects of the social and political context and of the EZLN strategy contributed to this surprising development. For several years, the number of various nongovernmental organizations (NGOs) had rapidly increased in Mexico as well as globally. Through their worldwide electronic links, news of the events in Chiapas spread quickly within and beyond Mexico. The network facilitated the rapid mobilization of Zapatista supporters, many of whom came in solidarity to Chiapas, in opposition to the attempted military suppression of the EZLN.

The message of the Zapatistas was expressed with attractive reasonableness. One of the leading figures in communicating the message, Subcomandante Marcos, analyzed the terrible conditions of indigenous peoples and ways of correcting them, writing in a style that delighted and enlightened Mexico City intellectuals. The messages were electronically disseminated through the global networks of NGOs and widely published. The Mexican government decided it was unable to pursue a war to destroy the EZLN.

A dominant party, however, may prolong negotiations and expect that the forces that compelled them to enter into talks will dissipate. Indeed, the negotiations between the Mexican government and the EZLN made little progress. By February 1995 the situation had deteriorated following the Mexican army's occupation of territory tacitly accorded to the EZLN. Only after the national Congress intervened did serious negotiations occur, resulting in the Accord of San Andrés, signed in February 1996. The accord included an agreement to constitutionally recognize the indigenous peoples' rights to self-determination and autonomy. But afterward, the government rejected the proposal. Then, after seventy-one years of rule, the ruling party, the Institutional Revolutionary Party (PRI), was defeated in elections.

The new president of Mexico, Vicente Fox of the National Action Party (PAN), upon assuming office in December 2000, asked the Mexican Congress to act on the accord. In March 2001 the EZLN marched to Mexico City and its representatives addressed the Congress. In April Congress passed an Indigenous Rights Law, but it incorporated only a portion of the accord's provisions; consequently, the Zapatistas and their supporters opposed the law. The conflict goes on, but largely within the political system and legal constraints.

Dilemmas abound in formulating policies to interrupt the movement toward growing intractability (Kriesberg 2003). Policies resorting to coercion and violence, seeking to intimidate the opposition, sometimes appear effective, at least in the short run. However, such methods usually fail and are often counterproductive. Attempted by relatively small and weak parties, perhaps out of desperation and romanticized visions of armed struggle, they provoke reactions that are likely to isolate them and make it easier for the dominant groups to overwhelm and destroy them (Gamson 1990). Similarly, general repression by authorities can generate greater opposition and resistance. Coercion that is precise and limited and that is placed in a context that allows for alternative ways of finding a mutual accommodation has a better chance of stopping increasing conflict intractability.

Policies embodying concessions also have risks. Concessions may be effective in placating some members of the opposing sides, which is sufficient to blunt further demands and recourse to intimidating coercion so that the conflict is managed within acceptable methods. However, the members of the side receiving the concessions may view them as signs of weakness and as resulting from their forceful actions; the concessions may then serve to whet their appetite for even greater concessions. The concessions won also can serve as resources to gain further concessions.

To minimize these risks of making concessions, the appropriate context should be provided. Direct and indirect negotiations can be useful in developing shared understandings about the propriety of the concessions and the trade-offs related to them. These may include back-channel official conversations as well as track-two discussions.

Intermediary Policies. Since intractability often depends on the external support of one or more sides in a conflict, withdrawing support can interrupt the conflict's escalation and even perpetuation. This is the rationale for arms embargoes for a region or against one of the contending parties. In recent decades increasing use has been made of various kinds of sanctions, including very targeted sanctions, but with only limited success (Cortright and Lopez 2002).

Governmental and nongovernmental organizations can also interrupt escalations by making their dreadful human consequences visible (Moser-Puangsuwan and Weber 2000). The mass media can shine a spotlight that arouses attention and sometimes intervention, which may contribute to direct coercive intervention, as was the case in Bosnia and Kosovo. In addition, transnational nongovernmental organizations acting in solidarity with beleaguered groups are sometimes able to interrupt a conflict's escalatory movement into intractability, as the previous discussion of Chiapas, Mexico, illustrates.

Undermining Institutionalization

Undercutting the institutionalization of an intractable conflict certainly is important in preventing its prolongation. Many possible factors and processes on each side can contribute to undermining such institutionalization.

Partisan Policies. Groups on each side often arise to oppose the institutionalization process, and they are sometimes branded as dissidents and traitors. To be effective, some of these groups point out the self-serving character of the leaders of the fight against the external enemy; furthermore, they may expose some who are personally profiting from the costly struggle.

As a struggle becomes protracted, some people are likely to doubt that persisting in it is worthwhile. People may resist by withdrawing from the struggle; for example, in long wars some people avoid conscription and some soldiers desert. Criticism of the continuing engagement in the conflict may become openly expressed, and opposition leaders may emerge who provide legitimacy for supporting another policy (DeBenedetti and Chatfield 1990). Peace movement organizations may arise, and demonstrations grow.

Such peace movement developments can interrupt escalation and hasten the conflict's termination as the idea of an acceptable settlement changes. However, as noted earlier, they can also be counterproductive. They may hearten the other side's resolve and raise their expectations of ultimate victory and so prolong the conflict. Assessing the consequences of these policies depends greatly on the terms of settlement that the assessor regards as practical and as morally just.

Intermediary Policies. External parties can contribute in many ways to undermining the processes entrenching intractability, although this matter has received relatively little attention. External intervention can help provide options for people in one or the other camp that would enable them to live reasonably well rather than depend upon being a warrior or otherwise engaged in the struggle. Such an intervention may be a safe asylum for some leaders or funds to help former fighters procure land for farming. An infusion of investments can help create jobs that promise security and a decent living standard.

External actors can also provide information about the costs of the conflict's perpetuation and escalation. The costs to family and community will seem even greater if they are seen as unnecessary or ineffective and if possible solutions based on the experience of others can be envisioned. Furthermore, educational programs, dissemination of information, and arranging meetings between people from the adversarial camps can undermine the polarization that accompanies the institutionalization of conflicts.

Interveners can provide information and consultations about constitutional arrangements that provide basic political rights, demobilization safeguards, and economic growth successfully achieved elsewhere. They may also assist in or promise future judicial proceedings and so inhibit the commission of atrocities and also offer survivors some measure of justice. To complicate these matters, admittedly, the expectation of future sanctions imposed on perpetrators of gross human rights violations may stiffen the resolve of alleged perpetrators to fight on.

Transforming Policies

Moving toward the transformation of an intractable conflict entails appropriate changes in identities, grievances, goals, and means of struggle by members of at least one party to an intractable conflict. Policies effectively fostering such changes must be pursued by the adversary parties as well as by intermediaries.

Partisan Policies. Changes in leadership often precede transforming policies. Sometimes new leaders are selected to undertake changes, and even when they are not, they may be able to look at matters more freshly and be less bound by what was done by the previous leaders. Furthermore, leaders of the opposing side may feel freer to test the possibility that the new leaders will be responsive to new initiatives.

At any time, conciliatory gestures or exploratory overtures may be made that contribute to de-escalating the conflict (C. Mitchell 2000; Kriesberg 1992). Such overtures are often made carefully so as to avoid seeming weak and inviting raised demands. One way to move cautiously is to use unofficial channels or to use intermediaries.

Unofficial, or track-two, channels are important in giving greater depth to the transformational movement (Davies and Kaufman 2002). Such contacts also provide opportunities for relations to develop and knowledge to be acquired that modify the conceptions held about the other side and collective self-identities. They may also reframe relations so that grievances and goals are less zero sum.

A series of agreements is usually needed to make the transition out of an intractable conflict into an enduring relationship that does not fall back into destructive conflict. The early agreements may take the form of confidence-building measures. They may be followed by agreements about how to deal with disagreements and contentious issues. Whatever the agreement, compliance to it is important if further transforming steps are to be taken.

Intermediary Policies. Mediation is one of the major ways for external parties to help transform seemingly intractable conflicts. It played a vital role in the 1990s transformation of the Israeli-Palestinian conflict. The U.S. government acted as the powerful mediator in bringing about the 1991 regional peace conference in Madrid. The Norwegian government played an important facilitating role in the PLO-Israeli negotiations near Oslo, producing the Declaration of Principles in 1993 (Kriesberg 2001).

Some mediators perform largely facilitative tasks, but these can be critical when done skillfully by someone with relevant authority and links to persons with resources. Thus, former U.S. senator George Mitchell provided many mediating services that contributed greatly to reaching the crucial Good Friday Agreement of April 1998, between the various parties struggling over the status of Northern Ireland (G. Mitchell 2000; Holland 1999). In 1995 he chaired an international committee to make recommendations on the issue of decommissioning (disarming under-ground organizations). In September 1997 Mitchell chaired peace nego-tiations with an extraordinarily wide range of groups represented. Besides chairing the sessions, he acted as a go-between for parties that would not talk to each other directly, he helped provide norms for the discussion, creating a safe space for negotiations, and he helped establish rules to reach decisions by significant consensus. In addition, he had access to President Clinton, who at times spoke directly to the parties.

Intermediaries can also be important in ensuring compliance to whatever agreements are reached. They can provide monitoring services and resources to compensate for losses and impose negative sanctions if noncompliance begins to occur. Furthermore, they can contribute to the reconstruction and construction of the economic, political, and social in-frastructure needed to build enduring constructive relations. The failure of intermediaries to remain engaged after initial peace agreements are reached contributes to the failure of such agreements to be sustained (Hampson 1996).

Consolidating Transformation

Recent history makes evident that agreements presumably ending previously intractable conflicts often unravel, with the conflict erupting destructively again. The task of building relations and institutions that avoid such regressions is challenging and requires continuing attention (Kacowicz et al. 2000). In this chapter, however, I only make some brief observations about consolidating the transformation of intractable conflicts and recovering from them.

Partisan Policies. A growing variety pf peacebuilding policies are being employed within and between societies after periods of large-scale violence. They include the establishment of institutions, with equitable engagement by persons from different sides in the conflict, to plan and to carry out cooperative activities. They also include educational programs fostering shared identities and norms of tolerance and mutual respect.

Considerable attention is currently given to the important role that reconciliation can play in the fundamental transformation of intractable conflicts. Reconciliation is a multidimensional phenomenon, including many aspects of justice, truth, respect, and security (Lederach 1997). It is not a single event or condition, since different degrees of the various dimensions of reconciliation are attained and change over time.

Intermediary Policies. Intermediaries can conduct a wide variety of policies that contribute to consolidating peace and helping people recover from the physical, social, and moral traumas of the intractable conflict. External actors often work directly with the former adversaries to support their peacebuilding efforts. External governments, IGOs, and NGOs provide useful intellectual, financial, and other resources to help build and sustain effective institutions and programs that help build peaceful relations.

For example, the United States Institute of Peace gathers information about reconciliation efforts in various countries and consults with governments and nongovernmental organizations regarding procedures to uncover the truth about the past and promote future justice (Kritz 1995; see also http://www.usip.org). UNESCO provides another kind of example.

It was established as the United Nations agency charged with erecting the structures of peace in the minds of human beings (Boulding 2000, 248). In 1994 it launched a Culture of Peace Program to work at the local as well as national level to introduce concepts of conflict resolution and peacebuilding to citizens in every sector of society (see http://www3 .unesco.org/iycp).

External actors also can help provide a context that supports and does not undermine the progress toward stable peace between former enemies. This includes managing related conflicts to minimize the damaging effects of refugee flows, economic disruption, and the diffusion of arms and armed fighters.

Conclusion

Conflicts receive most attention from policymakers, scholars, and the general public when the antagonists enter into a self-perpetuating, increasingly destructive struggle. That is the period, however, when peacemaking efforts by partisans or by interveners are most difficult to make effectively. Members of each side tend to be rallying against the hated enemy, and reversing the momentum is particularly difficult. Constructing a possibly effective move requires attention to what might be appropriate for the circumstances. No single tool fits all problems, and timing is important in applying every tactic (Kriesberg and Thorson 1991). Even a good peace proposal, if presented too early, may be rejected and then be unavailable at a more opportune time (Eliasson 2002).

In this chapter, I have also examined earlier and later phases of intractable conflicts; these are more susceptible to policies that would turn the conflict into more constructive paths. I discussed various strategies and tactics that partisans and interveners can undertake to help prevent conflicts from becoming intractable. These and other specific policies can also be employed to interrupt a conflict's escalation and institutionalization.

When both sides in a conflict or even one side begins to believe that it cannot impose its will on the other, explorations of possible alternatives to pursuing the struggle have some potential to begin a de-escalating and transforming move. Once an intractable conflict has begun to be transformed and terminating accommodations have been reached, a great many possible actions can be employed to consolidate the peace. As in the other phases, these actions can be conducted by partisans on each side of the conflict, by both official and nonofficial persons and groups. Intermediaries are also diverse, including agencies of national governments, representatives of regional and global international governmental organizations, and transnational and national nongovernmental organizations. The policies appropriate for this phase that were noted here are suggestive of the great variety of possible policies that may be pursued.

Clearly, many factors and processes contribute to increasing and also to reducing a conflict's intractability. Knowing about them helps provide insights about policies to manage and transform intractable conflicts. That knowledge also should help formulate and conduct effective policies. Also, knowing about many possible options helps in creating ones that are likely to be appropriate.

I have also noted here how various policies may fail to be effective and may even be counterproductive. Meaning well does not ensure doing well. Furthermore, simply ending a conflict may not be the correct objective in the eyes of many people. Considerations of justice and morality regarding the terms of the accommodation reached are also important.

Note

I wish to thank several people for their comments, questions, and nudges about earlier drafts of this paper. They are Pamela Aall, Chester A. Crocker, Fen Osler Hampson, Christopher Mitchell, and John Murray.

References

Aall, Pamela. 2001. "What Do NGOs Bring to Peacemaking?" In *Turbulent Peace: The Challenges of Managing International Conflict*, edited by Chester A. Crocker, Fen Osler Hampson, and Pamela Aall, 365–383. Washington, D.C.: United States Institute of Peace Press.

Boulding, Elise. 2000. *Cultures of Peace: The Hidden Side of History*. Syracuse, N.Y.: Syracuse University Press.

Brockner, Joel, and Jeffrey Z. Rubin. 1985. *Entrapment in Escalating Conflicts: A Social Psychological Analysis*. New York: Springer Verlag.

Cortright, David, and George A. Lopez. 2002. *Sanctions and the Search for Security*. Boulder, Colo.: Lynne Rienner.

Coy, Patrick G., and Lynne M. Woehrle. 2000. *Social Conflicts and Collective Identities*. Lanham, Md.: Rowman and Littlefield.

Davies, John, and Edward (Edy) Kaufman. 2002. *Second Track /Citizens' Diplomacy: Concepts and Techniques for Conflict Transformation.* Lanham, Md.: Rowman and Littlefield.

DeBenedetti, Charles, and Charles Chatfield. 1990. *An American Ordeal: The Antiwar Movement of the Vietnam Era.* Syracuse, N.Y.: Syracuse University Press.

Eliasson, Jan. 2002. "Perspectives on Managing Intractable Conflict." *Negotiation Journal* 18, no. 4 (October): 371–374.

Gamson, William A. 1990. *The Strategy of Social Protest.* Belmont, Calif.: Wadsworth Publishing.

Giddens, Anthony. 1979. *Central Problems in Social Theory.* Berkeley and Los Angeles: University of California Press.

Glenny, Misha. 1992. *The Fall of Yugoslavia.* New York: Penguin.

Gurr, Ted Robert. 2000. *Peoples versus States: Minorities at Risk in the New Century.* Washington, D.C.: U.S. Institute of Peace Press.

Hampson, Fen Osler. 1996. *Nurturing Peace: Why Peace Settlements Succeed or Fail.* Washington, D.C.: U.S. Institute of Peace Press.

Holbrooke, Richard C. 1998. *To End a War.* New York: Random House.

Holland, Jack. 1999. *Hope against History.* New York: Henry Holt.

Kacowicz, Arie M., Yaacov Bar-Siman Tov, Ole Elgstrom, and Magnus Jerneck, eds. 2000. *Stable Peace among Nations.* Lanham, Md.: Rowman and Littlefield.

Khalidi, Rashid I. 2002. "Toward a Clear Palestinian Strategy." *Journal of Palestine Studies* 31, no. 4: 5–12.

Kriesberg, Louis. 1992. *International Conflict Resolution: The U.S.-USSR and Middle East Cases.* New Haven, Conn.: Yale University Press.

———. 2001. "Mediation and the Transformation of the Israeli-Palestinian Conflict." *Journal of Peace Research* 38, no. 3: 373–392.

———. 2002. "The Relevance of Reconciliation Actions in the Breakdown of Israeli-Palestinian Negotiations, 2000." *Peace & Change* 27, no. 4: 546–571.

———. 2003. *Constructive Conflicts: From Escalation to Resolution,* 2d ed. Lanham, Md.: Rowman and Littlefield.

Kriesberg, Louis, Terrell A. Northrup, and Stuart J. Thorson. 1989. *Intractable Conflicts and Their Transformation.* Syracuse, N.Y.: Syracuse University Press.

Kriesberg, Louis, and Stuart J. Thorson. 1991. *Timing the De-escalation of International Conflicts.* Syracuse, N.Y.: Syracuse University Press.

Kritz, Neil J. 1995. *Transitional Justice.* Washington, D.C.: United States Institute of Peace Press.

Lederach, John Paul. 1997. *Building Peace: Sustainable Reconciliation in Divided Societies.* Washington, D.C.: United States Institute of Peace Press.

Mahony, Liam, and Luis Enrique Eguren. 1997. *Unarmed Bodyguards: International Accompaniment for the Protection of Human Rights.* West Hartford, Conn.: Kumarian.

Mandela, Nelson. 1994. *Long Walk to Freedom*. Boston: Little, Brown.

Mauzy, Diane. 1993. "Malaysia: Malay Political Hegemony and 'Coercive Consociationalism.'" In *The Politics of Ethnic Conflict*, edited by J. McGarry and B. O'Leary. London and New York: Routledge.

Mitchell, Christopher. 2000. *Gestures of Conciliation: Factors Contributing to Successful Olive Branches*. New York: St. Martin's Press.

Mitchell, George J. 2000. *Making Peace*. Berkeley: University of California Press.

Moser-Puangsuwan, Yeshua, and Thomas Weber. 2000. *Nonviolent Intervention across Borders*. Honolulu: Spark M. Matsunaga Institute of Peace, University of Hawaii.

Murray, John. 2002. Presentation at a seminar of the Program on the Analysis and Resolution of Conflicts, Syracuse University, Syracuse, N.Y., March 26.

Northrup, Terrell A. 1989. "The Dynamic of Identity in Personal and Social Conflict." In *Intractable Conflicts and Their Transformation*, edited by L. Kriesberg, T. A. Northrup, and S. J. Thorson, 55–82. Syracuse, N.Y.: Syracuse University Press.

Putnam, Linda L., and Julia M. Wondolleck. 2002. "Intractability: Definitions, Dimensions, and Distinctions." In *Making Sense of Intractable Conflicts*, edited by Roy J. Lewicki, Barbara L. Gray, and Michael Eliott. Washington, D.C.: Island Press.

Quandt, William B. 1992. *Peace Process: American Diplomacy and the Arab-Israeli Conflict since 1967*. Washington, D.C.: Brookings Institution; Berkeley and Los Angeles: University of California Press.

Ronfeldt, David, John Arquilla, Graham E. Fuller, and Melissa Fuller. 1998. *The Zapatista Social Netwar in Mexico*. Santa Monica, Calif.: RAND Arroyo Center.

Ross, Marc Howard. 1993. *The Culture of Conflict*. New Haven, Conn., and London: Yale University Press.

Thompson, John L. P. 1990. "Genocide and Social Conflict: A Partial Theory and a Comparison." In *Research in Social Movements, Conflicts and Change*, vol. 12, edited by Louis Kriesberg, 245–266. Greenwich, Conn.: JAI Press.

van der Stoel, Max. 1999. "The Role of the OSCE High Commissioner in Conflict Prevention." In *Herding Cats: Multiparty Mediation in a Complex World*, edited by Chester A. Crocker, Fen Osler Hampson, and Pamela Aall, 67–83. Washington, D.C.: United States Institute of Peace Press.

Volkan, Vamik. 1988. *The Need to Have Enemies and Allies: From Clinical Practice to International Relationships*. New York: Jason Aronson.

Waldman, Amy. 2002. "Talks Open in Sri Lanka Today to End 19-Year War." *New York Times*, September 16, 8.

5

Mediation in the Most Resistant Cases

Jacob Bercovitch

A NEW SPECTER IS HAUNTING the international system: the specter of conflicts that go on and on and defy most attempts at management. Conflicts such as those in Afghanistan, Kashmir, and Northern Ireland and the one between the Israelis and Palestinians have been a major feature of international relations for many years now. These conflicts are usually referred to as intractable conflicts, and it seems that they have become an inherent characteristic of international relations. The pervasiveness of seemingly endless, yet exceedingly dangerous, conflicts has inevitably been accompanied by numerous efforts, both formal and informal, by individuals, states, and international organizations, all designed to control or reduce the level of violence in these conflicts. The purpose of this chapter is to examine the role, relevance, and contribution of one of these efforts, namely, mediation.

Intractable Conflicts

Most international conflicts, whether fought over tangible or intangible issues, show a significant decline in escalatory patterns and violence over a period of time. Conflict management encourages adversaries away from violence in most, but by no means all, conflicts. Especially troublesome are those conflicts that are waged destructively and persistently and that defiantly resist many efforts to transform or settle them. These conflicts involve much violence; they kill and maim many people; they may relate to objective, tangible factors or to intangible ones; and they may take place between communities within a state or between states. We refer to such conflicts as intractable conflicts. What are the characteristics of intractable conflicts, and how much can any form of conflict management contribute to their resolution?

Edward Azar first drew our attention to this class of conflicts, which he described as protracted.[1] According to Azar, protracted conflicts take place between communal groups but quickly transcend national boundaries, they are usually linked to some intangible needs (e.g., identity, recognition, ethnicity), and they tend to generate or reinforce a high level of violence. We prefer to use the related term "intractable conflicts" to suggest a web of conflictual interactions and hostile perceptions that go on for many years, often becoming even worse in the process.

More specifically, what makes a conflict intractable are the following characteristics:

❏ Intractable conflicts tend to be long-lasting; many persist for twenty or more years.[2]

❏ The conflict is usually conducted through destructive means and is characterized by repeated acts of militarized activity and violence.[3] Militarized activity and violence may be sporadic (as it is in the Israeli-Palestinian and Indian-Pakistani conflicts) or suspended (as it is in the Cyprus conflict). The victims of violence in intractable conflicts include combatants as well as civilians.

❏ There is a long set of unresolved or apparently irreconcilable issues at stake. This means that the parties in conflict feel that at best they may reach temporary cessations of violence and that they cannot reach a fundamental and genuine resolution of their issues.[4]

❏ Psychological manifestations of enmity and deep feelings of fear and hatred generally underlie the relationship between parties in an intractable conflict. Continuous conflict tends to induce stereotypes and suspicions, and these reinforce antagonistic perceptions and behavior. In some cases the parties develop a vested interest in the conflict's continuation.[5]

❏ Intractable conflicts attract many actors and institutions that want to deal with, treat, manage, or resolve the conflict. Few of these actors or institutions are successful.

Intractable conflicts, as we use the term here, denote conflicts that (1) continue over an extended period of time, (2) are characterized by ever-present tension and violence, and (3) are arenas for many futile attempts at management or resolution. In many respects intractable conflicts are clearly different from other conflicts. They are not unlike malignant social processes, which enmesh actors in a web of threats and escalating maneuvers that cannot be easily brought to an end. Intractable conflicts parallel many of the characteristics of a zero-sum game. They may be likened to a prolonged process of entrapment, and this is what makes them so dangerous.

Intractable conflicts undoubtedly pose a great threat to international peace and security, but this does not mean that there are conflicts that are inherently intractable, nor does it imply that such conflicts are endless and can never be resolved. Intractable conflicts, like other conflicts, can be approached, dealt with, and managed. Understanding intractable conflict management must start with understanding the structure of the conflict, the issues and parties involved, and the nature of the conflict management effort.

In a study of international conflicts that occurred between 1945 and 1995, we found eighteen cases of actors in an intractable interstate relationship (that is, a conflict lasting more than fifteen years that featured periodic recourse to violence and many attempts at management). As shown in table 1, these relationships produced 75 serious, or militarized and violent, conflicts (out of 309 in the fifty-year period) posing a threat to regional or international security. These conflicts are different from the others in the period in being more violent, entailing more fatalities, resisting more management efforts, and being generally likely to recur again and again. Table 1 also records the number of times mediation by an outside party took place in these conflicts (note that the total number of mediation efforts, 382, includes 30 cases in which mediation was offered only— i.e., mediation was offered but not accepted). Table 2 presents information on the regional distribution of these serious, militarized intractable conflicts. We are concerned, however, with studying all mediation efforts

Table 1. Mediation in Intractable Interstate Conflicts, 1945–95

Intractable Conflicts	Number of Serious, Militarized Conflicts	Number of Mediation Efforts
1. China–United States	2	2
2. Greece-Turkey	4	87
3. Iran-Iraq	3	39
4. China-India	4	2
5. Afghanistan-Pakistan	4	11
6. Egypt-Israel	2	3
7. Argentina-Chile	1	9
8. Peru-Ecuador	4	15
9. Jordan-Israel	3	12
10. Syria-Israel	8	27
11. India-Pakistan	7	59
12. USSR–United States	5	4
13. Somalia-Ethiopia	4	15
14. North Korea–South Korea	5	8
15. Lebanon-Israel	6	22
16. Thailand-Cambodia	5	4
17. Nicaragua–Costa Rica	6	12
18. Israel–Palestine Liberation Organization/Palestinian Authority	2	21
Total	75	382[1]

1. The total of 382 includes 30 cases in which mediation was offered but not accepted.

Table 2. Regional Distribution of Serious, Militarized Intractable Interstate Conflicts, 1945–95

Region	Frequency	Percentage of Total
Central and South America	12	16.0
Africa	4	5.3
Southwest Asia	16	21.3
East Asia and the Pacific	14	18.7
Middle East	24	32.0
Europe	5	6.7
Total	75	100.0

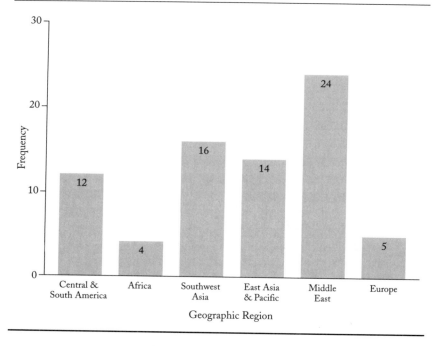

in these conflicts to see what, if any, impact they had on terminating intractable conflicts.[6]

Managing Intractable Conflicts

How can intractable conflicts be best managed, or how can intractable conflicts be made (more) tractable? The question of how to approach intractable conflicts is complex and defies an easy answer. So many factors are involved in making a conflict intractable that it is hard to know which factors have the greatest impact on the intractability of the conflict and which factors can be managed or transformed. How, then, can we manage or resolve intractable conflicts?

There is no single method, nor a single path, for ending seemingly endless conflicts. When we talk about ending intractable conflicts we mean engaging in conflict management or resolution. Conflict management or conflict resolution implies making a series of decisions, and taking active measures, to make a conflict more tractable, to terminate it, or to resolve it successfully. In the context of intractable conflicts it is more sensible to talk about conflict management only. Conflict resolution denotes a removal of the conflict and a resolution of all issues at stake, as well as a change in behavior and attitudes. The very intractability of the conflicts we are dealing with means that they can at best be managed, contained, or de-escalated; they are unlikely to be resolved. The challenge of dealing with intractable conflicts is to manage them in a way that leaves the distribution of benefits exceeding that of costs.

Managing intractable conflicts is a rational and conscious decisional process in which parties in such a conflict seek to take a series of steps to de-escalate, transform, or end their conflict in a way they both find temporarily acceptable. There is truly a full range of conflict management methods available to the parties.[7] They may engage in tacit or explicit negotiations, seek the help of the United Nations or other outsiders, issue threats, or just give in. For analytical purposes, it is useful to divide all conflict management methods into three broad categories: (1) unilateral methods (e.g., threats, avoidance, withdrawal), (2) bilateral methods (e.g., bargaining and negotiation), and (3) multilateral methods (e.g., UN peacemaking, mediation). Table 3 shows all conflict management approaches to intractable conflicts and indicates, quite strongly, that negotiation and

Table 3. Approaches to Conflict Management in Intractable Interstate Conflicts, 1945–95

Conflict Management Approach	Frequency	Percentage of Total
No management	13	1.5
Mediation	382	43.8
Negotiation	425	48.7
Arbitration	9	1.0
Referral to international organization	43	4.9
Total	872	100.0

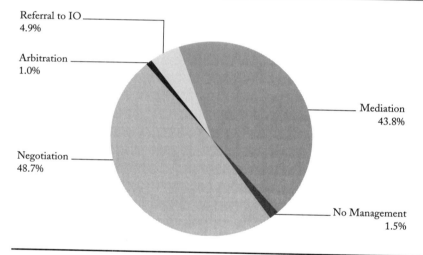

Referral to IO
4.9%

Arbitration
1.0%

Negotiation
48.7%

Mediation
43.8%

No Management
1.5%

mediation efforts make up most of the efforts to manage intractable conflicts peacefully.

Parties in an intractable conflict may use any of these methods to
manage some aspects of their relations or to transform their conflict. When
an intractable conflict is managed, it becomes quiescent or dormant, or the
costs associated with the conflict diminish, but the parties' overall ability to
act remains unaffected. Successful conflict management in the context of
intractable conflicts implies achieving some transformation in (1) the basic
structure of a conflict (e.g., change in incompatible goals and relations),
(2) the issue structure (e.g., change in salience of issues), or (3) actor transformation (e.g., change of leadership).[8] The remainder of this chapter examines how mediation, as a multilateral method of conflict management
in the context of intractable interstate conflicts, can achieve some of these
transformations and more generally build up a momentum to end a seemingly endless conflict.

Mediation and Intractable Interstate Conflicts

Mediation is widely regarded as the most common form of peaceful intervention in international conflicts.[9] Mediation is a noncoercive and voluntary form of conflict management that is particularly suited to the complexities of international relations, in which states and other actors guard their
autonomy and independence jealously. The voluntary and low-key aspects of
mediation make it more likely to be acceptable to parties in an intractable
interstate conflict. Where passions run high, and violence is often resorted
to, the parties in conflict may find it hard to engage in direct negotiations,
but they may well be happy to accept a nonbinding mediation offer.

There are many definitions of mediation. Chris Mitchell, for instance, defines it as an "intermediary activity . . . undertaken by a third party
with the primary intention of achieving some compromise settlement of
issues at stake between the parties, or at least ending disruptive conflict
behavior."[10] Charles Moore defines it as "an extension and elaboration of
the negotiation process that involves the intervention of an acceptable, impartial, and neutral third party who has no authoritative decision making
power to assist contending parties in voluntarily reaching their own mutually acceptable settlement."[11] Jay Folberg and Alison Taylor see mediation as "the process by which the participants, together with the assistance

of a neutral person or persons, systematically isolate disputed issues in order to develop options, consider alternatives, and reach a consensual settlement that will accommodate their needs."[12]

Here we prefer to choose the following fairly broad and generic definition. Mediation is here defined as a process of conflict management, related to but distinct from the parties' own negotiations, in which those in conflict seek the assistance of, or accept an offer of help from, an outsider (whether an individual, an organization, a group, or a state) to change their perceptions or behavior, and to do so without resorting to physical force or invoking the authority of law.

As such, mediation may take place between states, within states, or between groups of states, organizations, and individuals. Mediators may become involved in minor conflicts or intractable conflicts. When mediators enter a conflict, they do so to help those involved achieve a better outcome than could be achieved by the parties alone, and to do so through a wide variety of strategies and behaviors. Mediators usually adopt one dominant strategy, though in some conflicts they may need to change their strategy or behavior, but essentially what mediators do, can do, or are permitted to do may depend largely on who they are, who the parties are, and the nature and context of the conflict. Just as mediators seek to affect, modify, or transform aspects of a conflict, these very aspects may have an effect on the mediators' role, performance, and likelihood of success.

Factors Affecting Mediation in Intractable Interstate Conflicts

Factors affecting the process or outcome of mediation are numerous and varied. They relate to aspects of a conflict, the parties involved, and the manner of management itself. For our purposes, it is best to conceptualize the factors affecting mediation as contextual factors or behavioral factors.[13] Where a conflict is intractable, these factors are even more resistant to change or transformation. Let us review these factors in brief.

Contextual Factors

Contextual factors that affect mediators in intractable conflicts include (1) systemic features, (2) the nature of the conflict itself, and (3) the internal characteristics of the parties involved in the conflict.

The structure of the system within which an intractable conflict manifests itself may have profound implications for its potential for conflict management.[14] Systemic features such as polarity of the international system, patterns of alignment, distribution of power capabilities, and other geopolitical considerations are all associated with different approaches to and strategies of conflict management. Intractable conflicts in a bipolar environment where there is great-power rivalry, or support for each of the adversaries, will prove very resistant to most third-party efforts.[15]

Systemic features may make an intractable conflict more tolerable, as each party enjoys the support of a powerful patron. This patronage relationship may make intractable conflicts more difficult to manage or terminate. At times it may be easier for parties in an intractable conflict to settle into a pattern of political accommodation, outside support, and periodic violence than to give a third party too much leeway. In such cases parties become immune to increasing costs and a perception of a "hurting stalemate," and all that a third party can achieve is to freeze the conflict (e.g., Kashmir). Systemic factors are the least amenable to change and the most likely to pose a tough obstacle for any would-be mediator.

The nature of an intractable conflict is clearly crucial in determining how it is managed.[16] Certain issues in conflict, such as beliefs, core values, and identity, have a high saliency and are apt to encourage decision makers to accept higher levels of costs. This creates polarized zero-sum notions and makes it much more difficult to achieve any success with mediation or other diplomatic methods. Many intractable conflicts are over intangible or vital issues, and as Robert Randle notes, "no amount of mediation by a third party is likely to prevent the outbreak of (further) hostilities."[17]

Issues in conflict are the underlying cause of its evolution, escalation, and termination. In many intractable conflicts the issues, whether tangible or intangible, become indistinguishable from each party's perception of the world and its vision of history. Issues in intractable conflicts often become symbols and tenets of belief. When this occurs, third parties of any sort will have only the most minimal effect on the conflict's perpetuation.

Other characteristics pertaining to the nature of the conflict include the timing of mediation and the level of costs borne by each party. To have any chance of success, mediation must take place at the right, or "ripe," moment. While there is some disagreement about what constitutes the right moment or how to recognize it,[18] there is broad agreement that late mediation may encounter hardened and polarized positions, with new issues making their way onto the agenda and the parties developing strong vested interests in the ongoing conflict. The longer an intractable conflict continues, the more resistant to mediation it will be. Once violence becomes the norm, it is a norm that is exceedingly difficult to break (as current peacemaking efforts in the Israel–Palestinian Authority conflict exemplify only too well). The essence of mediation timing in the context of intractable conflicts is the creation of an atmosphere of political willingness, and a perception of mutual impasse. These moments, or windows of opportunity, may vary from conflict to conflict, but broadly speaking the sooner mediation takes place in an intractable conflict (especially if it occurs within the first three months), the better its chances of success.

Conflict intensity, costs, and fatalities relate to aspects of a conflict that have a great impact on mediation effectiveness. High-intensity conflict, high costs, and high fatalities are typical of many intractable conflicts. However we define and operationalize these features, there is considerable empirical evidence that they exercise a significant negative effect on mediation or indeed any other form of conflict management.[19] If we measure conflict intensity and costs as fatalities, we find that only 39 percent of all mediation efforts in the 1945–95 period had any degree of success (however minimal) in conflicts with high fatalities (i.e., more than ten thousand), compared with 64 percent of mediation efforts with some success in conflicts with fewer than five hundred fatalities.[20]

In discussing mediation in the context of intractable conflicts we have to bear in mind that some intractable conflicts experience high fatalities in a relatively short period of time; other conflicts experience the same level of fatalities over many years. Either way, an intractable conflict is costly, intense, and prolonged. It also takes place within an antagonistic relationship. These features have an adverse effect on the chances of mediation success. Mediators who engage in such conflicts, which we may liken to a serial confrontation, must realize that past costs cannot be easily discredited. To have any chance of success, any mediation effort requires resources, experience, strong political support, and a considerable measure of luck.

The internal characteristic of each party in an intractable conflict is the third of our contextual factors to have a major effect on mediation. This factor relates to structural properties of actors in conflict, their manner of governance, their internal cohesion, and their overall capacity to act on the international scene. Each of these may have an influence on the tendency to engage in or remain in conflict and the effectiveness of any form of conflict management.

Where parties in conflict, intractable or otherwise, are open democratic polities (which is not often the case), the chances of mediation succeeding in stopping or abating the conflict are higher. Conversely, where parties in conflict are nondemocratic polities, the need to rely on coercive methods to manage a conflict is greater.[21] Many intractable conflicts take place between fragmented actors whose very legitimacy may be at stake. This is not conducive to successful mediation.

The capacity to wage and sustain a conflict is derived from each actor's overall measure of power. Conflicts require military, personal, economic, and political measures. But what if one party in an intractable conflict has an abundance of power resources and the other does not? Where this occurs (where an "asymmetric intractable conflict" exists), the stronger adversary may have very few incentives to accept mediation or to see it succeed. Power parity in intractable and other conflicts is more conducive to effective mediation than power disparity.

Behavioral Factors

Behavioral factors refer to the very process of mediation, and how mediation behavior may influence conflict outcome. Significant factors in this category that may affect mediation include mediation identity and rank and mediation strategies.

Parties in a conflict, and mediators who intervene in it, invest considerable personnel, time, and resources. Given the inevitability and omnipresence of conflicts, a limited range of widely accepted procedures for dealing with them, and the unwelcome reality of the scope of their potential destructiveness, it is hardly surprising that so many actors, each adopting different strategies and tactics, are keen to mediate and do something about intractable conflicts. Mediators can range from individuals to states and international or regional organizations. Mediators bring resources and capabilities commensurate with their rank and status. Each mediator has different strengths and shortcomings in different contexts. What types of mediators, then, are the most effective in dealing with intractable conflicts?

Individuals who are not government officials or political incumbents may carry out some limited mediation efforts in intractable conflicts. Such individuals have contacts, experience, or academic backgrounds that may allow them to be accepted by one or both parties in an intractable conflict. Of necessity, their effectiveness is limited, but they can lay the foundation for more serious and formal efforts.

States, through official representatives, are more likely to mediate an intractable conflict. These conflicts, after all, pose a serious regional and international threat, and no state can afford to ignore them. When a state is invited to mediate a conflict, or when it initiates mediation, the services of one of its top decision makers are normally engaged. In these cases, presidents, secretaries of state, and other high officials become involved in some conflict, usually in the full glare of the international media, as representatives of their countries. Both big and small states have a part to play in intractable conflicts; big states can marshal resources to support their efforts, while small states do not threaten either party in conflict.

Regional organizations, such as the Organization of American States (OAS) or the African Union (AU), have clear mandates to mediate in any serious conflict in their region. International organizations, like the United Nations, represent ensembles of states that have signified their intention to fulfill the obligations—including those of formal mediation—of membership as set forth in a formal charter. In recent years we have witnessed a proliferation of mediation efforts by regional and international organizations. These actors are best suited to deal with the complexities of intractable conflicts (for example, the Arab League, the Pacific Islands Forum, the Organization for Security and Cooperation in Europe, ASEAN, and the Organization of African Unity). They have the flexibility, machinery, experience, personnel, and a pronounced lack of bias. As such they may be ideal mediators in intractable conflicts. Our analysis of the 382 different mediation efforts and offers reveals that representatives and leaders of regional and international organizations were involved in 60 percent of all cases. The identity of a mediator in an intractable conflict may well have a major impact on whether or not mediation is accepted and successful. In table 4, we can see the identity of all mediators in intractable conflicts, ranging from private individuals all the way to representatives and leaders of states.

Table 4. Rank of Mediators in Intractable Interstate Conflicts, 1945–95

Mediator Rank	Frequency	Percentage of Total
Private individual	1	0.3
National organization	1	0.3
Representative of regional organization	29	7.6
Leader of regional organization	9	2.4
Representative of international organization	108	28.3
Leader of international organization	83	21.7
Representative of small government	11	2.9
Leader of small government	22	5.8
Representative of large government	101	26.4
Leader of large government	17	4.5
Total	382	100.0

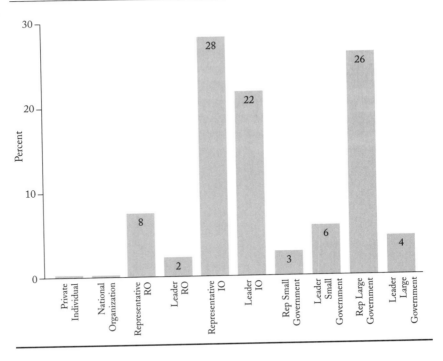

As table 5 shows, most mediation efforts in the context of intractable conflicts are initiated, not by either of the conflicting parties, but by a third party, and of these third parties, international organizations initiate most mediation efforts. International organizations respond to intractable conflicts, initiate mediations in these conflicts, and try to do something about them.

An important aspect of mediation in general, and in intractable conflicts in particular, is the manner of mediator behavior or the strategy used by a mediator. Evaluating the relationship between what mediators do and the outcomes of their efforts is, on the whole, based on ex post facto reflections from mediators (and they may be quite reluctant either to claim success or to take responsibility for failure) or on direct observations of their performance (rarely, if ever, available in international relations). While conceptualizing or measuring mediator behavior, roles, and strategies is difficult, many would agree with Saadia Touval that these ingredients make up the most crucial variable affecting mediation outcomes in any conflict.[22]

In the mediation literature the term "strategy" is employed in the context of decisions about means and ends. Usually, the concept refers to a process of planning to deploy available means to achieve ends or objectives. A strategy is thus a broad plan of action designed to indicate which measures may be taken to achieve desired objectives in conflicts. Mediation behavior refers to specific tactics, techniques, or instruments mediators may use. Are some strategies more likely to be used, or to be successful, in the context of intractable conflicts?

There are a number of ways to describe mediation strategy and behavior.[23] Here we follow Touval and Zartman, who classify mediator behavior along a spectrum ranging from low to higher intervention.[24] They identify three main strategies that encompass the spectrum of mediator behavior. At the low end of the spectrum are communication-facilitation strategies. In the middle are procedural-formulative strategies. Finally, the most active form of mediator behavior involves directive strategies. Let us describe each in turn.

Using communication-facilitation strategies, a mediator typically adopts a fairly passive role, channeling information to the parties and facilitating cooperation but exhibiting little control over the more formal process or substance of mediation. Tactics associated with this strategy include making contact with the parties, gaining the trust and confidence

Table 5. Mediation Initiation in Intractable Interstate Conflicts, 1945–95

Initiator	Frequency	Percentage of Total	Percentage
One party	20	5.2	5.5
Both parties	42	11.0	11.5
Mediator—third party	148	38.7	40.5
Regional organization	20	5.2	5.5
International organization	135	35.3	37.0
Total	365	95.5	100.0
Unspecified	17	4.5	
Overall	382	100.0	

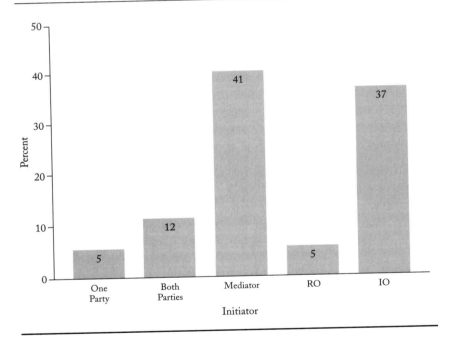

of the parties, arranging for interactions between the parties, identifying issues and interests, clarifying the situation, avoiding taking sides, developing a rapport with the parties, supplying missing information, developing a framework for understanding, encouraging meaningful communication, offering positive evaluations, and allowing the interests of the parties to be discussed.

Procedural-formulative strategies enable a mediator to exert more formal control over the mediation process with respect to the environment of the mediation. Here a mediator may determine structural aspects of the meetings and control constituency influences, media publicity, the distribution of information, and the situational positions of the parties' resources and communication processes. Tactics associated with this strategy include choosing the site of meetings, controlling the pace and formality of meetings, controlling the physical environment, establishing protocols, suggesting procedures, highlighting common interests, reducing tensions, controlling timing, dealing with the simple issues first, structuring the agenda, keeping parties at the table, helping the parties save face, and keeping the process focused on issues.

Directive strategies are the most powerful form of intervention. Here a mediator affects the content and substance of the bargaining process by providing incentives for the parties or issuing ultimatums. Directive strategies deal directly with and aim to change the issues and behavior of the dispute. The tactics associated with this strategy include changing the parties' expectations, taking responsibility for concessions, making substantive suggestions and proposals, making the parties aware of the costs of nonagreement, supplying and filtering information, suggesting concessions parties can make, helping the negotiators to undo a commitment, rewarding party concessions, helping devise a framework for acceptable outcomes, changing perceptions, pressing the parties to show flexibility, promising resources or threatening withdrawal, and offering to verify compliance with agreement.

Which of these strategies would be the most suitable in intractable conflicts?

The choice of a mediation strategy in any conflict is rarely random. It results from conscious decisions made by mediators who respond to the need to manage a conflict and protect their own interests and resources. Parties in an intractable conflict are in a condition of "negative interdependence." They view their conflict, and any efforts to manage it, from the vantage point of high intensity, a destructive social process, and a set of entrenched attitudes and perceptions that make many efforts at management very difficult. In such conflicts directive strategies serve only to antagonize the parties further and make them more entrenched. Less active strategies, such as communication-facilitation strategies that do not pose any threat to the parties and can be undertaken in some secrecy, are more likely to be accepted in high-intensity intractable conflicts.

By identifying each of our 382 mediation efforts in intractable conflicts with a specific strategy, we find, in table 6, that just more than 46 percent of all mediation strategies were of the communication-facilitation kind. In such cases, mediators mostly transfer information from party to party and try to assess issues and commitment to conflict management. In many international conflicts mediators use directive strategies to achieve their objectives; in intractable conflicts, though, they rely most often on strategies at the lower end of mediator involvement.

Mediation efforts in intractable conflicts are affected by many factors. Contextual and behavioral factors determine whether or not mediation can freeze a conflict, manage it, or help to resolve it. If we examine our 382 cases of mediation and think of success as a short-term outcome that may reduce violence and the level of hostility or achieve some formal settlement, we can see from table 7 that more than 50 percent of all mediation efforts were unsuccessful (i.e., the parties continue with their "serial confrontation"), but in just over 35 percent of efforts (those that resulted in cease-fires or full or partial settlements), mediation has had a beneficial impact on the conflict. This is encouraging, as it suggests that properly conducted mediation can produce a cease-fire or settlement or even help end an endless conflict.

Conclusion

Intractable conflicts today pose the most serious threat to international peace and security. While there may be no consensus on what precisely constitutes an intractable conflict, there is broad agreement that something must be done about such conflicts. Intractable conflicts, like other social conflicts, can and should be managed. The question is how exactly should they be managed?

Table 6. Mediation Strategies in Intractable Interstate Conflicts, 1945–95

Strategies	Frequency	Percentage of Total	Percentage
Mediation offered only	43	11.3	11.5
Communication-facilitation	177	46.3	47.5
Procedural	45	11.8	12.1
Directive	108	28.3	29.0
Total	373	97.6	100.0
Unspecified	9	2.4	
Overall	382	100.0	

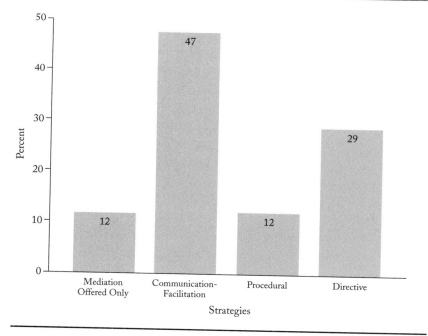

Table 7. Mediation Outcomes in Intractable Interstate Conflicts, 1945–95

Outcome	Frequency	Percentage of Total
Mediation offered only	43	11.3
Unsuccessful	200	52.4
Cease-fire	29	7.6
Partial agreement	90	23.6
Full settlement	20	5.2
Total	382	100.0

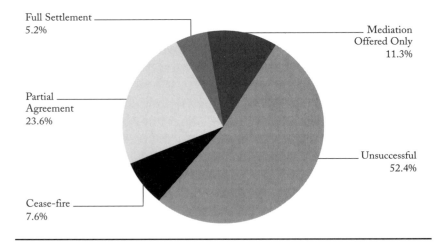

One of the general characteristics of intractable conflicts is that violence and coercion are recurring every so often. States in an intractable conflict "learn" to use, and rely on, coercive measures to deal with their conflicts and differences.[25] Once a malignant pattern of coercion and countercoercion is set in place, it may well be hard for anyone to break it. To avoid the "institutionalization" of an intractable conflict, serious efforts have to be made by the international community to encourage or initiate some form of mediation.

Mediation is ideally suited for intractable conflicts. It is a low-risk, low-visibility, low-cost, and voluntary method of conflict management. It has some control over aspects of the process of conflict management but leaves full control over the really important issue—the outcome—with the parties. From the Middle East to Korea, from Angola to Sudan, mediators may help manage an intractable conflict. This is not to imply that mediation is a panacea for all intractable conflicts, merely to suggest that under some circumstances mediation may well be effective.

Mediation in intractable conflicts is affected by numerous factors. I have tried to suggest that it is best to think of these as falling within a contextual or behavioral category. Many mediation efforts in intractable conflicts are doomed to fail because major powers have competing interests in an intractable conflict, or neighboring states may feel they have more to gain from a conflict's continuance than from its termination. Mediation may fail because the states in conflict have seen their capacity to govern, their legitimacy, or civil society collapse, or there are just too many "spoilers" who have serious problems about making any concessions and are determined to keep an intractable conflict going.[26] These factors further compound the difficulties inherent in intractable conflicts.

Should we, therefore, give up on intractable conflicts? The answer must be an emphatic no! The international community can keep a watching brief over many intractable conflicts to ensure that they remain "frozen," or in abeyance, while recognizing that mediation may contribute to ending the violence. Mediation efforts must be initiated and undertaken at an optimal moment (e.g., when there is a major systemic change or when the parties are truly ready for a dramatic shift), and where strong leaders can come forward, make commitments, and deal with the spoilers and other intransigent factions. When these contextual conditions prevail, a coordinated mediation effort organized by regional or international organizations and supported by some major actors may begin.

Seemingly intractable conflicts need not go on for many years. The United Nations can take the lead in initiating low-level third-party efforts, in the hope of freezing a situation and preparing the ground for more active and directive efforts by a regional hegemon or a major power. Mediation may not resolve an intractable conflict, but it may well make good progress toward its termination or even settlement. Mediation has a role to play even in the most resistant cases, and if used effectively, it can contribute to making an intractable conflict that much more tractable.

Notes

1. Edward Azar, "Protracted International Conflict: Ten Propositions," in *International Conflict Resolution,* ed. Edward Azar and John W. Burton (London: Wheatsheaf Books, 1986), 27–39.

2. See Paul Huth and Bruce Russett, "General Deterrence between Enduring Rivals Testing Three Competing Models," *American Political Science Review* 87, no. 1 (1993): 61–73.

3. See Gary Goertz and Paul F. Diehl, "Enduring Rivalries: Theoretical Constructs and Empirical Patterns," *International Studies Quarterly* 37, no. 1 (April 1993): 147–171.

4. See Zeer Maoz and Ben Mor, *Bound by Struggle* (Ann Arbor: University of Michigan Press, 2002).

5. See Cameron Thies, "A Social Psychological Approach to Enduring Rivalries," *Political Psychology* 22, no. 4 (2001): 693–725.

6. In our study we identified 309 international conflicts in the 1945–95 period. Each conflict was examined for all public and official conflict management efforts. Thus, the total number of different mediation efforts in our 75 intractable conflicts was 382. See Jacob Bercovitch and Richard Jackson, *International Conflict Management: 1945–94* (Washington, D.C.: Congressional Quarterly, 1997).

7. See Richard W. Fogg, "Dealing with Conflict," *Journal of Conflict Resolution* 29, no. 3 (1985): 330–358.

8. On other transformations, see Lous Kriesberg, *Constructive Conflicts* (Boulder, Colo.: Rowman and Littlefield, 1998).

9. See Jacob Bercovitch, *Social Conflicts and Third Parties* (Boulder, Colo.: Westview Press, 1984); and Kalevi J. Holsti, *Peace and War: Armed Conflict and International Order* (Cambridge: Cambridge University Press, 1991).

10. Chris Mitchell, *Peacemaking and the Consultant's Role* (Aldershot, U.K.: Gower, 1981), 87.

11. See Charles Moore, *The Mediation Process* (San Francisco: Jossey-Bass, 1986), 6.

12. See Jay Folberg and Alison Taylor, *Mediation: A Comprehensive Guide to Resolving Conflict* (San Francisco: Jossey-Bass, 1984).

13. For a review of these, see Jacob Bercovitch and Alison Houston, "The Study of International Mediation: Theoretical Issues and Empirical Evidence," in *Resolving Conflicts,* ed. Jacob Bercovitch (Boulder, Colo.: Lynne Rienner, 1996), 11-38.

14. On the relationship between structural features and international conflict management, see Benjamin Miler, *When Opponents Cooperate: Great Power Conflict and Collaboration in World Politics* (Ann Arbor: University of Michigan Press, 1995).

15. See Gary Goertz and Paul Diehl, "The Initiation and Termination of Enduring Rivalries," *American Journal of Political Science* 39, no. 1 (1995): 30–52.

16. On the relevance of issues in intractable conflicts and their management, see Paul Diehl, "What Are They Fighting For? The Importance of Issues in International Conflict Research," *Journal of Peace Research* 29, no. 3 (1992): 333–344.

17. See Robert Randle, *The Origins of Peace* (New York: The Free Press, 1973), 49.

18. For a useful review, see I. William Zartman, "Ripeness: The Hurting Stalemate and Beyond," in *International Conflict Resolution after the Cold War*, ed. Paul Stern and Dan Druckman (Washington, D.C.: National Academy Press, 2000).

19. See the studies by Russell Leng, "When Will They Ever Learn? Coercive Bargaining in Recurrent Crises," *Journal of Conflict Resolution* 27, no. 3 (1993): 379–419; and Jacob Bercovitch and Jeffrey Langley, "The Nature of the Dispute and the Effectiveness of International Mediation," *Journal of Conflict Resolution* 37, no. 4 (1993): 670–691.

20. See Bercovitch and Langley, "The Nature of the Dispute and the Effectiveness of International Mediation."

21. See William I. Dixon, "Democracy and the Management of International Conflict," *Journal of Conflict Resolution* 37, no. 1 (1993): 42–68.

22. See Saadia Touval, *The Peace-Brokers: Mediators in the Arab-Israeli Conflict, 1948–1979* (Princeton, N.J.: Princeton University Press, 1979).

23. See, for instance, Deborah M. Kolb, "Strategy and Tactics of Mediation," *Human Relations* 36, no. 2 (1983): 247–268.

24. See Saadia Touval and I. William Zartman, eds., *International Mediation in Theory and Practice* (Boulder, Colo.: Westview Press, 1985).

25. See Russell Leng, *Bargaining and Learning in Recurring Crises* (Ann Arbor: University of Michigan Press, 2000).

26. On the effects of these, see Stephen J. Stedman, *Peacemaking in Civil War: International Mediation in Zimbabwe, 1974–1980* (Boulder, Colo.: Lynne Rienner, 1991).

6

Negotiating Intractable Conflicts

The Contributions of Unofficial Intermediaries

Diana Chigas

DESPITE HOPES FOR PEACE following the fall of the Berlin Wall, the world continues to be beset by a host of protracted conflicts that appear intractable. Many conflicts—from Israel-Palestine to Kashmir and Central Africa—not only survived the end of the Cold War but became more intense in its aftermath. Now a new generation of "intractable" conflicts appears to be emerging in these areas, to add to those that survived the end of the Cold War. "New" conflicts in Bosnia, the Caucasus, and Kosovo are proving just as resistant to traditional instruments of diplomacy, mediation, and negotiation as the conflicts in Cyprus, Kashmir, Korea, and the Middle East. As suggested in the opening chapter of this book, although third-party intervention in conflicts has increased significantly over the past decade, third parties have not had a good track record in intractable conflicts. In part, the reasons for third-party failure lie in the structure and context of intractable conflicts, analyzed more fully in the preceding chapters in this volume. In some cases, third parties fail because the conflict itself is not "ripe" for resolution (Zartman 1985; Haass 1991); in other words, one or both parties may not have strong motives to de-escalate, in part because they believe the costs exceed the benefits of de-escalation. The lack of accountability and resource constraints, as well as the availability of external support for conflict actors, can undermine third-party efforts to resolve intractable conflicts; the conflict becomes too profitable for some actors, and, as I. William Zartman notes in chapter 3, the resources "become the end rather than the means of the conflict." "Bad" (Brown 2001) or weak leadership and internal fragmentation contribute significantly to intractability and also diminish the chances of third-party success. And as both Zartman and Louis Kriesberg note earlier in this volume, many intractable conflicts are intertwined with other conflicts regionally or globally, thus complicating the task of the third party by requiring it to be active in several layers of conflict simultaneously. In some cases, it is the third parties themselves who have contributed to deepening intractability by not intervening at the ripe moment (see chapter 1), by not intervening at all, or by intervening with methods inappropriate to the stage, intensity, and nature of the conflict (Fisher and Keashly 1991)—with what the editors of this volume call "poor or weak statecraft" (see chapter 16, page 381).

An additional reason for third-party failure in intractable conflicts is related to the capacity of traditional diplomatic approaches to deal with the nonobjective elements of protracted conflicts. As several authors in this volume note, intractability stems in part—even if not exclusively or primarily—from the nature of the conflict itself. Intractable conflicts tend to involve basic human needs and values that the parties experience as critical to their survival and, as a consequence, as nonnegotiable (Azar 1991; Kelman 1996; Rothman and Olson 2001; Coleman 2000). In other words, the grievances driving intractable conflicts tend to involve experiences of gross injustice and threats to identity and security, thus making the conflict existential—a struggle for survival (see chapters 1, 3, and 4 for fuller explanations of this aspect of intractability). While these issues of identity, survival, and fears of the "other" are often the product of the escalation of the conflict and are unrelated to the issues that initially triggered the conflict, they are critical to the resolution of the conflict. Negotiation or compromise as a path to resolution becomes impossible under these circumstances (see chapter 3).

Moreover, whether ethno-national, such as in Cyprus and the former Yugoslavia, or interstate, as in Kashmir and Korea, the experience of threat is so powerful and fundamental to human existence that the effects of the conflict pervade all aspects of a community's life (Coleman 2000). The conflict becomes institutionalized. The most obvious form of institutionalization is the creation of vested interests in the continuation of the conflict, as a number of groups within each community benefit from the conflict, whether from international attention and resources, career advancement, or legal or extralegal profiteering. A less obvious but equally powerful form of "institutionalization" occurs as a result of the creation of "conflict norms" (Kelman 1979; Pruitt, Rubin, and Kim 1994) that govern people's perceptions and behavior in the conflict. Negative attitudes and beliefs about the other are internalized. This worldview is perpetuated and passed on from generation to generation by social institutions and creates a psychological commitment to the conflict, as well as a set of norms prescribing militant and uncompromising behavior toward the other party (Kelman 1979) and punishing the expression of any views that the enemy may not be as bad, aggressive, or inflexible as assumed (see chapter 4). In effect, the conflict truly becomes an intersocietal phenomenon, between whole bodies politic (Saunders 1995) rather than between elites, making it difficult to develop a settlement.

Finally, the prolonged nature of intractable conflict gives rise to self-reinforcing escalatory dynamics that make it difficult for the parties to come to the table (see chapters 3 and 4). Several sociopsychological processes fuel intensification and perpetuation of a conflict, especially at a high level of escalation. Demonic images of the enemy and virtuous images of self develop on both sides. Each party sees itself as good, peaceful, and acting only for defensive reasons, while the other side is aggressive, untrustworthy, and responsive only to the language of force (Kelman 1997). When these perceptions are held in mirror-image fashion by both parties, their interaction reinforces stalemate by intensifying distrust, dehumanization, and de-individuation of the other party and interfering with communication, reducing empathy, and fostering win-lose thinking (Pruitt, Rubin, and Kim 1994; Kelman 1997). Moreover, these perceptions are highly resistant to change, even in the face of new information that is, from an outsider's point of view, clearly contradictory. Both parties tend to focus on information that confirms their perceptions, ignoring or neutralizing information that may disconfirm them. These dynamics create additional hurdles that make negotiation and resolution of intractable conflicts difficult.

Traditional instruments of negotiation, mediation, and conflict management are not adequate to address these aspects of conflict. They tend to be well suited to resolving resource-based issues (e.g., control over land, poverty, power sharing, distribution of economic opportunities) that may indeed serve as instrumental modalities for the protection of identity and human needs. But issues of identity, survival, and demonization of the other require a process that works directly to change the underlying human relationship and deals with perceptions, trust, and fears that fuel the institutionalization and self-reinforcing dynamic that sustains intractability.

Perceived limitations of traditional diplomatic tools have led to the growth of unofficial third-party interventions designed to analyze and improve the basic relationship between the parties engaged in conflict. In the 1990s there was great debate about the contributions of nongovernmental third parties. Many praise them, noting their potential for developing a broader set of ideas and approaches to address what are today more complex conflicts that involve relationships among whole bodies politic, that are based not on state interests, and that cross permeable boundaries diluted more and more by globalization (Peck 1998; Saunders 1995). Others warn of the dangers inherent in multiple agendas, lack of accountability of nongovernmental organizations (NGOs), and their potential for diverting needed funds from the United Nations and other responsible intergovernmental organizations (Peck 1998). With more than thirty-six thousand NGOs working internationally, and countless more grassroots organizations in areas of conflict, with different methods, different populations, and different goals, it is almost impossible to draw general conclusions about the value of unofficial third-party interventions.

This chapter proposes a framework for considering the roles that unofficial third parties are playing in intractable conflicts and explores the contributions, as well as the limitations, of the various forms of unofficial intermediation in the transformation of intractable conflict.

Official versus Unofficial Intervention: Track-One versus Multitrack Diplomacy

Unofficial intermediation was developed to supplement and fill the gaps of high-level, official third-party conflict resolution efforts and is often contrasted with official, or track-one, diplomacy, to emphasize the different methods and tools that are used by unofficial intermediaries. A brief word about official third-party intervention is warranted in order to situate unofficial efforts in a context of intervention. Official diplomacy, or mediation by governments or intergovernmental organizations (such as the United Nations, the OSCE, and the African Union), is commonly referred to as track-one diplomacy. The term was coined by Joseph Montville, a former diplomat, who distinguished traditional diplomatic activities (track-one diplomacy) from "unofficial, informal interaction between members of adversarial groups or nations with the goals of developing strategies, influencing public opinions, and organizing human and material resources in ways that might help resolve the conflict," which he called "track two" (Montville 1991, 262). Louise Diamond and John McDonald (1996) later refined the concept of track-two diplomacy to describe multiple (nine) "tracks" of diplomacy needed for sustainable peacebuilding, only one of them taking place among decision makers or delegated negotiators.

In track-one diplomacy, the intervener is almost always official—a government, such as the United States in the Israeli-Palestinian conflict and in Colombia, and Norway in Sri Lanka, or an intergovernmental organization, such as IGAD in Sudan, the United Nations in Cyprus, and the OSCE in the Georgia–South Ossetia conflict. Often governments and intergovernmental mediators work together, with interested and influential governments backing intergovernmental mediation efforts. For example, Norway, the United Kingdom, and the United States have been strong backers of the IGAD process in Sudan, as Stephen Morrison and Alex de Waal describe in chapter 7, just as the European Union, the United Kingdom, and the United States have been active in pushing the parties to negotiations for which the United Nations is the official mediator.

As Kriesberg notes in his chapter, official intervention, or track-one diplomacy, entails a broad range of possible activities, from the relatively nonforceful activity of facilitating communication between adversaries to proposing solutions and applying pressure to recalcitrant parties to come to a resolution. Track-one mediation or diplomacy generally includes a different set of activities than unofficial intermediation. Governments conducting track-one mediation often have a significant stake in the conflict and its outcome, and as principal mediators, they often suggest, promote, and help implement and sustain a settlement (Kriesberg 2001).

The intended product of these track-one interventions is an agreement, whether to a cease-fire to end violence in active intractable conflicts or to a more comprehensive settlement of the underlying conflict. Unofficial third parties, in contrast, have no resources or leverage to bring to the table and therefore generally take on a more facilitative or educational role.

Roles of Unofficial Intermediaries in Intractable Conflicts

As Rouhana (1995) notes, unofficial third-party intervention is a concept that means different things to different people. The range of unofficial interveners is broad, including religious institutions, academics, former government officials, nongovernmental organizations, humanitarian organizations, and think tanks, among others. The range of interventions is equally broad. This chapter is concerned with unofficial *intermediation*— in which an unofficial third party acts as a go-between, facilitator, or mediator between the sides of a conflict—yet the kinds of interventions undertaken by unofficial third parties extend far beyond mediatory or facilitation roles to include empowerment, advocacy, and economic and social development activities.

Yet even in this narrower class of unofficial third-party activity, roles are unclear; the lines between traditional mediation and newer forms of third-party interventions, as well as among unofficial third-party interventions themselves, are blurred. Unofficial intermediary activities have been described alternately as citizen diplomacy, supplemental diplomacy, prenegotiation, interactive conflict resolution, consultation, facilitated joint brainstorming, informal parallel negotiation, and back-channel diplomacy, among other terms.

There are many ways of categorizing unofficial intermediation activities. Figure 1 represents one typology dividing unofficial intermediation into three tracks, or levels, of third-party activity. The typology is based on the level at which the intervention occurs and the type of activity and broad products of the intervention. In each track, the third party works with a different class of participants (from top decision makers to grassroots communities) and generally engages in a different type of activity with different anticipated products (from mediation or premediation dialogue

Figure 1. Roles of Unofficial Third Parties

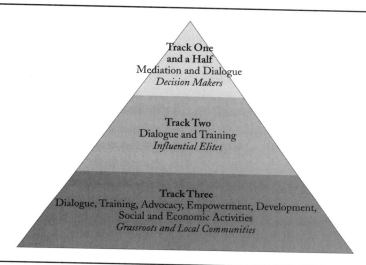

with officials aimed directly at furthering official negotiation processes in track one and a half, to a broader range of training, education, and empowerment activities to promote grassroots involvement in peace processes and develop cooperative attitudes and actions at the grassroots level to promote sustainability of peace in track three).

This typology is designed to highlight a fundamental characteristic of peacebuilding in intractable conflicts: namely, that it cannot occur merely at the elite level, nor aim only at settlements or agreements. The nature and the structure of intractable conflicts, described in great detail in previous chapters of this volume, require that peacebuilding and peacemaking address all levels of society (from the leadership to the grass roots) and deal with psychological and relationship aspects of the conflict.

The remainder of this chapter elaborates on the roles played by third parties at each level of intervention. It then analyzes the contributions of the third parties' activities to the transformation of intractable conflicts, as well as their limitations, and concludes with a summary of strengths and weaknesses of unofficial intermediaries for both active and abeyant intractable conflicts.

Unofficial Interventions with Decision Makers: Track-One-and-a-Half Diplomacy

In track-one-and-a-half diplomacy, unofficial actors (former government officials and religious or social organizations such as the Catholic Church or the Quakers) intervene with official government representatives to promote a peaceful resolution of conflict. Track-one-and-a-half diplomacy typically takes one of two forms: direct mediation and conciliation, in which the unofficial intermediary tries to mediate a settlement to the conflict or specific issues in dispute, or consultation, in which the unofficial third party acts as an impartial facilitator of informal problem-solving dialogue among decision makers or negotiators trying to "assist the parties in analyzing and dealing with their antagonistic attitudes and the basic issues in their relationship" (Fisher and Keashly 1988, 383).

Unofficial Direct Mediation and Conciliation. Unofficial actors have acted directly as mediators or conciliators between conflicting parties either by hosting and facilitating talks or by providing unofficial shuttle diplomacy. The latter is exemplified by the role of Quaker peacemaker Adam Curle in the Nigerian conflict of 1967–70. Curle shuttled between the Nigerian government and the Biafran rebel leaders, exchanging messages and engaging in bilateral discussions with both sides to help them develop a clearer picture of the issues, ideas for solution, and possibilities for progress.

The Community of Sant'Egidio, a private voluntary Catholic organization based in Rome and with contacts in the Vatican, has acted as a host and facilitator of direct negotiations. It has been able to play this mediation role based on its mission, its close association with the Vatican, and its extensive network of contacts. Building on fourteen years of developing relationships and providing humanitarian aid in Mozambique, the Community of Sant'Egidio assumed the role of primary mediator there in 1990. Bringing the main parties to its home in Rome, Sant'Egidio mediators facilitated, with the support of the international community, the agreement that ended the civil war in that country. Building on a similar extensive network of contacts among all parties and its widely acknowledged motivation for caring for the less fortunate, Sant'Egidio mediated one of the only agreements between the Serbian government and the Albanian community in Kosovo: the September 1, 1996, Educational

Agreement for Kosovo (Morozzo della Rocca 1998). Although this agreement was never implemented and was overtaken by the events that led to the NATO bombing in 1999, it did represent a significant achievement in that context.

Former president Jimmy Carter and the Conflict Resolution Program at the Carter Center at Emory University in Atlanta are another example. The Conflict Resolution Program operates with six permanent staff members who support the mediation efforts of Carter and his wife, Rosalynn. The former president and Mrs. Carter undertake most missions at the request of the parties. Carter consults with governments, as well as relevant governmental and intergovernmental organizations (Peck 1998). However, he acts in an unofficial capacity, albeit with official blessing. His status as a former president of the United States gives him legitimacy and entry at the highest levels. Yet, acting as an unofficial mediator, he is free to initiate discussions, facilitate communication, and explore new ideas.

In this role, Carter undertook a mission to North Korea in 1994 to defuse escalating tensions between that country and the United States.[1] Alarmed at the lack of direct contact between North Korea and the United States amid a growing crisis over North Korea's refusal to allow the International Atomic Energy Agency (IAEA) to inspect one of its nuclear plants, Carter took the initiative to meet with North Korean leader Kim Il Sung. The White House had declined direct contact until its conditions were met but did not object to Carter's acceptance of an invitation to go to North Korea, provided he made it clear that he was going as a private citizen and not with any authority from the U.S. government to negotiate. Explaining that he had come as a private citizen, but with the knowledge and support of his government, Carter succeeded in developing a deal that defused the crisis. He had no authority, of course, to commit the White House to the option he had developed with Kim Il Sung. But his announcement on CNN of North Korean readiness to agree to the deal just as he left North Korea made it difficult for the administration to reject it. Carter succeeded in providing a face-saving way for the administration to back down from a rigid position that was contributing to rapid escalation of tensions. He was, however, not greeted enthusiastically in Washington, as his CNN announcement had forced a divided administration to make a decision it had not yet been ready to make about how to deal with North Korea.

Direct mediation by unofficial third parties is not common. As the chilly reception given to Jimmy Carter upon his return to Washington from Pyongyang demonstrates, unofficial intermediaries can be seen as interfering with policies of interested governmental parties or mediators. There are also few individuals or organizations with sufficient stature or moral authority and sufficient connections within interested governments to play such a role.

Unofficial Consultation. More often, unofficial intermediaries play what Fisher (1972; Fisher and Keashly 1988) has called a consultant's role.[2] In this model, key individuals from the parties are brought together in their *personal* capacities, rather than as representatives of their side, for direct, private interaction. The meetings are low key, closed to the public, and non-binding. Participants share their perceptions and concerns, focusing on the interests and basic needs underlying their positions, jointly analyze the underlying issues and their relationship, and jointly develop ideas for resolution. The setting, ground rules, agenda, and third-party role facilitate a different kind of interaction than that normally occurring between the parties and thus change perceptions, bring new information into the discussion, and promote openness and creativity. The workshops are designed to promote relationship and trust building across conflict lines, development of lines of communication, and exploration of options that could meet both sides' interests and needs.

Negotiation and conflict resolution training has also been used as both a method and a forum for track-one-and-a-half dialogue. Generally, such training brings participants from conflicting parties for a common learning experience in which they learn concepts and skills and use them to focus on their own conflict. At times, unofficial intermediaries work separately (in parallel) with the parties to develop analytic and operational skills and a common vocabulary that can assist them when they do come together to negotiate (Chigas 1997). While sharing characteristics and goals with "consultation" and dialogue, joint training also seeks to provide an opportunity for participants to reflect on process, learn about common negotiation dynamics, and develop broadly applicable new skills.

Conflict Management Group's (CMG) initiative in the Georgian–South Ossetian peace process is an example of a track-one-and-a-half intervention that combined both problem-solving dialogue and training methods. The Georgia–South Ossetia Dialogue Project, undertaken by CMG from 1994 to 2002 in partnership with the Norwegian Refugee Council (NRC), comprised a series of facilitated joint brainstorming meetings over five years. "Facilitated joint brainstorming" is a method devised by Professor Roger Fisher of Harvard Law School and CMG to develop settlement options for negotiation. The meeting agendas included exercises and skill building in negotiation, designed to stimulate reflection on participants' assumptions about negotiation and future possibilities for mutual gains negotiation. In structured communication processes, participants were asked to talk about their own experiences, interests, needs, and fears and listen to and explore those of the other side. Participants brainstormed ideas related to the Georgian–South Ossetian negotiation process, particularly on issues they discovered to be of common concern, such as cultural and economic ties, refugees, and development. A significant amount of formal and informal time for relationship building was built into the program. Following the last overseas meeting, a core group of Georgian and South Ossetian high-level officials formed a steering committee, which met on a regular basis closer to home, especially before official negotiating sessions mediated by Russia and the OSCE, to informally share perspectives, correct misunderstandings, and develop ideas relevant to the negotiation process. Like the brainstorming meetings, the steering committee sessions were designed to develop deeper understanding of the core issues of concern to both parties and explore new approaches to resolving them, *not* to negotiate or agree on a single idea.

Unofficial Interventions with Unofficial Actors: Track-Two Diplomacy

The consultant's role described earlier originated with the development of track-two interventions. In track-two diplomacy, unofficial intermediaries work with nonofficial yet influential people from the conflicting sides to improve communication, understanding, and relationships and to develop new ideas for resolving the conflict. The Kashmir Study Group, described by Howard Schaffer and Teresita Schaffer in chapter 12, is a good example. Founded by a Kashmiri-American businessman, the Kashmir Study Group (KSG) has brought together academics, retired diplomats, NGO leaders, and members of Congress for dialogue. The KSG has developed new ideas for resolving the Kashmir problem that have generated serious discussion in both India and Pakistan. The social stature and networks of the participants, the range of perspectives they represent, and the creativity of the KSG's ideas have earned the group a reputation for nonpartisanship and a measure of influence in both countries.

A number of methodologies for conducting track-two diplomacy have been developed and well documented since the 1970s. The best-known and most developed of the track-two models is the interactive problem-solving workshop, developed by John Burton, Herbert Kelman, Ronald Fisher, and others (Kelman 2000; Rouhana and Kelman 1994; Mitchell 1981; Fisher 1972; Kelman 1972; Burton 1969). The workshop brings together nonofficial but influential members of the parties for direct, private interaction, joint analysis of the conflict, and joint problem solving. The identity and the role of third parties are similar: they are knowledgeable and skilled scholar-practitioners who are impartial and whose training and expertise enable them to facilitate productive dialogue and problem solving between the parties (Fisher and Keashly 1991; Rouhana and Kelman 1994). The participants in these efforts, however, are not officials or members of negotiating teams but rather "politically involved and often politically influential members" of conflicting societies (Kelman 2000; Rouhana and Kelman 1994). They may be parliamentarians, leaders, and activists of political movements, journalists, members of think tanks, and academics: people who are within the mainstream of their societies and close to the political center. Their unofficial position, along with the academic setting in which the meetings are conducted, permits them greater freedom to explore alternative perspectives and formulate new (joint) ideas (Kelman 2000).

Kelman and his colleagues have applied this approach to workshops, primarily between Israelis and Palestinians, since the 1970s. The workshops have been credited with contributing to the breakthrough achieved in the Oslo Accords of September 1993 by preparing cadres to negotiate productively, by providing substantive inputs (in terms of both ideas and awareness of sensitivities and perspectives of the other side), and by creating a better political atmosphere for negotiation (Kelman 2000).

Another model for track-two diplomacy, developed by former U.S. diplomat Harold Saunders, seeks to "engage representative citizens from the conflicting parties in designing steps to be taken in the political arena to change perceptions and stereotypes, to create a sense that peace might be possible, and to involve more and more of their compatriots." This "public peace process" (Chufrin and Saunders 1993) has been applied in the Inter-Tajik Dialogue, begun in 1993 under the auspices of the Dartmouth Conference Regional Conflicts Task Force. In this model, dialogue proceeds through a five-phase process. In the first phase, defining the problem and deciding to engage with the other side, the organizers contacted more than one hundred people in Tajikistan, seeking broad representation of the different factions in conflict, at a second- or third-tier of authority to ensure their ability to explore ideas freely (Slim and Saunders 2001). The second phase, involving mapping issues and relationships and identifying possibilities for working together, began with the first meeting in 1993, during which participants "were absorbed with unloading their feelings about the origins and conduct of the civil war." The third phase, analyzing the problem through dialogue and designing ways of changing the relationship, was ushered in by participants' emerging desire to focus on starting a negotiation to create conditions for refugee return. In this phase, the participants explored approaches to each key issue and came to broad conclusions about desirable ways to address problems. The fourth and fifth phases, building scenarios of interacting steps that can be taken in the political arena to change the relationships and acting together, have resulted in at least eighteen joint memoranda to convey ideas to the negotiating teams and the larger body politic (Slim and Saunders 2001). Dialogue participants shared these ideas with decision makers and international actors. They also held public events abroad and in Tajikistan. Some participants became delegates to the official negotiations and were able to transmit the ideas to their teams.

Unofficial Interventions at the Grass Roots: Track-Three Diplomacy

In track-three diplomacy, unofficial third parties work with people from all walks of life and sectors of their society to find ways to promote peace in settings of violent conflict. This work is aimed at building or rebuilding broken relationships across the lines of division among ordinary citizens in communities, in a range of sectors. In addition to dialogue, training, and other mediatory activities that bring people together across conflict lines, track-three interventions include psychosocial work to help communities deal with the trauma that violent conflict has produced, social and arts events that bring people together across conflict lines, joint business projects, peace education, social mobilization, economic and social development projects that establish concrete incentives for peace, and work with the media, religious organizations, and other shapers of public opinion, among others.

Many track-three activities operate at the local, or community, level. Most involve longer-term relationship-building and capacity-building endeavors designed to deal with root causes of conflict and sustain peace. Some, however, in hot intractable conflicts especially, are aimed at ending violence. In Sudan, for example, the People-to-People process undertaken by the New Sudan Council of Churches has had some success in promoting Dinka-Nuer reconciliation in Southern Sudan, achieving some concrete results in opening paths for humanitarian assistance, providing for reconstruction of homes and accommodation of internally displaced people, and ending violence (Jenner 2000). While some have criticized this church process as fostering political parties, it has achieved significant results in mitigating ethnic and factional fighting within the South.

Some interventions have national scope and influence. Studio Ijambo, an independent radio station established in Burundi in 1995 by the U.S.-based NGO Search for Common Ground, produces programs dedicated to peace and national reconciliation and dialogue among polarized groups. Studio Ijambo was a response to the need for balanced and anti-inflammatory media programming in a country where radio reaches an estimated 85 percent of the population and has been used to promote hatred and fear and manipulate listeners into committing unspeakable acts of violence.[3]

Seeds of Peace, a U.S.-based nongovernmental organization, works with the next generation of leaders from the Middle East and other conflict areas at its 150-acre International Camp for Conflict Resolution along the shores of Pleasant Lake in Otisfield, Maine. The Seeds of Peace goal is to create a safe place where teenagers who have grown up perceiving the other as a permanent enemy can begin to feel comfortable with their adversary, if not to form lasting friendships. Through their participation, governments help send the signal that the involvement of ordinary people in the peace process is as vital as that of the governments (Wallach 2000).

The premise of track-three diplomacy is that peace can and must be built from the bottom up as well as from the top down. Intractable conflicts affect a broad spectrum of people and pervade many aspects of a community's life. For any negotiation to be undertaken or to be successful, a "peace constituency" must exist, and for any settlement that is eventually reached, support and capacity for its implementation. Track-three interventions are therefore generally directed at rebuilding "social capital" (Putnam 2000) in communities that have been fractured by conflict. In many instances, the local level is a microcosm of the larger conflict; lines of identity in the conflict are often drawn through local communities, dividing them into hostile groups, and people at this level experience the day-to-day consequences of those divisions and of the decisions of the political elite. Track-three projects offer an opportunity for people to work at the community level, away from the political negotiation, on issues of peace and conflict resolution (Lederach 1997). As Louise Diamond (1999), originator of the concept of multitrack diplomacy, notes:

> The forces of war have an existing infrastructure that enables them to mobilize and actualize their aims—they have armies and arms suppliers; transportation, commerce and communication systems; banking, taxing and other funding methods; media, education and propaganda systems; and government ministries, clans, villages, political parties and other entities capable of taking action. The forces of peace have little of this. . . . Much more needs to be done to create both a human and an institutional infrastructure for peace-building, in order to concretize these methods and approaches in social, political and economic systems that can both stand on their own and work together toward a shared goal.

Impact of Unofficial Interventions

In the case of track-one-and-a-half mediation or conciliation by unofficial third parties, impact can be determined clearly by virtue of the achievement and maintenance of agreements. As Jimmy Carter's success in North Korea and Sant'Egidio's successes in Mozambique and Kosovo demonstrate, unofficial intermediaries can play valuable roles where official mediators are unavailable, uninterested, or seen as biased, or when any acceptance of mediation is perceived by the parties as a sign of weakness or legitimation of the enemy. In internal conflicts, because unofficial mediators cannot interfere with sovereignty, they may be able to gain entry more easily than governments or international organizations.

The noncoercive, informal nature of unofficial mediation also permits greater flexibility to unofficial actors in initiating and conducting discussions with the conflicting parties. Parties can maintain their incompatible positions while exploring whether there may be any possibilities for achieving their goals through negotiation. Any ideas generated in an unofficial mediation are later deniable. The political costs of noncooperation with unofficial mediators are also lower than those of noncooperation with unofficial initiatives. Ironically, this may lower resistance to and open space for exploration of negotiation possibilities when the parties still are committed to unilateral action.

Nonetheless, as Jimmy Carter's chilly reception in Washington upon his return from Pyongyang and the unraveling of the Educational Agreement for Kosovo demonstrate, NGO mediation is fraught with difficulties. The essence of intractability is, in a sense, the lack of ripeness for negotiated resolution; in these conditions, efforts to negotiate or mediate a settlement may be not only inappropriate but counterproductive (Haass 1991). Moreover, nongovernmental organizations do not have the resources or the authority to bring parties who are not ready or willing to the negotiating table, and there is a great risk of their being manipulated by the parties for their own initial (and incompatible) strategic objectives. While there is some evidence of NGO mediation and conciliation contributing to the prevention of further escalation and deepening of a protracted conflict, the underlying divisions remain untouched by their efforts.

Assessing the impact of the other forms of unofficial intermediation in intractable conflicts is more complex. These forms are not designed to achieve the goals of traditional diplomacy; they are not designed to produce agreements, nor to effect major shifts in policy in the short term. Rather, they seek to affect more intangible factors of intractability, such as attitudes and relationships that are more difficult to measure, whose contribution to change in the broader conflict environment is difficult to assess. Even when the impact of the interventions on participants' attitudes and relationships can be measured, the significance of these "micro"-level achievements for the larger conflict resolution process is often not clear. Attribution of impact among the myriad of independent and interdependent variables (Ross 2000; Lieberfeld 2002) is difficult. When there is movement—as there was in the Israeli-Palestinian conflict following Oslo, in South Africa, in Northern Ireland, and seemingly in Cyprus until the Greek Cypriots voted in April 2004 to reject reunification with the Turkish Cypriots—the most direct and visible causal links relate to changes in "objective" or structural factors in the conflict—changes in leadership, in the regional environment, or in the domestic political environment, often achieved through application of the resources and leverage of traditional (state and intergovernmental) third parties to change the cost-benefit calculus of key people in the conflict.

Nonetheless, some real contributions of unofficial third parties can be identified. While less direct and dramatic, they are an important part of the ripening and transformation of intractable conflicts. All forms of unofficial intermediation—from track-one-and-a-half consultation to track-three activities—have shown demonstrable successes in dealing with the psychological, cultural, and institutional elements of intractability identified in the case studies in this volume, in particular, changing attitudes and relationships among participants and building their capacity to work together cooperatively to develop peaceful means for resolution. In the words of Swedish diplomat Jan Eliasson (2002, 373), "the parties themselves—not just the conflict—must be 'ripe.'" The attitude and relationship transformations in the parties facilitated by unofficial intermediaries help the parties break out of the adversarial dynamic that characterizes their intractable relationship and help them recognize and seize ripe opportunities for negotiation as well as overcome hurdles to resolution at the table. The most significant impacts of unofficial intermediation can be grouped into four categories: (1) changes in attitudes and psychology of the parties, (2) improved communication and relationships across conflict lines, (3) development of new options to bridge the polarization or competition of solutions, and (4) improvements in the institutionalization of the conflict.

Changed Attitudes about the Other and about the Conflict

The most commonly observed change is the breaking down of negative stereotypes and generalizations of the other side. These enemy images serve both as tools for mobilizing public resources in support of policy and as psychological constructs that enable leaders to justify violence and confrontation against another group (Ayres 1997). Participants develop a deep understanding of the other's intentions and rationale for policies and behavior, their political culture, and decision-making context. Merely getting to know the other in an informal context can change conceptions of them, especially where there is little contact other than exchange of positions in official fora or the media. In many cases, participants note that workshops clarify misinformation about the other side and help them understand that the other community, like their own, has suffered in the conflict (Angelica 1999). The development of an empathetic understanding of the other side's experiences, perspectives, and needs forms an initial basis for trust.

Myths that the other is not interested in dialogue are often broken, and a working trust can begin to develop as the other's motivations become clarified and human connections develop. In CMG and NRC's track-one-and-a-half initiative in the Georgia–South Ossetia peace process, for example, one South Ossetian reported that he realized in a way that he had not before that the Georgians also genuinely wanted to get something out of the conflict resolution process. This deep realization allowed him to really listen to the Georgian perspectives for the first time since the war began (Allen-Nan 2002). Similar stories emerge from Cypriot, Israeli-Palestinian, and other unofficial processes (Kaye 2001; Kenyon 1999; Conflict Management Group 1994): the Greek Cypriot nationalist who became an activist for bicommunal rapprochement, or the journalist participant in a workshop for political, economic, and media leaders from both sides who first locked his door in fear of what his counterpart from the other side would do to him and was later suspended from his job for refusing to use language the other community found offensive. The structure and content of the dialogue allow participants to see a more differentiated and less negative image of the "enemy" and its "intentions." Participants learn that there is a diversity of views on both sides, including views that cut across conflict lines, and identify "coalition partners" on the other side with whom they might work to open a path to negotiation.

Unofficial intermediation processes also help participants transform their perceptions of the conflict in ways that open space for negotiation by facilitating mutual understanding and acceptance of these concerns about survival and identity and a transformation of win-lose existential framing of the conflict (Rothman and Olson 2001; Pearson 2001). Unofficial intermediation processes engage the psychosocial dimensions of the definition of the conflict directly. Participants identify underlying needs, values, and interests that are compatible and that can form the basis for a new definition of a common problem that the two sides share an interest in solving (Saunders 1995), and develop, as a result of deeper understanding of the other side's needs, a greater openness to abandoning previous non-negotiable positions (Meyer 2002; Kaye 2001). Participants also report a greater hope and confidence that joint solutions can be found (Conflict Management Group 1994, 1996; Klein 1994) and a greater willingness to engage with the other side. For example, participants in the Inter-Tajik Dialogue report that the dialogue helped them gain a new understanding of the sources of conflict in Tajikistan and helped them moderate their own positions (Slim and Saunders 2001). Even where "nonnegotiable" gaps persist, the empathy and mutual understanding that unofficial processes facilitate lessen the emotional reactivity and make it easier for the parties to work together to find compromise solutions (Deutsch 1988).

Improved Communication, Relationships, and Trust

Negative perceptions, and the distrust and confrontation they breed, are perpetuated by lack of communication. In some cases, the barrier is physical. Until recently, for example, the UN-patrolled Green Line in Cyprus dividing the two communities was difficult to cross, and telephone connections were limited to three United Nations lines. In other cases, where such physical restrictions are not imposed, political, social, and psychological constraints limit possibilities for communication in an equally powerful way. The communication vacuum "provides a greenhouse in which rumors flourish. Facts are embellished or distorted" (Pruitt, Rubin, and Kim 1994, 108). Interpretation and conjecture are taken as fact.

Unofficial intermediaries have made a significant contribution in opening channels of communication between parties who otherwise would find it difficult to meet or acknowledge any contact, and in improving the quality of communication—and consequently of understanding—across conflict lines. This is particularly important in hot intractable conflicts, where violence and heightened tensions usually lead to interruption of lines of communication, at both elite and grassroots levels.

At a time when there were no official contacts between the United States and the Palestine Liberation Organization, Landrum Bolling, former president of Earlham College in Richmond, Indiana, and a Quaker peacemaker, served as an unofficial liaison between Yasir Arafat and President Jimmy Carter during his administration. Track-two dialogues have constituted one of the few fora in which Israelis and Iranians could meet (Kaye 2001). Likewise, owing to political constraints on official contacts, track-two dialogues have offered a unique opportunity for Israeli-Syrian dialogue (Kaye 2001). In times of increasing tensions, these fora may be a significant channel for parties to clarify misperceptions and correct miscommunication that could lead to further escalation. The parties' concerns about legitimizing the status of the enemy, looking weak, or prejudicing their positions are lessened by the unofficial identity and the facilitative, diagnostic role of the intermediary and the fact that the meetings are not designed to produce agreement.

The common ground rules, structure, and venue for unofficial discussions also make possible a kind of communication that is generally not feasible among parties in intractable conflicts. Extreme polarization of communication, characterized by blaming, accusation, and use of language that is provocative or threatening to the other side, occurs at all levels of society. This dynamic perpetuates confrontation, mistrust, and hopelessness about the possibilities for change. Negotiation and problem solving under these conditions become impossible.

Unofficial intermediation processes help to close this gap in communication by changing the nature of the discussion. Participants exchange personal stories about their experiences in the conflict. They begin to analyze the conflict in a structured way, delving beneath positions and arguments to understand interests, needs, fears, concerns, priorities, constraints, and values (Kelman 2000). Participants become aware of the ways their language reinforces mutual mistrust because it is experienced as offensive, disrespectful, or threatening by the other side. They begin to develop a de-escalatory language that contributes to creating an environment in which they can communicate and solve problems more effectively. This is the basis for development of a working trust between the sides that permits joint analysis and joint problem solving to overcome barriers to settlement (Meyer 2002; Kelman 2000).

The transformation of attitudes and communication is inextricably tied to the establishment of deep relationships of mutual trust among participants in unofficial processes. Being with the "enemy" at breakfast, in the meetings themselves, and at the bar at night rehumanizes the conflict and helps participants recognize that they share many fears, needs, and concerns. As Howard Schaffer and Teresita Schaffer note in chapter 12, the track-two diplomacy initiatives on Kashmir have helped participants develop greater rapport and overcome suspicions of the Indian and Pakistani governments. While this newfound trust, and in some cases friendship, does not always extend beyond the boundaries of the workshop to the other side as a whole (Angelica 1999), these personal relationships are critical to the capacity of parties to develop a process for coming to the table and to deal with the hurdles in negotiation. In this context, unofficial intermediation can be seen as "attempts to strengthen the hands of the pro-negotiation elements on each side in their internal struggle" against the hawks (Kelman 1993, 240).

The impacts of improved relationships can be seen in the Georgian –South Ossetian negotiations. Participants in CMG's workshops reported that improved relationships brought with them the ability to talk informally on breaks from intense official negotiating sessions and to call each other when hot issues erupted. This, they concluded, significantly improved the official negotiations (Allen-Nan 2002). OSCE mediators also noted these shifts in relationship and attributed the improved tone of negotiations to the relationship building achieved in the unofficial workshops (Allen-Nan 2002). Similarly, personal relationships developed during unofficial regional dialogues in the Middle East have positively affected official interactions. For example, one Israeli participant associated with the Likud party used his track-two contacts to arrange meetings between then Likud leader Benjamin Netanyahu and Jordanian officials. Egyptian and Israeli track-two participants commented that negotiation at the official level was easier because of the contacts and relationships they had made when working on a global arms control agreement (Kaye 2001).

New Options for Productive Negotiation

Many unofficial initiatives have gone beyond understanding and dialogue to Harold Saunders's fifth stage of public dialogue—that of "acting together"—to have a concrete impact on changing the relationship between the parties (Chufrin and Saunders 1993). Unofficial processes can generate creative ideas for settlement that cannot be raised in official negotiations, as well as cadres of people with experience working with the other and capable of conducting productive negotiations.

A number of track-one-and-a-half and track-two initiatives have developed new ideas for de-escalation and settlement. The Kashmir Study

Group, described in chapter 12, has developed novel and useful ideas about resolving the Kashmir conflict and has influenced high-level decision makers to think about options outside their normal policy framework. The Dartmouth Conference's Inter-Tajik Dialogue produced eighteen joint memoranda with recommendations on organization of the negotiation process, and several participants in Kelman's problem-solving workshops have published joint papers discussing potential directions for resolution of the thorniest issues in the Israeli-Palestinian conflict. In the Inter-Tajik negotiations, the Commission on National Reconciliation (CNR)—the central implementation mechanism of the 1997 General Agreement, which included several dialogue members—later organized its work program through four subcommissions, echoing the model discussed in that first memorandum (Slim and Saunders 2001). The Harvard Study Group, a two-year initiative conducted under the auspices of Harvard's World Peace Foundation, produced a range of ideas for settlement of the Cyprus conflict that were shared with the leaders on both sides and the main official third parties involved (e.g., the United Nations and the United States); the ideas had some influence on the 2002 United Nations proposal (the Annan Plan). CMG's Georgia–South Ossetia Dialogue project resulted in a number of ideas for joint projects in education, culture, science, and economics and ideas for confidence-building steps, options for cooperation in law enforcement, and steps toward normalization of life in the conflict zone (Olson 2000). Many of these ideas were adopted in the formal negotiations, and although settlement of the conflict is still far away,[4] tensions between the parties have de-escalated significantly. The informal and unofficial nature of the meetings and the intermediary make it possible to present, explore, and discuss ideas openly, including ideas that may be too bold or too sensitive to bring up in official negotiations.

Impacts on Conflict Institutionalization: Changed Conflict Dynamic

Most of the contributions described rely on learning, changed attitudes, and new insights experienced by key individuals—participants in unofficial intermediation processes—that they then feed back into the negotiation or political process. Unofficial intermediation, especially interventions at the track-two and track-three levels, also can impact the structure of conflict in ways that can facilitate transformation of intractability by strengthening pro-negotiation forces, changing public discourse about the conflict, and building peace constituencies at all levels of society.

Creating Cadres for Negotiation. In addition to generating useful ideas, unofficial, citizen-based intermediation is a forum for nurturing cadres able to negotiate effectively with the other and resolve intractable issues when the window of opportunity opens. In South Africa key players in the negotiations between the African National Congress and the National Party were veterans of previous informal discussions, including the chief negotiators on both sides (Lieberfeld 2002). The Oslo process that led to the 1993 Declaration of Principles between Israelis and Palestinians similarly involved negotiators who had long experience with unofficial dialogue processes. In Ecuador and Peru, participants in a CMG-Harvard-led "facilitated joint brainstorming" process later became decision makers in the peace process and drew on their experience in those sessions in negotiating the agreements that ended more than forty years of conflict over their border. Armed with both strong working relationships with counterparts on the other side and a deep understanding of the other side's perceptions, interests, and needs, these people were able to work together to overcome obstacles to resolution at the table.

Strengthening Forces for Moderation. Citizen-based track-two and track-three processes help create space for voices of moderation that have been silenced or marginalized as a result of the polarization of the parties. In intractable conflicts it is difficult for moderates on either side to have a voice in policy or public debate. They are often driven into exile, intimidated into silence by political oppression, or threatened by their authorities or extremist groups. Even those who do take a pro-negotiation stance find themselves isolated or marginalized within their own groups because there appears to be no responsive voice on the other side. As Kelman notes, "[b]ecause of the psychological and political constraints under which they labor, [pro-negotiation elements on both sides] are likely to undermine each other's efforts to promote negotiations. . . . [I]n contrast to the hawks, when the doves on the two sides do what comes naturally, they work at cross-purposes: They tend to communicate to the other side less moderation and willingness to negotiate than they actually represent, and thus undermine each other's argument that there is someone to talk to on the other side and something to talk about" (Kelman 1993, 237–238).

Unofficial intermediation facilitates the formation of "coalitions across conflict lines" that can help organize and strengthen the "negotiating middle" and give a public platform to previously silenced voices for moderation. For example, a July 1997 workshop organized by American University among East Timorese who fell into the "negotiating middle" helped reinforce the position of political moderates and facilitated the formulation of joint negotiation options (Salla 1998). In South Africa a 1987 conference brought together sixty-one predominantly Afrikaans-speaking intellectuals to the left of the governing National Party with seventeen African National Congress (ANC) representatives in Dakar, Senegal. The success of this conference reinforced the influence of "diplomats," such as Thabo Mbeki, within the ANC over those who supported insurrection and mass mobilization (Lieberfeld 2002).

In addition to bolstering the influence of pro-negotiation elements on each side, unofficial diplomacy processes give voice to silenced or marginalized moderate perspectives in the public discourse. The Dakar Conference contributed to changes in white public opinion and increased public discussion of possibilities of negotiation with the ANC as white participants engaged in public speaking, attended "debriefings and house meetings," and even created an alternative Afrikaans newspaper. Lieberfeld (2002) concludes that Dakar "desensitized" whites to talks with the ANC, as evidenced by the comparative lack of media controversy over a follow-up meeting a year later.

Similar impacts on public opinion can be seen in other conflicts. In Cyprus, where powerful norms of group loyalty and cohesiveness had made it taboo to express the view that the enemy might not be as bad, aggressive, or inflexible as assumed, public discussion has been opened to allow previously silenced voices for negotiation and rapprochement to be heard. Bicommunal meetings have become uncontroversial, and "bicommunal rapprochement" has now become part of the public vocabulary and public debate in the mainstream media and political circles. Even a fledgling capacity for organization and preemptive action against extremist-provoked escalation of the conflict has developed. Following violent incidents at the buffer zone separating the two communities in 1996, the Bicommunal Trainers Group was able to bring together participants in a counter-demonstration to a belligerent nationalist demonstration. This led UN officials to organize a UN Day event, which attracted several thousand people and prevented a potentially explosive border clash from escalating further (Wolleh 2001). These activities may also have contributed to the emergence of a more active peace constituency on the island. Driven by the dismal economic situation in Turkey and northern Cyprus, and the prospect of membership in the European Union, tens of thousands of Turkish Cypriots demonstrated in 2003 in favor of the United Nations' Annan Plan. This pro-negotiation movement has been enhanced by a decade-long history of bicommunal dialogue, and most of its leadership are veterans of track-two and track-three initiatives. While the unofficial contacts have not brought about changes in the negotiation positions of the parties, they have softened the rigidly confrontational nature of the relationship between adversaries and have created public openness to a negotiated resolution.

Building Social Networks: An Infrastructure for Peace

Development of an infrastructure for peace is as important to the prenegotiation phase of transforming intractability as it is to the postsettlement phase of implementing an agreement and building peace at a societal level. Because intractable conflicts involve "continuous interaction among significant elements of whole bodies politic across permeable boundaries" (Saunders 1995, 272), it is important to build a political environment—a peace constituency—and a *capacity* to support and sustain peacemaking efforts at the top levels, and to resist repolarization of the conflict when inevitable setbacks occur. Broad participation by civil society actors of the opposing sides can help in preparing adversaries for taking de-escalating steps and negotiating and implementing a settlement. These peace constituencies and social networks across conflict lines help to open space for negotiations to occur and minimize rejectionist impacts in both camps (Kriesberg 2001).

Most track-two and track-three processes result in concrete, constructive joint actions designed to influence the political environment in which negotiations might take place. In Cyprus numerous joint projects —from a bicommunal choir to an EU Study Group to a lawyers' group identifying areas of divergence between the two communities' legal developments since the division of the island—have provided practical experience

and a model of cross-conflict cooperation. In Tajikistan dialogue participants have founded and become active in new civil society organizations.
The Tajikistan Centre for Citizenship Education produces materials and
organizes round-table seminars on subjects important for peacebuilding.
The Public Committee for Promoting Democratic Processes, also in
Tajikistan, is working on a range of projects that help to (1) foster economic development benefiting all members of strife-torn communities,
(2) develop university programs and courses in conflict resolution, (3) foster
dialogue in public fora at the regional level on issues of national importance, and (4) create a second national-level inter-Tajik dialogue (Slim and
Saunders 2001). Mercy Corps' Eastern Kosovo Stabilization Program developed interethnic agricultural market linkages that provided new business
possibilities to both Serbs and Albanians when they worked together. In
Georgia and South Ossetia, joint business ventures and other cross-conflict
projects promote interdependence and the development of substantive interests for peace. Radio Macedonia (Search for Common Ground's project in Macedonia) runs programming depicting interethnic cooperation
and dialogue.[5] Through public education, opportunities for people at all
levels of society to engage in dialogue, and promotion of tangible benefits
of cooperation across conflict lines, these projects contribute to the development of a peace constituency to support negotiation.

The experience of "community relations" work in Northern Ireland
provides a powerful example of the importance and potential impact of
this work. Community relations work, as cross-community intermediation is called, long preceded the start of the negotiations between the main
political actors that resulted in the Good Friday Agreement. Such work
at the grass roots established dense social networks and interdependencies
across conflict lines and institutionalized a number of practices, including
common history texts and curricula, that effectively restrain repolarization and return to violence (Fitzduff 2002). The strong community-based
networks developed through track-two and track-three processes have
contributed significantly to a common sentiment that the difficulties
encountered in the political process in resolving intractable issues such as
decommissioning of weapons and police reform cannot (and should not)
lead to a resurgence of violence.

In the words of one Greek Cypriot leader in the bicommunal
movement on Cyprus, "these activities disclose in many significant ways

the outlines of the anticipated society, the society of a federated Cyprus. Greek Cypriots and Turkish Cypriots gathering together, reflecting together, planning together, building together, even dreaming together, on equal terms, with their differences and similarities. . . . Among other things, the top-level agreements for a federal solution to the Cyprus problem require a serious follow-up of corresponding citizen activities, gestures, symbols, holidays, events, projects, which reflect the mentality and values of federation" (Anastasiou 1996). In this sense, unofficial processes create a model or a metaphor (Kelman 2000) for the possibility of a different relationship. They also establish links across fault lines that form the basis for a societal capacity to resist extremist images and rhetoric, as well as an infrastructure for negotiating and implementing a settlement. Indeed, some analysts hypothesize that greater "significant social movement action" (Kriesberg 2001, 388) and greater density of social links between Israeli Jews and Palestinians might have helped the Oslo process continue (Kriesberg 2001).

Limitations of Unofficial Intermediation

In assessing the effectiveness of track-two regional security dialogues in the Middle East, Dalia Kaye notes that "[i]t is an ironic aspect of track two that when such dialogue is most needed, it is often most difficult to bring about" (Kaye 2001, 68) or to sustain. Unofficial processes, in the Middle East and elsewhere, cannot completely insulate themselves from the political environment in which they are taking place. Participants in these efforts are always responsive to the political developments in their own communities and evaluate their joint work in the context of official activities, media coverage, and public opinion. In intractable conflicts, this context is invariably hostile. "Spoilers" actively try to undermine and marginalize efforts to build bridges across conflict lines. Participants are subject to direct harassment, intimidation, and sometimes violence from rejectionists, hard-liners, and their own governments. Other, less overt, hostile bureaucratic actions by political authorities—including failure to grant visas and permissions, and enforcement of laws forbidding contact— make participation difficult.[6] And while unofficial intermediation processes are generally designed to be low-key and private, they are not secret and are vulnerable to negative media exposure caused by leaks or media commentary.[7] These constant and unrelenting attacks on the political space for dialogue can have a harsh effect on morale and deter all but the most intrepid participants.

The hostile context also makes maintenance of attitude changes difficult owing to the "reentry problem" (Kelman 1993). Participants in unofficial intermediation efforts must preserve a delicate balance between forging coalitions across conflict lines and preserving their status, social networks, and effectiveness on their own side. A new and meaningful social identity, or definition of "us" and "them," may have been activated in unofficial processes, but many other social contexts reinforce participants' identity as a member of their group or side—with all the attendant prejudices, stereotypes, and fears. Consequently, if not reinforced by ongoing and frequent dialogue and cooperation, attitude change can quickly dissipate.

A different but equally significant way in which politics can undermine unofficial intermediation is related to asymmetries of the relationships between the parties. Differences in power or resources between the parties are often reflected in the views of the participants and their attitudes toward unofficial processes. Regarding the Israeli-Palestinian conflict, for example, Mohammed Abu-Nimer (1999) notes that Palestinians often come to groups with the express purpose of fostering changes in Israeli political views, while Jewish participants tend to be more concerned with establishing lines of communication and building social connections. While unofficial intermediaries try to redress this imbalance by equalizing numbers and balancing participants' contributions, they often do not have the resources to equalize the relationship (Kriesberg 2001) and may inadvertently reinforce the asymmetry in the agenda and structure of the meetings. As a consequence, weaker parties sometimes view these processes as denying the asymmetries and not addressing the central problems in the conflict.

Finally, the success of unofficial intermediaries depends to a large extent on their ability to develop and maintain a wide network of contacts, generate respect and trust toward the intermediary and the intermediation process, provide a neutral and safe setting, and promote and facilitate ongoing interaction and joint activity. Just as the editors note in chapter 1 with regard to track-one (official) third parties, "bad tradecraft" on the part of unofficial intermediaries can be a problem and can contribute inadvertently to the maintenance of intractability. Unofficial third parties can inadvertently reinforce polarized solutions, making peacemaking more difficult. In the Georgian–South Ossetian conflict, for example, different NGOs, working separately (and without coordination) with the South Ossetian and Georgian leadership, inadvertently widened the gap between the parties at the negotiation table. The NGOs had taken participants from each side abroad to learn about different ways to structure center-regional relations; one NGO took the Georgians to Scotland while another took the Ossetians to Germany. These efforts were intended to broaden the knowledge base of the parties and help them develop new options in their own negotiations, but they inadvertently reinforced the parties' confrontation at the table; after the visits, the Georgians began to insist on a Scottish model, while the Ossetians insisted on a German model.[8]

In addition, unofficial intermediaries often do not make adequate investment (in terms of resources, time, and effort) in processes and structures that allow participants to maintain their coalition and develop strategies and activities that have a meaningful impact in their societies. For international, governmental, or private donors, however, funding cycles are frequently short, resources limited, and agendas often in conflict with the agendas of unofficial intermediaries or participants themselves (Chigas and Ganson 2003; Rothman and Olson 2001). In this context, it is difficult to have a significant impact in an intractable conflict.

Conclusion

This chapter has suggested that while unofficial intermediation processes have made limited and generally indirect contributions to major policy shifts or breakthroughs in track-one official peacemaking, the contributions are important and should not be assessed solely by visible influences on track-one negotiations. Paradoxically, the strengths of unofficial intermediation in intractable conflicts are also the source of its weakness; the elements that make certain conflicts intractable both make unofficial intermediaries more useful and limit their effectiveness in intractable conflicts.

Psychological and perceptual factors, in the form of zero-sum identities and as drivers of other elements of intractability (such as hardening attitudes, institutionalization of conflict norms, and conflict mythology), contribute to the polarization of positions and to continued escalation, making unofficial intermediaries especially useful in intractable conflicts. Unofficial intermediation processes deal directly with these subjective elements of intractability and have had demonstrable success in changing attitudes and building relationships and communication. In addition, their lack of official status, political accountability, coercive capability, and, in most cases, policy stake in the conflict make it easier for unofficial intermediaries to bring the parties together, as the risks of entering into discussion with the other side are lower in this context, especially during periods of escalation and failed peacemaking. Unofficial processes create space and structures for improving understanding and trust, and for exploring creative ways of addressing the conflict that are necessary to bridge the polarization of positions and escape stalemate. In this sense, unofficial intermediation can and does play an important "prenegotiation" role in changing the political cultures on both sides to make the parties more receptive to negotiation, as well as a "paranegotiation" role in facilitating dialogue when official peacemaking efforts stall because the conflict is not ripe. Unofficial third-party processes are also particularly useful in building the capacity of the parties to negotiate and implement a resolution when a window of opportunity arises—in helping make the parties, as well as the conflict, ripe for negotiation. As the processes examined in this chapter indicate, unofficial intermediation can help the parties develop an increased sense of possibility and hope that solutions satisfactory to all may indeed be available and attainable and can equip parties with relationships, processes, and an environment that can help them negotiate those solutions effectively.

The broad range of activities and participants in unofficial processes also gives them a special advantage in dealing with another important aspect of intractable conflicts: the institutionalization of conflict brought about by the passage of time, the failure of peacemaking efforts, and the complex, multilevel dynamic of the conflict as a continuous interaction between whole societies. Peacemaking in intractable conflicts cannot be accomplished at the elite level alone, especially if peace is to be sustainable, but must transform relationships at all levels of society and create new infrastructure for peaceful relations to supplement and eventually replace those reinforcing the conflict. Unofficial third parties work at all levels of society, from elite to grass roots, with a broad range of activities that can give people a concrete experience of a relationship that is not confrontational.

They can help develop a constituency for peace—a positive environment for negotiation—and an infrastructure for implementation.

While unofficial intermediaries bring to the treatment of intractable conflicts special capacities that official (track-one) third parties do not have, the contributions of unofficial third parties should not be overestimated. The core dynamics of intractability are structural and instrumental. No amount of unofficial intermediation will bring about a change in incentives for continuing the conflict—whether material or political. Unofficial intermediaries generally do not have the capacity to change incentives; they have few resources to offer as "carrots"[9] and have even fewer "sticks" to wield to bring parties to the table or to encourage resolution. Often, the people who could benefit most from such interaction with the other side are unwilling to participate; unofficial processes often attract those who have more moderate views, do not involve those more supportive of the conflict, and consequently do not reach those whose participation would be most necessary for the resolution of the conflict.

Finally, in some cases, participation in unofficial efforts (which, at the track-one-and-a-half and track-two levels, often take place outside the conflict area in a pleasant environment) may even become part of the conflict institutionalization process, as "junkets" to countries such as Germany, the United Kingdom, the United States, and elsewhere and continued international attention become some of the benefits of continuing the conflict.

In the final analysis, no single intermediation process—from big-power mediation to track-three civil society bridge building—is adequate to deal with intractable conflicts. All are needed to address the complex web of factors that perpetuate intractability. Unofficial intermediation is most effective when coordinated, even if not formally, with official (track-one) efforts and able to draw on the resources of track-one actors—both to attract the right participants to these efforts and provide needed follow-up and to create the windows of opportunity that unofficial intermediation prepares participants to seize. At the same time, track-one efforts benefit greatly from parallel, independent (or quasi-independent) unofficial intermediation to help prepare the ground for effective negotiation, postsettlement peacebuilding, and open space for the parties to explore how to break deadlocks. Unofficial and official methods must take place alongside each other, in a complementary, if not integrated, manner in order to achieve de-escalation, settlement, and peacebuilding.

Notes

1. For a detailed account of the 1994 North Korean nuclear crisis and Carter's mediatory role, see S. Rosegrant and M. Watkins, *Carrots, Sticks, and Question Marks: Negotiating the North Korean Nuclear Crisis*, J. F. Kennedy School of Government Case Study (Cambridge, Mass.: J. F. Kennedy School of Government Case Program, Harvard University, 1995).

2. The "consultant's" role has generally referred to unofficial third-party efforts to bring together *influential non–decision makers* for dialogue and problem solving at the track-two level described below (Fisher 1972, 2002). Here the word "consultant" is used to describe the third party's role and activities vis-à-vis the participants in the effort, rather than the level at which they operate.

3. For more information, visit Search for Common Ground's website, www .sfcg.org/actdetail.cfm?locus=CGP&name=programs&programid=424.

4. For example, the informal meetings were partially responsible for a shift in Georgian policy of withholding from South Ossetia international aid for reconstruction. In addition, protocols signed by the leaders of the two sides on refugee return and on mutually acceptable identity documents, the installation of telephone lines, reduction of peacekeeping posts, and assistance to Georgian–South Ossetian joint business ventures had their origins in the unofficial dialogue meetings (Olson 2000).

5. More information is available at Search for Common Ground's website, www.sfcg.org/actdetail.cfm?locus=CGP&name=programs&programid=64.

6. In Cyprus, for example, the Greek Cypriot government refused to protect participants in bicommunal activities from physical harassment by demonstrating nationalists at the buffer zone, while after 1997 the Turkish Cypriot government prosecuted civil servants participating in bicommunal activities under a law forbidding such contact.

7. Regional dialogues in the Middle East, for example, have suffered from negative media exposure.

8. The "Barcelona meeting" of the Georgia–South Ossetia Dialogue Project facilitated by the Conflict Management Group and the Norwegian Refugee Council was designed in part to bridge that gap by bringing both parties together to examine the Spanish model and learn about different ideas.

9. This is changing as nongovernmental organizations involved in development and humanitarian assistance in conflict areas are becoming more concerned with their impact on conflict. The commitment of these agencies, however, to neutrality —and to maintaining the apolitical nature of their work—means that they have rarely become involved in activities with an overt political dimension. (The Norwegian Refugee Council in Georgia–South Ossetia is an exception.)

References

Abu-Nimer, M. 1999. *Dialogue, Conflict Resolution and Change: Arab-Jewish Encounters in Israel.* New York: State University of New York Press.

Allen-Nan, S. 2002. "Unofficial Conflict Resolution as a Complement to Diplomacy: A Case Study of the Georgian–South Ossetian Peace Process Highlighting 'Track-One-and-a-Half' Diplomacy." Paper presented at the International Studies Association Convention, March 24.

Anastasiou, H. 1996. "Peace Builders at the Crossroads." In *The Multi-cultural Carpet: Reflections on Bi-communal Work in Cyprus,* accessed March 23, 2003, at http://www.americanembassy.org.cy/archive.htm#HARRY.

Angelica, M. 1999. "Evaluation of Conflict Resolution Training Efforts Sponsored by the Cyprus Fulbright Commission, 1993–1998." Nicosia: Cyprus Fulbright Commission, www.Cyprus-conflict.net.

Ayres, R. W. 1997. "Mediating International Conflicts: Is Image Change Necessary?" *Journal of Peace Research* 34, no. 4: 431–447.

Azar, E. E. 1991. "The Analysis and Management of Protracted Conflict." In *The Psychodynamics of International Relationships,* vol. 2, *Unofficial Diplomacy at Work,* edited by V. Volkan, J. Montville, and D. Julius. Lexington, Mass.: Lexington.

Brown, M. E. 2001. "Ethnic and Internal Conflicts: Causes and Implications." In *Turbulent Peace: The Challenges of Managing International Conflict,* edited by C. A. Crocker, F. O. Hampson, and P. Aall, 209–226. Washington, D.C.: United States Institute of Peace Press.

Burton, J. 1969. *Conflict and Communication: The Use of Controlled Communication in International Relations.* London: Macmillan.

Chigas, D. 1997. "Unofficial Interventions with Official Actors: Parallel Negotiation Training in Violent Intrastate Conflicts." *International Negotiation* 2: 409–436.

Chigas, D., and B. Ganson. 2003. "Grand Visions and Small Projects: Coexistence Efforts in Southeastern Europe." In *Imagine Coexistence: Restoring Humanity after Violent Ethnic Conflict,* edited by M. Minow and A. H. Chayes. San Francisco: Jossey-Bass.

Chufrin, G. I., and H. H. Saunders. 1993. "A Public Peace Process." *Negotiation Journal* 9, no. 2: 155–177.

Coleman, P. 2000. "Intractable Conflict." In *The Handbook of Conflict Resolution,* edited by M. Deutsch and P. Coleman, 428–450. San Francisco: Jossey-Bass.

Conflict Management Group. 1994, 1996. "Final Report to AMIDEAST: Cyprus Conflict Management Project." Unpublished reports, Conflict Management Group, Cambridge, Mass.

Deutsch, M. 1988. "Commentary: On Negotiating the Non-negotiable." In *Leadership and Negotiation in the Middle East,* edited by B. Kellerman and J. Z. Rubin, 248–263. New York: Praeger.

Diamond, L. 1999. *The Courage for Peace: Daring to Create Harmony in Ourselves and the World.* York Beach, Maine: Conari Press.

Diamond, L., and J. McDonald. 1996. *Multi-track Diplomacy: A Systems Approach to Peace,* 3d ed. West Hartford, Conn.: Kumarian Press.

Eliasson, J. 2002. "Perspectives on Managing Intractable Conflict." *Negotiation Journal* 20: 371–375.

Fisher, R. J. 1972. "Third-Party Consultation: A Method for the Study and Resolution of Conflict." *Journal of Conflict Resolution* 16: 67–94.

———. 2002. "Methods of Third-Party Intervention." In *Berghof Handbook for Conflict Transformation*, edited by A. Austin, M. Fischer, and N. Ropers, accessed December 18, 2002, at www.berghof-center.org/handbook/fisher/index.htm.

Fisher, R. J., and L. Keashly. 1988. "Distinguishing Third-Party Interventions in Intergroup Conflict: Consultation Is *Not* Mediation." *Negotiation Journal* 4: 381–393.

———. 1991. "The Potential Complementarity of Mediation and Consultation within a Contingency Model of Third-Party Intervention." *Journal of Peace Research* 28, no. 1: 29–42 (special issue on international mediation).

Fitzduff, M. 2002. *Beyond Violence: Conflict Resolution Processes in Northern Ireland.* Tokyo: United Nations University Press.

Haass, R. 1991. *Conflicts Unending.* New Haven, Conn.: Yale University Press.

Jenner, H. 2000. "'When the Truth Is Denied, Peace Will Not Come': The People-to-People Process of the New Sudan Council of Churches." Cambridge, Mass.: Collaborative for Development Action (Reflecting on Peace Practice Case Study), www.cdainc.com.

Kaye, D. D. 2001. "Track Two Diplomacy and Regional Security in the Middle East." *International Negotiation* 6: 49–77.

Kelman, H. C. 1972. "The Problem-Solving Workshop in Conflict Resolution." In *Communication in International Politics,* edited by R. L. Merritt, 168–204. Urbana: University of Illinois Press.

———. 1979. "An Interactional Approach to Conflict Resolution and Its Application to Israeli-Palestinian Relations." *International Interactions* 6: 9–22.

———. 1993. "Coalitions across Conflict Lines: The Interplay of Conflicts within and between the Israeli and Palestinian Communities." In *Conflict between People and Groups,* edited by J. Simpson and S. Worchel. Chicago: Nelson-Hall.

———. 1996. "The Interactive Problem-Solving Approach." In *Managing Global Chaos: Sources of and Responses to International Conflict*, edited by C. A. Crocker, F. O. Hampson, and P. Aall, 501–519. Washington, D.C.: United States Institute of Peace Press.

———. 1997. "Social-Psychological Dimensions of International Conflict." In *Peacemaking in International Conflict: Methods and Techniques*, edited by I. W. Zartman and J. L. Rasmussen, 191–236. Washington, D.C.: United States Institute of Peace Press.

———. 2000. "The Role of the Scholar-Practitioner in International Conflict Resolution." *International Studies Quarterly* 1, no. 3: 273–288.

Kenyon, K. 1999. "The Development of a Comprehensive Interdisciplinary Learning Model for International Peacebuilding: The Case of Cyprus." Diss., University of Idaho.

Klein, D. 1994. *Evaluation Report: Cyprus Conflict Management Project.* Unpublished report, Conflict Management Group, Cambridge, Mass.

Kriesberg, L. 2001. "Mediation and the Transformation of the Israeli-Palestinian Conflict." *Journal of Peace Research* 38, no. 3: 373–392.

Lederach, J. P. 1997. *Building Peace: Sustainable Reconciliation in Divided Societies.* Washington, D.C.: United States Institute of Peace Press.

Lieberfeld, D. 2002. "Evaluating the Contributions of Track-Two Diplomacy to Conflict Termination in South Africa, 1984–90." *Journal of Peace Research* 39, no. 3: 355–372.

Meyer, R. 2002. "Paradigm Shift—the Essence of Successful Change?" Derry/Londonderry: INCORE Occasional Papers, www.incore.ulst.ac.uk/home/publication/occasional.

Mitchell, C. R. 1981. *Peacemaking and the Consultant's Role.* Aldershot, U.K.: Gower.

Montville, J. 1991. "Transnationalism and the Role of Track-Two Diplomacy." In *Approaches to Peace: An Intellectual Map*, edited by W. S. Thompson and K. M. Jensen, with R. N. Smith and K. M. Schraub. Washington, D.C.: United States Institute of Peace.

Morozzo della Rocca, R. 1998. "Community of Sant'Egidio in Kosovo." In *Private Peacemaking: USIP-Assisted Peacemaking Projects of Nonprofit Organizations*, edited by D. Smock, *Peaceworks* 20. Washington, D.C.: United States Institute of Peace Press.

Olson, L. 2000. "The Georgia–South Ossetia Dialogue Process: A View from the Inside." Case Study, Reflecting on Peace Practice Project. Cambridge, Mass.: Collaborative for Development Action.

Pearson, R. F. 2001. "Dimensions of Conflict Resolution in Ethnopolitical Disputes." *Journal of Peace Research* 38, no. 3: 275–287.

Peck, C. 1998. *Sustainable Peace: The Role of the United Nations and Regional Organizations in Preventing Conflict.* Lanham, Md.: Rowman and Littlefield.

Pruitt, D., J. Rubin, and S. Kim. 1994. *Social Conflict: Escalation, Stalemate, and Settlement,* 2d ed. New York: McGraw-Hill.

Putnam, R. 2000. *Bowling Alone: The Collapse and Revival of American Community.* New York: Simon and Schuster.

Rosegrant, S., and M. Watkins. 1995. *Carrots, Sticks, and Question Marks: Negotiating the North Korean Nuclear Crisis,* J. F. Kennedy School of Government Case Study. Cambridge, Mass.: J. F. Kennedy School of Government Case Program, Harvard University.

Ross, M. H. 2000. "Evaluation in Conflict Resolution Training and Practice." Paper presented at United States Institute of Peace symposium, Washington, D.C., June 27–28.

Rothman, J., and M. Olson. 2001. "From Interests to Identities: Towards a New Emphasis in Interactive Conflict Resolution." *Journal of Peace Research* 38, no. 3: 289–305.

Rouhana, N. 1995. "Unofficial Third-Party Intervention in International Conflict: Between Legitimacy and Disarray." *Negotiation Journal* 11: 255–270.

Rouhana, N., and H. C. Kelman. 1994. "Promoting Joint Thinking in International Conflicts: An Israeli-Palestinian Continuing Workshop." *Journal of Social Issues* 50, no. 1: 157–178.

Salla, M. 1998. "East Timor." In *Private Peacemaking: USIP-Assisted Peacemaking Projects of Nonprofit Organizations,* edited by D. Smock, *Peaceworks* 20. Washington, D.C.: United States Institute of Peace Press.

Saunders, H. H. 1991. "We Need a Larger Theory of Negotiation: The Importance of Prenegotiating Phases." In *Negotiation Theory and Practice,* edited by J. W. Breslin and J. Z. Rubin, 57–70. Cambridge, Mass.: PON Books.

———. 1995. "Possibilities and Challenges: Another Way to Consider Unofficial Third-Party Intervention." *Negotiation Journal* 11: 271–275.

———. 1996. "Prenegotiation and Circum-negotiation: Arenas of the Peace Process." In *Managing Global Chaos: Sources of and Responses to International Conflict,* edited by C. A. Crocker, F. O. Hampson, and P. Aall, 419–432. Washington, D.C.: United States Institute of Peace Press.

Slim, R., and H. H. Saunders. 2001. "The Inter-Tajik Dialogue: From Civil War towards Civil Society." In *ACCORD: An International Review of Peace Initiatives.* London: Conciliation Resources.

Wallach, J. 2000. *The Enemy Has a Face: The Seeds of Peace Experience.* Washington, D.C.: United States Institute of Peace Press.

Wolleh, O. 2001. "Local Peace Constituencies in Cyprus: The Bicommunal Trainers' Group." Berghof Report No. 8. Berlin: Berghof Research Center.

Zartman, I. W. 1985. *Ripe for Resolution: Conflict and Intervention in Africa.* New York: Oxford University Press.

Cases of Intractable Conflict

7

Can Sudan Escape Its Intractability?

J. Stephen Morrison and Alex de Waal

IN THE EARLY HOURS of May 26, 2004, in the Kenyan town of Naivasha, twenty-one years and ten days after the outbreak of civil war in Southern Sudan, the government of Sudan and the Sudan People's Liberation Movement signed the final framework agreement for peace. It had been a nasty, brutish, and very long war. Peace was celebrated by Sudanese from both North and South. The exhausted mediators and principal negotiators congratulated themselves. But there was an atmosphere of anticlimax. The negotiations had been so protracted, with several agreements signed over the previous two years, that the final settlement had come to seem inevitable. Most recognized that the real challenges lay in implementing an immensely complex agreement that provides for power sharing, wealth sharing, security arrangements, special arrangements for contested areas and the national capital, and a pre-interim period of six months followed by an interim period of six years, to be followed in turn by a referendum on self-determination for Southern Sudan. And the peace in Southern Sudan was signed in the shadow of a separate war in Darfur, western Sudan, that flared in 2003 and has been associated with ethnic cleansing, massacres, and in the opinion of a growing number of observers, including the U.S. government, genocide.

For two decades, few wars were more depressingly persistent than the Sudanese civil war. The causes of the war are overdetermined: they include race, religion, economics, and politics. The war itself was hideously

161

complex, involving multiple internal players and external interests. It frustrated the efforts of a series of negotiators. In important respects, it became a conflict in equilibrium. However, beginning in 2002, a new, determined intervention by a coalition of regional and international actors, with the United States playing a pivotal role, gradually broke this protracted deadlock. At the time of writing (June 2004), a series of agreements on self-determination for Southern Sudan, sharing of wealth and power, and security arrangements have put in place all the building blocks for a comprehensive political settlement.

The civil war in Sudan began in 1983. It pitted an Arab-oriented Islamist regime in Khartoum against an insurgent armed movement, the Sudan People's Liberation Movement/Army (SPLM/SPLA; hereafter SPLA), chiefly based in Southern Sudan. Each sought to enhance its military position through opportunistic alliances with an array of armed ethnic militias and regional states. Sudan gained its independence in January 1956, a few months after a mutiny by Southern soldiers initiated a civil war that lasted until 1972. This conflict was resolved by the Addis Ababa Agreement, which granted substantial autonomy to the South, but the agreement was progressively undermined by Khartoum, setting in place a slide to renewed civil war in 1983. Sudan's independent history has been dominated by chronic, exceptionally cruel warfare that has starkly divided the country on racial, religious, and regional grounds; displaced an estimated four million people (of a total estimated population of thirty-two million); and killed an estimated two million people. A further million were displaced by the conflict in Darfur in 2003–4.

Multiple attempts at mediation between the parties date back to soon after war resumed in the early 1980s. These initiatives range from the first meetings between the SPLA and the Northern political parties in 1984–85 up to the most recent rounds of the Inter-Governmental Authority on Development (IGAD, a subregional grouping of northeast African states, not including Egypt), the Joint Libyan and Egyptian Initiative (JLEI, a peace process launched by Libya in 1998 that was quickly taken over by Egypt), and several attempts at facilitation of peace talks by the Nigerian government. At no point during the war did the parties cease talking to one another, even in the face of unabated fighting. Nonetheless, before 2002, only the 1988–89 peace initiative and the Nigerian government–led Abuja talks of 1992–93 showed any real promise of ending the war. All other initiatives achieved modest gains that initially raised hopes and eventually foundered. These initiatives did generate a dense legacy of written agreements—a "literature of accord"—that contained the elements of a possible negotiated settlement. However, the fecklessness of those on both sides who signed these agreements, and their routine nonimplementation, discredited mediation efforts and enshrouded them in widespread cynicism.

Several interlocking factors cemented Sudan's intractability, the most important being the character of the two principal antagonists.

Over time, as the war's duration extended and its human costs worsened, the polarization and the mistrust between the government of Sudan (GoS) and the SPLA steadily deepened. In this twenty-year period, each side came to be dominated by an autocratic leadership that lacked the coherence, internal unity, and clarity of purpose essential to lead Sudan decisively out of war and toward peace. Instead, each settled into a comfortable accommodation with persistent warfare that sustained its respective bases of power and seldom threatened its core constituencies. Each also believed (sometimes correctly, more often erroneously) that military triumph remained within reach and aggressively sold its followers on this ambition. Each typically perceived peace initiatives as mere tactical opportunities to buy time and strike a pose. And each ultimately concluded that achieving peace held too many risks and uncertainties to pursue in earnest. Powerful external realities reinforced these fateful leadership choices and encouraged a failure of vision.

Until recently, regional mediation efforts were ineptly managed and insufficiently resourced—in human, financial, and political terms. This reflected to a significant degree the internal divisions and the institutional weaknesses in the bordering countries and regional organizations. It also reflected the absence of any serious investment by the United States and other major powers in a mediation enterprise.

Interestingly, however, during 2001–2 a shift of circumstances lessened Sudan's apparent intractability and increased the opportunity for serious negotiations. The multiple factors undergirding Sudan's rigid fatalism began to appear somewhat less fixed and more mutable. In July 2002 the parties signed a protocol at Machakos in Kenya covering many of the key issues of the war, and in October this was followed by a cessation of hostilities during which the parties entered into intensive negotiations, leading to a series of agreements in the fall of 2003. Although the forum and the lead negotiator were provided by IGAD, and especially its Kenyan chair, much of the hard work was done by the troika consisting of

Norway, the United Kingdom, and the United States. This process culminated in the final framework agreement signed in Naivasha in May 2004.

The most important factor has arguably been the Bush administration's increased leverage and focus on Khartoum, accelerated by a global post-9/11 counterterrorism agenda that placed a premium on coercing sudden cooperation from Khartoum on not just counterterrorism but peace negotiations and humanitarian access as well. Implicit was the U.S. threat that if results were not soon manifest on these three fronts, aggressive action to isolate and possibly destabilize Khartoum would follow, endorsed by highly mobilized U.S. constituencies, most important, evangelical Christians (for whom Southern Sudanese suffering, including enslavement, at the hands of the government has become an important rallying call) and African-American antislavery activists, in league with congressional allies and hard-line elements within the Bush administration itself.

These pressures quickly raised the threat level felt by Khartoum and motivated it to seek a new path to get out from under U.S. condemnation, normalize its international standing, and preserve its power in the North. The SPLA leadership came under newfound pressure from Washington to see an expedited, negotiated settlement, backed by Bush administration guarantees, as its best hope.

Changes in Sudan and the surrounding region fortified the shift in U.S. calculations. In Khartoum President Omer al Bashir deposed his ideological mentor and political rival, the Islamist theoretician and political leader Hassan al Turabi, in December 1999. This reflected a feeling that the Islamist project in Sudan had reached its limits, and its costs in terms of international isolation and domestic division had become unbearable. Sudan's radical Islamists were becoming older, and their ranks depleted by the war. Searching for other political constituencies to replace the radicals who had followed Turabi into opposition, the GoS became more politically accommodating. The war was exhausting the government. On the Southern Sudanese side, an increasingly organized civil society constituency was becoming less tolerant of the SPLA leadership's unending promises that victory lay "just around the corner." The internal divisions and the vicious internecine strife between Southern factions mobilized Southern church and community leaders to pursue reconciliation initiatives that had the logical outcome of pressing the SPLA leadership to take peace initiatives more seriously.

In the region, the Moi government in Kenya sought expanded counterterrorism cooperation (already extensive after the August 1998 bombing of the U.S. embassy in Nairobi) and a diplomatic alliance with the United States to achieve peace in Sudan, in hopes that these combined initiatives would raise Kenya's standing internationally and reduce its risk of isolation before Daniel arap Moi left office in 2003. Hence the sudden seriousness of purpose shown by the Moi government in 2002 in revitalizing the IGAD process, including pressing the SPLA (reliant upon Kenya for its residences and transit of matériel, humanitarian aid, and people) to get to the negotiating table. Since January 2003 the Kenyan government of President Mwai Kibaki has continued this role without interruption.

Elsewhere in the region, Eritreans, Ethiopians, and Ugandans mounted a unified campaign in 1996–97 that sought to press Khartoum militarily through joint support of the SPLA. In 1998 this unity fell apart with the Ethio-Eritrean war and conflict between Uganda and its erstwhile ally, Rwanda. In turn, each of the three neighbors sought better relations with Khartoum.

Harmonization of the policies of donors has also been important. Until 2002 the Sudanese government hoped that it could divide the Americans and the Europeans, containing the threat posed by the United States and seeking development assistance from Europe. A new unified front with a division of labor between the parties has overcome this problem, and European Union assistance has been made conditional on progress in the peace talks. Meanwhile, much of the diplomatic legwork has been done by British, Norwegian, and Swiss diplomats, who have also been able to call upon a strong network of academic specialists on Sudan. In 2002, for the first time, the major international players were all in line.

The most compelling signal of these changes, internal and external to Sudan, was the agreement reached on July 20, 2002, at the IGAD peace talks, chaired by the Kenyan government in Machakos. This was a major breakthrough, with the two sides agreeing to the framework for a settlement. This included a provision for Southern Sudan to administer itself for a six-year interim period leading up to a referendum on self-determination. Under the agreement, the existing Islamic laws in Northern Sudan would continue in force. President Bashir would remain in office, with the SPLA leader, John Garang, taking the position of vice president. The other building blocks of a settlement were subsequently put in place, one by one, especially after face-to-face negotiations between Vice President Ali Osman Mohammed Taha and SPLA leader John Garang began in Naivasha, Kenya, in the fall of 2003. Until the last moment, the peace was not secure. Khartoum remained divided and anxious about any U.S.-brokered agreement and aware of the difficulties that lay ahead in implementing some of the components of the deal. Until the last moment, too, elements of the SPLA leadership continued to listen to the siren song of military triumph even as the peace talks progressed, encouraged in that belief by its Christian evangelical U.S. supporters, Eritrean adventurism, and the hope that a U.S. global strategy of aggressive preemption against Iraq and others might redound somehow to its favor.

Nature of the Conflict: Internal Factors

Aims and Ideologies of the Parties

The official positions of the principal parties are ideologically opposed. While the GoS is wedded to a vision of an Islamic state, in one form or another, the SPLA is committed to a united secular "New Sudan." These positions are by definition incompatible. But the positions are more uncertain, complex, and changeable than their official statements suggest.

As the conflict continued, the parties' positions polarized. The war itself has led to the growth of Islamic extremism in Northern Sudan, while in the South it has led to both the demand for self-determination and the emergence of a Christian agenda. These factors have been exacerbated during the war, partly because of the losses both sides have incurred and the grievances both have accumulated. Each atrocity has further polarized the situation. Issues that did not exist at the outbreak of war, such as the enslavement of Southern women and children by Northern militiamen and alleged war crimes that Khartoum committed in the western Upper Nile oil-producing region and elsewhere, have emerged as major issues of contention. Paradoxically, a parallel process of continued dialogue and intermittent mediation has created a "literature of accord." The ongoing, often repetitive and exhaustive discussions among the parties have led to consensus on a range of key issues that offer the basis of a negotiated settlement. At various times, this process of accommodation and compromise has been dominant. At other times, the disparity in the parties' vision dominates the discourse.

The GoS has articulated different visions. One is the Islamist agenda, still often repeated in public statements. This entails the Islamization of the whole of Sudan. A second, contrary, perspective is encapsulated in several agreements, notably the 1997 Khartoum Agreement and Amendment 14 to the Constitution, which provides for self-determination for the South in the context of the broadly Islamic constitution. A third vision is found in the GoS position outlined in the Joint Libyan and Egyptian Initiative, which is based upon power sharing and limited democratization in the North, again in a broadly Islamic framework. At the heart of each vision is the simple aim of staying in power.

On the opposing side, John Garang, leader of the SPLA, has articulated "three tracks" for peace. Track one is seeking outright victory plus social and economic development of the liberated areas—an imposed "New Sudan." Track two is seeking victory through a military and political alliance with the National Democratic Alliance (NDA). The NDA, founded in 1989 as a coalition of the civilian parties ousted by the June 1989 coup, expanded its base and ambitions in 1994–95. The alliance is chiefly composed of Northern opposition parties and sought to foment a popular uprising that would usher in a national government based on the democratic principles contained in the Asmara Declaration of 1995, which outlined the NDA's objectives. However, as the prospects of peace with the SPLA have come closer, the NDA has become increasingly ineffectual, with much of its leadership making bilateral deals with Khartoum. Track three is a negotiated peace achieved through the IGAD peace initiative, at which the SPLA has sought a "one country–two systems" solution to Sudan's conflict. Garang's three tracks offer radically different strategies with different outcomes. Most believe that Garang would have preferred track one, but the deal offered thus far appears to have committed him to peace through track three.

Strategies of the Parties

Throughout the war both parties believed that total victory was possible. The GoS felt that it came close to outright victory in 1992–93, that SPLA military weaknesses were steadily worsening as external support waned, and that it was only a matter of time before the SPLA disintegrated. The GoS was tempted to believe that it could systematically co-opt Eritrea, Ethiopia, and Uganda, and perhaps even the United States, to marginalize and weaken the SPLA. It pursued an ambitious armament program financed by oil revenue. The GoS therefore suspected that if it could hang on when the SPLA was on the offensive, the moment might come when Khartoum could seize the offensive and win.

More modestly, the GoS has regarded sustaining its power as victory. That has permitted it to control and develop the major oil fields, maintain its hold on the major Southern cities of Juba and Wau, and hence reliably achieve a baseline security agenda. This strategy has also enabled the GoS to delegate most of the fighting to its Southern allies, armed ethnic militias at odds with the SPLA, thus rendering the war essentially an internal Southern conflict with a low human cost to the North.

Oil extraction is concentrated in Southern Sudan. The war and strong U.S. opposition to oil companies' activities in Sudan (manifest in the Sudan Peace Act passed by the U.S. Congress and in the threat of further legislation to impose capital market sanctions on such companies) has ensured that no major U.S. oil corporation has been active in the country. Chinese, Malaysian, and Indian oil corporations have taken leading roles, with Canada's Talisman and Sweden's Lundin Oil also playing roles. Nonetheless, the revenue from oil, which began to flow in 1999, has transformed the financial prospects for the GoS, enabling it to bear the cost of the war for the foreseeable future. Oil production has raised the stakes for the SPLA. It fears the military might of an oil-financed GoS war machine. But the oil has also given them more to fight for.

The SPLA came near enough to victory on three occasions since the late 1980s to continue to believe that military triumph was feasible. In December 1989, Ethiopian military intervention came close to bringing down the Khartoum government (which was saved by a counteroffensive assisted by the then Eritrean insurgents, the Eritrean People's Liberation Front). In 1992 the SPLA overran Juba, capital of Sudan's South, and then withdrew when the leadership decided that it was incapable of holding that position at an affordable military cost. In January 1997 support from Eritrea, Ethiopia, and Uganda (each of them responding to the GoS's destabilization of their countries) brought the SPLA tantalizingly close to bringing down Khartoum. The next year, the SPLA overran the Southern provincial capital, Wau, but again withdrew.

This history points to two factors. One is that the SPLA leadership came very close to victory on its own terms because of external military support. Hence, it was logical for the SPLA to pursue a strategy that prolonged the war, hoping that another external factor (e.g., U.S. support) could decisively swing the war its way at some indeterminate point in the future.

The second factor is that if the SPLA concentrates its forces on a "Southern" victory, by taking a major Southern city, it can achieve this. But this victory may be won at the cost of boosting a Southern nationalist/separatist agenda that is opposed by the SPLA leadership.

The NDA, meanwhile, believed that there was a real possibility of a popular uprising overthrowing the government, as occurred in 1985 when the government of President Jaafar Nimeiri was removed in this way.

Partial agreements have reconciled the major parties with important opposition elements. For example, the 1997 Khartoum and Fashoda Agreements brought the GoS and breakaway Southern factions together. The SPLA has also reunited with several breakaway factions. But each of these agreements has been more in the way of a defense pact than a peace agreement.

Structure (Internal Weaknesses) of the Parties

The main parties—the GoS and the SPLA—have major internal weaknesses. They are not democratic. The leaderships have not been properly called to account by their constituencies. Any comprehensive peace process that includes an element of democratization entails exposing the leaderships to an element of risk.

If the GoS implements a peace accord, then many of its senior members will lose position and status. The leadership does not have the authority to ensure the loyalty of senior figures who will lose out. It fears that if it compromises on religion and the state, or yields important posts to the NDA or SPLA, it will be outflanked by more radical elements. For the GoS, the number one concern is keeping Northern rivals at bay, especially veteran Islamist leader Hassan al Turabi's Popular National Congress.

The SPLA cannot move toward a democratic peace without addressing some fundamental issues that it has so far failed to resolve, such as internal democratization and the nature of self-determination. Implementation of a peace agreement also means a level of institutional development that the SPLA has refused to undertake. Development of institutions would, it is feared, undermine the autonomy enjoyed by the leadership. Lastly, a peace agreement would require the leadership to answer fundamental questions about its war aims that it has so far been reluctant to address. Consistently, the SPLA leadership's priority has been removing internal Southern rivals. For some time in the late 1990s, the NDA served as an effective forum for opposition groups to reconcile with one another and present consensus positions. However, the NDA has been undermined by the readiness of the SPLA to present incompatible positions in IGAD and by the tendency of the NDA chairman to negotiate unilaterally with Egypt and Libya. The NDA found itself unable to decisively move toward a position compatible with the IGAD or the Libyan-Egyptian peace initiatives, for fear that it would split apart. Hence, it tends to agree on doing a minimum. As the IGAD negotiations have progressed since 2002, the NDA has become virtually irrelevant and has largely fragmented into its individual members pursuing their own interests.

Similarly, the Umma Party, which split from the NDA in 2000, is itself divided. One wing joined the GoS in mid-2002, while the other (headed by former prime minister Sadiq el Mahdi) has remained in opposition inside the country. Both wings, however, have continued to be supportive of the IGAD peace process.

The Legacy of Past Agreements

The history of agreements going back to 1972 has both positive and negative dimensions. On the positive side, the long record of negotiation and agreement has created a literature of accord. At one time or another, the parties have signed documents that cumulatively represent solutions to most of Sudan's most pressing problems: state and religion, self-determination, wealth sharing, and so on. If these agreements are collectively tabled, then there is relatively little left to negotiate.

The negative side is that most of these agreements have not been honored. There is a very low level of trust. In particular, the Southerners deeply distrust the Northerners, believing with justification that the government in Khartoum will sign an agreement for tactical reasons and then dishonor it at the first opportunity.

In addition, the sheer accretion of agreements and (in some cases) their elevation to totemic status have impeded negotiation. Agreement documents were used as weapons in negotiation sparring. And single documents were subject to different interpretations. The most important example of the latter is the IGAD Declaration of Principles (DoP), drawn up in 1994. This includes a reference to the principle of self-determination for Southern Sudan. The SPLA contended that the DoP committed the parties to self-determination, while the GoS (which only agreed to sign the DoP in 1997) claimed that the reference to the principle was merely an agenda item for discussion.

There were also contestations over the meaning of provisions in the July 20, 2002, Machakos Protocol, and in particular over whether the negotiations should include the war-affected regions adjoining Southern Sudan. The disputed "three areas" of Abyei, the Nuba Mountains, and the Southern Blue Nile proved the last major stumbling block in the quest for peace, resolved only in May 2004. Doubtless there will be disputes over the interpretation of the details of the Naivasha agreement, too.

The Gains of Conflict

For both the GoS and the SPLA, there have been material gains from the war. For both of them, the continuing conflict has served as a reason for postponing democratization. For the GoS, the conflict has justified maintaining large extra-budgetary expenditures, and for the SPLA, it has allowed all finances to remain secret.

The population of the South and the adjoining areas of the Nuba Mountains and the Southern Blue Nile has borne the brunt of the war. But in a curious way, the suffering of the Southern people has been a commodity that enabled certain groups and individuals to benefit. John Garang has spoken of "the vultures of peace," referring to professional mediators who shuttle around Sudan. There are also relief organizations and slave redemption programs that have brought spin-off benefits to local partners. And given the way in which the SPLA's struggle has garnered massive sympathy among important constituencies in Europe and North America, the South's humanitarian needs have also brought financial, political, and personal benefits to the leaders of that struggle.

The secondary parties—the Northern civilian parties inside and outside the NDA, the non-SPLA Southern factions and parties—have a deeper interest in a settlement. The general strategy of these smaller parties has been to promote more representative structures, in both Khartoum and the NDA. The main parties have been aware that a settlement is likely to entail greater democratization, which will strengthen the smaller parties, probably at the main parties' expense.

A Conflict in Equilibrium?

The war caused immense human losses, but in many respects, Sudanese society, economy, and politics accommodated to the conflict. Conflict became a way of life. In substantial areas of the country, including much of the South, a certain normality prevailed despite the war, which did not jeopardize the core constituencies of either side. The communities that bore the brunt of the fighting (Nuer and Nuba, in particular) do not carry great political weight with either party. For both principal parties, the continuation of the war was a comfort zone.

Such an equilibrium could not be broken by internal developments: it required external players to substantially shift the structure of incentives and disincentives for a continuing conflict. Speaking to Voice of America on May 30, 2004, John Garang echoed this clearly. "This peace agreement was reached, not necessarily because the parties wanted to, but because both parties were forced to," he said. "We negotiated an agreement, because we were forced to by a set of pressures. The cost of continuing the war was felt by both sides to be much higher than the cost of stopping the war. So, we stopped the war."

Nature of the Conflict: External Factors

External Linkages and Calculations of the Parties

As mentioned, both principal parties have believed that external factors would be crucial in delivering them a decisive advantage. They have recognized that internal factors alone were unlikely to resolve the war.

The Egyptian linkage has been crucial to Khartoum's calculation. The GoS believed that with Egyptian backing the regime itself was secure. But the cost of Egyptian support was that it was more difficult to achieve a settlement in the South, because of Egypt's intransigent opposition to any mention of self-determination for the South. This was a price Khartoum was prepared to pay for a long period. However, during 2002 U.S. pressure began to override the Egyptian factor, persuading the GoS to countenance self-determination.

The SPLA leadership has counted on an external factor to deliver outright victory on its own terms.

Regional Interests in the Conflict

All of the regional countries would benefit from a settlement, though not necessarily from peace at any price. The East African countries have much to gain from the lessening of the refugee burden: the end to cross-border destabilization, including from flows of small arms; and an increase in regional trade and cooperation. The opportunities for importing Sudanese oil are particularly important.

In contrast, Egypt believes that the costs borne of an independent Southern Sudan would outweigh any gains from peace. Egypt remains firmly opposed to any hint of Southern Sudanese secession. Its reasons are several. One is its unwillingness to renegotiate the 1955 Nile Waters Agreement, which would be necessary if another state were to come into being in the Nile basin. Egypt is dependent on a very favorable share of the north-flowing Nile for its water supply and, indeed, its very existence. The Egyptian government is also sensitive to charges that it might be party to the division of a fellow member of the Arab League, especially in view of the widespread perception across the Arab world that it has acquiesced in the "division" of Palestine and Iraq.

However, most of the countries of the region have come to live with the conflict. At two major moments—the late 1980s and the mid-1990s—the Sudanese civil war has indeed threatened regional stability. However, for most of the period it has not. Since the late 1990s, Khartoum has been actively cultivating the role of good neighbor. Provided that neither of the parties becomes embroiled in neighboring conflicts (as the SPLA did in Ethiopia in the late 1980s, and the GoS did with most of its neighbors in the mid-1990s), then the conflict is regarded as manageable. As of early 2004, the implosion of Eritrea has created instability on Sudan's eastern border. However, unlike in the recent past, consequent on its president's regression to dictatorship, it is Eritrea that is now regarded as the rogue state. Sudan has entered into a subregional alliance with Ethiopia and Yemen to contain the threat of Eritrea. Sudan has also started selling oil to most of its neighbors. The exception to this rule is Chad, whose government is dangerously destabilized by the conflict in Darfur. In the 1980s, the successive Chadian governments of Goukouni Waddai and Hissene Habre were overthrown by insurgencies based in Darfur, and the eruption of the 2003 conflict has threatened the delicate political equilibrium that keeps President Idris Deby in power.

International (Dis)interest

The conflict in Sudan has attracted a lot of attention for a variety of reasons, including terrorism (especially in 1995–98) and humanitarian relief (at regular intervals since 1988). The war is a perennial issue, and all actors are concerned with a solution, but this has generally been secondary to other matters. Until 2002, Sudan's donors did not have a common approach to a peace settlement. With a settlement, the prospects of Sudan receiving expedited debt relief and greater levels of foreign investment have increased. Sudan's donors dangled the prospect of major postwar reconstruction programs as a carrot to the parties. They will continue to do so during the implementation phase of the agreement, though it is unlikely that the international consensus that prevailed during 2002–4 will be sustained indefinitely.

Much of the current high level of U.S. interest in Sudan stems from a coalition of interest groups that have been concerned with specific issues, such as human rights, slavery, and religious freedom, rather than with peace itself. Many members of this coalition are motivated by high principle and ideological commitment, and have limited interest in a compromise negotiated settlement.

These special interests did, however, provide leverage to the mediators, giving them a number of carrots and sticks, such as stringent sanctions and military support to the opposition. But the demands of the specific issues and the constituencies behind them usually mean that they cannot be used in this way. For example, no relief agencies would permit humanitarian aid to be made conditional on progress toward peace. And the U.S. counterterrorist agenda will not wait for a comprehensive settlement.

At no point has the war itself been the overriding agenda item for international engagement with Sudan, and at no point until 2002 was a settlement of the war seen as an absolute precondition for pursuing other agendas in Sudan. During 2002–4, however, international interests at last lined up behind a common approach to resolving Sudan's war. This closed the door to the parties' strategies of forum shopping and playing mediators and external parties against one another.

Nature of the Mediation

Extent of the Mediation

There have been a large number of peace initiatives for Sudan. Peace in Sudan has rarely been neglected. Getting the parties together is not, in itself, an achievement.

By 2001 the mediators had become exhausted. The very extent of the mediation over the decades meant that the parties were experts at maneuvering, while the mediators were relative novices. They were not ready to bring to bear the sustained pressure needed to jump-start a serious process.

This accretion of initiatives and agreements demanded either an encyclopedic knowledge on the part of the mediators or a "cut-the-Gordian-knot" approach of starting from scratch. Mediators lacked the former. No mediator had the leverage and confidence to undertake the latter. The approach taken by the revitalized IGAD process since 2002 has been essentially to extract the content from the "literature of accord"—the partial agreements signed by the parties—and pressure parties into making these into a real peace deal. The substance of the agreements reflects the parties' positions and compromises; that these agreements have been obtained is a testament to external pressure and diplomacy.

Structure of the Mediation

There was a general agreement that the settlement should be comprehensive and should combine both peace and democratization. But until 2004, none of the processes managed to achieve these different goals.

IGAD aims at a comprehensive peace and has the DoP that covers all aspects of the Sudanese conflict, but its approach is based on the North-South polarity. Both the GoS and the SPLA concurred that the NDA should not be included, thereby undermining the potential for a comprehensive peace process. The SPLA explanation for why it does not want its NDA partners in IGAD appears to be based on John Garang's "three-track" approach—that is, it sees IGAD as only one option among several.

The JLEI included all the parties but was focused on the "big four": Bashir, Garang, and the two most prominent Northern civilian leaders, Sadiq el Mahdi and Mohamed Osman al Mirghani (chairman of the NDA). In addition, the JLEI was not regarded as substantively comprehensive by the Southerners because of its principled exclusion of the right of self-determination. It was essentially a North-North reconciliation and limited democratization initiative.

The smaller parties in the NDA and the breakaway Southern factions have the strongest interest in peace. While the war continued, their position was necessarily marginal. Their best chance for influence arises in the context of democratic politics. The major parties and the mediators alike have preferred to keep these parties marginalized or excluded from mediation processes, sometimes arguing that this simplifies the mediation process.

The 1988–89 peace process, which nearly succeeded, was based on a constitutional conference and a democratic system. The 1992–93 Abuja negotiations, which also came close to success, were based upon power sharing without strong democratic components.

The 2002 IGAD process, strongly backed by Norway, the United Kingdom, and the United States, was based on a sharp prioritization of issues and parties. It identified peace between the major protagonists (GoS and SPLA) as the key issue and hence relegated the other parties to a secondary position. In the region, the IGAD process focused on Egypt and Kenya (although the former's unreadiness to play a constructive role means it became marginalized), also sidelining other players (such as Ethiopia, Libya, and Nigeria). It focused on first obtaining a framework agreement and then moving to the details, trusting that the momentum obtained by such a process would help the parties to soften their positions. Ultimately, this succeeded in bringing about a settlement. But the challenge will lie in the implementation of its ambitious provisions. As the IGAD process approached completion, it generated a momentum that encouraged other parties to back it. These parties hoped that they could gain positions in a new government. This is encouraging insofar as it means that all the major contenders for office in the future will have committed themselves to supporting the agreement. However, the fact that the IGAD process has recognized only armed opposition has also prompted some groups to take up arms. The major insurrection in the western state of Darfur that began in 2003 reflects this logic of obtaining political concessions through use of force.

Leverage and Impartiality

Mediation efforts in Sudan have been either impartial and lacking in leverage or partial but with leverage. Only since 2002 have impartiality and leverage been seen together.

When the IGAD initiative was launched in 1994, the IGAD countries had leverage on both parties. At first the IGAD countries were seen as sympathetic to the GoS (which is why it agreed to their role), but three of them

(Eritrea, Ethiopia, and Uganda) rapidly came to support the SPLA/NDA against the GoS. During 1995–97 these countries had massive leverage because of their own military engagement in Sudan. In fact, by 1997–98 they were close to the point of being able to dictate terms to the GoS, and the GoS reluctantly came around to endorsing the IGAD Declaration of Principles. Had the Eritrea-Ethiopia axis not collapsed, it is possible that an unfavorable peace settlement would have been forced on the GoS.

Thereafter, the IGAD effort became more impartial but also lost its leverage. It is notable that the "revitalized" IGAD peace process in 1999–2001 was headed by a mid-level Kenyan diplomat with a weak secretariat. In contrast, the peace efforts in Burundi, a country with great humanitarian suffering but no comparable strategic importance, have been headed by two of Africa's most formidable statesmen (Nelson Mandela and Julius Nyerere), backed by a full array of donors and engaged NGOs.

The Joint Libyan and Egyptian Initiative, launched in 1999, was accompanied by serious leverage, in the form of key support to Khartoum and pressure on the NDA leadership. But it was clearly not impartial.

The troika-backed IGAD process of 2002 had more leverage than any previous effort. Although the GoS regularly complains that the United States is not impartial—citing, for example, the Sudan Peace Act, signed into law by President Bush in October 2002, which is highly sympathetic to the SPLA—the post–September 11 counterterrorist imperative has brought the United States and the GoS closer together on key issues. In addition, Washington's key partner in the negotiations—Britain's Foreign and Commonwealth Office—is seen by Khartoum as being more "balanced." (The SPLA, meanwhile, looks favorably on the U.S. role while being more distrustful of Britain.) This relative impartiality and high leverage have worked well.

The division of diplomatic labor has been important in making the peace process work. The Kenyan-IGAD chairmanship of the process has been accepted by all. U.S. leadership has been key: the United States alone has the leverage to ensure a settlement. But the diplomatic personnel it has been able to deploy have been relatively few. Hence, the active engagement of other partners, working in close coordination, has been essential. The British involvement stems in part from Britain's historical role in Sudan and the attendant expertise available in the Foreign Office and British universities. Norway is valued precisely because it is seen as humanitarian, disinterested, and discreet. Switzerland was engaged for the specific task of negotiating a cease-fire in the Nuba Mountains region, in an exemplary piece of diplomatic delegation. The European Union, potentially Sudan's major donor along with some of its member-states, notably Italy and the Netherlands, has insisted that the normalization of its development assistance program depends upon a satisfactory outcome to the peace negotiations.

Culture and Principles of Negotiation

Throughout the peace process, there appeared to be progress in resolving many major issues covered in the literature of accord. But this was often an illusion. Before 2002, there was no process whereby the parties formally agreed on issues: this was merely an inference from the different documents. Rather, the mediation process had a tendency to go back to first principles each time, allowing each party to revise its position and reach disagreement where agreement may have existed before. Thus, the SPLA was able to present radically new proposals in 1999. In fact, before 2002 IGAD never set up principles for negotiation, and most sessions were conducted by means of posturing and tactical point scoring.

Negotiation was hampered by different expectations from the two parties. The Northern parties, including the GoS, are accustomed to compromise and political process. They are ready to agree to less than what they want, confident that they can gain the balance after the agreement is signed. The Southerners and marginalized people are well aware of this and want cast-iron guarantees before they sign. They are not prepared to take anything on trust. They put great store on external guarantors.

Tradecraft of the Mediators

Until 2002, all the major initiatives were handicapped by poor tradecraft. The IGAD mechanism was one of the most cumbersome imaginable until its "revitalization" in 1999, but after that it remained pedestrian and poorly led for a further three years. The JLEI had no secretariat at all and was plagued by delays, conflicting signals, and inconsistencies. It was essentially a reactive initiative that was spurred into action whenever there was progress at IGAD, with the principal aim of stalling that progress. The Nigerian facilitation was undone by mismanagement.

The IGAD Partners' Forum (IPF), set up to support the IGAD initiative, also became a liability at first. It rapidly expanded to include all interested parties and was run on the basis of consensus, thus becoming unwieldy and subject to conflicting interests. An IGAD "core group" of Norway, the United Kingdom, and the United States was established to overcome this problem. In 2001–2 this troika achieved agreement on the way ahead, converging on the model of a vigorous IGAD process and resolving key issues in sequence. The Machakos and Naivasha rounds of talks robustly followed this approach. The sheer weight of the numerous international mediators, all pressing the same message, has been essential to the success thus far.

The Darfur Conflict

Beginning in early 2003, and escalating into a major conflict in January 2004, the war in Sudan's westernmost region of Darfur illustrates the complexity and intractability of the Sudanese conflict while also threatening to undermine the nascent peace agreement between the GoS and the SPLA, painstakingly thrashed out under IGAD auspices. The Darfur war arose from a long history of marginalization of the region, compounded by immediate factors. Among the latter were the split in Sudan's Islamist movement, which left most Darfurian Islamists (who were in al Turabi's camp) out of power, and the fact that Darfur's interests were conspicuously absent from any of the framework agreements signed at the IGAD talks. Two rebel movements, the Sudan Liberation Army (SLA, a broadly secularist regional group) and the Justice and Equity Movement (JEM, which has strong Islamist leanings), emerged and made some rapid military gains. The GoS responded with its familiar tactics of arming and supporting a militia (known as the Janjawiid), arrest and detention of suspected opponents, and aerial bombardment. But if the GoS calculated that it could quickly suppress the insurrection before it became an international issue, it was wrong. The cruelty of the campaign in the region, and especially the excesses of the Janjawiid, were labeled as ethnic cleansing. A refugee crisis in neighboring Chad garnered international humanitarian attention. And the brutality of the assault appeared to be a betrayal of Khartoum's promise that it was committed to human rights and democracy.

The Darfur war also caused a major political crisis in Khartoum. The people of Darfur are a mixture of many ethnic groups, some calling themselves "Arab" and others "African," but all are Muslim and many are active in Islamist politics. No religious justification for the war can be pretended. The Janjawiid espouse an Arab supremacist ideology, which chimes with the way in which the Sudanese state is dominated by "Arab" groups from the Nile. Therefore, the Arab-Islamist alliance that had sustained the Sudanese state was well and truly fractured. This in turn left the GoS unable to build a political consensus on how to approach the Darfur crisis. As a result, the Sudanese military have been given free rein.

Meanwhile, the SLA and JEM are young organizations that have yet to develop a common political program. They, too, are engaged solely in crisis management. They believe, with some justification, that their insurrection poses an even greater threat to the government than the war in the South ever did. As more young men from the refugee camps, angry at the atrocities they have suffered, their bitterness nursed by exile, join the rebel movements, political positions may harden. Alongside this, there is a serious prospect of the government fracturing further and of the security clique responsible for the Darfur campaign and other abuses in the South conspiring to block the consummation of any peace deal.

First mediation efforts by Chad collapsed in late 2003, reflecting the poor preparation of the facilitators. Subsequently, the European Union, the United States, and the African Union have all become involved. However, while the structure of the mediation appears similar to that of the IGAD talks, the Darfur conflict lacks the literature of accord that made possible agreement at IGAD. There is a genuine danger that the humanitarian access negotiations headed by the United States, the Europeans, and the United Nations could undermine the political mediation efforts of the African Union. Moreover, the escalation of the Darfur conflict and the high stakes involved pose severe challenges for the implementation of the provisions of the IGAD settlement. There is a real fear that Sudan's moment of peace may slip away.

Implications

It is hard to escape the conclusion that the principal parties, regional powers, and main mediators were comfortable with the ongoing war in Southern Sudan. The parties, neighboring governments, and special international interest groups could all meet their main objectives while the war continued.

During 2001–2 a combination of circumstances promised to alter this depressing configuration. Key governments, especially Kenya, Norway, the United Kingdom, and the United States, decided that Sudan was worth more effort. This coincided with increased leverage by the United States and a U.S. position that, while still not wholly impartial, was closer to "balance" than at any time in the previous decade. The policy of regime change by force had been abandoned. International unanimity over the substance and method of the peace process left the parties with no serious option but to talk, and to commit themselves in practice to principles they have long accepted. The mediators took a robust approach to the peace process, prioritizing and sequencing issues, and displayed a welcome readiness to pressure the parties.

The eruption of the Darfur war in 2003–4 threatens to plunge Sudan into another round of conflict, with only dim prospects of rapid resolution. The lessons of the ultimately successful mediation of the civil war in the South need to be learned and applied. Sudan can escape the intractability of its conflicts. The Naivasha agreement of May 2004 is the country's best-ever chance for peace. But the obstacles to the effective implementation of the settlement remain formidable. The long-suffering Sudanese people deserve some good luck, and if the fortunate constellation of international and regional forces that came into being in 2002 and held until the time of writing in early 2004 holds during the implementation of the IGAD settlement and the Darfur mediation, they may finally achieve peace.

Postscript

As of late 2004, the Darfur crisis has become a strategic threat to the entire Sudanese peace process and a new source of intractability. There is no agreement on the crisis's root causes among the leaders of the GoS and the Darfur rebels. Both sides underestimated how vulnerable Darfur was to runaway conflagration, and both are internally divided on what political strategy could feasibly end the crisis.

The rebellion was initially fanned by SPLA and Chadian meddling and by Turabi's aspirations to unseat his former colleagues. Eritrea hosted the rebels, while Egypt marshaled the Arab League in support of the GoS.

The invasion and occupation of Iraq helped blind the outside world to the early genesis of the Darfur crisis and has gravely constrained the West from finding a diplomatic strategy of carrots and sticks that can attract solid support within the UN Security Council, the Arab League, and the African Union. On September 9, the U.S. administration declared the atrocities in Darfur to be "genocide." Some members of the Security Council and some Arab powers fear that punitive international action against Sudan will be seen as an assault on Islam and will only worsen instability inside the Khartoum regime; they also suspect that a strategy of regime change is at work.

Mediation efforts have been deficient. Although the African Union chairperson, Alpha Konare, has engaged the crisis energetically, he has lacked a strong technical secretariat, and the peace talks in Abuja, Nigeria, in August and September were marred by missteps. The prospects for a quick fix for Darfur have all but vanished.

The eruption of the Darfur war, at a time when the Naivasha framework remains to be concluded, jeopardizes the North-South peace agreement itself. While the SPLA regards the consummation of Naivasha, and its own entry into government, as a precondition for solving the Darfur crisis, the GoS holds an opposite position and prefers to suspend the Naivasha framework until it can put the North—its "own house"—in order. This may take a long time, during which a slide back into war in the South cannot be ruled out.

8

Intractability and Third-Party Mediation in the Balkans

Steven L. Burg

THE DISSOLUTION OF YUGOSLAVIA can be viewed as a continuous process of conflict or as a series of related but discrete conflicts. Conflict began with the inability of elites within the old regime to reach agreement on the peaceful and democratic transformation of their common state and continued through more and less violent confrontations in Slovenia, Croatia, Bosnia, Kosovo, and Macedonia. These conflicts were characterized by competing claims to the rights to self-determination, sovereignty, and territorial integrity and by efforts by international mediators to resolve these competing claims in a manner consistent with the interests and norms of the international community. The efforts to conform to international norms affected mediators' behavior in every instance, while the understanding of these norms on the part of the conflicting parties was determined by their pragmatic political interests. With respect to the question of intractability, Croatia, Bosnia, and Kosovo present us with "conflicts that . . . persisted over time and refused to yield to efforts . . . to arrive at a political settlement" and thus fit the definition of intractability proposed by the editors of this volume in their introductory chapter. The conflict in Slovenia, in contrast, proved susceptible to a timely and enduring negotiated settlement. The agreement negotiated in Macedonia in August 2001 but not yet fully implemented raises the hope that that conflict, which turned violent only briefly, will also prove not to be intractable. The differences between the structural characteristics of these conflicts suggest some of the factors that may contribute to intractability and the greater difficulties posed by such conflicts for third-party mediators.

The intractability of conflict and the efficacy of mediator efforts constitute quite distinct analytical issues. Nonetheless, the conflicts arising out of the dissolution of Yugoslavia suggest that the actions of third-party mediators are an important, although not necessarily determining, factor affecting whether the parties to a conflict pursue their goals through negotiation or violence, and whether violence, once initiated, can be ended. This chapter examines the structural differences between the conflicts in Croatia, Bosnia, and Kosovo, on the one hand, and the conflicts in Slovenia and Macedonia, on the other, to suggest some sources of intractability. It also reviews the role of third-party mediators in each of these conflicts to identify the potential impact of negotiations on the course of events. This analysis is used to suggest certain modest lessons for third-party intervention in potentially intractable conflicts.

Dynamics of Conflict and Dissolution

The dissolution of socialist Yugoslavia can be attributed to the effects of several mutually reinforcing conflicts. The most fundamental of these were the conflicts engendered by rising ethno-nationalism among the peoples of Yugoslavia, fueled by unresolved historical memories and grievances; by contemporary conflicts of economic and political interests; by the external environment of change in communist Eastern Europe and the Soviet Union; and by structural features of the Yugoslav communist system that made it difficult, if not impossible, for the federal regime to respond effectively to the manifest conflicts of the 1980s and 1990s.

Conflicts among the major ethno-national groups in Yugoslavia had been a recurring condition since the state was created in 1918. The conflict between Croatian and Serbian nationalisms in the period between the world wars paralyzed state institutions and led to two major reorganizations of the state. The first of these was an attempt to preserve a unitary state by replacing administrative units that approximated historical national homelands (i.e., "Croatia" and "Serbia") with units whose boundaries and names were based on the major geographical features of the country (principally, rivers). The failure of this effort to "de-ethnicize" the state was followed by an agreement in 1939 between the Serbian and Croatian leaderships to accommodate Croatian nationalism by creating a Croatian state-within-the-state. This second reorganization appeared likely to produce the federalization of the country into Slovene, Croatian, and Serbian states. However, the onset of World War II ended this process, which otherwise might have ended interethnic conflict through de facto territorial partition. At the same time, it is not clear that partition would have resolved competing Croatian and Serbian claims to the same lands[1] or accommodated the national aspirations of the Muslim and Albanian minorities, who remained unrecognized.

Occupation of the country by the Germans and the Italians and the creation of a Nazi-sponsored independent Croatian state magnified interethnic conflicts by establishing expansive borders for that state and by introducing extremist and genocidal ideologies into conflicts that up to then had been expressed in terms of cultural, procedural, institutional, and even constitutional demands. The intergroup violence of the wartime period, most intense in multinational Bosnia, had an enduring effect on nationalist conflict in the postwar Yugoslav state not only by creating deeply felt intergroup grievances about the past but also by increasing the perceived "stakes of the game" for any group relegated in the future to "minority" status in an ethnically defined territory.

The communist regime that came to power in the postwar period attempted to deal with the legacy of World War II first by suppressing both the manifestations and the memories of interethnic conflict. It made only a limited effort to address the accumulated grievances of the ethnic populations in a constructive manner. The regime adopted a largely ethnically determined federal structure for the state, as a form of symbolic concession to national identities. None of this symbolism would have mattered much, of course, if the country had been ruled by a monolithic, Stalinist Communist Party organization. However, Tito broke with Stalin and Stalinism almost immediately, and the Yugoslav party was compelled to relegitimate itself on the basis of support from below. The transformation of Yugoslav ideology from Stalinism to self-management involved a significant deconcentration of economic and political power. This process was initially directed toward limited marketization and limited democratization of Yugoslavia in its entirety. However, the inevitable confrontation between reformers and conservatives within the communist leadership, which culminated in 1966, redirected change toward devolution to the regions, thereby empowering the organizational and political bases of the most significant supporters of reform to act autonomously of the federal center. Over time, territorial devolution opened the door to renewed expression of the country's conflicting nationalisms in the context of interregional policy disputes over federal economic, political, and constitutional reform.

The ease with which legitimate regional economic and political agendas could activate repressed ethno-nationalisms and escalate internal conflict was demonstrated dramatically in 1968, when economic discontent fueled nationalist unrest among the Albanian population in Kosovo. It was demonstrated even more powerfully in 1971, when a process of constitutional reform intended by the regime to devolve power to the republics was taken over in Croatia by nationalist intellectuals and a younger generation of sympathetic communist politicians. A nationalist Croatian "mass movement" that seemed to threaten the integrity of the federal state emerged, provoking a military response from the regime. The Croatian mass movement should have been a warning to the regime about the dangers of allowing devolution to proceed more quickly than economic reforms could create common interests that cut across regional borders, fostering integrative political forces. But economic reforms that might have broken down barriers to interregional economic activity proved impossible to adopt. The devolution of the 1960s and 1970s, enshrined in a new constitution in 1974, had already created a hyperdecentralized state in which economic and political power—in both the state and the ruling Communist Party—rested in the hands of regional leaders. Federal decision-making institutions operated according to deeply entrenched principles of power sharing that gave each of the regional leaderships veto power, which they used to defend regional economic interests. The death of Tito in 1980 eliminated the only authoritative counterweight to the interregional deadlock that was the inevitable result of adopting such decision-making rules in the socioeconomic and political circumstances of the Yugoslav state.

Economic disparities among the regions made it difficult to forge a post-Tito consensus on federal policy for dealing with the overhang of accumulated international debt, high inflation, and economic decline, which were eroding Yugoslav living standards in the 1980s. The level of development, and consequent living standard, in Slovenia was already more than eight times greater than in Kosovo in 1984,[2] and the gap was increasing. Slovenia and Croatia, more highly developed than the other regions, defended their resources against federal levies, and especially against demands to continue Tito-era policies of shifting resources from the wealthier northern regions to subsidize social services and economic development in the less developed southern regions, which included Bosnia, Kosovo, and Macedonia. Lagging development in these regions was fueling popular discontent, which burst forth in rioting and extended small-scale violence in Kosovo again in 1981. Nonetheless, proposals to reform the economy by eliminating regional barriers to market forces and to alleviate the political deadlock by democratizing federal institutions and replacing regional power sharing with majoritarian parliamentary arrangements were met with fierce regional resistance. The inability of the post-Tito regional leaderships to reform the regime even in the face of a manifest crisis of economic (non)performance undermined the legitimacy of the communist order, which had long been based on the instrumental support engendered by economic well-being. Such support is inherently more fragile than affective, or emotional, support. In Yugoslavia, moreover, emotional support was directed toward ethnic or national identities, not the civic identity of Yugoslavism. Hence, declining material performance in the 1980s not only weakened the legitimacy of the Yugoslav regime but increased the relative attractiveness of its alternative: national regimes based in the regions.[3]

The Yugoslav regime was weakened still further by changes in the international environment associated with the collapse of communism in Eastern Europe and the Soviet Union. Democratization processes in Poland and Hungary were closely associated with the assertion of Polish and Hungarian nationalisms. The fall of the Berlin Wall was associated with affirmation of the principle of national self-determination as justification for the unification of East and West Germany. Inside the Soviet Union, the declarations of "sovereignty" by ethnically defined republics and lesser units of the Soviet federal system and the mostly peaceful response of the Soviet and, later, Russian governments to most of them lent additional political weight to the principle of national self-determination. The use of force by the central state to suppress regional national self-determination movements appeared to have become the exception rather than the rule. Thus, the Soviet external threat that had contributed to internal Yugoslav cohesion since 1948 disappeared.

At the same time, ethnic nationalism had gained legitimacy throughout Eastern Europe and the former Soviet Union as the basis not only for opposing communism but also for challenging the legitimacy of the multinational state per se. Indeed, for some international actors, external diplomatic and political support for regional nationalisms in Yugoslavia, which in the past had been understood as not only undesirable and illegitimate but a violation of international legal norms of noninterference in the internal affairs of a sovereign state, had now gained legitimacy as a form of support for democratization. Thus, opposition to communism merged with ethnonationalism in Yugoslavia and claimed the mantle of democratization, legitimated by reference to the newly invigorated principle of national self-determination, supported diplomatically and politically by outside actors no longer constrained by norms of noninterference, and manifested in regional demands for de facto, and later de jure, independence. The political divisions produced by unresolved historical grievances, domestic economic and political conflicts over substance and process, and international legitimation of the principle of national self-determination were for the most part mutually reinforcing in Yugoslavia.

Sources of Intractability

Claims to self-determination and sovereignty were linked in the dissolving Yugoslav state to both territory (the existing republics and provinces of the federation) and ethnic identity. Where ethnic populations transcended republic and provincial boundaries, the assertion of ethnic group claims to self-determination and sovereignty engendered conflicts over definition of the borders of the emerging successor states, over the rights to be enshrined in their new constitutions, and even over the legitimacy of their very existence. Because sovereign control of territory was understood by nationalist political entrepreneurs as a license to treat minorities under their control unfairly, competing claims to sovereign control of territory were seen by all parties as zero-sum issues. Fear of the consequences of minority status in a national state ruled by the "other" set off what international relations specialists have called the "security dilemma": a dynamic of competing ethnic mobilizations that may be understood by each group as defensive but are seen by others as threatening and therefore fuel escalation of inter-group conflict, which leads to intergroup violence and war. Under commu-nism, the existence of the federation and a transcendent, common identity ("Yugoslav"), as well as the use of central state power to enforce the princi-ple of multinationality in the regions, moderated the clash between major-ities and minorities within the republics and provinces. Once the survival of the communist-era federation was called into question in 1990, how-ever, these conflicts escalated.[4]

In Croatia the large Serb minority in that republic mobilized against Croatian nationalist forces intent on transforming Croatia into a national state of the Croats. In Kosovo the resistance of the local Albanian major-ity (a minority in the context of the Serbian state of which Kosovo was a province) to domination by the Serb minority backed by Belgrade (the majority in the context of Serbia) gave rise to a popular movement for es-tablishment of an independent Kosovar Albanian state. In Macedonia the ethnic Macedonian majority moved quickly to establish an independent state defined in a manner that privileged Macedonian identity and culture over that of its large ethnic Albanian minority.

Croatia, Kosovo, and Macedonia all pitted a relatively large, territo-rially compact ethnic minority—an irredenta—against the ethnic majority in a struggle over the definition of the existing or emerging state and polit-ical regime. In each case, the demands of the minority challenged the con-centration of power in the hands of the majority and raised the prospect of a territorial devolution of power or even partition that was unacceptable to the nationalist majority. In Bosnia the same factors produced a more complicated pattern of conflicts, because the number of significant actors was greater. Both the Serb and Croat minorities in Bosnia laid claim to sovereign control over large areas of the republic, challenging the legiti-macy of the emerging Bosnian state. The establishment of a unitary Bos-nian state was supported by Bosnian Muslims intent on dominating it, by Bosnian political forces genuinely committed to multinationality (con-sisting largely of former communists), and by the international community. The territorialization of demands for self-determination by ethnic minori-ties in the three regions, and the understanding of self-determination by majorities (and minorities) as a license to dominate other ethnic groups within one's own national state, thus created a set of zero-sum struggles

over definition of the successor states emerging from the dissolution of
Yugoslavia and a series of intractable conflicts. This dynamic is not exceptional. The intractable violence that erupted in the republics of the Caucasus following disintegration of the Soviet Union can be attributed to the
same factors.

Escalating conflict over the nature of the Yugoslav state in the late
1980s and early 1990s reflected the greatly increased opportunities for
gain, and risks of loss, associated with the almost continuous process of
reform and redefinition of the state that had been taking place since
Yugoslavia was first created. Constitutional reforms adopted in the late
1960s and mid-1970s had involved negotiations on many of the same
issues that confronted Yugoslav leaders in the early 1990s. But by the
early 1990s, changes in Eastern Europe and the Soviet Union undermined
the legitimacy of the communist federation, transforming Yugoslavia
from a "leading" to a "lagging" socioeconomic and political system in the
region. The potential gains from independence and the increased risks
associated with remaining part of a declining state dominated by an ethnic
"other" led regional leaders in Yugoslavia to use their veto powers to block
efforts to introduce economic reforms or democratic elections at the federal level. This denied the Yugoslav state any opportunity to repeat the
process of relegitimation it had achieved in the 1950s and 1960s, this
time through genuine democratization.

Regional leaders blocked democratization of the federal government
through competitive elections and the adoption of majoritarian principles
in federal institutions. They insisted on holding competitive elections in the
republics first. Under communism there had been little opportunity for
civil society to develop and no opportunity for social or economic interests to organize themselves independently. There were few interest-based
organizations in the regions other than those defined in ethno-cultural
terms and even fewer that cut across regional borders. As a result, regional
elections advantaged nationalist forces, the most outspoken advocates of
independence and the only actors able to appeal to the most easily mobilized, if not the only truly "organized," interest in the electorate. Thus,
paradoxically, the onset of democratization left regional political leaders
in Yugoslavia less able to resolve ethno-regional issues through compromise than they had been under the old regime. Those who might nevertheless have been inclined to do so—the social democratic left, composed

mostly of former communists—were swept away in the first round of democratic elections in the regions.

Elections in the republics over the course of 1990 brought to power leaderships that no longer shared any overarching common interests.[5] Indeed, most regional leaders had more to gain from unilateralism than from cooperation, as cooperation would have required compromise on the issue that defined the electoral strength of their ruling parties: nationalism. The Croatian Democratic Union (HDZ), led by Franjo Tudjman, appealed exclusively to the ethnic Croatian electorate in elections held in April and May 1990. The party ignored the large (15 percent of the population) ethnic Serb minority and even openly alienated Serbs by its appeals to Croatian nationalism and assertions of continuity between the emerging Croatian state and the wartime Croatian state. The exclusionary nationalism of the Croatian leadership helped fuel the conflict between the Croatian state and territorially concentrated Serb minorities in what came to be known as the "Krajina." Similarly, in the November 1990 elections in Bosnia, each of the three major parties (the Party of Democratic Action [SDA], led by Alija Izetbegovic; the Bosnian branch of the Croatian HDZ; and the Serb Democratic Party [SDS], led by Radovan Karadzic) appealed exclusively to its own ethnic base. The parties cooperated with one another only in an effort to defeat candidates of the non-nationalist parties in second-round runoff elections. Once in power, they adopted dramatically conflicting perspectives on the nature of the emerging Bosnian state.[6]

In Serbia multiple parties competed to establish Serbian nationalist credentials, including otherwise "democratic" opposition parties. Given the fact that significant numbers of Serbs resided outside Serbia, Serbian nationalism inevitably took the form of irredentism, aimed particularly against Bosnia and Croatia. The threat to other nations and territories inherent in increasingly aggressive, violent Serbian nationalist irredentism, and the even greater threat of Serb domination of the Yugoslav military establishment in each of the republics, contributed to the intensity of conflict over the dissolution of Yugoslavia. The Socialist (former Communist) Party of Slobodan Milosevic secured the largest share of the vote in Serbia and an overwhelming parliamentary majority in December 1990 by transforming itself into a nationalist party. But over time, the party lost ground to the more extreme nationalist Radical Party of Vojislav Seselj, which entered the Serbian government briefly in 1992–93.[7] Ethnic minorities in Serbia—principally, the Hungarians of Vojvodina, the Muslims of the Sandzak region, and the Albanians of Kosovo—were effectively excluded from power.

In Kosovo the primary Kosovar Albanian political organization in this period and its leader, the Democratic League of Kosovo (LDK) and Ibrahim Rugova, chose to boycott Serbian elections and institutions, choosing instead to construct alternative, "parallel" institutions of their own. Unlike many of the nationalist parties in other regions, the LDK followed a strategy of peaceful resistance, necessitated by the overwhelming power imbalance between the Kosovar Albanians and the Serbs. But at the same time, Rugova and the LDK rejected any solution short of independence. Thus, in Croatia, Bosnia, and Kosovo, the structure of the emerging party systems (in Kosovo, a movement rather than a party) institutionalized and reinforced ethnic divisions, and political leaders adopted maximalist, confrontational positions. Thus, both structure and leadership, as well as the dynamic of competitive elections and the intensity of the Serbian nationalist threat to Croatia, Bosnia, and Kosovo, contributed to the intractability of conflict.

In Macedonia, as well, parties defined themselves largely in ethnic terms, and there was almost no crossover voting between Albanians and Macedonians. However, more than one party competed for votes within each ethnic community, imparting greater value to the potential patronage benefits of participation in government. This created important incentives for the strongest Albanian party to enter into government with the strongest Macedonian party. The willingness of the strongest ethnic Macedonian party after each election to enter into such a coalition, despite winning a sufficient number of seats in parliament to govern on its own or in alliance with another ethnic Macedonian party, can be attributed in large part to the proximity of Macedonia to the ethnic unrest in neighboring Kosovo and its implications for ethnic Albanians in Macedonia. Paradoxically, while the danger of "spillover" is often considered a destabilizing factor, in Macedonia the threat of violence spilling over from Kosovo contributed to moderation on the part of most party leaders. The construction of coalition governments was also facilitated by the absence of a history of interethnic violence and the consequently more moderate sense of grievances underlying intergroup relations in Macedonia. The country's first postcommunist president also worked to encourage moderate, nonconfrontational politics among party leaders in Macedonia. Each of the postcommunist governments have thus included both the strongest Macedonian party and the strongest Albanian party—a structural condition that encourages interethnic bargaining, compromise, and the emergence of shared interests, even if successive government coalitions have not been wholly successful at this. Thus, in Macedonia, structure, leadership, and the dynamic of electoral competition all facilitated compromise.

Yugoslav leaders, their political power based after 1990 on nationalist ethnic constituencies, proved unable to negotiate a comprehensive agreement on either preserving the country or dissolving it. Neither a series of seven meetings of the federal collective presidency together with other federal officials held over the first three months of 1991 (the so-called Yu-summits) nor a series of six meetings of the republic presidents held during the period March–June 1991 (the so-called summit of the six) could produce any agreement to ameliorate the mounting crisis. Few of the factors that contributed to intractability in Croatia, Bosnia, and Kosovo were present in the conflict over Slovenian secession from Yugoslavia. Because there was no Serb population in Slovenia, neither ethnic-status nor territorial disputes between the Slovenian and Serbian leaderships occurred. Indeed, Milosevic and Slovenian president Milan Kucan publicly endorsed each other's views on self-determination, and thereby reached a de facto agreement on Slovenian secession, in January 1991.[8] The fighting that broke out when Slovenia finally did secede in June 1991 was brought to an end relatively quickly because Yugoslav (in reality, Yugoslav Army and Serbian) and Slovenian leaders were able to construct a non-zero-sum compromise. Each side had different interests and goals; each could trade a significant concession for a significant gain: Slovenia achieved independence, and the Yugoslav Army and Milosevic secured control over the considerable military hardware in Slovenia and could redeploy it for use in subsequent fighting in Croatia and Bosnia. The double-edged character of this solution—good for Slovenia, Serbia, and the Yugoslav Army on the one hand, but very bad for Croatia and Bosnia on the other—underscores the fact that the intractability of conflicts in Croatia, Bosnia, and Kosovo was in part a consequence of the dynamics of conflicts in neighboring republics/states.

Mediation and Intractability

The zero-sum nature of the issues that divided most of the regions made compromise very difficult for their leaders to achieve on their own. Moreover, the issues that divided Yugoslav leaders eventually became linked to zero-sum principles endorsed by the international community and its mediators, that is, the application of self-determination to territorial units (at first, republics only, but eventually including the province of Kosovo) and the inviolability of these borders. The initial response of European actors linked the prospect of recognition to the negotiation of a comprehensive settlement that guaranteed minority rights and allowed for the peaceful renegotiation of internal (republic) borders.[9] This approach would have left international actors outside the internal Yugoslav negotiating process and tied the fate of each successor entity to that of all the others. If this approach had been sustained, a comprehensive negotiated settlement might have been possible. However, the European Union quickly backed away from it. The principle of nonviolability still, in theory, allowed for the peaceful renegotiation of borders. But this principle (as well as the principle of self-determination) was applied to internal boundaries, and international mediators entered into direct participation in negotiations between the Yugoslav republic leaderships in the formal framework of the European Community Conference on Yugoslavia. This approach effectively endorsed the secessionist claims of the republics, weakened the incentives for majority groups in the republics to compromise on rights for minorities, and magnified the fear of independence on the part of minorities. The European approach effectively "internationalized" the conflicts between the Yugoslav republics and delegitimated the federal Yugoslav state.[10] At the same time, the structure of the conference gave encouragement to the nationalist ambitions of the Albanians of Kosovo and Macedonia through negotiations in subcommittees that treated these minority groups as negotiating equals of Serbia and Macedonia. In effect, the international effort to mediate a peaceful solution of the Yugoslav crisis was inevitably transformed into a process for facilitating the dissolution of Yugoslavia.

The negotiated solution to the conflict in Slovenia begs the question of whether (and how) the international community and its mediators might have constructed a non-zero-sum compromise among all the republics (including Kosovo) short of dissolution. There was only one goal under the control of the international community that was sufficiently important to each of the regional leaders to constitute a positive inducement: recognition. Economic sanctions and rewards, however much they might have helped or hurt in the long run, could not address the immediate issues of identity and control that were driving the crisis. A non-zero-sum outcome could have been achieved for all the regions only if a cohesive international community had made it clear that recognition would be granted only to all of the Yugoslav regions simultaneously, or to none of them, and only in response to their peaceful settlement of all their disputes. Such a settlement could have come only as the result of direct, multilateral, good-faith negotiations among the regional leaderships as well as the federal and military leaderships. In the absence of powerful incentives and constraints articulated and enforced by the international community, such negotiations could not—and did not—happen. If recognition was a powerful incentive to cooperation, only a dual threat of recognition (of the victim) and military intervention (against the aggressor) offered a sufficiently powerful constraint on the use of force by any of the Yugoslav actors.

In the face of such incentives and constraints, the Yugoslav actors might have been compelled to find mutually acceptable solutions to their conflicts *on their own*. These would most likely have taken the form of a combination of the territorial status quo, strengthened and consistent rights regimes across all the regions, and enhanced autonomies for minority-populated territories. But it is not inconceivable that some redrawing of internal boundaries and redefinition of statuses might also have resulted. Whatever the result, however, it would have to have been achieved by the Yugoslavs themselves.

The European Union considered but rejected the use of force in Croatia. The proposal, as reported by European negotiator David Owen and others, amounted to a defense of the existing borders of the Yugoslav federal republic of Croatia against what was seen as aggression by Serbia and the Yugoslav military, thus reflecting an inclination of some European leaderships to intervene in support of the Croatian claim of independence rather than to mediate. Simple military intervention in support of independence, however, offered no solution to the political struggle inside Croatia between the nationalist leadership and the large ethnically Serb minority population. The subsequent mediation efforts in Croatia undertaken by Cyrus Vance in his capacity as special representative of the United Nations secretary-general achieved partial success by ending the fighting between Croatia and Serbia and containing the fighting between the Croatian state and the Serb minorities who had seized control of the Krajina.[11] The latter were under the influence, if not outright control, of Serbia. Thus, the conflict in Croatia was for the most part conducted between two sets of state actors. The issues concerned territory and minority rights, as well as the withdrawal of the Yugoslav military and its assets. The existence of Croatia as an independent state—as opposed to its borders—was not in dispute.

For the Serbian leaders, the Vance Plan appeared to "freeze" the status quo, creating an opportunity to strengthen their control over Croatian territory. But no internationally recognized outcome other than affirmation of the Croatian claims was possible once the European states recognized the Croatian state and its claims to independence. Recognition eliminated any further incentive for the Croatian leadership to compromise. Indeed, recognition very nearly led the Croats to renege on their agreement. But the Vance Plan created an opportunity for Croatia to build up its capacity to end the conflict at a later date on its own terms, by force. Thus, while the Vance-negotiated agreement was made possible by the emergence of a "hurting stalemate" between weakening Serb forces and a Croatian state not yet strong enough to win, the two sides remained as intractable in their political stances as they had been before the agreement. No meaningful effort was undertaken, despite international pressure, to negotiate a solution to the internal conflict over rights, and the provisions of the Vance Plan for ameliorating conflict in the Serb-held territories were never implemented. With the agreement in place, however, each of the parties to the conflict in Croatia could turn its attention to the war in neighboring Bosnia.

The conflicts in Bosnia and Kosovo, in contrast to those in Slovenia and Croatia, involved not only fundamentally incompatible claims to territory but deeply held differences over whether the states claimed by the Muslims in Bosnia and by the Albanians in Kosovo should exist at all. In both cases, Serbs pressed their opposition to the state through extreme violence against the "other." To a great extent, the existential character of these conflicts for the groups involved accounts for their intractability, even in the wake of armed intervention by a third party intent on ending them.

The international effort to achieve a negotiated end to the fighting in Bosnia passed through several stages, characterized by differing approaches to the conflict.[12] The initial effort was led by the European Community, through its Conference on Yugoslavia. From the beginning, mediators chose to engage only the three nationalist parties in government. While this decision was consistent with formal diplomatic logic, it ignored the reality that, while these parties were formally coalition partners, they were in fact bitter political opponents. The "government" hardly functioned as such. The nationalist parties had no greater claim to represent the interests of Bosnia than the nonethnic former Communist Party that had also secured significant electoral support in the 1990 elections. The exclusion of this party from the negotiations empowered nationalist perspectives in defining the Bosnian state at the expense of nonnationalist perspectives.

Not surprisingly, the European Community negotiations, carried out in the framework of the Conference on Yugoslavia and overseen by Jose Cutileiro, foundered over the inability of the three nationalist parties to agree on either a constitutional order or an administrative map for the emerging state in talks conducted in February and March 1992. Each of the parties was unwilling to compromise its view of the Bosnian state. Indeed, while the goal of mediators was to create a viable state, the goal of two of the three conflicting parties appeared to be to prevent the emergence of a viable state. Nonetheless, the international community extended recognition to Bosnia. Recognition, however, did not mitigate the hostility of the Bosnian Serbs and the Bosnian Croats to the idea of a Bosnian state. Their opposition was expressed not only in the negotiations on Bosnia but in warfare.

Mediation of the Bosnian conflict was taken over by a joint European-UN organization, the International Conference on the Former Yugoslavia (ICFY) in September 1992, cochaired by Cyrus Vance for the United Nations and David Owen for the European Community. Mediation in Bosnia was complicated by the structure of the conflict. It was both an internal struggle among three nationalist parties with mutually exclusive territorial and political claims and an international conflict between Bosnia and the neighboring states of Serbia and Croatia. The latter were involved both indirectly, through support for the Bosnian Serbs and Croats, and directly, through military and diplomatic intervention. The Bosnian Serb military, for example, was dependent on support from Serbia. Mediation was also complicated by the structure and composition of the ICFY. European and UN approaches to dealing with conflict were not identical; and the United States, perhaps the most influential and capable international actor with respect to the Balkan conflicts, remained uncommitted to the process.

International negotiators attempted to end the war by developing a formula for an extensively decentralized state. The process of negotiation was for the most part conducted through proximity talks, bilateral discussions between mediators and each of the conflicting parties, and indirect communication between the parties via the mediators, and in meetings with the leaders of Croatia and Serbia. There were relatively few direct negotiating sessions among all the parties. The Vance-Owen plan itself was developed largely by international experts. All the parties sought to use the mediation process as a means to pursue their own goals rather than as an opportunity to pursue a good-faith effort to find a common solution. The absence of any Western threat of force—either to implement an agreed-on settlement or to impose a solution in the absence of agreement—led one member of the Vance-Owen team to liken the negotiations to playing "baseball without a bat."[13] Unable to compel the parties to compromise, David Owen was led to offer last-minute concessions to the Serbs in April 1993 that moved the Vance-Owen plan for decentralization toward outright partition. The lack of engagement on the part of the United States and the concomitant absence of a credible threat of force continued to plague negotiators even as they moved toward an explicit plan for partition in 1993 and 1994. Not even a partition plan could work as long as parties on the ground remained wedded to force and the most significant outside power, the United States, remained uninterested in compelling them to agree.

The failure of the Vance-Owen plan led the warring parties to begin exchanging proposals of their own for the partition of Bosnia. In August Owen's and Vance's successor, Thorvald Stoltenberg, put forward a plan that was based in part on these proposals, but the Bosnian Muslims rejected it. Further exchanges culminated in direct, multilateral negotiations encompassing all parties to the conflict—internal and external—in September 1993. These resulted in another proposal for de facto partition, which the Bosnian Muslims also rejected. Not even direct pressure from the French and German governments could persuade the Bosnian

Muslims to accept a proposal for partition. Divisions had emerged among Bosnian Muslim leaders over conduct of the war and negotiations. Hard-line sentiments were widespread among Bosnian Muslim parliamentarians, military leaders, and officials who perceived the tide of war shifting in their favor and reducing their incentive to compromise. Moreover, the United States continued to remain aloof from the negotiating process, sustaining Muslim hopes for continued U.S. support, hopes further encouraged by direct U.S. involvement in covert arms shipments to Bosnian Muslim forces beginning in early 1994.

Declining interest in negotiations on the part of the Bosnian Muslims was paralleled by an increasing readiness on the part of the Croatian leadership to resolve its own conflict by force. Such an approach necessarily required the elimination of Serb strongholds in neighboring Bosnian territory. Bosnian Muslim and Croatian interest in ending the conflicts in their respective republics on their own terms, by force, converged with increasing U.S. interest in bringing these conflicts to an end, largely for domestic political reasons and out of concern for the cohesion of the NATO alliance. The prospect of an escalation in the fighting thus led in late 1994 to a change in the character of international efforts to end the conflict; ICFY efforts to mediate a negotiated settlement were displaced by U.S. efforts to end the war through a strategy of coercive diplomacy.[14]

The success of coercive diplomacy in Bosnia in 1995 was based on three main factors. First, a military standoff between the parties—but not a hurting stalemate—was created and enforced by the United States, through a combination of arming and restraining both the Bosnian Muslims and the Croatian military. This created a credible threat that both the Serbs occupying the Krajina and the Bosnian Serbs would be defeated. The first threat was fully realized. The threat to the Bosnian Serbs was limited to the battlefield. Second, the United States became fully committed to ending the war and thus recognized the need to address the real and often conflicting interests of all sides, including the outside actors, Serbia and Croatia; this meant recognition for the Bosnian Serb republic and a promise to lift sanctions against Serbia. Thus, Bosnian Serbs—unlike the Serbs in Croatia—were offered some political compensation for their military defeat. Third, the use of force pressured both the Serbs and the Muslims into accepting the partition of Bosnia. The United States and its NATO allies were careful not to use so much force as to lead either side to believe that all was won or lost, thereby creating real incentives for each to accept the U.S.-brokered settlement.

The strategy of coercive diplomacy ended the fighting in Bosnia, but it did not end the conflict. The negotiations in Dayton, Ohio, on defining the postwar Bosnian state were characterized by the same difficulties that had characterized the earlier negotiations conducted by the European and ICFY mediators. The Dayton negotiations differed, however, in two important respects. The United States continued to exercise coercive influence over the parties to the negotiations, and the most intransigent of the actors—the Bosnian Serbs and the Bosnian Croats—were excluded, to be represented by the leaders of Serbia and Croatia. Thus, while the negotiations at Dayton were difficult, they were conducted among representatives of states, rather than among nonstate actors. Negotiations and the exchange of concessions between Croatia and Serbia were second in importance only to the role of the United States in concluding an agreement at Dayton.

The Dayton agreement established a de facto international protectorate over Bosnia and redirected the conflict among Muslims, Serbs, and Croats to more peaceful means. But the institutions established at Dayton have been insufficient to resolve the fundamental existential conflict between these groups. The Dayton arrangements have left power divided among the three major ethnic groups and between the central state and its constituent entities (the federation and the Serb Republic) and lower units (cantons and local governments). Even after more than eight years, central institutions remain incapable of formulating and implementing policies for the whole state. As a result, the representative of international authority in Bosnia, the Office of the High Representative, has had to intervene repeatedly to impose policy decisions where local actors proved unable or unwilling to do so on their own. Paradoxically, to the extent that international institutions continue to perform such a role, Bosnian institutions will remain internally divided and incapable. Yet there is no clear exit option for international forces in Bosnia that does not increase to unacceptably high levels the risk of renewed violent conflict among the three Bosnian ethnic communities. Intervention in Bosnia has thus taken on the characteristics of an open-ended commitment to administer the territory. The conflict is not "frozen," but progress is being achieved at a glacial pace.

A similar outcome has been reached in the intractable conflict in Kosovo. There, as in Bosnia, conflict was driven by mutually exclusive claims to control over territory. The claim of Albanians to an independent state of Kosovo conflicted with the claim of Serbs that Kosovo represented an integral part of the historical state of Serbia. Serbs, a small numerical minority locally, enforced their claim by means of brutal repression backed by the power of the Serbian state. Albanians pressed their claim, beginning in the 1980s, by mounting a peaceful mass movement of resistance to Serbian authority. The movement was led by the Democratic League of Kosova (LDK) and Ibrahim Rugova, who insisted that the only acceptable solution to the conflict was independence for Kosovo. None of the several efforts by governmental and nongovernmental third parties during the 1980s to encourage discussion between the Kosovar Albanians and the Serbs produced significant progress. The Serbs resisted any third-party involvement, and especially the involvement of governments or multilateral organizations. The Albanians insisted on it. Both sides understood the implications of such involvement similarly: it would have "internationalized" their conflict.

The de facto partition of Bosnia at Dayton, and especially the creation of a Serb entity inside Bosnia, appeared initially to the Kosovar Albanians as a first step toward independence for the Bosnian Serbs. This increased Albanian impatience with the lack of progress toward their own independence and constituted a potent destabilizing form of "spillover" of the conflict in Bosnia.[15] Dayton provided an impetus for the emergence in early 1996 of a Kosovar Albanian organization willing to use force to achieve that goal, the Kosovo Liberation Army (KLA). The emergence of the KLA put pressure on the LDK to show progress toward achieving independence. At the same time, Milosevic and the Serbian leadership were interested in persuading the United States to lift sanctions imposed on Serbia during the war in Bosnia and sustained by the United States because of the conflict in Kosovo. In addition, the rise of a popular democratic opposition to Milosevic inside Serbia created incentives for the Serbian president to achieve progress toward a peaceful settlement. The result of this convergence of interests between Rugova and Milosevic was the negotiation of an agreement in September 1996 to normalize the educational system in Kosovo, mediated by a nongovernmental international organization. The promise of a negotiated settlement inherent in the education agreement was, however, never fulfilled. Neither side had the resources or the will to implement the agreement, and international actors failed to provide resources or political pressure to act. The attention of international actors was focused on post-Dayton Bosnia.

While it remains arguable whether the conflict in Kosovo was susceptible to negotiated settlement in 1996,[16] the conflict did not, in fact, draw a concerted effort by international actors to mediate a settlement until the KLA posed a serious challenge to Serb control of the province, thereby evoking a disproportionately violent response and concomitant humanitarian crisis. It was the onset of fighting between Serbian (formally, Yugoslav) military and police units and the KLA, and especially the use of disproportionate force by the Serbs against civilians in Kosovo, in early 1998 that prompted U.S. and international efforts to mediate the conflict. Those who sought to end the crisis through negotiations confronted two challenges. The first was familiar from the conflicts in Croatia and Bosnia: how to reconcile greater autonomy for Kosovo with the sovereignty and territorial integrity of Yugoslavia. The second was how to prevent increasing, and increasingly violent, confrontations in Kosovo between the Yugoslav military and police and the KLA from undermining the negotiation effort. Negotiators were thus entering into yet another zero-sum game, this time involving the LDK, the KLA, and Belgrade. U.S. policymakers attempted to resolve the contradiction between autonomy and sovereignty by undertaking diplomatic efforts in the spring of 1998 to formulate an agreement between Belgrade and the LDK leadership. An intensive drafting process was carried out by the U.S. State Department, involving both Belgrade and an LDK-sponsored group in Prishtina in bilateral negotiations with U.S. diplomats, but not with each other. By the fall of 1998, however, neither Milosevic nor the LDK leadership enjoyed even the limited freedom to bargain that had allowed them to conclude the education agreement two years earlier. The emergence of the KLA made it impossible for the LDK to compromise on its long-standing demand for independence. At the same time, the increasing popular authority of the KLA relative to the LDK, and the apparent likelihood that the KLA would quickly gain power in a self-governing Kosovo, made it impossible for the Serbian side to settle for anything less than reaffirmation of Kosovo as an integral part of Serbia.

In Bosnia negotiators also faced multiple actors with conflicting interests. But in Bosnia, when the United States undertook its effort to end the fighting, it enjoyed direct or, in the case of the Bosnian Serbs, indirect leverage over all the parties. In Kosovo, in contrast, U.S. leverage over the LDK and Milosevic was rapidly declining by 1998, and the United States enjoyed no leverage at all over the KLA. The October 1998 agreement reached between Richard Holbrooke and Milosevic, for example, fell apart when Serbian compliance with Holbrooke's demands for force reductions and withdrawals were exploited by the KLA to expand its presence and power in Kosovo. Thus, by the end of 1998, negotiations had become futile.

The United States and its allies then attempted to impose a settlement on all the parties in early 1999. They demanded that both the KLA and Serbia cease the violence in Kosovo and enter into negotiations mediated by U.S. and allied negotiators, to be based on a draft developed by them but already rejected by both sides in late 1998. These negotiations, conducted at Rambouillet, represented an attempt by the United States to coerce both sides into an agreement that was acceptable to neither by means of a threat of force. The U.S. effort failed to offer the positive inducements required for a strategy of coercive diplomacy to succeed, as it did in Bosnia. The United States simply could not compel the KLA to comply with any settlement with which Milosevic might agree, as the KLA was unprepared to compromise its commitment to achieve independence by force of arms. Thus, the U.S. strategy in Kosovo quickly degenerated into a straightforward exercise in coercion, carried out in the form of an allied air campaign against Serbia. From the perspective of the KLA, this represented a successful outcome; it seemed to replicate the use of force by the United States to partition Bosnia.

Despite the capitulation of Milosevic and the Serbs in June 1999, the conflict in Kosovo has not yet been fully resolved. It seems clear that the legacy of interethnic violence that accompanied the fighting between the KLA and Serbian forces, and especially the violence carried out by Serbian forces against Kosovo civilians in 1998 and 1999, precludes the restoration of Serbian control over the province, even if changes under way in Serbia were to result in the establishment of a stable democratic state. The province has been placed under United Nations administration, and determination of its final status has been put off for some as-yet-undefined period. Conflict between Serbs and Albanians in the province persists. At the same time, conflict among competing political factions of Kosovar Albanians makes it unlikely that a stable, democratic system will be established within Kosovo in the near future. Kosovo, like Bosnia, has become a de facto international protectorate, the ultimate status of which remains indeterminate. Negotiations to resolve this issue are proving difficult to establish, as the two sides continue to disagree on the preconditions and structure of such discussions.

Conclusion

This review suggests that the structure of conflicts contributes to intractability by limiting the options available to mediators. Structure includes the nature of the issues in contention, the quality of political leadership among the conflicting parties, and the dynamics of electoral competition and the definition of elite constituencies. Although third-party mediation could not move intractable conflicts in Croatia and Bosnia toward resolution through negotiation, mediator involvement did not aggravate these conflicts. The behaviors of all parties, including their use of force, were constrained by concern for the consequences of their actions in negotiations. Where negotiations were accompanied by an international presence on the ground—whether observers or peacekeepers—this constraint was even stronger, even though it was insufficient to prevent egregious violence. It is more difficult to make this argument for Kosovo, where mediation rapidly gave way to coercive bombing, which triggered a Serbian plan to expel much of the ethnic Albanian population, carried out with great violence against innocent civilians. It seems clear, however, that the conflict between the KLA and Serbian forces that prompted the mediation effort and bombing would have continued to escalate, perhaps triggering the expulsion effort.

Nonetheless, mediation in these intractable conflicts suffered from certain deficiencies that might have been avoidable even in the face of such constraints. In Croatia and Bosnia, mediation efforts were not supported by a credible threat of force that might have compelled the parties to negotiate in good faith. The success of coercive diplomacy in Bosnia suggests that the threat of force may be most effective when significant positive incentives to compromise are also present. But as the Kosovo case makes clear, reliance on the threat of force may lead to the use of force; when coercive diplomacy fails, the only option left is simple coercion. As these cases suggest, coercing parties to cease fighting and accept an agreement drafted by outside experts is unlikely to resolve the issues underlying an intractable conflict, especially existential issues of the kind that motivated violence in Bosnia and Kosovo.

The cases reviewed here also suggest that mediators of intractable conflicts ought not to attempt to develop a "solution" of their own. The conflicting parties will have no vested interest of their own in making such a solution work. Mediators should focus instead on ensuring that the parties to the conflict work in good faith to find one of their own and facilitate their efforts to do so. Identifying or constructing a common positive inducement or incentive for all parties to compromise is critical to this approach. The dissolution of Yugoslavia presented an opportunity to use international recognition as such an inducement, but this opportunity was lost.

The failure of mediators to use recognition as a positive inducement to good-faith negotiation in these cases reflects a dilemma inherent in the very notion of third-party mediation: as outsiders to the conflict, mediators bring the understandings, preferences, and interests of their sponsoring states, institutions, and organizations to the process of negotiation. In the cases at hand, the multilateral mandates of mediators were characterized by conflicting understandings, preferences, and interests that complicated the task of ensuring appropriate international support for the outcomes of negotiations. The fateful decision to recognize the Yugoslav republics as states before reaching agreed-on solutions to the territorial, political, and existential conflicts associated with their dissolution, as well as the decision not to use or even threaten to use force in support of negotiations, reflected the understandings, preferences, and interests of some sponsors of the mediation effort, but by no means all.

These factors may also lead mediators to continue negotiations when a realistic assessment of the probability of success might suggest otherwise. A strong argument could be made that mediators should have responded to the failure of the conflicting parties in Bosnia to accept the Vance-Owen plan in April 1993 by withdrawing. However, by this time some of the sponsoring states had committed troops, treasure, and prestige to the mediation effort, leading them to block any alternative other than to continue that effort. While David Owen accepted this, Cyrus Vance did not. Vance's resignation as cochair of the ICFY should have been a signal to all states concerned that they needed to change their Bosnian strategy. In the end, however, neither the interests of the conflicting parties themselves, nor the force of international law and norms, nor the preferences of individual mediators, nor even moral principles weighed as heavily as the political-security interests of the most powerful outside actors in shaping the negotiating strategies, processes, and outcomes in these intractable conflicts.

Notes

1. For a collection of maps illustrating such competing claims, see Stevan Zec, ed., *Karte nasih podela: Politicki atlas jugoslovenskih zemalja u 20. veku* (Belgrade: BMG, 1991).

2. For comparative social and economic data for the regions in 1984, see Federal Statistical Office, *Yugoslavia 1945–1985: Statistical Review* (Belgrade: Federal Statistical Office, 1986), 180ff. For an analysis of regional differences, see Dijana Plestina, *Regional Development in Communist Yugoslavia* (Boulder, Colo.: Westview Press, 1992).

3. See Steven L. Burg, "Elite Conflict in Post-Tito Yugoslavia," *Soviet Studies* 38, no. 2 (April 1986): 170–193.

4. For an overview, see Lenard J. Cohen, *Broken Bonds: The Disintegration of Yugoslavia* (Boulder, Colo.: Westview Press, 1993).

5. For analyses of the elections in Croatia, Bosnia, Serbia, and Macedonia, see Karen Dawisha and Bruce Parrott, eds., *Politics, Power and the Struggle for Democracy in South-East Europe* (Cambridge: Cambridge University Press, 1997).

6. See Steven L. Burg, "Bosnia-Herzegovina: A Case of Failed Democratization," in *Politics, Power and the Struggle for Democracy in South-East Europe*, 122–145. For a more comprehensive treatment of the conflict in Bosnia, see Steven L. Burg and Paul S. Shoup, *The War in Bosnia-Hercegovina: Ethnic Conflict and International Intervention* (Armonk, N.Y.: M. E. Sharpe, 1999).

7. The electoral dynamics of Serbia are analyzed in Robert Thomas, *The Politics of Serbia in the 1990s* (New York: Columbia University Press, 1999).

8. Burg and Shoup, *The War in Bosnia-Hercegovina*, 80–81.

9. See, for example, *Declaration on Yugoslavia* of the Extraordinary EPC [European Political Cooperation] Ministerial Meeting, Rome, November 8, 1991.

10. Saadia Touval draws the same conclusion in *Mediation and the Yugoslav Wars: The Critical Years, 1990–95* (New York: Palgreave, 2002), 46–47.

11. For a detailed account of these negotiations, see ibid., 87, 102.

12. For a detailed account, see Burg and Shoup, *The War in Bosnia-Hercegovina.*

13. Herbert S. Okun, as cited in *New York Times*, July 11, 1993, IV, 7.

14. The emergence of this strategy is detailed in Burg and Shoup, *The War in Bosnia-Hercegovina*, 322–360.

15. For an assessment of the situation in Kosovo in the aftermath of Dayton, see the report of a December 1995 field mission to Kosovo in Barnett R. Rubin, ed., *Toward Comprehensive Peace in South East Europe* (New York: Twentieth Century Fund Press, 1996), 47ff.

16. The author makes this argument in "Coercive Diplomacy in the Balkans: The U.S. Use of Force in Bosnia and Kosovo," in *The United States and Coercive Diplomacy*, ed. Robert J. Art and Patrick M. Cronin (Washington, D.C.: United States Institute of Peace Press, 2003), 57–118.

9

Angola

The End of an Intractable Conflict

Paul Hare

Causes of Conflict

The Struggle for Independence

The original causes of the civil conflict in Angola can be traced back to the struggle for independence against the Portuguese colonial regime. Three liberation movements, each finding its roots in different geographic and ethnic areas, fought against Portuguese rule and, more often, among themselves. The Frente de Libertação de Moçambique (FNLA) drew its strength primarily from the Bakongo people in the north; the base for the National Union for the Total Independence of Angola (UNITA) was in the south among the Ovimbundu ethnic group, the largest tribal group in Angola, constituting about 40 percent of the population; and the power base of the Popular Movement for the Liberation of Angola (MPLA) resided among the Kimbundu along with some whites and *mesticos* concentrated heavily in the capital, Luanda. None of the liberation movements dominated or drew support from the majority of the population, which could have facilitated a more orderly transition to independence, as was the case in Zambia (the United National Independence Party), Mozambique (Frelimo), South Africa (the African National Congress [ANC]), and Namibia (the South West Africa People's Organization [SWAPO]). Even in Zimbabwe, Robert Mugabe's Zimbabwe African National Union clearly bested Joshua Nkomo's Zimbabwe African People's

Union in the elections in 1980, which most likely ensured a greater degree of stability, at least during the early years of independence, than might otherwise have been the case.

The Cold War

During the years of the Cold War, Angola's internal war became further intertwined with regional and international rivalries that polarized Angolan society and enveloped the conflict in the ideological trappings of the East-West confrontation. The MPLA followed a Marxist-Leninist line and received military equipment and advisers from the Soviet Union and troops from Cuba. While the FNLA, previously supported by the United States, was eliminated on the battlefield during 1975–76, UNITA retreated to the south to regroup and rebuild. In the eyes of many in the West, especially in Washington, UNITA and, more specifically, its leader, Jonas Savimbi, became symbols of resistance to the spread of communism in Africa. Four armies (FAA, FAPLA, Cuba, and South Africa) waged war on Angolan soil in seesaw battles during the 1980s. In a larger sense, Angola's civil war became a subset of rivalries pitting the United States against the Soviet Union and Cuba, and South Africa against the SWAPO and ANC bases in Angola and communist hegemony in the southern African region.

     This episode in Angola's history came to a close with the agreements leading to the independence of Namibia and the withdrawal of Cuban troops from Angola at the end of the decade. The coupling of these agreements and the end of the Cold War changed the internal dynamics of the conflict in Angola. The asserted ideological differences separating the MPLA and UNITA largely evaporated as both parties, at least in principle, began to embrace free markets and democratic institutions. The international and regional dimensions of the conflict diminished with the removal of the Cuban and South African armies from Angola.

The Post–Cold War Period

The next phase of the conflict was waged between the armies of the government and UNITA. While some observers argued that the roots of the conflict were essentially tribal, the significance of this tribal character can be unduly magnified, as considerable crisscrossing of tribal and racial boundaries occurred. Indeed, during three decades of fighting, neither the MPLA nor UNITA ever really attempted to identify the "enemy" strictly along ethnic lines. Perhaps more important than tribal considerations was the geographic and physical divide between the city and the countryside—that is, between the elites living in the cities and controlling the levers of power and wealth and the peasantry cultivating the land. In this sense, geographic, economic, tribal, and racial differences reinforce one another in creating a great divide in Angolan society.

The winding down of the Cold War brought another significant change to Angola's internal conflict. Whereas before, the parties had relied principally upon external sources for support, financing, and patronage, these sources dried up. Both sides found other ways to arm and feed their military machines. The government relied on oil, which was steadily growing in volume because of new discoveries offshore. UNITA mined diamonds, principally from alluvial deposits in Angola's riverbeds located in the northeastern part of the country. The amount of money generated from Angola's natural resources was staggering and promoted a culture of corruption. In one sense, the conflict became a war over resources from which the elites could profit.

Another factor contributed to the impasse. On the one hand, the MPLA-controlled government dominated virtually all areas of life where it exercised authority. Originally, the government established a one-party state based on socialist principles, but it subsequently adopted a multi-party system and began to liberalize the economy, though the legacy of past ideologies and thinking still persisted in some quarters. On the other hand, Jonas Savimbi was a leader of undoubted charisma but also immense ambition, so much so that many observers concluded he would never be satisfied unless he ruled over Angola. These were combustible elements, which help to explain why the conflict endured for so long.

The Death of Savimbi

The death of Savimbi at the end of February 2002 dramatically altered the situation in Angola and raised the prospect that the conflict might finally be resolved. More will be said about this development at the end of the chapter.[1]

Five Phases of Peacemaking

1. Liberation Struggles and the Alvor Agreement

During the 1960s and the first part of the 1970s, the struggle against Portuguese rule in Angola had several characteristics. The first was the proliferation of and divisions within the liberation movements themselves. At one point, up to eleven separate liberation movements were organized, though eventually three dominant movements emerged (MPLA, FNLA, and UNITA). Each of these movements experienced serious internal difficulties. For example, a prominent MPLA leader, Daniel Chipenda, defected and joined forces with Holden Roberto's FNLA in what was known as the Eastern Revolt. Jonas Savimbi had been the FNLA's foreign minister before resigning in 1964 and establishing his own movement, UNITA. Coupled with this pattern of internal dissension was the degree to which the liberation movements fought against one another to defend their turf and gain ascendancy.

The large-scale intervention of outside actors, regional and international, was another recurring motif of the early Angolan conflict. While outside assistance was originally provided and justified in order to combat colonialism, Angola quickly got sucked up in the Cold War. External intervention and support hardened the positions on all sides, militarized the conflict even more, and made deal making among the parties much more difficult.

A third characteristic was the tactic of pitting one movement against another, a tactic previously employed to extend Portuguese control over Angola. Each movement accused the others of cooperating with the Portuguese to advance its own military and political agenda. For example, Savimbi allegedly entered a pact with the Portuguese authorities in 1972, under which UNITA would cooperate against the MPLA in return for Portuguese recognition of a UNITA operational zone in eastern and central Angola. These perceptions fueled distrust among the combatants and their leaders about the motives of the other parties to the anticolonial struggle.

The Organization of African Unity (OAU) and some African leaders attempted intermittently to promote reconciliation and unity among the liberation movements, but any agreement reached was quickly struck down. Only after the coup in Lisbon in 1974 did the three liberation leaders, Agostinho Neto, Holden Roberto, and Jonas Savimbi, agree to negotiate jointly Angola's independence from Portugal, thus setting the stage for the negotiations leading to the Alvor Agreement of January 15, 1975. This was the first time that a colonial power had negotiated an agreement with three separate national liberation movements, all of which were recognized by the OAU.

The Alvor Agreement rapidly fell apart, as FNLA and MPLA militants clashed in Luanda. In a last-ditch effort to salvage the accords, President Jomo Kenyatta summoned the three liberation leaders to Nakuru, Kenya, in June 1975. The Nakuru Declaration reaffirmed the Alvor Agreement and described why the situation in Angola had deteriorated so drastically. Among the reasons it cited was "the introduction of great quantities of arms by the liberation movements," which was attributed "to the fact that the liberation movements have maintained their mutual lack of confidence resulting from their political and ideological differences and their divergences in the past."

While the Nakuru Declaration did not explicitly refer to the role of Portugal, the colonial power bears the major responsibility for the failure to implement the terms of the Alvor Agreement. Following the "Revolution of Carnations" in 1974 by disgruntled Portuguese military officers, the new regime in Lisbon was determined to dismantle Portugal's empire with virtually no regard to what would follow. The Alvor accords, which provided an unduly compressed timetable and organization for the transition to independence in Angola, never got off the ground. Portuguese security and police forces were withdrawn from the interior, and only a skeleton police presence was maintained in Luanda. The Portuguese governor general maneuvered to ensure that the reins of power were handed over to the MPLA, which, in fact, happened. By the time independence arrived, hundreds of thousands of Portuguese had left Angola in haste, leaving behind a power vacuum and three contending liberation movements to fight it out among themselves. When a steady hand could have made a difference, Portugal demonstrated that it did not have the will and commensurate resources to maintain law and order during the crucial transition from colonial to independent rule.

In the end, the Portuguese transferred power to the "Angolan people" on November 10, 1975, and Neto proclaimed himself president of the People's Republic of Angola the next day. The FNLA and UNITA retaliated by announcing the formation of a second government in Huambo. The dynamics of the battlefield shaped the final outcome. The MPLA/Soviet/Cuban triumvirate crushed the FNLA's advance toward Luanda from the north and thwarted the South African/UNITA attack from the south. Leery of further involvement and still recovering from the aftershocks of Vietnam, the United States absented itself from Angola with the passage of the Clark Amendment in December 1975. Isolated and feeling betrayed by the Americans, South Africa withdrew its troops from Angola. UNITA retreated to the bush to rebuild its organization and conduct guerrilla warfare. In February 1976 the OAU recognized the MPLA as the legitimate government of Angola and abandoned its previous position of calling for the formation of a national unity government that could promote a spirit of national reconciliation among the contending parties.

In retrospect, this first effort to secure a peaceful and independent Angola was doomed to failure. Too many forces were pulling the country apart. Regional and ethnic differences had led to three separate liberation movements, each distrustful of the others for their own very good reasons. The intervention of outside powers, small and big, had provided the resources and equipment for each movement to continue its struggle and resist compromise. The few African initiatives to promote cooperation and reconciliation lacked muscle and paled in significance to the larger forces tearing the country apart. Finally, the colonial power failed to prepare Angola and its people for the day when they would be responsible for governing themselves, and when the moment of independence arrived, they proved woefully inadequate to the task.

2. The Cold War and the Primacy of Regional Diplomacy

During the 1980s Angola's civil war became engulfed in a larger regional conflict in which the Americans, South Africans, Cubans, and Soviets were central actors. South Africa's strategy was to provide assistance to UNITA in the southern regions of Angola and deny SWAPO forces, based in Angola, access to Namibia. Throughout the decade, South African/UNITA military contingents clashed with Angolan/Cuban forces in periodic battles. Each could claim its share of victories, but neither side prevailed.

The diplomacy of this period focused on a regional strategy driven by the United States. The objectives were twofold and linked—the withdrawal of Cuban (and South African) troops from Angola and the independence of Namibia, then under South African control. The American diplomatic effort was sustained, continued over eight years, and involved highly complex (and exhausting) diplomatic minuets among the Angolans, Cubans, and South Africans. At a later stage, the Russians and the United Nations were brought into the game. Diplomacy ultimately prevailed with the signing of the New York Principles in July 1988. Even more important, the terms of the agreement were implemented. The Cuban troops left Angola ahead of schedule; the South Africans withdrew behind the Orange River; and Namibia achieved its independence.

The various accords did not directly address Angola's civil war or its resolution. No reference was made to UNITA in the formal agreements, though part of the deal struck between the Angolans and the South Africans was a trade-off under which South Africa would stop providing military support to UNITA and Angola would close ANC bases in its territory.

Was this an opportunity missed? Various voices, including South Africa and UNITA, had called for reconciliation between the two Angolan parties during the negotiations, though South Africa stopped short of making this point a prerequisite to a regional settlement. The United States supported the concept in principle but resisted any attempt to link the internal struggle to the broader diplomatic agenda. It feared that any effort to proceed along these lines would divert attention and could scuttle the negotiations. Instead, the United States believed (or hoped) that by resolving the Namibian and Cuban questions, the way would be paved for a subsequent political settlement of Angola's internal war. In Chester Crocker's words: "There was simply no action-forcing event or coercive pressure that could possibly produce 'reconciliation first'—in either Angola or South Africa. We could not just 'demand' it; had we tried, our partners would have run for the exits. Cuban troop withdrawal *had* to be the engine to drive the train of Angolan reconciliation."[2] After the repeal of the Clark Amendment in 1985, which permitted the resumption of military assistance to UNITA, the United States believed that U.S. aid to UNITA could be used as a quid pro quo to promote a settlement of Angola's civil war.

In the latter half of 1988, the United States and South Africa urged President Denis Sassou-Nguesso of the Republic of Congo to take an active role in promoting the national reconciliation agenda in Angola. Sassou-Nguesso organized a series of meetings with several African countries, which helped establish the concept of and lay the groundwork for an "African solution" to Angola's conflict. At a more concrete level, the United States provided a paper on basic principles for national reconciliation to the Congolese, the MPLA, UNITA, and the Cubans in an effort to get the parties thinking about the framework for an internal settlement.

These were limited steps intended to lay the seeds for future negotiations. Throughout the 1980s, U.S. diplomacy had remained focused on the big regional picture and the larger stakes that were involved in getting the Cubans out of Angola, and the South Africans out of Angola and Namibia. Resolution of Angola's internal struggle was deemed important but contingent upon grasping firmly the elusive prize of a regional settlement. In the immediate term, the United States continued to support UNITA. The objective was not to topple the MPLA government in Luanda, which was beyond the reach of UNITA and U.S. capabilities, but to maintain a military balance and prevent the MPLA from dominating the battlefield. The United States had no intention of ditching UNITA in the aftermath of a regional settlement. The political costs would have been too high. A cynic might have been tempted to proceed otherwise in the belief that such an approach would hasten the end of war through military means and better secure America's long-term interests in the oil sector.

3. Failed African Initiatives

In the latter part of 1988 and 1989, a number of African leaders became involved in an effort to promote reconciliation in Angola building upon the earlier initiatives of Sassou-Nguesso. President Mobuto Sese Seko of Zaire obtained the support of more than a dozen African leaders to press for a settlement. The United States actively supported and encouraged this process. The USSR also signaled its interest in a political settlement as it sought to disengage from costly overseas adventures. Although President José Eduardo dos Santos initially took a hard line and called for the neutralization of UNITA, the Angolan government began to soften its position. In June 1989, Mobuto hosted a conference in Gbadolite, Zaire, attended by seventeen African heads of state. President dos Santos and Savimbi were present, but, significantly, no face-to-face talks occurred between the two leaders.

At the end of two days, the conference produced a written communiqué that included an agreed-upon date for a cease-fire and the procedural steps to conduct full-fledged negotiations. A dispute, however, arose immediately over what had been agreed to. The specific bone of contention involved Savimbi's fate under the prospective peace arrangements. President Kenneth Kuanda of Zambia told a press conference that Savimbi had agreed to go temporarily into exile in order to facilitate the peace process, an assertion that Mobuto quickly repudiated. This contretemps effectively jettisoned the talks. A number of efforts were subsequently made to put the pieces back together, but they all failed. By the end of 1989, major fighting had erupted in the southeast of the country, reportedly involving some thirty to forty thousand Angolan army and UNITA troops.

The African initiatives failed for a number of reasons, among which were the legacy of distrust between the government and UNITA and the fact that both had the resources to continue the war. The Angolan government seemed particularly intransigent, possibly because it was buoyed by the withdrawal of South African troops from Angola (while a substantial number of Cubans remained in-country) and brighter economic prospects occasioned by its acceptance into the International Monetary Fund and World Bank and the signing of new oil concessions. The Angolan government also did not want to confer legitimacy upon Savimbi through the negotiating process, hence its reluctance to enter into face-to-face talks with UNITA. The proliferation of mediators with different agendas hampered the negotiations, of which the debacle at Gbadolite was a prime example. Finally, the Africans had to rely almost exclusively on persuasion to achieve their ends.

4. The Bicesse Accords

A combination of factors contributed to the next phase of peacemaking in Angola. The winding down of the Cold War had the twofold effect of lessening superpower interests in Angola and facilitating superpower cooperation to end the civil war. The Soviet Union wanted to diminish its financial commitments to Angola, which had accumulated a $6 billion debt, mainly for the purchase of Soviet arms. In addition, the Angolan army's major offensive in the southeast had bogged down. The chances for a decisive victory by either side seemed remote, despite the intensity and scale of the military offensive, which had inflicted heavy costs on both sides. Even with the withdrawal of South African troops from Angola, UNITA had demonstrated that it had a formidable military machine, which was capable of operating in different sectors of the country and could not be easily destroyed.

Largely in response to the military stalemate and under prompting by the United States and the Soviet Union, dos Santos finally agreed to hold direct talks with UNITA. This agreement represented a major breakthrough and paved the way for secret exploratory talks between the two parties in Portugal in April 1991. This was to be the first of six rounds of talks that would lead to the signing of the Bicesse Accords in Portugal on May 31, 1991. Under the new mediation scenario, Portugal hosted the talks and the United States and the Soviet Union attended as observers, forming what became known as the Troika, comprising the former colonial power and the two former superpower patrons of UNITA and the MPLA. This group had far more influence over the parties than the Africans ever had and offered real hope that peace in Angola might be achieved.

The Bicesse Accords called for a cease-fire, confinement, and demobilization of the respective armed forces, formation of a national army of forty thousand drawn equally from UNITA and the MPLA, and multiparty elections monitored by the United Nations. The agreement included the "Triple Zero" provision, under which the Troika would not provide military equipment to either side and would use their good offices to discourage others from providing arms. The pivot of Bicesse was the holding of multiparty elections, the first in Angola's history. Elections were held in September 1992 and were declared to be "generally free and fair" by the UN special representative, but the peace collapsed soon after and the country tumbled back into an even more vicious war than before.

Various reasons are cited for the failure of Bicesse. Some, including the UN special representative, Margaret Anstee, claimed that the UN mission (the United Nations Angola Verification Mission, UNAVEM II) was inadequately funded to carry out the responsibilities that had been entrusted to it. Given that UNAVEM II had a budget of $118 million and 350 military observers, 126 police observers, and 100 electoral observers, this point had validity, especially when compared with other peacekeeping missions, such as those in Namibia and Mozambique. The United Nations also did not have a clear-cut role for overseeing the process. For example, the Joint Political-Military Commission, which had this oversight responsibility, was chaired alternately by the MPLA and UNITA, while the United Nations and the Troika sat in as observers.

The UN secretary-general, Boutros Boutros-Ghali, said the primary cause for the breakdown was the incomplete implementation of the military provisions of the accords. The two armies had not been effectively disarmed or demobilized, nor had the new national army been organized in any accepted sense of the word prior to the elections. This defect proved to be crucial. During the cantonment period, UNITA kept its military force largely intact and was able to move quickly on the offensive following the elections. In contrast, the government's less disciplined forces virtually disintegrated during the demobilization period. In the fighting that followed the elections, the government survived principally through the deployment of the Rapid Intervention Police, which had been established with Spanish assistance during the period leading up to the elections.

It is also said that the Bicesse process failed because it was based on a "winner-take-all" formula, which made the elections essentially a zero-sum game. You either won or lost at the ballot box, with no provision for sharing power following the electoral process. This point has merit, but it does not take sufficiently into account the potential role the opposition could have played in the National Assembly and in Luanda's public arena. UNITA won about one-third of the legislative vote, 70 seats out of a 220-member assembly, and this bloc would have carried significant political weight, despite the limited powers of the National Assembly.

Many factors contributed to Bicesse's failure, including the history of deep distrust between the parties, inadequate resources to fund the peace process, the residual military capabilities of the parties, the parties' access to natural resources, the lack of a clearly defined role for the United Nations, the "winner-take-all" election conundrum, and the incomplete implementation of the military integration process prior to the elections. These reasons do not, however, fully or even satisfactorily explain why the process failed. The basic problem was that Savimbi lost the elections, which he thought he would win. An astute observer, Tony Hodges, put it this way: "The failure to achieve peace in Angola cannot therefore be explained purely in structural terms. Besides the rivalry over access to resources and the general problem of mutual lack of confidence, a key factor has been the psychological makeup of Jonas Savimbi. His role in the Angolan conflict confirms the importance of the individual in history." Hodges further explained that Savimbi had a messianic sense of destiny that had driven him to seek absolute power for three decades. These are qualities that do not lend themselves to "compromise or to playing second fiddle in a regime headed by someone else."[3]

Savimbi was not prepared to accept defeat at the ballot box or to go through with the second round of presidential elections, which was required by law since dos Santos had failed by a whisker to obtain an absolute majority of the popular vote. Instead, Savimbi chose to continue his quest for power in other ways. He nearly succeeded.

5. The Lusaka Protocol

Several initiatives were taken to put the Bicesse peace process back on track following the outbreak of hostilities after the September 1992 elections. During April and May 1993, the UN special representative, Margaret Anstee, conducted marathon negotiations lasting six weeks in Abidjan, Côte d'Ivoire, which produced a draft document called the Protocol of Abidjan. Although the government delegation was prepared to initial the draft protocol, UNITA balked at the provision calling for the quartering of its troops. Its delegation maintained that any troop withdrawals should be delayed until UN peacekeepers were deployed and *both armies* were quartered, which meant that the two parties would be treated equally, as had been the case under the Bicesse Accords. This position was a deal breaker for both the government and the mediators.

The prospects for resolving the Angolan conflict darkened following the collapse of the Abidjan talks. The UN Security Council reacted by condemning UNITA and adopting an arms and petroleum embargo in September. The resolution contained the additional threat of further sanctions, including trade and travel restrictions, unless UNITA complied with the terms of the resolution. In a demonstration of where it stood, the United States established diplomatic relations with Angola in May 1993. UNITA tried to avoid the sanctions measures. It declared a unilateral cease-fire and issued a seven-point communiqué that reaffirmed the validity of the Bicesse Accords and reiterated UNITA's acceptance of the September 1992 elections.

Why did UNITA extend an olive branch to the government and the international community at this time? The imposition of sanctions and the prospect of more played a role, though the dynamics of the battlefield were probably more influential in shaping UNITA's decisions. By September 1993 UNITA controlled 70 percent of Angolan territory, including the important provincial towns of Huambo and Uige, the major airfield of Negage, and the diamond center of Cafundo. It had occupied the oil town of Soyo. Despite these battlefield successes, UNITA had created a long logistical tail that made it difficult to provide fuel and supplies to its far-flung troops. Meanwhile, the government had not been idle. It recruited mercenaries, increased the size of its army, trained elite commando units, and purchased massive amounts of arms and military equipment to redress the military imbalance. UNITA must have calculated that as the prize of Luanda itself remained beyond reach, the best course would be to consolidate its military position and to repair its political image with the international community by engaging in peace talks. The announcement of a unilateral cease-fire was intended to freeze the battlefield situation, which still favored UNITA.

The stage was thus set for another major initiative to resolve Angola's civil war. For more than a year, the two parties conducted another round of negotiations to end the internal conflict, under the aegis of the new UN special representative, Alouine Blondin Beye, assisted by the Troika observers. While the talks proceeded at a snail's pace in Lusaka, Zambia, the war inside Angola escalated and the humanitarian crisis grew, though the balance of power increasingly favored the government. Despite repeated calls by the mediation team for a halt to the fighting, the government followed a classic "fight-and-talk" strategy. UNITA fought back but steadily lost ground to the government's forces.

The Lusaka negotiations produced a complex document comprising annexes, general principles, specific principles, and modalities. Its central thesis was, however, quite simple. On the one hand, UNITA would disarm its military wing and become a legitimate political party. Its soldiers could either join the national army or police or be reintegrated into civilian life. The UNITA generals would be incorporated into the military command structure. On the other hand, UNITA party members would be offered positions in the government at all levels—national, provincial, and local—and a government of national unity and reconciliation would be established. Its deputies would return to the National Assembly so that the party could participate fully in the political life of the country. A general amnesty would be proclaimed. A new round of elections would be held once the situation had stabilized. The UN special representative, in consultation with the parties, would establish the date.

Lusaka tried to learn from past lessons. The UN special representative led the negotiations and chaired the meetings of the Joint Commission, which was established to oversee the peace process. A substantial peacekeeping force, of more than seven thousand peacekeepers and military and police observers, was dispatched to Angola to implement the terms of the agreement. The calendar called for a careful sequencing of military and political steps, starting with a cease-fire and ending with the formation of a Government of National Unity and Reconciliation. By delaying the timetable for elections, the Joint Commission would avoid the "winner-take-all" scenario and provide an opportunity for the wounds of war to be healed.

Despite these efforts by the international community, Lusaka failed to bring peace to Angola, and the peace process ultimately collapsed in the latter part of 1998, plunging the country back into war. Some observers have argued that the peace process collapsed because the United Nations and the observers followed a policy of "see no evil" and failed to fault the parties when they violated the agreement, especially with respect to widespread human rights abuses. Both sides were thus encouraged to treat the United Nations with impunity. The government claimed that UNITA had used the cease-fire period as a shield to rearm and reequip its military forces and blamed the United Nations for allowing this to happen. UNITA charged that the government had employed a scorched-earth policy when state administration was extended into areas formerly under UNITA control, thus demonstrating the government's hegemonic objectives.

Some observers believed that none of the leaders intended to follow through with the peace accords since they had a vested interest in the prolongation of the war. Representatives of civil society maintained that their exclusion represented a fatal flaw in the peace process that would need to be redressed. Others thought that the peace agreement itself was fundamentally flawed in that inadequate provision was made to secure UNITA's essential interests in a new political order. On the opposite side, it was argued that Savimbi was never committed to the peace process. UNITA had signed the Lusaka Protocol only under duress and intense military pressure from the government.

The UN Security Council repeatedly stated that the primary reason for the failure of the Lusaka Protocol lay in UNITA's refusal to allow state administration to be fully extended into areas it controlled in the central highlands and to fulfill its disarmament obligations. For that reason, the Security Council kept in place the three sets of sanctions it had adopted against UNITA and sought to tighten their enforcement by the international community. In addition to the original arms and petroleum embargo, the sanctions included restrictions on travel, closing of UNITA offices overseas, freezing of bank assets, and curtailing of UNITA's diamond trade.

As in the case of the Bicesse process, much of the singular failure of the Lusaka peace process can be attributed to the inability of the United Nations to supervise effectively the disarmament and demobilization processes. The United Nations should not be blamed outright for this outcome, since the implementation of any peace agreement depends importantly on the political will of the parties to fulfill their obligations. There are finite limits to what can be expected of a peacekeeping force, unless it has clearly defined enforcement powers and the resources to back them up.

When all is said and done, however, the major responsibility for the collapse of the Lusaka process rests with UNITA and, more specifically, with its leader. In his darker moments, Savimbi would tellingly comment: "What leader has given up his arms and survived?" This statement reflected his deeply seated fears of abandoning the military struggle and his army. In fact, Savimbi had used the interim provided by the Lusaka peace process to strengthen his military position in order to fight again.

The Aftermath of Savimbi's Death

The death of Jonas Savimbi at the end of February 2002 dramatically altered the political landscape of Angola. Savimbi had been the undisputed, often ruthless, leader of UNITA and had been the principal stumbling block during the Bicesse and Lusaka peace processes. His death, coupled with the weakened military posture of UNITA, opened up new opportunities to end Angola's civil war.

The government had two options following the death of Savimbi. It could continue to conduct military operations with the objective of eliminating UNITA's remaining leadership in the bush, or it could reach out to UNITA's military and political command in order to obtain a cease-fire and end the conflict. For several weeks after Savimbi's death, the government sent mixed signals about the course it would pursue. Its position was clarified when the government announced on March 13 a cessation of offensive military operations in order to pave the way for talks with UNITA's leadership.

Following this breakthrough announcement, the two military commands met in the eastern town of Luena and quickly hammered out an agreement for a cease-fire and the modalities for the demobilization and integration of UNITA's military force. Significantly, these talks were conducted without any third parties present, though representatives of the United Nations and the Troika witnessed the initialing of the accords in Luena by the two military commands. The chiefs of staff of the two armies formally signed the Memorandum of Understanding, designated as an annex to the Lusaka Protocol, in Luanda on April 4, 2002, in the presence of numerous dignitaries, including President dos Santos and the interim leader of UNITA, Paulo Lukamba "Gato."

Most observers agree that the peace deal will stick this time. Although UNITA had the choice of continuing a guerrilla-style war, its prospects were bleak. Isolated internationally and faced with dwindling resources, what remained of its army would have been steadily decimated by the government's superior force. At a psychological level, the death of the only leader UNITA had known dealt a monumental blow to the movement and left the remaining leadership in a severely weakened position. The speed with which UNITA agreed to the cease-fire and the terms for the demobilization of its army reflected the precarious situation in which it found itself.

Implications

The Role of the Individual

The sudden turnaround in Angola has certain implications for intractable conflicts. It confirms the view of Tony Hodges and others who have spoken of the importance of the individual in shaping history. Savimbi had a larger-than-life presence on the Angolan stage for decades and had become an almost mythic figure, reviled by some and beloved by others. In his quest for power, he had in the end overreached against an adversary that possessed superior resources. The question may be asked if the outcomes would have been different during the two peace processes of the 1990s had Savimbi not been present. The answer is not clear-cut. Much would have depended upon who had followed him and the degree to which that person exercised control over a movement that had deep roots in the interior of the country. What can be said is that the prospects for a peaceful outcome would have improved dramatically without Savimbi, since there was no heir apparent in the wings who had his charisma, international reputation, and "messianic sense of destiny" to rule Angola.

The Difficulty of a Symmetrical Military Balance

Angola illustrates the difficulty of ending civil conflicts peacefully when the two sides are almost evenly matched militarily. During the two major international interventions in the 1990s, each side had the upper hand at times but could not deal a knockout blow or gain a decisive advantage over the other. In fact, the pendulum almost invariably swung back the other way. This equilibrium created an unstable environment for implementing agreements and building a durable peace. The situation at the beginning of 2002 was quite different from what had existed before. If not knocked out, UNITA was on the ropes. The government could essentially dictate the terms of settlement, albeit in conformance with the previously negotiated Lusaka Protocol that set the parameters and framework for the discussions.

The Question of Resources

Angola's abundant wealth of natural resources has been a curse, not a blessing. Access to oil and diamonds fueled the war machines of the government and UNITA, respectively, and had two major consequences. First, their access to resources gave the parties the option of returning to war if the political process did not unfold to their liking. This was Savimbi's choice after the elections in 1992 and later during the implementation phase of the Lusaka peace process. Second, access to resources gave the parties a large measure of independence and insulation against outside pressure and reduced the third parties' field of maneuver. This was in contrast to the situation in Mozambique, where the antagonists were strapped financially and had compelling reasons to settle their differences through means other than war. Angola's conflict would have been far less intractable and would probably have ended much sooner had oil and diamonds been removed from the equation. Lack of resources would also have given third-party interveners greater purchase over the antagonists.

The Mediators

The history of Angola's war illustrates continuity and change, with respect to both its causes and the nature of third-party intervention. The Portuguese, Americans, Africans, Russians, and the United Nations all played their roles in different degrees and with different results. Portugal's original objective was to get out of Angola as quickly as possible. The United States sought to freeze the internal situation pending resolution of the larger regional agenda involving the withdrawal of Cuban and South African troops from Angola and Namibian independence. The Africans attempted to promote reconciliation among the contending parties, but their efforts were not sustained, lacked backup, and faltered quickly.

The two most serious attempts to end Angola's war definitively occurred during the Bicesse and Lusaka peace processes. In both instances, the mediators involved a combination of the United Nations, Portugal, the United States, and the Soviet Union (Russia). The Bicesse formula had a certain logic, because the United States and the Soviet Union were the principal backers of UNITA and the government of Angola, respectively. Both supplied arms and military equipment and provided political support to their Angolan clients, which gave the two powers some leverage and influence over the parties. In addition, the United States could dangle the diplomatic recognition card before the government of Angola. The Portuguese brought a history of common language and experience to the negotiating table. The fact that the mediators were able to obtain an agreement represented a diplomatic triumph.

Lusaka represented a different context. The mix of mediators remained the same, reflecting Lusaka's direct link to Bicesse, but the United Nations was now put in overall charge of the process. The strengthened role of the United Nations was intended to rectify what had been perceived as a shortcoming of the Bicesse process, when the United Nations had been brought in almost as an afterthought. The role of the Troika remained essentially the same as it had been at Bicesse but, owing to changed circumstances, its utility has been questioned. Portugal and Russia were perceived to be aligned with the government, which reduced the credibility of the Troika.

The Troika also did not have the same cards to play at Lusaka. The United States had severed its military assistance relationship with UNITA and had recognized the Angolan government. Russia had effectively abandoned the triple-zero agreement banning the provision of military equipment to both sides. The only stick the mediation team had was the prospect of censure or sanctions by the Security Council. While this carried some weight with both parties, it was a blunt instrument that was difficult to apply tactically.

At one point, the British suggested establishing a "Friends of Angola" group in Luanda, similar to the one that had been successfully employed in Mozambique. While the proposal received sympathetic consideration in Washington, it was promptly shot down by Lisbon and Moscow, which did not wish to lose their privileged position in the peace process. The UN special representative also did not want to upset the existing mediation framework. In retrospect, it would have been useful, though certainly not decisive, to have a bloc of concerned but disinterested observers involved more closely in the process.

The United States played a key role in four of the five peace phases previously described. Even during the period leading up to independence, the United States provided material support to two of the three liberation movements. Its most prominent and direct leadership role occurred during the successful diplomatic effort to forge a regional settlement in the 1980s. At Bicesse and Lusaka, the United States coordinated with the Portuguese, Russians, and the United Nations, but it did not take the lead. It can be argued that the chances for success would have improved had the United States taken a larger leadership role, especially during the Lusaka process. This assumes that an arrangement with the United Nations could have been reached. The risks and responsibilities accruing to the United States would have been higher under this scenario, but the lines of authority would have been more clear-cut and could have carried more clout with the parties. That being said, it is unlikely that the final outcome would have materially changed had there been a different mix of mediators. If anything, the history of Angola underlines the limits of third-party intervention.

Mediation Tactics and Strategy

Were there any critical turning points when a different approach might have yielded a different outcome during the Bicesse and Lusaka peace processes? The failure to establish an integrated national army prior to the elections was the most important defect during the Bicesse process. Neither the government nor UNITA—nor many in the international community, for that matter—wanted to delay the elections timetable, which had been inscribed on the Bicesse calendar. It would have been difficult to stop the elections in midstream, unless the Security Council had demanded that the military provisions be completed before the elections were held. If the threat were to be real, the Security Council would have had to be prepared to withdraw the UN mission unless the parties complied with its demand.

The timelines contained in the Lusaka Protocol were longer than those in Bicesse and were not driven by an elections calendar, but the pace of implementing the protocol's terms was ragged and painfully slow because of the dilatory tactics of the parties, especially UNITA. Despite the slow pace, progress was registered in many areas and the country enjoyed relative stability compared with the 1993–94 period. The United Nations had good reason to remain engaged as long as progress could be observed. The big question mark related to the extent of UNITA's disarmament under the plan. Possibly only one-third, if that, of the troops that UNITA mobilized at the quartering areas were real soldiers. Many brought in no arms or arms of antique vintage. These were observable facts.

Should the United Nations (and the Joint Commission) have insisted that only "real soldiers with real weapons" be registered at the camps, even if this led to a breakdown of the process? The UN special representative believed it was important at all costs to keep the momentum moving forward in order to save the peace process. While the government criticized UNITA's military performance under the agreement, it stopped short of pulling out of the process, realizing that *all* of UNITA's troops would not be confined nor *all* of its weapons turned over to the United Nations. The government wanted, above all, to obtain UNITA's declaration, required under the protocol, that it was totally disarmed, which would mean that any nonquartered military or police would be deemed bandits.

Nevertheless, clearer and more robust public signals from the United Nations regarding compliance or lack thereof by the parties would have removed any ambiguities about what constituted unacceptable behavior. It would have solidified the United Nations' position as the final arbiter of the peace process and made it less vulnerable to the manipulations of either side.

Funding Peacekeeping Operations

As was previously pointed out, one of the defects of the Bicesse peacekeeping operation was inadequate funding for its mission. The support provided to the Lusaka peace process was far more substantial. Some observers assert that the Bicesse outcome would have been different had the UN mission been properly funded—that is, had there been more peacekeepers, electoral observers, and transportation capabilities and a generally more robust posture, the very weight and authority of the UN presence might have carried the day. This is questionable. First, funding did not spell the difference between success and failure during the Lusaka peace process, when $1 million per day was spent on the operation. Second, the quality of the people deployed, especially with regard to leadership, professional conduct, and language capability, can often be more important than sheer numbers. While a larger and more mobile UN electoral observer group would have helped, it is doubtful that such a group would have changed the final judgment on the outcome of the elections by the United Nations. Third, as a general proposition, adequate resources are secondary to the more fundamental issues of political will and a reasonable level of commitment by the parties themselves to the peace process.

The Importance of Continuity

The continued presence of the United Nations in Angola had on the whole a positive impact. It served as a point of contact with the government, opposition political parties, and representatives of civil society and offered the hope, and indeed the expectation of the international community, of an alternative to protracted war. When circumstances changed, the United Nations was able to reengage quickly with the parties. Equally important, the Security Council's insistence that the Lusaka Protocol

remained the most viable basis for achieving peace provided a lifeboat on
which all could climb aboard after Savimbi was killed.

Final Comment

The signing of the cease-fire agreement marks the end of Angola's armed
conflict but signals just the beginning of Angola's search for real peace.
Promoting national reconciliation, carrying out an effective demobilization
program, attending to the plight of Angola's internally displaced, moving
forward on the path of economic reform, repairing a devastated infrastructure, addressing corruption, and opening up real political space are
some of the challenges that the government faces. Resources and political
will are required to build a durable peace. The war can no longer be used
to explain why the government has not done more for its people.

Notes

1. An earlier version of this chapter was presented to the Working Group on
Intractable Conflicts at the United States Institute of Peace in January 2002, about
one month before Savimbi's death. The postscript—"The Aftermath of Savimbi's
Death"—was subsequently added.

2. Chester A. Crocker, *High Noon in Southern Africa: Making Peace in a
Rough Neighborhood* (New York: W. W. Norton, 1992), 291.

3. Tony Hodges, *Angola from Afro-Stalinism to Petro-Diamond Capitalism*
(Bloomington: Indiana University Press, 2001), 18–19.

10

Third Parties and Intractable Conflicts

The Case of Colombia

Cynthia J. Arnson
and Teresa Whitfield

THIS CHAPTER EXPLORES the intractability of Colombia's conflict and the challenge it has presented both to efforts to reach a negotiated settlement and to the engagement of third parties. We argue that, while the collapse of the peace process championed by President Andrés Pastrana (1998–2002) placed the obstacles to the settlement of the conflict in sharp relief, it also opened the conflict up to the international community as never before. The demise of the process was followed by an intensification of the war by both the guerrillas and the new administration of President Álvaro Uribe Vélez, inaugurated in August 2002. While declaring his openness to negotiations and to a UN role in peace talks, Uribe also set forth a series of preconditions for a resumption of dialogue with the insurgents, who themselves showed scant interest in returning to the bargaining table.

The chapter describes the causes of Colombia's conflict as internal and predominantly social. They are distinguished from the causes of the conflict's intractability by the fact that the latter resulted from the transformation of the conflict over the past four decades. We contend that the sources of intractability—which include the multiplicity and fragmentation of armed actors, the degradation of the conflict, and, perhaps above all, the fueling of the conflict by the availability to the armed actors of substantial economic resources, principally from the drug trade—present more challenges to the conflict's resolution than its original causes. The involvement of third parties has historically been limited by Colombian reluctance to countenance the participation of outside actors. Although the Pastrana process saw a greater openness to such actors than before, their involvement was further conditioned by U.S. policy, the weakness of the process itself, and ambivalence on all sides (including the United Nations). The experience served to drive home the fact that, when parties to the conflict lack the will, interested third parties cannot leverage a peace process and that there may be risks involved in trying to do so.

Within days of his election, Uribe turned a new page in the history of the Colombian peace process by holding forth the prospect, shunned by his predecessors, of opening direct talks with right-wing paramilitary groups.[1] Soon afterward he authorized contacts, facilitated by the Catholic Church, between his peace commissioner, Luis Carlos Restrepo, and paramilitary leaders. By December 2002 the majority of Colombia's paramilitaries, including most of the dominant group, the United Self-Defense Forces of Colombia (AUC), had announced a unilateral cease-fire and agreed to a formal process of negotiation with the government. This development altered the structural dynamics of the Colombian peace process in that it granted the paramilitaries the status of political actor, a development long pursued by the paramilitaries' cofounder, Carlos Castaño, but resisted by the Colombian government. However, by mid-2004 the talks had been thrown into crisis following the abduction and assumed murder of Castaño by rival paramilitary commanders. Castaño's disappearance was soon followed by the murder of a dissident AUC commander who, like Castaño, had criticized the organization's involvement in drug trafficking.

The AUC, like the two principal guerrilla groups, the Revolutionary Armed Forces of Colombia (FARC) and the smaller National Liberation Army (ELN), has been officially designated by the U.S. State Department as a foreign terrorist organization. Although the paramilitaries are frequently represented as somehow equivalent to the guerrillas—violent armed actors from the right in opposition to those on the left—their relationship to the government is quite different. Notwithstanding their current illegal status, their history is one of extensive links to and support by the state. Unlike the guerrillas they so bitterly oppose, paramilitaries do not purport to contest the state so much as to take its place in the large areas of the countryside from which the state is absent. Talks with them are therefore fraught with complications, not the least of which is deciding exactly what they will be offered in exchange for demobilization, given the paramilitaries' long history of participation in drug trafficking, human rights abuses, and the illegal acquisition of land and other resources during the course of the conflict. Indeed, critics of the peace process with the AUC charged that the group was using the talks to gain political legitimacy while escaping prosecution for human rights and drug trafficking crimes, all the while maintaining its hold on the lucrative drug trade.

The Pastrana Peace Process and the Role of the International Community

On February 20, 2002, President Andrés Pastrana ended a three-and-a-half-year peace process that had been at the center of his presidency. In an emotional address to the nation, Pastrana denounced that day's hijacking of an airplane and the kidnapping of the president of the Senate's Peace Commission by the FARC. He ordered the Colombian military to retake a demilitarized zone in southern Colombia, known as the *despeje*, the creation of which he had authorized at the beginning of his presidency in order to further talks with the FARC. While peace talks with the second of the country's insurgent groups, the ELN, would continue for a few more months—Pastrana abandoned them in May 2002—Colombia prepared for the escalation of its four-decade-old internal armed conflict to new levels.

The collapse of the Pastrana administration's peace process with the FARC had been long anticipated. In 1998, as presidential candidate of the Conservative Party, Pastrana had made the negotiation of an end to the conflict the principal focus of his campaign. Before Pastrana's inauguration, contacts with the FARC and a meeting with Manuel Marulanda, the organization's historic leader, had been enormously popular. However, these contacts kindled hopes that proved to be unfounded. Talks were slow to be initiated and soon became bogged down by procedural issues, the government's failure, in the eyes of the FARC, to take sufficiently strong measures against the paramilitaries, and a series of crises initiated by the FARC such as hijacking and the kidnapping and assassination of foreign nationals and prominent Colombians. Meanwhile, periodic renewals of the *despeje* invited public scrutiny of the minimal achievements of the peace process and the benefits derived from the zone by the FARC.[2] Rather than abandon the zone, and with it a process on which he had staked his presidency, in October 2001 Pastrana authorized stepped-up military operations around the area, leading the FARC to halt all contact with government representatives.

In the absence of progress, Pastrana announced on January 9, 2002, that he was ending what was by now seen by many as only a "virtual" peace process and giving the FARC just forty-eight hours to abandon the zone. The announcement was widely applauded within Colombia. But those forty-eight hours stretched into days as the United Nations and the international community were, for the first time in Colombia's many years of varied negotiations, drawn into a central role in the process. On January 10 the FARC announced that it was prepared to meet with James LeMoyne, the acting special adviser to the UN secretary-general on Colombia; Daniel Parfait, the French ambassador to Colombia, who was the coordinator of a group of ten "facilitating" countries of the talks between the government and the FARC; and representatives of the Catholic Church. Pastrana responded, on television, that he was extending the deadline to allow LeMoyne to meet with FARC negotiators. After intense discussions, the FARC accepted that the necessary guarantees existed for continuation of the peace talks and committed themselves to reach, with the government, a framework for a cease-fire by January 20, 2002.

The UN special adviser, all ten ambassadors of the facilitating commission, and representatives of the church witnessed the agreement that was eventually reached. It contemplated a more active role for the international community and proposed an ambitious timetable for the discussion of substantive issues such as paramilitaries, kidnapping, and an international verification commission. The timetable was to conclude with concrete agreements leading toward a cease-fire by April 7, 2002. The agreement represented a more specific program of work for negotiators than had yet been seen within the FARC process. But, in retrospect, it was also deeply unrealistic in its expectations of what either side was willing and able to negotiate and the time that would be necessary to do so. Skepticism within Colombia over its significance was exacerbated by a renewed military campaign by the FARC.

Interpretations of FARC actions on February 20, 2002—the airplane hijacking and kidnapping that prompted the breakdown of the process—varied. Most of those closest to the talks, including diplomats and government officials, were convinced that the actions had been ordered at a senior level. Some doubted that the FARC had actually meant to force an end to the process, while others believed that the FARC, faced with a "moment of truth" signified by the deadline for a cease-fire, simply lacked the political will to move forward.[3] Representatives of the international community who had played a part in exposing this hard reality were left wondering, not only whether intervening to avert the collapse of the talks in January had been the right thing to do, but also whether it might not have been a more healthy development in the long term if the Pastrana peace process had collapsed some two years earlier. As feared, the breakdown of the peace process was followed by the intensification of the conflict under pressure of a FARC offensive that included a stepped-up urban bombing campaign, an increase in kidnapping, and renewed efforts to regain territory lost to the paramilitaries.

One direct beneficiary of the situation was the independent rightist candidate for the presidency, Álvaro Uribe Vélez, who won an unprecedented victory in the first round of the presidential elections on May 26, 2002.[4] His triumph reflected popular support for a dramatic increase of military pressure on the guerrillas, widely blamed for the failure of the peace talks and for increased attacks on civilians. In promising to restore security, Uribe was in tune with developments in the United States, where a major shift in policy toward Colombia had begun in the wake of the attacks of September 11, 2001. As the United States mobilized to fight a global war on terrorism, administration and congressional officials were moving beyond an emphasis on counternarcotics in Colombia to the direct targeting of military assistance for counterterrorism operations. Unsurprisingly, Uribe's declared intention to escalate the war, including by doubling the size of the police and military, was met in kind by the FARC. In the weeks following his election, the FARC issued death threats against municipal and regional authorities across the country and pursued a sustained assault on the economic infrastructure. The stated aim of these campaigns was to render the country ungovernable.

As Uribe assumed the presidency on August 7, 2002, the FARC staged an apparent assassination attempt, launching an assault with homemade mortars and killing twenty-one people in a poor neighborhood adjacent to the presidential palace. Prospects for a negotiated settlement in Colombia had rarely been more distant. Yet Uribe surprised many when, within days of his election, he called on the United Nations to lend its "good offices" in pursuit of a negotiated settlement, a tacit acknowledgment that a third-party role in an eventual peace process had gained widespread acceptance within Colombia.

Uribe laid down strict conditions for a resumption of talks with the guerrillas: a cease-fire, an end to kidnapping and other terrorist acts against the civilian population, and the severing of ties to the drug trade. Although the same conditions were to apply to the paramilitaries, contacts and then talks with the latter were—unlike those with the insurgents—permitted within Colombia. Simultaneously, Uribe launched a "democratic security" policy aimed at more effectively prosecuting the war against the guerrillas and, at least in theory, the paramilitaries. He declared a "state of internal commotion," giving the government an array of emergency powers provided for in the Constitution; imposed a one-time tax on the wealthy to help finance the expansion of the armed forces;[5] established "zones of rehabilitation and consolidation," expanding military powers in two highly conflictive areas; and announced the establishment of a vast network of civilian informants to provide support for the military. These measures were for the most part welcomed by a war-weary Colombian public, and Uribe's approval rating in his first months in office soared to 70 percent, remaining there for much of his first two years in office.

The priority attached to improving military security—defined almost exclusively in counterguerrilla terms—overshadowed any progress toward negotiations. While discreet conversations with the ELN were held, at least initially, in Cuba, engagement with the FARC—for which Uribe had enlisted the good offices of the United Nations—was limited to exploration of a humanitarian agreement that would include the release of kidnap victims. For its part, the FARC appeared utterly uninterested in talks with the Uribe government. Only with the paramilitaries did any movement seem evident, and in January 2003 the government announced the formation of an "exploratory commission" of mostly regional officials in zones of paramilitary influence to sound out the possibilities for more formal peace talks.[6] Formal talks between the Colombian government and the AUC began in July 2003 with the signing of the Acuerdo de

Santa Fe de Ralito. In this document the AUC pledged to complete the demobilization of its forces by December 2005 and expressed support for a "Colombia without narcotrafficking."[7]

Causes of the Conflict and Its Intractability

Difficulty in establishing clear-cut causes of the conflict in Colombia relates, in the first instance, to what the conflict is not: it is not based on ethnic, racial, or religious exclusion; it cannot be attributed to "horizontal inequalities"—within the Latin American context, Colombia's levels of poverty and inequality, although serious in themselves, are not remarkable enough to have acted as a conflict trigger;[8] nor is the "neighborhood" to blame. The countries of the Andean region have a history of state crisis and instability accompanied, in the case of Peru most notably, by periods of guerrilla warfare. Unlike Colombia, they have suffered rapid, unpredictable, and at times unorthodox changes in government. However, they have never experienced the levels of internal violence common in Colombia for decades. The causes of Colombia's conflict are internal and predominantly social. As such, they are inextricably interwoven with the successive, multiple, and progressive waves of violence that have assailed the country for much of its history, and most notably in the second half of the twentieth century.[9]

It is therefore an oversimplification to equate the beginning of the conflict with the formation of the major guerrilla groups, the FARC and the ELN, in the mid-1960s. Rather, the set of social, geographical, and institutional conditions that fanned social conflict at the local level into violence that would come to assume a national dimension needs to be understood in the context of the violence of the country's past. While Colombia has suffered civil confrontation and conflict since its independence from Spain in 1810[10] (between 1899 and 1902, for example, the War of the Thousand Days claimed some one thousand lives), the internal armed conflict of the latter part of the twentieth century had it roots in the social and political upheaval of the years between 1948 and 1958, now widely referred to as *La Violencia,* in which some two hundred thousand Colombians were killed. *La Violencia* was unleashed by political partisanship that began during the electoral campaigns of 1945–46 and was fueled by the assassination of the popular Liberal leader Jorge Eliécer

Gaitán in 1948. It was famously described by political theorist Eric Hobsbawn as one of the "greatest armed mobilization[s] of peasants . . . in the
recent history of the western hemisphere."[11] Its latter period saw the level
of slaughter diminish but also the emergence of violence as a form of
criminal economic enterprise engaging partisan and factional networks.
The period of *La Violencia,* but not violence itself, ended when Liberals
and Conservatives reached power-sharing agreements in 1957 symbolized by the creation of the National Front.

Against this background, it is possible to identify a variety of sources
of conflict with diverse regional expressions within the country. The first
of these was the National Front itself, which brought an effective end to
the partisan struggle between Liberals and Conservatives, but at the heavy
price of exclusion of other actors from participation in the political process.
The power-sharing agreements, which were to last until 1974, provided
for the alternation of the two parties in the presidency, and their equal representation in Congress and the rest of the government, including the cabi-
net (this provision would last until 1986). Although the arrangement paved
the way for the development of a stable democratic system, the monopo-
lization of this system by the two major political parties and their inability
to transform the structure of the regime in response to social and other
demands directly contributed to the rise of violent opposition to the state.

A second cause of conflict relates to the struggle for land. Successive
National Front governments failed to counter either the massive expulsion
of peasants from their lands during the 1950s[12] or the persistent inequity
in the country's land tenure. Agrarian reform legislation introduced under
the first National Front president, Alberto Lleras Camargo (1958–62),
was slow to be implemented, and efforts by subsequent governments—
including sponsoring the creation of the National Association of Peasant
Users (ANUC) to create a constituency for reform efforts—failed to
address the underlying problem of land distribution.[13] The extremely
limited scope of land reform left peasants frustrated and alienated from
the state. According to one study, by 1996, 44.6 percent of land was in the
hands of 0.4 percent of landowners, while 66.8 percent of farmers had only
4.3 percent of land.[14] Sympathy for the guerrillas—particularly the FARC,
which had its origins in a sui generis form of agrarian communism[15]—
was one immediate consequence of this frustration. Another was the extensive colonization of Colombia's frontier territories, where the state was

essentially absent. The process of colonization transformed the use and occupancy of almost a quarter of the nation's territory during the second half of the twentieth century and created conditions—social disorder, a lack of public services, the privatization of state functions—rife for exploitation by guerrilla and paramilitary organizations.[16]

A third source of conflict relates to the first two: the growing urban-rural divide as a result of the other aspect of internal migration—an exodus from the countryside to the nation's cities. While urban growth came relatively late to Colombia in comparison with other Latin American countries, it followed the same patterns. In 1938 only 29 percent of the population lived in the cities; by 2000 the proportion was 70 percent.[17] This shift in the social and economic fabric of the country stretched urban centers to their limits. But it also exacerbated the inability of the state to extend its presence to the rural areas of the country, particularly those recently colonized, leading to what one commentator described as "the foundation of a new, stateless, country."[18] As the urban centers took over from the agricultural (principally coffee) sectors as the engines of economic growth, neglect of social conflict in rural areas fueled the escalation of political violence between armed actors over issues such as labor conditions (e.g., in the banana-growing region of Urabá). In this context of urban growth it is unsurprising that the guerrilla movement with the most resonance during the 1970s and early 1980s was the M-19, an urban guerrilla organization (modeled on the Montoneros of Argentina and Tupamaros of Uruguay) that was founded in 1970 to protest the alleged fraud in the presidential elections held on April 19 of that year.

The causes of the intractability of Colombia's conflict are, of course, not unconnected to the complexity of the social conditions that gave rise to it. However, they differ in that they have emerged from the evolution and transformation of the conflict over the past four decades—a transformation marked most notably by the flowering of a multiplicity of armed actors and a general degradation of the conflict. In some respects, and not unlike with conflicts elsewhere, the sources of intractability that have caused the conflict to continue and grow have superseded the issues that spurred the conflict in the first place. As distinct from the obstacles to the settlement of the conflict discussed later (which are in essence the manifestations of intractability), the causes of intractability can be grouped in two broad areas: (1) the historical weakness of the Colombian state and its delegation of authority to parastate and paramilitary actors, the military and territorial dimensions of which Uribe set out to reverse; and (2) the transformation of illegal armed actors, both guerrillas and paramilitaries, by the abundance of resources available to them, principally but not exclusively as a result of the illegal trade in narcotics.

The violent history of Colombia is one in which self-defense or parastate actors of one kind or another have long been present. The prevalence of these groups has been directly related to the inability of the Colombian state to meet the population's demand for security or enforce accountability through the justice system. However, the creation of such groups was also directly sanctioned by the state, dating from 1965, when the introduction of Law 48 on public security legalized the arming of civilians by the Ministry of Defense. By legitimizing private armies, this law encouraged self-defense and paramilitary structures to be seen as both an inherent part of the social order and an integral part of the state's own efforts to counter the country's growing insurgencies. By the time the law was abolished in 1989, the genie was out of the bottle: a variety of self-defense and paramilitary groups were active in many of the country's most productive regions, posing a major obstacle to the resolution of the Colombian conflict.

Paramilitaries active in the early 2000s traced their origins to a range of small and irregular armed entities present in various regions of the country in the early 1980s. These included private armies created by emerald barons and drug cartels for protection, other groups established directly by the armed forces, and others initiated by landowners, cattle ranchers, and other private actors (often with the support of the army) for the protection of their interests against kidnapping and extortion by the guerrillas.[19] Paramilitaries grew into a national movement of some twelve thousand armed men under the banner of the United Self-Defense Forces of Colombia (AUC),[20] a loose federation that entered into a period of crisis in July 2002. Their growth can be attributed to a number of factors, but predominantly to the changes in landownership financed by drug money, which saw the accumulation of vast agricultural estates. By 1994 the lands bought with the proceeds from the drug trade amounted to 4.4 million hectares, or 10 percent of the country's most fertile lands.[21] This changed the course of the war, as the new landowners became part of the paramilitary structure as well as a principal component of its social base.

There are numerous reasons that the transformation of the paramilitaries represents a central element of the Colombian conflict's intractability. Their open pursuit of an irregular war was based on a strategy of targeting the civilian population (alleged collaborators with the guerrillas) —in massacres, assassination, forced displacement, and social cleansing— that bears considerable responsibility for the degradation of the conflict. Their evident success at countering the guerrillas in exerting control of territory and populations by these means led many sectors—including powerful regional elites who benefit from paramilitary protection—to offer them their open or tacit support. Although stated government policy was to oppose armed groups of the right as well as the left, persistent reports of ties between the Colombian military and paramilitaries suggested a damaging ambiguity with respect to the attitude of the state and other elites, in that these forces were tolerated as a lesser evil if not accepted as a tactical ally in the war against the guerrillas.[22] Meanwhile, the paramilitaries' pursuit of political recognition and equal representation within any peace process was violently repudiated by the FARC, which throughout the Pastrana years made its participation in peace talks contingent on the nonrecognition of the AUC. The opening of talks with the AUC during the Uribe administration, without simultaneous talks with the FARC, raised the central issue posed repeatedly in the long history of Colombian peace negotiations: how to provide military security for demobilized fighters from one side in the conflict while their armed opponents remain active.

The transforming nature of the resources available to the various illegal armed actors was not, of course, limited to the paramilitaries. Colombia has been a significant producer of drugs—first marijuana, then cocaine and heroin—for more than four decades. During the late 1970s and 1980s, as cocaine consumption exploded in the United States, Colombia processed raw materials—coca paste made from coca grown in Peru and Bolivia and chemical precursors imported from Europe—into cocaine. Drug cartels controlled the production and traffic of the drug, while Colombia's guerrillas, particularly the FARC, derived significant income from the taxing of coca crops, transportation routes, and processing facilities in the territories under their control.

A second and much more lucrative period of the cocaine boom began in the mid-1990s, after the demise of the big Colombian cartels and the reduction in the growth of coca in both Peru and Bolivia as a result of successful interdiction and substitution programs financed by the United States. Coca cultivation in Colombia expanded exponentially: between 1994 and 2000 it soared from 49,610 hectares to 183,200 hectares, much of it in areas in the south of the country controlled by the FARC. Over the same period, the combined area of coca cultivation in Peru and Bolivia dropped from 156,700 hectares to 62,453 hectares.[23] Only in 2003 did coca cultivation in Colombia begin to drop precipitously as a result of extensive fumigation pursued by the Uribe government. According to U.S. State Department figures, the amount of land in Colombia used to cultivate coca dropped 21 percent in 2003; the United Nations reported an 11 percent overall drop in coca cultivation in Colombia, Peru, and Bolivia in 2003, the lowest level of production in fourteen years.[24]

As cultivation had expanded in Colombia in the mid- to late 1990s, so had the income derived from it. Although hard data quantifying this income are notoriously difficult to come by, it was estimated in 2001 that the FARC's annual income was some $360 million, 48 percent of which was derived from the drug trade, 36 percent from extortion, 8 percent from kidnapping, 6 percent from cattle rustling, and the rest from robbery of financial enterprises and others. For its part, 60 percent of the ELN's annual income was estimated to come from extortion (principally of the oil industry), 28 percent from kidnapping, 6 percent from the drug trade, and 4 percent from cattle rustling.[25] In early 2000 AUC commander in chief Carlos Castaño told Colombian television that 70 percent of his organization's income was derived from drugs.[26]

Fueling the drug trade and the profits it engendered was voracious demand for drugs in the United States and other countries. In 2000 alone, U.S. consumers spent a staggering $36.1 billion on cocaine, and another $11.9 billion on heroin, according to figures from the White House Office of National Drug Control Policy.[27] Indeed, the nexus of drugs and armed conflict in Colombia is impossible to understand without taking into account the demand-side motor that fuels production and trade.

The consequences of this financial bonanza for the conduct of the war were profound.[28] An abundance of economic resources meant that the armed actors had the capacity to arm and sustain indefinitely substantially larger numbers of fighters than would otherwise have been possible (in 2002 the FARC was estimated to have some 17,000 combatants supported by 10,000 militiamen, organized in seventeen fronts across the country; the ELN, although increasingly battered by the paramilitaries, was estimated to number about 3,500 fighters, organized in five principal fronts).[29] Over time, the struggle for territorial control, inextricably linked to the extraction of income from drugs and other resources such as gold, emeralds, and oil, gradually came to replace the social conflicts over land in which the conflict originated. It would be a mistake to confuse these territorial struggles, which have been described by former minister of defense Rafael Pardo as a "transitory objective," with the ultimate goal of either belligerent (political power for the guerrillas, the destruction of the guerrillas for the paramilitaries).[30] However, these struggles for territory created a new geography of conflict from which the Colombian state itself was largely absent.

Obstacles to Settlement

Principal among the factors militating for many years against the resolution of the Colombian conflict has been the fragmentation of the major actors in the conflict and the consequent problems of leadership. Until Uribe set out explicitly to overcome it, fragmentation within the state, despite a series of reform efforts marked most notably by the Constitution of 1991, consistently hindered its ability to implement an effective strategy with regard to peace. The executive branch was chronically unable to work effectively with other branches of government or with powerful sectors of the economic and political elite, which, for the most part, failed to demonstrate a willingness to address the resolution of the conflict with any degree of urgency.[31] Moreover, the negotiation efforts by presidents and their close advisers appeared divorced from, if not openly undercut by, military attitudes and actions that have favored the pursuit of war, including the tacit support of paramilitary operations.

Problems of fragmentation characterize both the insurgents and the paramilitaries as well. Guerrillas in Colombia have historically been both diverse (in the late 1980s there were at least six active guerrilla organizations)[32] and fractious. Issues of leadership within both the FARC and the ELN are, for obvious reasons, largely a question of conjecture. However, they are regularly blamed for some of the organizations' more inconsistent behavior (including the actions that led to the breakdown of the FARC process in February 2002) and for lack of clarity in establishing a negotiating platform. Indeed, officials involved with the negotiations during 2001 and 2002 cite the difficulty in establishing exactly what the FARC wanted to achieve from the process as a central obstacle to its progress.[33] This lack of clarity perpetuates debates on whether the FARC, in particular, can be understood as a political or ideological actor or is more accurately characterized as a terrorist criminal enterprise concerned principally with profiting from the drug trade.

Problems of fragmentation and leadership within the paramilitaries became increasingly evident in the early 2000s. Carlos Castaño had, since the creation of the AUC, made every effort to project the image of a national homogeneous force that was both an antisubversive group and a civilian resistance movement. Nevertheless, doubts had always persisted about the level of cohesion and unity of the forces represented within it. In the first half of 2002, Castaño's efforts to seek political legitimacy and thereby position the organization to participate in a future peace process exposed internal differences over drug trafficking and a lack of control by the AUC leadership over regional commanders.[34] These came to the surface in mid-July 2002 when, following an internal dispute crystallized by differences over the kidnapping for ransom of a Venezuelan businessman, Castaño resigned from a leadership position within the AUC and presided over the organization's dissolution, all within a matter of days.

The demise of the AUC would prove short-lived: it was reconstituted in September 2002, albeit in a form that formalized a schism with one of its most potent members, the Bloque Central Bolívar.[35] The split brought to the fore internal differences over the paramilitaries' derivation of financial gain from drug trafficking. Worsening this friction were indictments issued in September 2002 by a federal grand jury in Washington, charging Castaño and two of his deputies with smuggling more than seventeen tons of cocaine into the United States and Europe.[36] The request for extradition further undermined Castaño's attempt to put himself at the head of a modernizing, anti-drug-trafficking AUC, with pretensions to legitimacy at the negotiating table. As the AUC embarked on negotiations with the government in 2003, further divisions ensued,[37] some of them caused, ironically, by Castaño's efforts to distance himself from drug trafficking. In response to the U.S. indictments, for example, Castaño posted a letter on the AUC website claiming that one-fifth of the organization was involved in the drug trade and that he knew the names of its major players.[38] When Castaño disappeared in April 2004 following what appeared to be an assassination attempt by his former allies, one interpretation held that the attack was an effort to silence him before he could inform on fellow paramilitary leaders to U.S. authorities. Castaño's removal from the scene appeared to leave the AUC firmly in the control of major drug traffickers.[39]

A second major set of obstacles to settlement of the Colombian conflict has to do with its duration, the inadequacy of a state response to its consequences, and the changes that these have wrought on the country. While the conflict created conditions in which the production and traffic of drugs could flourish, drugs then transformed the conflict. The escalation of crime, whether rooted in violence, corruption, or both, has had a corrosive effect on society, and indeed on the methods and practices of the armed actors. The result has been profound social disintegration. In 2002 some 75 percent of the national territory was controlled or contested by insurgent or paramilitary forces;[40] the provision of social services such as health care and education has been severely limited by this central failing of public security, a condition Uribe set out to reverse. Tax revenue as a percentage of GDP is low (10.1 percent in 1998, according to the World Bank, compared with 15.1 percent in Bolivia and 18.4 percent in Chile, and rising to 13.3 percent in Colombia in 2002),[41] both because in many areas the state has had to compete with, or has been displaced by, alternative systems of taxation imposed by guerrillas and paramilitaries and because of elite resistance to increases in income tax. Shortly after taking office, Uribe imposed a one-time, 1.2 percent tax on wealthy Colombians to finance increased defense spending, an initiative welcomed by the private sector. But the country's tax system remained highly regressive and characterized by widespread tax evasion; according to researchers at the New York–based Council on Foreign Relations, in 2002, only 740,000 of Colombia's 44 million people paid income taxes.[42]

The conflict also spawned a human rights catastrophe of massive proportions. During 2001 human rights groups documented between 3,000 and 3,700 deaths due to political motives, including targeted murders, disappearances, and combat casualties;[43] the figure included the assassination of scores of trade unionists, journalists, human rights defenders, and elected officials. However, the number of homicides, among the highest per capita in the world, was some nine times higher at 27,840, a

rate of sixty-five homicides for every one hundred thousand inhabitants.[44] Sadly able to top numerous tables of this kind, during 2002
Colombia suffered 2,986 reported kidnappings (60 percent of which were
attributed to the guerrillas), more than in the rest of the world combined.[45]
But perhaps the most vivid expression of the humanitarian crisis caused
by the conflict was the country's exceptionally high level of internal displacement. While no consensus exists on the number of displaced persons,
the overall number has been estimated to be between 1 and 2.5 million.[46]
In the first two years of the Uribe administration, however, the situation
improved markedly. By the end of 2003, the administration was able to
point to significant improvements in virtually all of these indicators: according to government figures, kidnappings fell by 26 percent, homicides
by 20 percent, and forced displacement by 52 percent, statistics confirmed
for the most part by nongovernmental organizations.[47]

Paradoxically, a third obstacle to the settlement of Colombia's conflict derives directly from the country's twenty-year history of negotiations
between the government and a range of insurgent forces. These negotiations, which began under President Belisario Betancur in 1982, have seen
a number of partial successes. Between 1990 and 1994, some 4,500 and
6,000 guerrillas, mainly belonging to the M-19 and the Popular Liberation
Army (EPL), laid down their arms under agreements signed with Presidents Virgilio Barco and César Gaviria, which offered reintegration into
the political process and some economic benefits in return for demobilization. While newly reintegrated guerrillas were initially able to make
an important showing as a third political force and played a significant
role in the drafting of Colombia's new Constitution in 1991, they soon
faded from the national scene. More disturbing as a precedent for other
insurgents considering demobilization was that many former guerrillas
were assassinated, either by paramilitaries or, in the case of the EPL, the
FARC and dissident members of their own organization. Most dramatic
and of greatest relevance to the FARC was the fate of the Patriotic Union
(UP), a party established by the FARC in the mid-1980s as an outcome
of the peace process with the Betancur government. Although the UP
participated in the elections of 1986 and won more than a dozen congressional seats (some in coalition with factions of the Liberal Party), it
was essentially annihilated by a sustained campaign by the paramilitaries.
By conservative estimates, some 334 members of the UP and affiliated

popular organizations were assassinated between January 1986 and April 1988 alone, including their presidential candidate for the 1986 elections, four congressmen, two mayors, and eleven mayoral candidates. By the early 1990s, the UP itself claimed to have lost well over two thousand of its members, including party activists and other elected officials at the local and municipal levels.[48]

Beyond the immediate disincentive to the FARC to lay down its weapons and enter the political process, it could be argued that the partial successes of negotiations in Colombia did little to temper the gravity of the conflict overall. The demobilization of the M-19 did bring a halt to the spectacular urban operations (including its disastrous occupation of the Palace of Justice in 1985) that had been its hallmark. But the territorial logic of partial peace is that space vacated by one armed actor is immediately taken over by another, and this indeed proved the case. In Colombia, fragmented negotiations led not to an accumulation of peace but to further violence and prolongation of the war.[49]

In the wake of the breakdown of the peace process with the FARC in early 2002, a particular kind of negotiation fatigue set in. This fatigue reflected disgust with the persistent abuses of the FARC and a conviction that its actions during the negotiations demonstrated a lack of political will, but also a widespread perception that the process was also a victim of government mismanagement. This mismanagement was detected in the failure to insist on sufficient and verifiable conditions for the demilitarized zone, a lack of competence on the part of the government's various negotiating teams, and the government's inability to develop a coherent negotiating strategy. In the end, President Pastrana's insistence on his personal conduct of the peace process, his preference for confidants over more experienced negotiators, and his reluctance to countenance that negotiations in Colombia would require substantive undertakings on both sides proved very costly.

In addition to the escalation of the conflict, the course taken by the FARC process complicated efforts to renew negotiations in the future. Uribe rejected the concession of territory for talks with the FARC under any circumstances. Meanwhile, a rise in urban terrorism and in attacks on civilians by the FARC—the notable incident was a car bomb assault on Bogotá's Club Nogal in February 2003 in which more than thirty people were killed—further poisoned the atmosphere for a renewal of talks.

Public confidence in the aggressive strategy pursued by Uribe increased, leaving many Colombians believing that pursuit of a military victory over the rebels was the only viable strategic option.[50]

A final obstacle to the settlement of Colombia's conflict has been ambivalence regarding the involvement of outside actors in efforts to solve the conflict. Successive Colombian governments traditionally were reluctant to countenance any efforts to elevate the conflict or to extend political recognition to the guerrillas, through international involvement. This position represented carefully guarded considerations of sovereignty, but also an unwillingness to accept that the Colombian state itself be put in the position of a "party" to the conflict as opposed to a victim of it.[51] Although one of President Pastrana's signature achievements was to internationalize the conflict, initially through the involvement of the United States in Plan Colombia, he did so while insisting that "Colombia would not accept any type of intervention in the conflict between the Government and the rebels opposing it."[52]

The Colombian guerrillas have shared with the government a wariness of international involvement, particularly that of the United Nations. The guerrillas regard the United Nations as a puppet of the United States or the imperial powers; Colombian governments have shied away from UN involvement because of concerns about a diminution of national sovereignty.[53] However, a principal reason that the FARC in particular has resisted the involvement of outside actors appears related to the fact that, quite simply, it has not needed it. One of the more immediate consequences of the abundance of resources fueling the conflict in Colombia is that, as in other resource-rich conflict environments, the most obvious kinds of leverage—the provision or withdrawal of external assistance to fight the war, or promises of reinsertion packages, donor conferences, and the like—hold little attraction. Members of the international community who have wished to assist in efforts to resolve the conflict thus face a particular kind of dilemma. Just as channels of assistance cannot be used to influence a positive outcome of the process, so the usual "rules of the game," whereby international assistance to an insurgent movement might guarantee a certain degree of respect for international personnel, are absent. This point was graphically brought home to some of the European countries who became engaged as "friends" of the talks with the

FARC during the Pastrana years, only to have their citizens kidnapped by the guerrilla forces.[54]

The potential benefits of international involvement, both in maintaining contacts with insurgent groups at a time when negotiations had broken down and in lending legitimacy to a process widely questioned in Colombia and abroad, were readily grasped by the Uribe administration. Uribe surprised many observers when, within days of taking office, he urged the United Nations to remain involved in efforts to engage the FARC, all the while setting out strict preconditions for a resumption of talks. Later, Uribe invited the Organization of American States to assist in the demobilization of paramilitary forces and to sit at the peace table as an observer. Both initiatives reflected the utility of international participation in advancing government interests, particularly in demonstrating to the international community that the Uribe government retained interest in a negotiated, rather than a purely military, solution to the conflict.

Third Parties: Interests, Objectives, and Limits

Why, then, did the international community become involved initially in Pastrana's efforts to negotiate an end to the Colombian conflict, and what effect did that involvement have? Answering this question calls to mind three major points: (1) the fact that the principal international actor in Colombia, the United States, was only peripherally involved in supporting the peace effort, even if the thrust of U.S. policy in Colombia did much to galvanize European and Latin American support for the negotiations, (2) opportunities for international involvement were constrained by the weakness of the process itself: much of the effort focused on attempts to influence and engage the parties, particularly the guerrillas, to build confidence and thereby foster the conditions for settlement, and (3) the period of the most intense international involvement was relatively short, lasting less than a year between 2001 and 2002. While the outcome of the peace process was unsuccessful, one of its few positive legacies was the near-universal acceptance that greater international involvement would be required in any future peace process in Colombia. In the end, a principal objective—to keep the process alive in the hopes of creating "ripeness" and avoiding the alternative, a widening of the conflict—proved impossible.

This reflected less a flawed international approach than a lack of political will by the parties.

During the Pastrana years, third-party involvement in the peace process was heavily conditioned by, and at times appeared a reaction to, U.S. policy. The Clinton administration initially gave strong rhetorical support to Pastrana's peace initiative and in December 1998 sent midlevel State Department officials to Costa Rica to meet with the FARC privately. This initiative fell apart following the FARC's murder in March 1999 of three activists from the United States who were campaigning for indigenous rights, a brutal act that unleashed a barrage of criticism of the State Department by conservatives on Capitol Hill.[55] From that point onward, the administration maintained an attitude of critical support for the peace process, preferring that it exist but for the most part skeptical that it would lead anywhere and doing little to advance its prospects. Instead, the administration focused most of its energies on getting the Colombian government to develop a coherent strategy for dealing with the multiple threats to its ability to govern. This included the issue of drug trafficking, a long-standing U.S. concern that had become magnified by what one senior U.S. official called "the explosion" of coca production in southern Colombia, an area mostly dominated by the FARC.

The unveiling of Plan Colombia in September 1999 as a $7.5 billion, multiyear proposal to counter drug production, foster economic development, enhance human rights and democratic governance, and support the peace process further constrained and defined avenues for international collaboration in Colombia.[56] Justified or not, Plan Colombia soon became identified with the largest component of the U.S. contribution: military and police aid, including funds for Blackhawk helicopters and the training of new counternarcotics battalions.[57] This meant that other donors had to identify or distance themselves from the thrust of U.S. policy, especially as the Colombian government itself sought to channel international participation in Colombia under the plan's umbrella.

This latter effort greatly complicated United Nations involvement in Colombia. During the previous government of President Ernesto Samper, and in response to a burgeoning humanitarian crisis, the Colombian government had acceded to pressure to invite the United Nations to establish Bogotá offices of the UN High Commissioner for Human Rights (1997) and the UN High Commissioner for Refugees (1998). It is fair to say that the Colombian government was rather ambivalent about the relinquishing of sovereignty symbolized by the offices—and indeed welcomed the human rights office on the (probably misguided) basis that it would be less intrusive than the appointment of a special rapporteur reporting on Colombia to the UN Human Rights Commission in Geneva. On the one hand, the Colombian government recognized that it needed help and welcomed international assistance; on the other, it sought to minimize public criticism of its action or inaction and strove to avoid being identified as part of the problem rather than as a victim of the ruthless tactics of the conflict's various armed actors.

A similar ambivalence pervaded the appointment of a senior UN official to advise the secretary-general on Colombia. To the surprise of the United Nations, which had historically been extremely sensitive to Colombia's well-known concerns about its sovereignty, the suggestion to make some kind of senior appointment on Colombia came from the government itself. However, the idea—which was promptly, if quietly, endorsed by the United States—was that such an individual would play a useful role in marshaling international support for Plan Colombia. While this was clearly not acceptable to the United Nations, when Secretary-General Kofi Annan announced that veteran Norwegian diplomat Jan Egeland would be his special adviser in December 1999, Egeland's title and mandate reflected the limited, if not conflicting, conceptions of his role. Egeland's title was to be "special adviser to the secretary-general for international assistance to Colombia"; his mandate was "to serve as the focal point for the United Nations system in its efforts to mobilize international assistance for social, humanitarian, human rights, drug control (alternative development projects) and peace-building activities in Colombia."[58]

This was a far cry from a specific role in facilitating, let alone mediating, the peace talks between the Colombian government and either the FARC or the ELN and indeed reflected the particular concern of the Colombian government that the United Nations *not* be asked to perform a political role within the process. Over time, and in a manner wholly unsurprising to anyone who had followed Egeland's highly political and highly effective career in peacemaking,[59] through patient and persistent footwork he established a role of "discreet facilitation" that allowed his title to be curtailed to the more open-ended "special adviser to the secretary-general on Colombia."

Given the fits and starts of the FARC process—and the fact that direct talks with the ELN had not even begun by the time of Egeland's appointment—much of the initial UN effort was directed at building confidence between the parties and breaking the historic isolation of the FARC. On Egeland's initiative, senior guerrilla leaders and Colombian government officials toured several European capitals in February 2000,[60] a trip designed to take the guerrillas, literally and figuratively, out of the jungle into the modern world. The so-called Eurotour was followed a month later by a visit of leading Colombian private sector leaders to the *despeje*. Rather than take these visits as an incentive for new behavior, the FARC, as it would on many subsequent occasions, continued to operate as if the conduct of the war had no bearing on developments at the peace table. In April 2000 the FARC issued "Law 002," calling on Colombians with assets of $1 million or more to pay a "peace tax" or risk being kidnapped. In the ensuing firestorm of criticism of the peace process, Pastrana's first peace negotiator, Víctor G. Ricardo, resigned. Still, efforts to engage the FARC politically continued. In June 2000 the entire secretariat of the FARC met in the *despeje* with representatives of more than twenty European and Latin American countries to discuss questions of drug production and alternative development. Loosely organized and producing few results, the meeting nonetheless exposed the FARC to a number of concerns held by the international community, including issues of kidnapping and international humanitarian law. "It was a dialogue of the deaf," said one participant, reflecting on the desire of many in the international community to play a constructive role in the peace process while the nature of that involvement remained improvised and ill defined.[61]

Despite persistent difficulties in the negotiations and frequent breakdowns of the talks altogether, the United Nations as well as other actors in the international community shared several common premises: that there was no purely military solution to the Colombian conflict; that the peace process initiated by the Pastrana government, while imperfect, warranted diplomatic and political, as well as financial, support; and that the depth of the humanitarian crisis and the extent of the suffering inflicted on the civilian population as a result of the conflict demanded a response from the international community. Egeland's own words over a period of months reflected those multiple imperatives. "There are different views and approaches on how best to help Colombia," he told an international gathering in London in June 2000. "What is not acceptable is to do little or nothing when the country is trying to end generations of bitter war while dealing with an overwhelming humanitarian, economic, social and political crisis."[62] By the end of the year, and amid mounting frustration in Colombia over the process's meager results, he acknowledged that "this peace process has produced little and has many difficulties. But an imperfect peace is better than a perfect war."[63]

If the imperative to "do something" about Colombia drove an initial response from the international community, just as important during the Clinton years was a repudiation of the perceived militaristic thrust of U.S. policy. At a July 2000 international donor conference held in Madrid, countries of the European Union, as well as Brazil, Canada, and Japan, pledged only a fraction of the $1 billion in aid sought by the Colombian government in the context of Plan Colombia.[64] Moreover, European countries that had not been consulted during discussions regarding the contours of Plan Colombia sought openly to distance themselves from a U.S. approach focused heavily on the fumigation of coca crops. European donors organized themselves as a Support Group of the Peace Process in Colombia, de-emphasizing narcotics and aiming assistance at projects to address the social and economic roots of the conflict.[65] As European assistance to Colombia expanded over the next several years, the emphasis on social and economic development over security and counterdrug policy largely continued.

While some of the international involvement in Colombia surfaced as a repudiation of Plan Colombia, it would be a mistake to see the admittedly limited European and Latin American involvement exclusively in those terms. Both Spain and Germany, for example, had been engaged in the peace process with the ELN during the Samper administration, encouraging "pre-accords" between the guerrillas and members of civil society that were to set the stage for future direct negotiations with the government. Spain, along with Mexico and several of the Nordic countries (a so-called Nordic mafia, in the words of one Bogotá-based diplomat),[66] had been deeply involved in peace processes in Central America in the 1980s and 1990s, bringing both expertise (not always welcomed by Colombians, who rightly saw their conflict as far more complex) and a desire to contribute to the process in Colombia. Self-interest was also a factor, as many European countries had substantial investments in Colombia in extractive industries as well as in manufacturing and services. Nationals of many of these countries also counted among the thousands of kidnap victims held by the FARC and the ELN, contributing to a view widely (if cynically) held by Colombians that foreign involvement in the peace process was motivated by a desire to "vaccinate" citizens of a particular country from kidnapping by the guerrillas. True or not, representatives of a host of countries appeared to welcome a chance to bounce around in the back of a jeep to reach the guerrillas in the *despeje,* in the perhaps naive but well-intentioned view that such engagement would advance national interests and/or impact positively on the peace process.

Over the course of the Pastrana years, two "groups of friends" of the peace process were formed with the goal of exerting leverage on the parties and massaging the process forward. A group of five countries—Cuba, France, Norway, Spain, and Switzerland—formed in June 2000 to support an incipient process with the ELN, and in February 2001 the FARC and the Colombian government agreed to constitute a "group of friendly countries and international bodies, to inform them about the state and evolution of the process and motivate their collaboration."[67] The group subsequently named for the FARC process included no fewer than twenty-five countries as well as the Vatican and representatives of the United Nations and the European Community. The mechanism was as unwieldy as it was inclusive, reflecting a widespread desire for inclusion but hobbled from the beginning by a vague and uncertain mandate. These limitations were only partly overcome by the constitution of a smaller facilitation commission of ten countries.[68] A March 2001 meeting of the larger group with the FARC and government in the *despeje,* to which the United States was invited but which it declined to attend, demonstrated the largely showcase nature of international involvement.

The United Nations directly encouraged the formation of groups of friends for a number of reasons. Egeland and his deputy, James LeMoyne, were acutely conscious of the extent to which the United Nations was working on its own with an ill-defined mandate and considered that the process could only benefit from greater interaction of the Colombian parties, particularly the guerrillas, with the outside world. However, the formation of such groups in a peace process as weak as Colombia's had a number of inherent problems. Ambassadors were not necessarily well versed in peace processes: "We are just ambassadors," commented one Western diplomat in Bogotá. "Peace, conflict resolution, shuttle diplomacy in the jungle—this was not what we were sent to do."[69] The ambassadors became engaged as "friends" but had varying degrees of support from their capitals; moreover, they were "friends" with insurgent groups having well-known histories of human rights violations. All the while, their undoubted commitment to the pursuit of peace in Colombia ran the risk of getting far ahead of the situation on the ground—as well as far ahead of the policies of foreign ministries back home.

The ELN process during 2001 proved a case in point. In December 2000 the government and the ELN had reached "pre-accords" on the creation of a demilitarized "meeting zone" *(zona de encuentro)* in southern Bolívar for the purpose of holding the National Convention long sought by the ELN. The pre-accords, which were witnessed by the group of friends, indicated that the zone would require international verification. This, in turn, spurred the interest of other members of the international community, who agreed to serve as "verifiers" of the process.[70] In February 2001 the government and the ELN asked the United Nations—the first time that the government of Colombia and either guerrilla group had jointly asked the United Nations for anything—for technical assistance to establish the feasibility and requirements for verification of the proposed zone. The United Nations commissioned an outside entity[71] to conduct the feasibility study, which was undertaken with the active support of a number of the "friends" and "verifiers." But the central political reality was that the ELN was losing ground to the paramilitaries in the region where the demilitarized zone was to be established. And the paramilitaries were determined to prevent the creation of the zone at any cost.

In the end, despite apparent efforts to persuade the paramilitaries otherwise,[72] the government proved unable to defend the agreement. As the paramilitaries attacked the process directly, the army, which was determined to avoid a second *despeje,* refused to attack them, leaving the government as well as members of the international community with limited, if any, options. In a particularly egregious episode, during key meetings attended by the ELN in Cuba, paramilitaries attacked the villages from which the ELN members attending the meetings had come. The ELN went to the friends and asked them to denounce the paramilitary action and the inability of the government to follow through on its agreement, but the friends, as diplomats accredited to the government, felt that they could not do so. The ELN's relationship with the friends turned understandably chilly for several months and the process slowed.[73]

A similar kind of problem arose within the FARC process. In July 2001, contrary to any expectation that the formation of the "friends" might have a moderating influence on FARC behavior, guerrillas kidnapped three German nationals, including a representative of the government aid agency GTZ. That same month, the FARC kidnapped Alan Jara, former governor of Meta province, from a UN vehicle in which the resident representative of the United Nations Development Program (UNDP) was riding. One of the Germans escaped in September 2001 and the other two were released in October, but Jara remained a captive as of this writing in mid-2004. Both incidents outraged members of the international community: a strongly worded statement from the European Community said that the abductions "gravely compromised the support of the international community in Colombia's peace process."[74] But the incidents illustrated once again that the FARC saw no contradiction whatsoever between the peace process, and international involvement in it, and business as usual as they defined it.

In this context it is perhaps understandable why the ten members of the facilitating commission that engaged in talks with the FARC seemed almost surprised by the positive contribution they made to the dramatic turn taken by negotiations in early 2002, described at the beginning of this paper. They attributed the utility of the group to its diversity (several diplomats interviewed by the authors indicated that Cuba and Venezuela were particularly helpful in dealing with the FARC), the shared commitment of these countries to a negotiated solution to Colombia's conflict, their ability to maintain the group's cohesion and confidentiality in difficult circumstances, and their good working relationship with UN representative James LeMoyne, who took over from Egeland in late 2001.

Following the breakdown of the peace process with the FARC in February 2002, questions arose about whether members of the international community had served as "useful fools" of the guerrillas, prolonging a process that should have collapsed long before under its own weight. Our reading of events suggests that this analysis is too harsh, even if it appears compelling in hindsight. "The logic was simple," explained one senior diplomat involved in the process. "There is no exclusively military solution to the conflict. There is a negotiation under way. We should do everything possible to make it the last one."[75] The approximately five weeks of the most intense international involvement in the Colombian peace process, between early January and late February 2002, succeeded in producing the most detailed and substantive agreements of the entire three-and-a-half-year process, including a deadline for a cease-fire. That the FARC balked—even as close observers of the process recognized that the government was in no position to deliver on the agreements—should reflect more on the goals and intentions of the parties to the conflict than on those of the international community.

International involvement in Colombian peace negotiations took a decidedly different turn during the Uribe years, as the Organization of American States (OAS), not the United Nations, came to play the central role in the only peace talks to get under way: those with paramilitary groups. While continuing in its attempts to negotiate a humanitarian accord with the FARC that would release kidnap victims, the United Nations turned down repeated requests from the Uribe government, as well as from the AUC, to monitor compliance with the December 2002 cease-fire and participate in the talks formally launched in July 2003. The United Nations did not want to afford the paramilitaries the recognition as a political actor that their participation in the process would imply. Moreover, as UN special advisor James LeMoyne pointed out, there was no obvious need for UN facilitation, as the government self-evidently had no problems communicating with the paramilitaries.[76]

Domestic and international criticism of the negotiations with the AUC peaked in late 2003, following the government's proposal of an "alternative penalties law" that would allow paramilitary leaders responsible for atrocities to escape prison sentences. In an effort to afford the process greater legitimacy, Uribe convinced OAS secretary-general César Gaviria in January 2004 to commit the organization to monitor and assist in the demobilization and reintegration of some 850 members of the AUC's Cacique Nutibara bloc, a demobilization that took place in November 2003. Gaviria's failure to consult OAS member-states in advance of making this commitment to Uribe aroused considerable fury among the delegations of several countries; the mission was approved, however, after its mandate was modified to address a number of human rights concerns.

Lessons Learned

By mid-2004 prospects for a settlement of the Colombian conflict—negotiated or otherwise—appeared as remote as ever. Heightened terrorist attacks by the FARC in the heart of urban areas in 2002–3 had stiffened the resolve of the Uribe administration and the Colombian public to use all means necessary to combat and defeat the guerrillas. Meanwhile, the continuing splintering of the paramilitary movement and repeated violations of the cease-fire raised serious questions about the future of peace talks. And this was before any of the substantive issues of a negotiation had been tackled: what to do about the history of drug trafficking and violence against the civilian population; how to provide security guarantees while preventing unfettered passage of demobilized fighters into the regular army; what to do about vast economic gains, including landholdings, acquired by violence. If the need for simultaneous negotiations with violent actors on all sides—something this chapter has suggested is a central lesson of the Colombian experience, despite the benefits derived from the partial successes garnered in the past—appeared more vital than ever, the possibility for comprehensive negotiations had never seemed more distant.

Ultimately, it may prove more possible for a peace process to address some of the root causes of the Colombian conflict than it will be to address key sources of intractability. Grievances—such as political exclusion, the lack of human rights protections, the absence of agrarian reform, and the general neglect of rural areas—that have contributed to the endurance and escalation of violence in Colombia's countryside constitute aspects of an agenda that could be negotiated at the peace table. However, it should be recognized that the prospects for addressing the agrarian issue in the absence of security in the countryside are virtually nonexistent. Successful agrarian reform, as well as alternative development for cultivators of coca and poppy, can be implemented only in a secure environment and requires the infrastructure necessary to extend market opportunities to rural farmers, not simply reinforce a system of unviable individual plots.

One source of intractability—the weakness of the Colombian state—has already received widespread attention, both from Uribe and from the United States, particularly in its military and security dimensions. (The delegation of security functions to parastate paramilitary groups whose degree of autonomy has constituted a central source of intractability is one of the bitter ironies of the Colombian conflict.) The tendency to privilege the security aspects of state strengthening, understandable in the face of vicious attacks by the guerrillas, nonetheless risks underemphasizing other critical aspects of state reform in the political, economic, and social arenas. State presence that limits the contact of Colombian citizens to the military or the police, and not the public health official, educator, or judge, will do little to overcome the state weakness on which the conflict feeds.

One of the readings of the FARC process under Pastrana was that the guerrillas were not "hurting" enough to make the necessary concessions for the negotiations to work. How to approach the conditions of stalemate without merely increasing the Colombian conflict's cycles of violence and degradation is a fundamental challenge. At its core, the challenge is to strengthen and professionalize state military and law enforcement capacity within a democratic context, not one that further erodes the rule of law or deepens the cycle of dirty war. Cease-fire or no, this implies a fundamental and clean break between the armed forces and the paramilitaries—in fact as well as in rhetoric—and a change in attitude throughout the government and the political and military elite, such that paramilitaries are viewed as part of the problem, not part of the solution. Indeed, the paramilitaries' apparent penetration of key Colombian institutions and segments of the political and economic elite poses a long-term problem for the future of democratic governance in the country.

The resource income from illegal drugs constitutes the greatest source of intractability in Colombia and poses the most serious obstacle to settlement. The original formulation of the Pastrana administration saw peace as the key to solving the drug issue. This has been turned on its head, in that a host of actors, including the United States, came to understand addressing the drug issue as fundamental to resolving the war. There are various avenues for fighting the drug war that can either help or hurt. The U.S.-sponsored fumigation of coca crops, vigorously embraced by the Uribe administration, has resulted in notable decreases in cultivation, but it is unclear whether such wide-scale fumigation can be sustained over the medium and long term. Indeed, the record suggests that, in the absence of jobs, credit, and investment, peasant growers will have an on-going incentive to grow coca and will find the means and the land to do so.[77] As the UNDP and others have argued, attacking—especially at the local level—the criminal enterprises that launder money and that traffic in drugs and precursor chemicals will prove more productive over the long term than penalizing peasant growers of coca or poppy.[78]

However, one should bear no illusion that strategies for reducing the income from resources such as diamonds or oil—entirely legal commodities for which sanctions regimes can be constructed—are applicable to the illicit trade in narcotics. More can certainly be done to engage insurgents in particular on questions of manual eradication and alternative development, but the huge profits and corruptive influence of the drug trade (witness the tens of billions spent on drug consumption annually in the United States alone) and their intersection with the war make any comprehensive settlement difficult to envision. Strategies to reduce the demand for drugs in the United States and elsewhere are also key to conflict resolution strategies in Colombia.

What role, then, can be played by the international community in contributing to a resolution of Colombia's conflict, beyond reducing the demand for illegal narcotics? Perhaps the most obvious lesson of the Pastrana peace process is that interested third parties cannot leverage a peace process absent the will of the parties. This is as true for an international organization such as the United Nations as it is for loosely or formally designated "groups of friends." It is easy to point out that should negotiations be possible in the future, the international community will have to break the model by which mediation is conceived as a strategy of conflict limitation or management. Less clear, in the absence of talks, is what, if any, intermediate steps—including keeping existing channels of communication open—can help contribute to the creation of ripe conditions in which a future process can prosper. Thus, judgments about when and how third parties should be involved in Colombia are inevitably ambiguous and subjective and entail some element of risk. The challenge, it seems, is to balance investments of political capital and credibility with indications that the parties themselves are seeking an alternative to war, while at the same time renewing efforts to respond effectively to the country's humanitarian crisis.

Finally, third parties involved in a future peace process need to be straightforward about the conditions in which they will participate, including insisting on clear demonstrations of political will and confidence building early in the talks. Concrete deadlines and objectives must move any process forward in a relatively short period, given the depth of public cynicism about negotiations and the enormous cost in suffering imposed by the war. If many, both in Colombia and abroad, remain skeptical that there is a military solution to the Colombian conflict, it is still not inevitable that the conflict can or will end through negotiations. Sustained political, economic, military, and diplomatic pressures must converge if a negotiated settlement is to be even remotely possible.

Notes

The authors gratefully acknowledge the research assistance of Woodrow Wilson Center intern Craig Fagan. The authors would also like to thank the editors, Marco Palacios, Robin Kirk, and several others who wish to remain anonymous for their helpful comments and suggestions.

1. The president-elect indicated that he would talk to the paramilitaries if they accepted a cease-fire and stopped the killing of innocent Colombians. A few days later U.S. assistant secretary of state Otto Reich responded to a journalist's question on the subject by saying, "We believe that all the terrorist groups should take part in a dialogue." See Associated Press, "Anti-Rebel Group in Colombia Backs Talks," *Washington Post*, May 31, 2002, 26; and Sergio Gómez Maseri, "Colombia negociará también con los grupos paramilitares, dice EU," *El Tiempo*, May 30, 2002.

2. These included military reinforcement, the detention of kidnapping victims, and the pursuit of drug activities.

3. Author interviews, Bogotá, March 18–20, 2002.

4. The Colombian Constitution determines that the president may serve only a single four-year term, a restriction that Uribe has sought to overcome.

5. The military is small and poorly funded relative to the size of the country and the number of insurgents it is opposing. At the time of Uribe's election, the army was funded by less than 2 percent of the country's GDP (nearly 3.5 percent was spent on defense as a whole) and has a total of 116,000 to 120,000 men; however, at any one time there were only some 30,000 to 35,000 out of a total of some 53,000 professional troops available for combat as others were tied down in training, the protection of fixed sites, and other activities. U.S. State Department official, interview by author, Washington, D.C., May 16, 2002. Under the one-time tax, roughly 420,000 Colombian citizens and businesses are expected to pay 1.2 per cent of the value of their liquid assets. See International Crisis Group Briefing, *Colombia: Will Uribe's Honeymoon Last?* (Bogotá and Brussels: International Crisis Group, December 2002), 4.

6. "Diálogo: El primer paso," *Semana*, January 13, 2003, http://www
.semana.com.

7. Text, "Acuerdo de Santa Fe de Ralito para Contribuir a la Paz de Colombia," July 15, 2003.

8. Frances Stewart argues that "horizontal inequalities," defined as inequalities between groups in access to or control over resources and/or political power, bear a causal relationship to the incidence of conflict. See Frances Stewart, "Horizontal Inequalities as a Source of Conflict," in *From Reaction to Conflict Prevention: Opportunities for the UN System*, ed. Fen Osler Hampson and David M. Malone (Boulder, Colo.: Lynne Rienner, 2002), 105–138. According to Colombia's National Planning Department, in 2001, approximately 60 percent of the population was below the poverty line, with the percentage in rural areas close to 80 percent. According to the World Bank, in 2001 Colombia ranked fifth out of seventeen Latin American countries in income inequality.

9. There is an extensive literature on the causes of Colombia's conflict. See David Bushnell, *The Making of Modern Colombia: A Nation in Spite of Itself* (Berkeley: University of California Press, 1993); Daniel Pécaut, *Crónica de dos décadas de política colombiana, 1968–1988* (Bogotá: Siglo XXI, 1989); Gonzalo Sánchez G., *Ensayos de historia social y política del siglo XX* (Bogotá: El Ancora, 1984); and León Zamosc and Francisco Leal, eds., *Al filo del caos: Crisis política en la Colombia de los años ochenta* (Bogotá: Tercer Mundo Editores, 1990).

10. Jonathan Hartlyn counts "seven major civil confrontations in the second half of the [nineteenth] century, as well as other smaller-scale regional conflicts," and civil conflict and violence in the 1930s and 1940s. "Civil Violence and Conflict Resolution: The Case of Colombia," in *Stopping the Violence: How Civil Wars End*, ed. Roy Licklider (New York: New York University Press, 1993), 37.

11. Eric Hobsbawn, "The Anatomy of Violence," *New Society* 1 (April 11, 1963): 16.

12. Marc Chernick cites estimates of more than two million displaced persons created by these expulsions in "Negotiating Peace amid Multiple Forms of Violence: The Protracted Search for Settlement to the Armed Conflicts in Colombia," in *Comparative Peace Processes in Latin America*, ed. Cynthia J. Arnson (Washington, D.C.: Woodrow Wilson Center Press; Stanford, Calif.: Stanford University Press, 1999), 163.

13. According to historian John Bushnell, "the overall pattern of land distribution in the country was virtually the same at the end of the [reform] period as at the beginning." See Bushnell, *The Making of Modern Colombia*, 234.

14. The figures are from a study by National University researcher Absalón Machado, cited in Marisol Gómez Giraldo, "Campesinos, más de la mitad son pobres," *El Tiempo*, September 23, 2002.

15. The FARC has its origins in the displacement of peasants by partisan violence in southern Colombia in the 1940s and 1950s and the subsequent formation of communist self-defense groups against the interests of large landowners. In 1966 these groups came together to constitute themselves in the FARC as a guerrilla movement under the wing of the Communist Party. Only in the early 1980s did the FARC become an independent organization that espoused its own military and political doctrine.

16. Colonization has been most dynamic in eight zones covering some three hundred thousand square kilometers. In the past fifty years some 1.3 million colonists have cleared and settled approximately 3.5 million hectares. Frank Safford and Marco Palacios, *Colombia: Fragmented Land, Divided Society* (New York, Oxford: Oxford University Press, 2002), 311.

17. Ibid., 301.

18. Gonzalo Sánchez G., "Guerra prolongada y negociaciones incertas en Colombia," in *Violencia colectiva en los paises andinos,* ed. Gonzalo Sánchez G. and Eric Lair, a special edition of *Bulletin de l'Institut Français d'Études Andines* 29, no. 3 (Lima, 2000): 269–305.

19. For the history of the paramilitaries, see Carlos Medina Gallego, *Autodefensas, paramilitares y narcotráfico en Colombia* (Bogotá: Editorial Documentos Periodísticos, 1996); Fernando Cubides C., "From Private to Public Violence: The Paramilitaries," in *Violence in Colombia, 1990–2000,* ed. Charles Berquist, Ricardo Peñaranda, and Gonzalo Sánchez G. (Wilmington, Del.: Scholarly Resources, 2001); and an unpublished background paper prepared by Teresa Whitfield, "Colombia: The Paramilitaries" (October 2002).

20. In December 2000 Colombia's Ministry of Defense reported that the "illegal self-defense groups" had grown from 1,200 in 1993 to 4,500 in 1998 and 8,150 in 2000, a rate of growth five times greater than the FARC's. Ministerio de Defensa Nacional, *Los grupos ilegales de autodefensa en Colombia* (Bogotá: Ministerio de Defensa Nacional, December 2000), 10. In May 2002, a source close to Colombian military intelligence told one of the authors that the latter estimated that the AUC had just under twelve thousand combatants. Interview by author, May 15, 2002.

21. Nazih Richani, *Systems of Violence: The Political Economy of War and Peace in Colombia* (Albany: State University of New York Press, 2002), 112.

22. In recent years pressure from the United States has led to some progress in forcing the state to crack down on these ties, but reports from the UN High Commissioner for Human Rights and others, including Human Rights Watch, have indicated that the progress has been uneven and inadequate given the gravity of the problem.

23. Figures are from U.S. Department of State, *International Narcotics Control Strategy Report,* 1996, 1997, 1998, 1999, 2000, 2001, 2002, 2003, http://www.state.gov/g/inl/rls/nrcrpt.

24. Frances Robles, "Coca Land Diminishing, U.S. Says," *Miami Herald,* March 23, 2004; BBC News, "Andes Record Fall in Coca Crop," June 18, 2004.

25. Alfredo Rangel, *Guerra insurgente* (Bogotá: Intermedio Editores, 2001), 391.

26. Dario Arizmendi, "Cara a Cara: Entrevista Carlos Castaño," transcript, March 1, 2000, 29. Nazih Richani estimated in early 2002 that the paramilitaries' income ("much of it derived from the drug trade and money laundering activities") was between $200 and $300 million. See "Colombia at the Crossroads: The Future of the Peace Accords," *NACLA Report on the Americas* 35, no. 4 (January-February 2002): 18.

27. Cynthia Arnson, "U.S. Interests and Options in Colombia: An Alternative Framework," in *U.S. Policy toward Colombia* (Washington, D.C.: Aspen Institute, 2002), 26.

28. A growing literature has examined the intricate connection between economic resources and war, spurred initially by the thesis of World Bank researcher Paul Collier that conflicts are less rooted in grievances than they are in economic agendas and opportunities. See Paul Collier, "Doing Well Out of War" (paper prepared for the Conference on Economic Agendas in Civil War, London, April 26–27, 1999); Paul Collier and Anke Hoeffler, "Greed and Grievance in Civil War," World Bank Policy Research Working Paper 2355, May 2000, mimeographed; Mats Berdal and David M. Malone, *Greed and Grievance: Economic Agendas in Civil Wars* (Boulder, Colo.: Lynne Rienner, 2000); and Woodrow Wilson International Center for Scholars and International Peace Academy, *The Economics of War: The Intersection of Need, Creed, and Greed* (Washington, D.C.: Woodrow Wilson Center, 2002).

29. International Crisis Group, *Colombia's Elusive Quest for Peace* (Bogotá and Brussels: International Crisis Group, March 2002), 9–10.

30. Rafael Pardo Rueda, "The Prospects for Peace in Colombia: Lessons from Recent Experience," Inter-American Dialogue Working Paper (Washington, D.C.: Inter-American Dialogue, July 2002), 1.

31. See Ana María Bejarano et al., "La fragmentación interna del estado y su impacto sobre la formulación e implementación de una política estatal de paz y convivencia ciudadana," in Centro de Investigaciones Sociojurídicos (CIJUS), *Estudios Ocasionales* (Bogotá: Ediciones Uniandes, June 2001).

32. These include the FARC, ELN, M-19, Popular Liberation Army (EPL), Revolutionary Workers Party (PRT), and the indigenous-based Armed Quintin Lame Movement (MAQL).

33. Negotiation officials, interviews by authors, New York, December 6, 2001, and Bogotá, March 18, 19, and 20, 2002.

34. In the most notorious instance, open conflict developed between Castaño's forces and those of Hernán Giraldo Serna, a paramilitary leader in the Sierra Nevada of Santa Marta, over the latter's drug trafficking and order to kill three undercover drug agents, two of them from the U.S. Drug Enforcement Agency, in October 2001. Before the resolution of the conflict in February 2002, seventy paramilitaries had been killed and some four thousand campesinos displaced.

35. The Bloque Central Bolívar controlled coca fields in Putumayo and southern Bolívar departments, key targets of U.S. antidrug policy. Scott Wilson, "Cocaine Trade Causes Rifts in Colombian Drug War," *Washington Post,* September 16, 2002, A1.

36. Inside Colombia, Castaño faced more than two dozen indictments for crimes ranging from assassinations to massacres. See John Otis, "Talks Signal Power Shift in Colombian Civil War," *Houston Chronicle,* November 27, 2002.

37. The Elmer Cárdenas bloc pulled out in January 2003. See Luis Jaime Acosta, "Colombia Paramilitary Bloc Severs Peace Contacts," Reuters, February 3, 2003.

38. Online NewsHour, "U.S. Indicts Colombian Paramilitary Chief," September 25, 2002, http://www.pbs.org/newshour/updates/colombia.

39. See, for example, Andy Webb-Vidal, "Peace Talks in Colombia on Brink of Collapse," *Financial Times,* May 3, 2004; and Juan Forero, "With Chief Missing, Colombia Militias Gain Leverage," *New York Times,* May 19, 2004.

40. International Crisis Group, *Colombia's Elusive Quest for Peace,* 7.

41. International Bank for Reconstruction and Development, "Central Government Finances," Table 14, *World Bank Development Report, 2000/2001: Attacking Poverty* (Washington, D.C.: Oxford University Press, 2001), 300. See also Council on Foreign Relations, *Andes 2020: A New Strategy for the Challenges of Colombia and the Region* (New York: Council on Foreign Relations, 2004), 110.

42. Cited in Jimmy Langman and Joseph Contreras, "Beyond 'Drugs and Thugs,'" *Newsweek International,* February 2, 2004.

43. Cited in U.S. Department of State, "Colombia," *Country Reports on Human Rights Practices 2001* (Washington, D.C.: U.S. Government Printing Office, March 4, 2002).

44. Ibid.

45. The figures are according to the Colombian NGO País Libre, which tracks kidnappings. See http://www.paislibre.org.co/noticias. See also Reuters, "Colombia Abductions Dip, but Still Kidnap Capital," January 30, 2003.

46. The lower estimate is from the U.S. State Department; the higher figure is from the Consultoría para los Derechos Humanos (CODHES), a Colombian NGO, which notes that some of those displaced since 1985 may have returned home. The Colombian government's human rights ombudsman noted a 50 percent increase in displacement between 2000 and 2001. See Defensoría del Pueblo, *El desplazamiento forzado por la violencia en Colombia* (Bogotá: Defensoría del Pueblo, April 2002), 2.

47. See Héctor Latorre, "Colombia 'avanza' en derechos humanos," BBC-Mundo.com, March 5, 2004; Reuters, "War Refugees in Colombia Down by Half in 2003," April 1, 2004; and Fundación Seguridad & Democracia, *Balance de Seguridad* *en Colombia Año 2003* (Bogotá: Fundación Seguridad & Democracia, December 12, 2003), 1–5.

48. The figures are from the Colombian government, as cited by Hartlyn, "Civil Violence and Conflict Resolution," 55; see also Human Rights Watch/Americas, *State of War: Political Violence and Counterinsurgency* (New York: Human Rights Watch, 1993), 17.

49. This point is made by Gonzalo Sánchez G., "Guerra prolongada y negociaciones incerta en Colombia," 295.

50. *Washington Post* correspondent Scott Wilson reported that "a number of opinion polls taken show Uribe has a majority of Colombians believing the government can defeat the insurgency." Scott Wilson, "A Worsening War in Colombia," *Washington Post*, February 1, 2003.

51. On October 10, 2000, Colombia's minister for foreign affairs, Guillermo Fernández de Soto, told a press conference at the United Nations that "the government is part of the solution and not part of the problem, as might occur in other parts of the world." Guillermo Fernández de Soto, Press Conference at the United Nations," UN press release, October 10, 2000.

52. "Press Conference by the President of Colombia at the United Nations," UN press release, September 22, 1999.

53. FARC leader Marulanda has also made repeated references to the failure of the international community to respond to government bombing attacks in 1964 against so-called Independent Republics set up by rural guerrillas who were the forerunners of the FARC. The FARC has also held a generally dim view of the UN role in peace negotiations in Central America, as peace accords in El Salvador and Guatemala did little to address issues of poverty or economic and social marginalization.

54. The ELN has appeared less resistant to international or third-party involvement, attempting to maintain contacts with groups in Colombian civil society through talks held in Spain and Germany under church auspices in the late 1990s. The ELN has also welcomed the involvement of the Cuban government, with which it maintains an ideological affinity, and talks during the Pastrana years were held in Havana. In mid-2004 the Mexican government attempted to broker renewed talks between the Colombian government and the ELN, efforts apparently welcomed by the guerrillas. As of this writing, it was too early to tell whether the initiative would prosper.

55. It is still not clear whether these murders represented lack of command and control by the FARC's high command over a regional front, or a direct attempt to sabotage dialogue with the United States. Neither interpretation reflects well on the FARC. See Cynthia J. Arnson, "The Peace Process in Colombia and U.S. Policy," in *Peace, Democracy, and Human Rights in Colombia,* ed. Gustavo Gallón and Christopher Welna (South Bend, Ind.: University of Notre Dame Press, 2004).

56. While the origins of Plan Colombia are still somewhat murky, it differed substantially from what Pastrana had originally proposed in 1998 as a kind of Marshall Plan or bank to finance agreements at the peace table. Some have claimed that English versions of Plan Colombia were available months before a version in Spanish, suggesting not only a heavy U.S. hand in its authorship but also that the plan's main audience was in Washington.

57. Some 80 percent of the Clinton administration's January 2000 aid request for $1.6 billion was for military and police assistance related to drug eradication and interdiction efforts.

58. United Nations, "Jan Egeland Appointed Special Adviser to the Secretary-General for International Assistance to Colombia," press release, SG/A/715, December 9, 1999.

59. Egeland had helped initiate and organize the "Norwegian channel" between Israel and the Palestine Liberation Organization that led to the Oslo Accords in September 1993. He also directed Norwegian facilitation of peace talks between the government of Guatemala and the guerrillas of the Unidad Revolucionaria Nacional Guatemalteca (URNG).

60. The countries visited were France, Italy, Spain, Sweden, and Switzerland.

61. Senior European diplomat, interview by authors, Bogotá, March 19, 2002.

62. Jan Egeland, draft statement, London Conference on Colombia, June 19, 2000, mimeographed, 4.

63. Ibon Billelabeitia, "U.N. Envoy: Time for Peace Running Out in Colombia," Reuters, December 11, 2000.

64. Spain pledged $100 million, Norway $20 million, and Japan $70 million. The United Nations offered an additional $131 million, with another $300 million from the Inter-American Development Bank and the Andean Development Corporation. Subsequent meetings in Bogotá in October 2000 and in Brussels in April 2001 brought the total European contribution to about $300 million. A contribution of about $30 million in 2002 was directed to towns in the highly conflictive region of the Magdalena Medio.

65. Willy Stevens, Belgian Foreign Ministry (presentation at Georgetown University, Washington, D.C., June 24, 2002); and Marc Chernick, "Protracted Peacemaking/Permanent War: The Insertion of the International Community into the Colombian Peace Process" (paper prepared for the International Peace Academy, "From Promise to Practice: Strengthening UN Capacities for the Prevention of Violent Conflict," January 2002).

66. Western diplomat, interview by authors, Bogotá, March 20, 2002.

67. Comunicado Conjunto del Gobierno Nacional y las FARC, "Acuerdo de los Pozos," Los Pozos, Caquetá, February 9, 2001.

68. The group of friends included Austria, Belgium, Brazil, Canada, Chile, Costa Rica, Cuba, Denmark, Ecuador, Finland, France, Germany, Italy, Japan, Mexico, Netherlands, Norway, Panama, Peru, Portugal, Spain, Sweden, Switzerland, United Kingdom, Venezuela, the Vatican, and representatives of the United Nations

and European Union. The facilitating commission consisted of Canada, Cuba, France, Italy, Mexico, Norway, Spain, Sweden, Switzerland, and Venezuela.

69. Western diplomat, interview by authors, Bogotá, March 20, 2002.

70. The countries were Canada, Germany, Japan, Portugal, and Sweden.

71. This was the Conflict Prevention and Peace Forum, a program of the New York–based Social Science Research Council.

72. According to paramilitary leader Castaño's version of events, these efforts included attempts to intercede directly with the paramilitaries facilitated by a range of figures, including Gabriel García Márquez and senior Spanish officials such as former prime minister Felipe González. Mauricio Aranguren Molina, *Mi confesión: Carlos Castaño revela sus secretos* (Bogotá: Editorial Oveja Negra, 2001), 261–285.

73. This account draws on Teresa Whitfield's involvement with events at the time as well as interviews with diplomatic sources in New York, December 6, 2001, and Bogotá, March 19, 2002.

74. Reuters, "EU Says Role in Colombia 'Gravely Compromised,'" July 31, 2001.

75. Senior diplomat, interview by authors, Bogotá, March 18, 2002.

76. Agence France Presse, "Descarta la ONU mediar con los 'paras,'" *El Nuevo Herald*, May 19, 2003; Associated Press, "UN May Stay Out of Colombian Talks," May 20, 2003. LeMoyne angered members of the Colombian government and elite when he made public statements suggesting that "the upper classes are not making enough sacrifices in Colombia's war," and that it was "a mistake to think that the FARC members are only drug-traffickers and terrorists." The Colombian government accused LeMoyne of justifying guerrilla violence. See Andrew Selsky, "Debate Surrounds UN Envoy Colombia Quip," Associated Press, May 21, 2003; and Agence France Presse, "Bogotá rechaza los comentarios del delegado especial de la ONU," *El Nuevo Herald*, May 21, 2003.

77. This shift of production is referred to as the "balloon effect": reductions in cultivation in one area that cause cultivation to pop up in another. See also Scott Wilson, "Coca Invades Colombia's Coffee Fields," *Washington Post*, October 30, 2001, 17.

78. United Nations Development Program, *Informe Nacional de Desarrollo Humano 2003: El Conflicto, callejón con salida* (Bogotá: United Nations Development Program, 2003); "Ojos en el cielo," *El Tiempo*, June 9, 2004.

11

The Uses of Deadlock
Intractability in Eurasia

Charles King

THE FACTORS THAT IGNITE WARS are not the same as the forces that keep them going. For both the strategist and the soldier, the experience of violence is transformative. Calculations of costs and benefits change during the course of a conflict. The seductive power of sunk costs, the dynamics of shifting war aims, the possibility of political gain against domestic opponents, and the vested interests of foreign actors can all have an effect on when and how military leaders decide to negotiate or to fight on.[1]

These elements of warfare, whether within or between states, have long been known to theorists and practitioners. What is novel, however, is how they play out in environments of state weakness. Recent research on civil wars, particularly in Africa, has illustrated the intimate relationship between the robustness of state institutions and the durability of civil violence.[2] The constant threat of violence keeps state structures weak and provides opportunities for personal enrichment. With no centralized police force or effective customs or tax service to restrain them, soldiers can become entrepreneurs, taking advantage of natural resources and trade in both legal and illegal goods. In some instances, those networks can over time become transformed into the institutions of quasi states.

Weakness is not something that simply happens to states. In many countries, it is in the direct political and economic interests of the supposed guardians of public order to keep order from ever breaking out. Such has been the case in several of the disputes that have ground on for more than a decade in the former Soviet Union. Beginning in the late 1980s, more than a half-dozen small wars raged across Eurasia: in Azerbaijan, Moldova, Georgia, Tajikistan, and the north Caucasus republics of the Russian Federation. All involved a host of different actors, including the central governments of new states, territorial separatists, and foreign armies, and sprang from a combination of ethnic grievances, disputes over land, and struggles for power among old and new elites. With the exception of the second Chechen war, which began in 1999, the military side of most of the conflicts ended in the mid-1990s, and peace negotiations were launched under the sponsorship of the United Nations and the Organization for Security and Cooperation in Europe (OSCE), including substantial involvement by the United States. To date, however, the various sides in several of these conflicts have remained at an impasse, unable to sign a final peace accord that would allow the war-torn countries to be reunited but unwilling to stomach a return to the violence of the early 1990s.

In four of these conflicts—in the Nagorno-Karabakh region of Azerbaijan, in the Transnistria region of Moldova, and in the Abkhazia and South Ossetia regions of Georgia—it is tempting to blame the depth of ethnic hatred between the principal belligerents for the continuing standoff.[3] It is not difficult to find leaders on all sides who denounce their opponents as foreign interlopers who have no business living in "their" country, or as fascists bent on ethnic cleansing, or as stooges of Russia, NATO, or even the Freemasons. However, the rhetoric of ethnic confrontation covers up the basic conundrum that has prevented these conflicts from moving toward a final resolution: no party with decision-making power is sufficiently hurt by the status quo that it has an incentive to push forward with a real settlement. Or to put the argument less charitably, plenty of individuals on all sides benefit from the current state of affairs to such a degree that a lack of resolution—and the profound weakness of legitimate state institutions that results—is preferable to a stable, defined final status. The amount of time that has elapsed since the origins of the post-Soviet wars has now meant that something very close to functional but unrecognized states have emerged in the former rebel territories. Peace negotiations today are therefore not so much about trying to bring together two parties in a civil war as about trying to merge two separate states and even societies.

The first section of this chapter outlines some of the key pillars of intractability, the major obstacles that have so far blocked settlement.

(This chapter does not consider the conflict in Chechnya, although it exhibits some of the characteristics of the four conflicts examined here. Because the second Chechen war continues today as a guerrilla conflict, the dynamics of peace negotiations—which have not yet begun—and state building analyzed here have not been present.) The second and third sections focus on international involvement; the key regional player in all of these disputes, the Russian Federation; and third-party mediators. The final section offers some conclusions and points toward the difficulty of deriving broadly applicable lessons from the Eurasian wars.

The Uses of Deadlock

Each of the major Eurasian wars had similar long-term and proximate causes.[4] Conflicts often involved an ethnic minority that was distinct from the majority population in the country (or Soviet-era republic) as a whole and that had enjoyed a relatively privileged position during the Soviet period, usually within an ethnically defined administrative subunit. The resurgence among the Soviet Union's republican nationalities went too far and too fast for many minorities, who worried that the revival of majority cultures would come at the expense of the "socialist internationalism" of the Soviet era. The lack of real mechanisms for dealing with interethnic tensions meant that the weak Soviet center had little at its disposal besides the use of force; interventions by interior and defense ministry troops in the waning days of the Soviet Union, designed to quell the situation, sometimes exacerbated it. In other instances, Soviet troops in the conflict zones—based there when the Soviet Union still existed and then taken under Russian Federation control after 1991—aided the most radical separatists with manpower and weapons. In some cases, there seem to have been orders from the Russian interior or defense ministry to aid the separatists; in others, the ministries were less important than the entrepreneurial actions of military commanders on the ground. The result, however, was the flow of arms, equipment, and personnel to rebel groups inside the newly independent states.

Full-blown wars were waged in the period from 1988 to 1994, and the destruction was considerable: entire cities virtually destroyed, hundreds of thousands of refugees and internally displaced persons (IDPs), tens of thousands dead. The depth of interethnic animosity wrought by the wars is still very high. Armenians in Karabakh fear a renewal of war by the government of Azerbaijan, a "Turkic" state that is often compared in the rhetoric of Armenian politicians with the Ottoman Empire, perpetrator of the Armenian genocide of 1915. Ethnic Russians and Ukrainians in Transnistria claim that Moldova's Romanian-speaking majority will, at some point, choose to unite with neighboring Romania. Abkhaz and South Ossetians remember the rhetoric of the early 1990s in Georgia, when ethnic minorities were treated as unwelcome guests by a Georgian government that seemed to be striving for ethnic purity. On the other side, central governments feel that these minority concerns merely mask the interests of the Russian Federation, which they claim uses the problem of minority rights as a lever to keep the conflicts simmering. As long as the disputes remain unresolved, the logic goes, weak countries such as Azerbaijan, Georgia, and Moldova will remain inside the Russian sphere of influence.

It is easy to see this mutual enmity as the major brake on settlement, especially given that many of the elites who had a hand in making the wars were still in office in 2004, ten years after the most active violence ended: Vladislav Ardzinba, leader of Abkhazia; Igor Smirnov, leader of Transnistria; Robert Kocharian, former leader of Karabakh and now president of Armenia, among others.[5] However, the chief obstacle has been that, beneath these unresolved grievances, political elites in the rebel areas have gone about the process of building states that now function about as well as the recognized countries of which they are still nominally constituents—and states that, moreover, are shielded by independent armies, foreign forces, and armed paramilitary groups: numbering up to twenty-four thousand troops in Transnistria, two thousand in South Ossetia, five thousand in Abkhazia, fifty-six thousand in Karabakh.[6] Today, the Eurasian wars look far less like "stalled" or "frozen" ethnic conflicts than examples of a process known in other parts of Europe from the late Middle Ages forward: the creation of new states out of the crucible of war.

That Azerbaijan, Georgia, and Moldova are weak states is crucial to understanding the development of the Eurasian conflicts since the early 1990s. The per capita GDP of these states, at purchasing-power parity, lies between those of Papua New Guinea and Swaziland. Public revenue collection, although improving, is often too low to support even the most basic state functions, such as adequate policing, payment of pensions, or provision of health services. Sizable portions of each country's territory, population, and wealth-producing potential—the separatist zones—remain outside central control. Karabakh and the occupied zone around it constitute 14 percent of Azerbaijan's territory; Transnistria is 12 percent of Moldova's; Abkhazia and South Ossetia together are 17 percent of Georgia's.[7] Even beyond the unrecognized states, there are many parts of the country where the central government's writ does not run.

Chronic state weakness is of clear benefit to the separatist governments. Tariffs and production taxes can be avoided. Lucrative imports such as alcohol and cigarettes can be brought in for resale or transshipment. The degree to which the separatists have been able to benefit from the weak states differs, however. The least successful has been Nagorno-Karabakh. Its population, estimated at around one hundred fifty thousand, survives mainly on subsistence farming or resale of consumer goods imported from Iran and Armenia. Swaths of towns and villages remain in ruins. Removal of the thousands of land mines laid during the conflict has progressed with international assistance, but the fear of unexploded ordnance continues to restrict agricultural production. Despite these difficulties, local authorities have been able to construct something resembling a state, with its own foreign ministry (whose representatives regularly visit the United States to meet with Armenian diaspora leaders and U.S. politicians), army, police, and judicial system.

Abkhazia and South Ossetia have fared slightly better. Both were reasonably important regions of Georgia during the Soviet period, boasting impressive tourist facilities, mining complexes, and light industry. Now, however, few enterprises function, since the outflow of refugees and IDPs more than halved their populations, which now stand at under two hundred thousand in Abkhazia and perhaps eighty thousand in South Ossetia. (There has been no systematic census since 1989.) The local economy is centered on other pursuits. In Abkhazia export of fruits and nuts, particularly tangerines and hazelnuts, remains an important source of revenue; in fact, upsurges in local violence among rival economic clans tend to be seasonal, as bandits attempt to steal hazelnut shipments in the late summer and early autumn. Trade in scrap metal, from both dysfunctional industries and power lines, is also important—even though it has destroyed what little industry (and power distribution capacity) the region has left. In South Ossetia geography has been the local government's chief asset.

(continued on p. 278)

Table 1. Eurasia's Major Intractable Conflicts

	Main Actors	Conflict Period and Cease-fire	Major Mediators	Peacekeeping Operations	Major Mediation Achievements
Nagorno-Karabakh	Armenia and Nagorno-Karabakh Republic versus Azerbaijan.	Began 1988. Cease-fire since May 1994. No major violence since then.	Minsk Group of the OSCE (cochaired by France, Russia, and the United States) established in 1992. Personal representative of the chairman in office of the OSCE based in Tbilisi, Georgia. Minsk Group provides good offices and sponsors periodic face-to-face meetings of the Armenian and Azerbaijani presidents.	None. OSCE committed to fielding a mission after peace settlement.	Drafting of series of principles for continued negotiation. No agreement on basic framework for peace.

| Transnistria | Dnestr Moldovan Republic (a.k.a. Transnistria) versus Moldova. On the Transnistrian side, some freelance fighters from Russia and Ukraine (Cossacks, Ukrainian militias). Russian Federation troops (about 1,000, separate from the Russian peacekeepers) still stationed in Transnistria were to have been withdrawn by the end of 2002, but the deadline was not met. | Began 1989. Ceasefire since July 1992. No major violence since then. | OSCE field mission based in Chişinău, Moldova, since 1993. Provides good offices and forum for negotiations. Periodic meetings of presidents of Moldova and Transnistria and meetings of expert groups. | Tripartite Russian-Moldovan-Transnistrian peacekeeping force in place since 1992; currently around 1,000 troops (500 Russian). Small Ukrainian observer mission deployed 1998. | Series of agreements on financial and trade cooperation and security and confidence-building measures. Agreement on basic principles for negotiations (particularly on the goal of creating a "common state") signed in 1997. OSCE draft document on creation of a federation of Moldova and Transnistria put on the table in 2002. Separate Russian plan for a federation put forward in 2003 but rejected by Moldovan side. |

continued on next page

Table 1. Eurasia's Major Intractable Conflicts (*cont.*)

	Main Actors	Conflict Period and Cease-fire	Major Mediators	Peacekeeping Operations	Major Mediation Achievements
Abkhazia	Republic of Abkhazia versus Georgia. On the Abkhaz side, some freelance fighters from North Caucasus, plus Russian (former Soviet) troops still based in Abkhazia. On the Georgian side, various guerrilla groups active inside Abkhazia. Russian Federation troops stationed in Abkhazia and Georgia (about 3,000 troops, separate from the Russian peacekeepers) are the subject of ongoing negotiations between Georgia and Russia.	Began 1992. Cease-fire since May 1994. Occasional fighting in security zone between the two sides and in the Kodori Gorge region (area inside Abkhazia still controlled by Georgia). Latest small-scale fighting (in Kodori) was in fall 2001.	United Nations Observer Mission in Georgia (UNOMIG) authorized in 1993 and based in Tbilisi, Georgia. Provides good offices and negotiating forum coordinated by special representative of the secretary-general. Periodic meetings of working groups with representatives of both sides.	Around 100 international UNOMIG observers monitor security zone between Abkhazia and Georgia proper, plus another 100 international civilian support personnel. Separate peacekeeping mission of the Commonwealth of Independent States (in practice, a Russian-only mission) of around 1,600 troops deployed in security zone since 1994.	Drafting of series of principles for continued negotiation. No agreement on basic framework for peace.

| South Ossetia | Republic of South Ossetia versus Georgia. On the South Ossetian side, some freelance fighters from North Ossetia (a republic of the Russian Federation). | Began 1990. Cease-fire since July 1992. No major violence since then. | OSCE field mission in Tbilisi, Georgia, in place since 1992. Provides good offices and negotiating forum. Periodic meetings between South Ossetian and Georgian presidents. | Small Russian Federation peacekeeping force (around 500 troops) deployed in 1992. | Drafting of series of principles for continued negotiation. No agreement on basic framework for peace. |

Source: Troop figures are from *The Military Balance, 2003–2004* (London: International Institute for Strategic Studies, 2003).

Lying across a major north-south artery linking Georgia with the Russian Federation, the republic has been able to extract considerable revenue in the form of "transit taxes."

Transnistria's economic position is probably better than that of any of the other unrecognized states. Transnistria was the mainstay of Moldovan industry during the Soviet period, with heavy machine industries and power-generating plants concentrated there. The Moldova Steel Works, a high-quality rolled steel facility in northern Transnistria, was the pride of Soviet Moldovan industry, and it has continued to function under Transnistrian control. It has been so successful, in fact, that in 2001 the United States and Canada found Moldova guilty of dumping steel on the U.S. and Canadian markets. Although the steel came from the Transnistrian mill (and therefore bypassed Moldovan export controls), the dumping triggered punitive sanctions from the United States—a tariff of 232.86 percent, the highest of any country sanctioned by the United States.[8] Given the dire state of Moldova's own economy, Transnistria's economy looks rather better in some areas. In every major field except consumer goods, the separatist region has been a net "exporter" to the rest of Moldova.[9]

Central authorities frequently complain about the economic benefits that accrue to the separatist governments. But those benefits also flow to the institutions and individuals ostensibly responsible for resolving the conflicts. The links between corrupt central governments and the separatist regions, especially in Georgia and Moldova, have further imperiled already weak state structures while enriching those who claim to be looking after state interests. For example, the illegal trade with Russia benefits people in both South Ossetia and Georgia proper. The South Ossetian government receives money from transit taxes and smuggling, while Georgian authorities, especially the interior ministry, are able to take a cut by exacting fines from truck drivers who carry the transited goods onto Georgian-controlled highways. It is partly for these reasons that relations between the two sides have actually been rather cordial, notwithstanding the lack of a final settlement. The South Ossetian president, in fact, openly supported Eduard Shevardnadze in his campaign for Georgian president in early 2000—even though Shevardnadze was technically running for office in a state that the South Ossetians consider separate and inimical.

Average citizens are not blind to these activities, which have produced a deep skepticism about state institutions. In a 2000 survey in

Georgia, two-thirds reported having no faith in parliament or the president, and some 80 percent had no faith in tax and customs officials.[10] In a 2002 survey in Moldova, 57 percent reported little or no faith in parliament and 63 percent had little or no faith in the police.[11] Throughout these conflict zones, the weak state is not a condition that has arisen out of nowhere. Continued weakness is to a great degree in the interests of those in power.

Even beyond the problem of corrupt state institutions, there are powerful domestic incentives for central governments not to change the status quo. In the Georgian parliament, the Apkhazeti faction—the remnants of the former Georgian administration in Abkhazia that fled to the Georgian capital during the war ("Apkhazeti" is the Georgian word for "Abkhazia") —has proved to be a brake on genuine compromise. The Apkhazeti hold set-aside seats in parliament and, although they do not control enough parliamentary votes to push through legislation, they are vocal opponents of any move that might seem to compromise their own interest in one day returning to power in Abkhazia. They have long blocked legislation that would provide for resettlement and integration of the 250,000 ethnic Georgians and the closely related Mingrelians displaced during the Abkhaz war, people who have spent much of the 1990s and early 2000s living in "temporary" accommodation in dilapidated state-owned hotels. Permanently resettling the IDPs outside Abkhazia would in fact reduce the Apkhazeti faction's political and economic power, since they control state budgetary disbursements to the IDPs in the form of social services.[12]

In all three states there are also other simmering ethnic issues that will be strongly affected by movement on the most serious disputes. How governments handle relations with the unrecognized states will have a profound impact on the form and degree of autonomy that might be demanded by other groups in the future. In northeastern Azerbaijan some 160,000 ethnic Lezgis (Muslim, mainly Sunni, highlanders) live separated from a larger Lezgi community inside the Russian republic of Dagestan. Political movements calling for the union of the northern and southern Lezgin lands have arisen on both sides of the border. A final settlement that allowed far-reaching autonomy for Karabakh might provide, from Azerbaijan's perspective, an unwelcome encouragement to the Lezgis.

A similar dynamic has been at work in Moldova. The Gagauz, a Turkic Christian population of around 150,000 in southern Moldova, were granted territorial autonomy in 1995. But since then, Gagauz leaders have demanded even greater devolution of authority to their institutions; local leaders have even shored up ties with Transnistrian authorities, demanding that Moldova eventually become a full-fledged confederation of three parts: Moldova proper, Transnistria, and the Gagauz lands.

In Georgia the status of mainly Armenian districts in the south will be affected by how the Abkhaz and South Ossetian disputes are resolved. In two districts, ethnic Armenians account for more than 90 percent of the population. These areas are already largely outside central government control; Georgian currency is rarely used, and poor roads mean that contacts with the capital are limited. There is a small but ardent separatist movement in the region, demanding independence or unification with Armenia, but even among more moderate groups there is a strong sense that the Armenian-speaking areas should have local autonomy. (Relations between Georgia and Armenia have generally been cordial since 1991, but the two countries did fight a border war over these and other regions at the end of World War I.) The presence of a large Russian military base in the area—the only real source of employment—has also put the Armenian population at odds with the Georgian government, which demands that the Russian base be withdrawn.[13] Even if central governments were genuinely interested in changing the status quo, they would still be faced with the uncomfortable precedent that might be set for other potential disputes if full devolution of power to the de facto states occurred.

There is yet another dimension to the state-building process in the unrecognized regions: the effort to inculcate a sense of identity and loyalty among average citizens. Early in all four conflicts, local authorities moved to take over educational and cultural institutions within the conflict zones. New national festivals were inaugurated. History curricula were redesigned to highlight the citizens of the separatist regions as the indigenous inhabitants of their territory. Local intellectuals also worked, as far as possible, to discover cultural or historical heroes around which semiofficial cults could be built, and previous experiences of statehood, no matter how short-lived, were marshaled to serve the cause. The wars of the 1990s are also now treated as hallowed struggles against external aggression. "The war [against South Ossetia] killed and maimed thousands of our citizens; left tens of thousands of innocent people without shelter, work, and means of survival; razed our infrastructure; robbed the people of kindergartens and

schools; and made peaceful citizens into refugees," reads a South Ossetian textbook. "Nevertheless, these years have a special historical significance for us, because we not only managed to defeat the aggressor but
also to build our own statehood."[14] Children who were not even born
when the national movements began in the late 1980s are now adoles-
cents, and they have spent the 1990s and early 2000s reading similar versions of history in their schoolbooks.

Of course, one can find equally tendentious views of history and
recent politics in textbooks published by the ministries of education of
Azerbaijan, Georgia, and Moldova; no one in the former Soviet Union has
a monopoly on uncritical patriotism. But in both the recognized and the
unrecognized states, more than ten years of such propagandizing has
resulted in the creation of populations that will not easily shed the version
of the truth that they have invested so much in defending. Moreover,
those whose job it is to create and propagate these ideologies—university
professors, academicians, schoolteachers, even writers and poets—have a
huge personal incentive to continue doing so: since many have progressed
in their careers precisely because they came to control a set of cultural
institutions divorced from the recognized central governments (a local
polytechnic that overnight became a "national university," for instance),
they are loath to make any move that would undercut the advantages they
derive from existence inside a functionally separate state.

The Russia Factor

From the onset of social mobilization, each of the Eurasian wars had substantial external involvement. Soviet, later Russian, troops were either stationed on the ground in the conflict zones (Abkhazia, Transnistria) or
implicated in providing weapons and personnel to separatist forces
(Nagorno-Karabakh, South Ossetia). Volunteer forces from other parts of
the former Soviet Union—Armenian volunteers in Karabakh, North
Caucasus irregulars in Abkhazia, Cossacks in Transnistria, North Ossetian
fighters in South Ossetia—were dispatched to aid the embattled minority
populations. International organizations such as the United Nations and
the OSCE brokered negotiations. The preeminent regional power, Russia,
provided peacekeeping troops and served as an informal guarantor of the
interests of the separatist powers in ongoing talks.

The active interests of outside parties in these conflicts have not led to any easy resolution. In fact, in many ways, outsiders have contributed not only to the victory of the separatists on the battlefield but also to the consolidation of statehood afterward. Russia has not been the only external player, of course. Diaspora groups in the United States and Western Europe have been strong supporters of the Armenian cause in Karabakh, sending humanitarian assistance and investing in the local economy. The unrecognized states even cooperate with one another, so that each has become something of an external influence on the behavior of the others. The presidents and foreign ministers regularly exchange visits and coordinate bargaining positions. Each unrecognized state has officially recognized every other one. Among all these external influences, however, the most significant has been the Russian Federation.

The official Russian history of the Eurasian wars argues that the government had a largely pacifying role in each of the conflicts.[15] However, Russian assistance was a major component in the early stages of state building. In Moldova, Russian Federation troops were the main source and conduit of weapons and personnel—including highly trained senior officers—to the Transnistrians.[16] There were no troops in Azerbaijan after mid-1993, but Russian troops in neighboring Armenia aided both Armenian government troops and Karabakh separatists during the war. Leakage of weapons and soldiers from the Russian base in Abkhazia, along with the arrival of freelance fighters from the Russian north Caucasus republics, was critical to Abkhaz success against the ragtag Georgian army.[17]

As of mid-2004, Russian troops were still stationed in Moldova and Georgia, against the will of the two host governments. At the OSCE Istanbul summit in 1999, both states secured Russian agreement to a full-scale withdrawal, and since then there has been some progress, particularly with the closure of one Russian base in Georgia and the staged withdrawal of military equipment and munitions from Moldova. At the time of this writing, Russian troop strength (not counting soldiers who are part of peacekeeping deployments) stands at about three thousand in Georgia and one thousand in Moldova.[18]

In both cases, however, withdrawal has been more complicated than it would at first appear. The Moldovan government, under both Russian and OSCE pressure, signed an agreement in 1994 that mandated that the withdrawal of the Russian army be "synchronized" with resolving the final status of Transnistria. Until the Istanbul summit, that agreement effectively blocked real progress, since it was unclear whether withdrawal should precede resolution or vice versa. The Transnistrians were also eager to throw obstacles in the path of departing soldiers—sometimes literally, by blocking railroads to prevent the removal of military equipment. Even if Russian troops eventually leave Moldova, the Russian Federation's "presence" will remain in other ways. With the vast numbers of retired Russian military personnel who have elected to stay in Transnistria—where they and their families have lived for years and where their military pensions go further than in parts of Russia—the Transnistrians have a ready supply of mobilizable soldiers. Indeed, the total number of men under arms, regular armed forces plus reservists, is far larger than the number in Moldova proper.

In Georgia the Russian military began downsizing in 2000, closing an airbase just outside the capital of Tbilisi. However, three major bases remain, two of them in politically sensitive regions (one in Abkhazia and one in Javakheti, the area in the south with a largely Armenian population). The Russian military base in Abkhazia serves much the same function as the troop presence in Transnistria, providing employment and security for an effectively separate regime. The Russian and Georgian governments have carried out negotiations regarding the transformation of the base into a convalescence station for Russian peacekeepers, but that change of label would not substantially alter the strong role that the facility plays in Abkhaz political and economic life. In both Georgia and Moldova, even the salaries of Russian soldiers, paid in rubles, have ensured that Abkhazia, South Ossetia, and Transnistria remain economically tied to Russia rather than to their recognized central governments, since goods and services are purchased using rubles rather than national currencies.[19] The relationship is reinforced by Russian visa and passport policy. Since late 2000 citizens of Georgia, but not inhabitants of Abkhazia and South Ossetia, have been required to apply for regular Russian visas, and obtaining Russian passports has been relatively easy in any of the separatist regions, especially if individuals first agree to work as contract soldiers in Russian military units.[20] Russian citizenship has also been relatively easy to obtain in most of the conflict areas; it may well be the case that a plurality—if not a majority—of the inhabitants of Abkhazia, South Ossetia, and Transnistria are now Russian citizens. That situation, of course, gives the Russian Federation a direct interest in the outcome of these disputes.

External Mediators

Negotiations under the aegis of multilateral organizations have been on-going since the mid-1990s. In Azerbaijan the OSCE-sponsored Minsk Group has provided good offices and a mechanism for negotiations since 1992. In Moldova an OSCE mission has been active since 1993 and has sponsored numerous rounds of negotiations. In Georgia a United Nations observer mission, UNOMIG, was deployed in 1993 to provide a basis for negotiations on Abkhazia's future and to monitor the peacekeeping operation conducted by Russian forces (nominally under the control of the Commonwealth of Independent States) in the Georgian-Abkhaz security zone. In South Ossetia Russian peacekeepers have been in place since the end of the war, and negotiations on South Ossetia's final status have continued apace, involving North Ossetia, the OSCE, and Russia as mediators.

The multiple rounds of negotiations, both during and after the fighting, have often seemed endless. Consider the example of Karabakh, the longest-running dispute in the former Soviet Union. In the late 1980s the Gorbachev administration appealed to socialist brotherhood and the Soviet army to restore order, to little avail. Boris Yeltsin and Nursultan Nazarbaev, the president of Kazakhstan, brokered an agreement on territorial autonomy for Karabakh within Azerbaijan in September 1991, but the agreement was scuppered when an aircraft carrying Russian and Azerbaijani officials was shot down over Karabakh. The OSCE began its own mediation track in 1992, leading to an unsuccessful draft peace accord in 1993. The same year the UN Security Council passed three resolutions demanding the withdrawal of Armenian and Karabakh forces from Azerbaijani territory. In May 1994 the Russian Federation finally managed to secure a full cease-fire agreement, the Bishkek Protocol. Russia attempted unsuccessfully to broker a final settlement, and the peace process was put under the sole aegis of the OSCE's Minsk Group (so called because the final peace conference was to take place in Minsk, Belarus), cochaired by France, Russia, and the United States. However, the Minsk process has long been primarily a form of shuttle diplomacy, since the parties to the conflict have rarely been able to meet. It was not until 1999 that the Armenian and Azerbaijani presidents announced their willingness to join in serious face-to-face talks, which culminated in a cordial meeting in Key West, Florida, in April 2001. Since then, however, the situation seems to have returned to deadlock, the Azerbaijani government denouncing Armenian "terrorists" and the Armenian government denouncing the Azerbaijani "genocide" against ethnic Armenians during the war. (The two sides cannot even agree on what happened in Key West. The Armenians insist that a land-for-peace deal was put on the table—whereby Azerbaijan would give up Karabakh in exchange for other concessions from Armenia—while the Azerbaijanis maintain that no specific points were ever put forward.) A similar litany of meetings postponed and canceled characterizes the other conflicts as well.

That the belligerents are willing to talk with each other at all is no small achievement, especially given that in all four conflicts the separatists won outright on the battlefield. These post-Soviet disputes must surely be one of history's rare instances of clear military victors' being willing to come to the bargaining table to compromise with the vanquished. In that sense, the bar for success in the negotiations should probably be set relatively low. The fact that there has not been a reversion to large-scale violence (with the exception of occasional flare-ups in Abkhazia) is in part due to the continued engagement of outside actors. Still, there are three broad obstacles that have prevented international organizations from making real progress toward a final settlement.

First, for all the decision-making elites concerned, there are some benefits to continued "dialogue" but no costs to nonimplementation of agreements. The belligerents have been favorably disposed to negotiate, even if scheduled sessions are routinely postponed or canceled, largely because they understand that they will thereby remain within the good graces of the facilitating parties—and receive development assistance and other rewards for staying in the game. But never have talks produced more than an agreement to continue talking, an outcome that all sides find agreeable. At a minimum, there is no disincentive to continue meeting; at a maximum, the belligerents get the best of both worlds: the continued approbation of the international community for their "steadfastness" and "willingness to maintain dialogue" and the ability to continue to reap the rewards of stalemate. Precisely because the current situation is less bad than potential alternatives—the escalation to full-scale war, for example —no international mediator has ever attempted to pressure either the central governments or the unrecognized states into making a binding agreement and then sticking with it.

Second, there is a persistent dilemma at the heart of the conflicts concerning the relationship between individual citizens and their governments. In instances in which there is a mobilized group of citizens with clear interest in resolving the conflict, they have little access to political power; and in instances in which citizens have access to political power, there is no mobilized group with an interest in resolving the conflict. Examples of the first instance are Azerbaijan and Georgia, where the existence of substantial IDP populations, who have spent years in squalid "temporary" housing, should have produced a powerful domestic lobby for the resolution of the conflict. Indeed, in Azerbaijan more than half the total population views the Karabakh conflict as the most serious problem facing the country.[21] But in neither case have the governments—both of which have regularly falsified elections—felt a serious need to be responsive to the interests of their electorates, including the IDPs.

The exact opposite situation obtains in Moldova. There, the record on responsiveness has been relatively better, but there is no vocal and organized constituency that might press the government to settle the separatist dispute. When asked to name the most important problem facing Moldova, only 3 percent of Moldovans named the Transnistrian problem; only 18 percent put it among the top three problems. (In contrast, 75 percent named economic development, and 41 percent said the fight against corruption.)[22] People have gone about their lives on the assumption that Transnistria is simply no longer a part of their country. In all three countries, the net effect is the same: no real domestic pressure on governments to change the status quo.

Third, at times the actions of international negotiators have inadvertently bolstered the claims to statehood of the separatist regions. The criticism that outside negotiators automatically legitimize belligerents by the very act of speaking with them is a mantra often repeated in civil wars, usually by governments reluctant to engage in dialogue with insurgents. That, however, is not the real issue in the Eurasian conflicts. There, international organizations have actually gone rather further, working with and through the institutions of the unrecognized states or otherwise pursuing policies that strengthened their claims to statehood. To a certain extent, the very idea of peace negotiations has entailed some recognition of the legitimacy of those institutions. The separatists, after all, were the military victors and could dictate the basic terms of the talks—at a minimum, some form of "substantial autonomy" within the confines of the internationally recognized states that would allow their institutions (particularly their armies) to remain in place.

But in more subtle ways, the policies of external actors have raised to the level of a "state" the very congeries of institutions that negotiators have continued to label no more than the germ of a future "autonomous" area inside Azerbaijan, Georgia, or Moldova. In Karabakh the difficulty of crossing the front line between Karabakhtsi and Azerbaijani forces (and the excellent road link to Armenia, constructed with assistance from ethnic Armenians abroad) has meant that humanitarian and development programs, including those sponsored by the U.S. government, are managed from Armenia, not from Azerbaijan.[23] In Moldova the OSCE urged the Moldovans to sign an accord in 1997 that committed both sides to existence within a "common state," a form of language that the Transnistrians now interpret as Moldovan acquiescence to no more than a loose confederation[24]—and a form of wording that was also proposed by the Minsk Group in Karabakh in 1998 before being rejected by the Azerbaijani side. In Abkhazia international relief agencies remain an important part of the local economy, injecting around $4 to $5 million into the economy each year through rents and payment of local staff.[25] Of course, there is no insidious plot on the part of the OSCE or the United Nations to beef up the "stateness" of the unrecognized governments, although more than a few Azerbaijani, Georgian, and Moldovan conspiracy theorists insist there is. Rather, in a context in which there are already functional but unrecognized state institutions in place, outside mediators have had little choice but to work through them.

Russia has long insisted that the existence of the separatists is a fait accompli and that any final settlement will have to square the circle by somehow affirming the territorial integrity of the existing states while also providing for something close to independence—"maximum autonomy," "confederation"—for the unrecognized ones. Since 1999, there has been a clear change in Russian policy in each of these conflicts. The OSCE Istanbul summit, which committed Russia to withdrawing from Georgia and Moldova, also signaled a major new willingness to see the conflicts resolved. International negotiators report that Russian representatives seem far more willing to support resolution than to gain some particular advantage. The problem remains, however, that Russian policy has always been made in the plural, with various institutions—the presidency, the foreign ministry, the parliament, and the military—pursuing their own individual aims. The administration of President Vladimir Putin does seem to have moderated its views on the strategic usefulness of the unrecognized entities, but there is still little reason to believe that Russia will accept anything short of major autonomy for the separatist zones as part of a final settlement. That outcome, while allowing the international community to claim that the conflicts had been "solved," would probably do little more than legitimize the status quo—one in which outsiders have very little influence at all on democracy, human rights, and crime in the unrecognized states.[26]

Conclusion

At first glance, the four Eurasian conflicts surveyed in this chapter would seem to be textbook cases of how the international community should handle civil wars. After 1991, when the conflicts shifted from being internal problems of the Soviet Union to serious regional disputes involving newly independent states, international organizations were quick to become involved. The United Nations passed numerous resolutions on the Karabakh and Abkhazia conflicts and, in the latter, authorized the deployment of a local observer mission to provide monitoring and good offices to the belligerent parties. The OSCE likewise fielded missions in Moldova and Georgia. (Separate OSCE offices in Georgia are responsible for the negotiations in both South Ossetia and Karabakh.) The organizations also worked to bring on board regional players, particularly Russia, Turkey, and Ukraine, as guarantors of the negotiations and of an eventual peace settlement. Even the recognized states themselves have gone far toward rectifying the problems that originally spawned the conflicts, adopting legislation on minority rights and promising significant devolution of authority to the rebel areas as part of a final peace deal.

It is therefore difficult to derive easy lessons from the Eurasian wars; the mediators themselves—the diplomats and representatives of international organizations—have by and large done an exemplary job of facilitating the talks. The problem has not been one of techniques employed by outsiders or the leverage that they might have over the belligerents. Rather, the obstacles to settlement lie in the benefits of deadlock that continue to accrue to all parties: for the separatists, a more or less functional state that provides considerable rents to the major decision makers who have managed to control its institutions; for the central governments, a useful scapegoat for the many economic and political problems that the recognized states continue to face and, for some, a source of personal profit in the form of smuggled merchandise, drugs, weapons, and trafficked people; for the international community, a stalemate that, while clearly suboptimal, is better than all-out war. In that sense, the conflicts may well be "happy intractables"—no really stable peace but at least no immediate likelihood of war either.

The benefits of deadlock, of course, are relative. Azerbaijan, Georgia, and Moldova, three of the poorest states in the former Soviet Union, racked by economic problems and on, at best, an uncertain path toward democracy, would profit immensely from stable governance in a unified and peaceful state. For example, a World Bank study concluded that Azerbaijan could wipe away a quarter of its trade deficit by resolving the dispute over Karabakh, simply because of increased exports and transport savings.[27] But achieving that end, an aggregate good for the country as a whole, would demand a high price from the key decision makers on all sides. The separatists would have to dismantle the considerable statelike structures that they have built over the past decade. Entrepreneurs and smugglers would have to submit to the scrutiny of state regulatory bodies in the central government. Corrupt customs officials would have to give up their gains from illegal transnational commerce. Politicians would have to face constituents who might accuse them of selling out to the "ethnic cleansers" and "fascists" on the other side of the conflict line. And even at a much lower level—from writers who have spent the past ten years extolling the independence of a country called Abkhazia or Transnistria to schoolchildren who have been born and grown to adolescence inside a country they call Karabakh or South Ossetia—there are plenty of disincentives to settle for less than the de jure independence that was won de facto on the battlefield a decade ago.

None of these calculations would have been exactly the same several years ago, even in the middle of the war. But as the disputes have dragged on, languishing in a middle ground between war fighting and stable peace, rational actors in both the central governments and the separatist zones have learned to live with, and even benefit from, the status quo.

Intractability has become the equilibrium option for the major players concerned. Even the most dedicated peacemakers have thus found themselves in a quandary: pushing a settlement with separatists who have no real incentive to negotiate in good faith, central leaders who are not seriously hurt by the current state of affairs, and an international community that has had little real interest in putting serious pressure on any of the parties. Until at least one of these factors begins to change, it is difficult to see how any of the major actors in Eurasia's conflict-ridden states and their unrecognized rebel regions will find settlement a preferable option to continued intractability.

Since September 11, all sides have found yet another reason to remain at loggerheads: the recognized governments now have a new label to apply to the separatists—"terrorists"—that they believe will turn heads in Washington. In the worst case, the very idea of a global "war on terrorism" may eventually convince the recognized governments that using force against the separatists is a legitimate analog of the U.S. war against al Qaeda or the Philippines' war against Abu Sayyaf. On the other hand, it is precisely this logic that the separatists point toward when they argue that they need the special protection provided by Russian peacekeepers and the Russian army, or perhaps even membership in the Russian Federation itself. When the United States announced a major train-and-equip program for the Georgian government in 2002—after reports that al Qaeda fighters were to be found in Georgia's remote Pankisi Gorge region along the Russian border—the response of the Abkhaz and South Ossetians was to declare their intention to seek "associate status" within the Russian Federation.

There is one final, uncomfortable point about the dynamics of intractability in these disputes, and one that makes it even more difficult to draw practical lessons from the Eurasian conflicts. It concerns the problem of legitimacy, and it is a problem masked by the easy labels we normally apply to the parties in these conflicts—including labels such as "separatist" that I have used throughout this chapter. The fact of the matter is that, from the perspective of the "separatist" states, the ongoing disputes are still part of the sorting out of borders and identities that attended the collapse of the Soviet Union. That is, they have to do with basic questions of which states are meant to succeed the old Soviet federation and where the boundaries of those states should lie. The international community decided that places called Azerbaijan, Georgia, and Moldova should exist and that their boundaries should be those of the internal administrative divisions of the Soviet state. There was, of course, no clear-cut reason why this should have been the case. None of those three states could lay claim to a clear "historical right" to independence (at least not without a rather tendentious reading of history) and none of the national movements that produced de facto independence in 1991, subsequently recognized de jure, showed themselves to be particularly committed to genuine democracy and minority rights.

The "separatists," however, defeated these recognized governments in military conflicts. They organized referenda on independence. They have built functioning state institutions and local economies. They have held numerous rounds of elections for public offices, elections that were manipulated and unfree, no doubt, but no more so than those in Azerbaijan and Georgia. (According to international observers, only Moldova has had consistently free and fair elections since the early 1900s, and in 2001 those elections produced history's first ever freely elected parliament dominated by communists.)[28] It is in this context that outside mediators have tried to persuade the "separatists" that the states they have built are wholly illegitimate and that their rightful place is within the confines of three states whose flags fly at the United Nations but have not flown over the rebel territories for more than ten years. The strategy of outsiders has been low cost but ultimately self-defeating: to block the recognition of really existing states while doing very little to prevent them from becoming more and more functional. To leaders—and, indeed, to average citizens—in Abkhazia, Karabakh, South Ossetia, and Transnistria that looks like a bum deal. International negotiators are in the unenviable position of trying to convince them that it isn't.

Notes

1. Parts of this chapter draw on arguments originally made in Charles King, "The Benefits of Ethnic War: Understanding Eurasia's Unrecognized States," *World Politics* 53, no. 4 (July 2001): 524–552.

2. See, for example, William Reno, *Warlord Politics and African States* (Boulder, Colo.: Lynne Rienner, 1998); Mats Berdal and David M. Malone, eds., *Greed and Grievance: Economic Agendas in Civil Wars* (Boulder, Colo.: Lynne Rienner, 2000); Herbert M. Howe, *Ambiguous Order: Military Forces in African States* (Boulder,

Colo.: Lynne Rienner, 2001); and Mark R. Beissinger and Crawford Young, eds., *Beyond State Crisis? Postcolonial Africa and Post-Soviet Eurasia in Comparative Perspective* (Washington, D.C.: Woodrow Wilson Center Press, 2002).

3. These regions go by a variety of names, some of which are associated with a particular political position on the conflict itself: Artsakh for Nagorno-Karabakh; Transdniester and Pridnestrov'e for Transnistria; Apsny for Abkhazia; Iryston for South Ossetia. I use the name most commonly used and most easily pronounceable in English.

4. For a detailed treatment of the origins of these conflicts, see Stuart Kaufman, *Modern Hatreds: The Symbolic Politics of Ethnic War* (Ithaca, N.Y.: Cornell University Press, 2001).

5. In 2003 regime changes took place in Azerbaijan and Georgia. Elections (denounced as fraudulent by international and local observers) awarded the Azerbaijani presidency to Ilham Aliev, son of the previous president, Heydar Aliev, who died shortly after this dynastic succession. In Georgia peaceful demonstrations forced the resignation of President Eduard Shevardnadze. New elections, deemed generally free by observers, awarded the presidency to a young opposition politician, Mikheil Saakashvili. For an early assessment of the political changes in Georgia, see Charles King, "A Rose among Thorns," *Foreign Affairs* (March-April 2004): 13–18.

6. *The Military Balance, 2003–2004* (London: International Institute for Strategic Studies, 2003), 66, 73, 77. The figures include mobilizable reserves.

7. Even determining where the current boundary lines of the secessionist entities lie is a challenge. For a careful assessment of the amount of territory under Armenian/Karabakh control, see Thomas De Waal, *Black Garden: Armenia and Azerbaijan through Peace and War* (New York: New York University Press, 2003), 284–286.

8. U.S. International Trade Commission press release, July 13, 2001. The factory's impressive Web site is at www.amp.ru/mmz.

9. *Republic of Moldova: Economic Review of the Transnistria Region, June 1998* (Washington, D.C.: World Bank, 1998), 27.

10. GORBI, *Georgian Lifestyle Survey 2000*, cited in *Human Development Report, Georgia 2000* (Tbilisi: United Nations Development Program, 2000), 74.

11. *Barometrul opiniei publice din Republica Moldova*, Chişinău, March-April 2002.

12. Interviews by author, Tbilisi, October 20, 2000. In early 2004, one of President Mikheil Saakashvili's first initiatives was to engineer the replacement of the old Apkhazeti leadership with moderates who may be more willing to allow the resettlement of IDPs.

13. Interviews by author, Akhalkalaki and Akhaltsikhe, October 27, 2000.

14. K. G. Dzugaev, ed., *Iuzhnaia Osetiia: 10 let respublike* (Vladikavkaz: Iryston, 2000), 4.

15. See V. A. Zolotarev, ed., *Rossiia (SSSR) v lokal'nykh voinakh I voennykh konfliktakh vtori poloviny XX veka* (Moscow: Institute of Military History, Russian Ministry of Defense, 2000), especially chapter 8.

16. Stephen Bowers, "The Crisis in Moldova," *Jane's Intelligence Review,* November 1992, 484.

17. The most complete account of Russian assistance in all these conflicts is Mihai Gribincea, *The Russian Policy on Military Bases: Georgia and Moldova* (Oradea, Romania: Cogito, 2001).

18. *The Military Balance, 2003–2004,* 94.

19. Russian peacekeeping forces, although under a separate command from regular army personnel, have had a similar influence on the local economy. By mid-2004 there were around 2,600 Russian peacekeepers total in Abkhazia, South Ossetia, and Transnistria.

20. In 2003 Russia extended that special relationship to the Georgian region of Achara, along the Black Sea coast. Achara has not formally seceded from Georgia, but it maintains a tense relationship with the central government as an "autonomous republic."

21. See Fariz Ismailzade, *The OSCE Minsk Group and the Failure of Negotiation in the Nagorno-Karabakh Conflict,* Caspian Brief No. 23 (Cornell Caspian Consulting, April 2002).

22. *Barometrul opiniei publice din Republica Moldova,* Chişinău, March-April 2002.

23. Senior manager of United States assistance program, confidential interview by author, Stepanakert, Nagorno-Karabakh, September 28, 2000. Even the OSCE's special representative for Karabakh is based in Tbilisi, Georgia, since placing the office in either the Armenian or the Azerbaijani capital would have been unacceptable to one of the sides.

24. See "Memorandum ob osnovakh normalizatsii otnoshenii mezhdu Respublikoi Moldova i Pridnestrov'em," signed in Moscow, May 8, 1997.

25. Senior official in the United Nations Office for the Coordination of Humanitarian Assistance (UNOCHA), confidential interview by author, Tbilisi, August 29, 2000.

26. In July 2002 the OSCE put forward a discussion document that argued for the creation of a federation of Moldova and Transnistria. The Moldovan side signaled its acceptance of the idea in principle, but the Transnistrian side was unenthusiastic. In 2003 Russia put forward its own federal plan, which was eventually rejected by the Moldovan side. The United States strongly objected to the Russian plan, since it would have guaranteed long-term Russian basing rights in Moldova.

27. The estimate was as high as 54 percent for Armenia. Evgeny Polyakov, *Changing Trade Patterns after Conflict Resolution in the South Caucasus* (Washington,

D.C.: Poverty Reduction and Economic Management Sector Unit, Europe and Central Asia Region, World Bank, 2000).

28. See the reports in the annual editions of *Nations in Transit,* edited by Adrian Karatnycky, Alexander Motyl, and Amanda Schnetzer (Washington, D.C.: Freedom House, 2004).

12

Kashmir

Fifty Years of Running in Place

Howard B. Schaffer
and Teresita C. Schaffer

THE KASHMIR CONFLICT is a by-product of the partition of India and the simultaneous independence of Pakistan and India. It has been with us ever since, a hardy perennial in the catalog of international disputes, often serving as a kind of metaphor for the broader problems that plague India and Pakistan. And yet the character of the conflict has changed over the years, as have the types of solutions that outsiders have considered.

In the thirty years following the 1971 India-Pakistan war, there was no serious third-party involvement. Developments since September 11, 2001, have created a moment of opportunity for the United States to deal more effectively with the India-Pakistan dispute, and in particular with Kashmir. Previous such opportunities have been short-lived, and the cynics have history on their side. But the costs of the conflict are tremendous, so reflecting on how one could change the sterile pattern it has followed to date is worthwhile.

What Is Kashmir?

The pre-1947 princely state of Jammu and Kashmir, about the size of Minnesota, consisted of five major areas. The first three are today under Indian administration:

❏ The Valley of Kashmir has a population of 4.7 million, most of them Kashmiri-speaking Sunni Muslims. Its prominent Hindu minority now mostly lives outside the Valley after over a decade of insurgency. This is the heart of Kashmir. It is distinguished from other regions of the state by its practice of Kashmiriyat, the culture of Kashmir. It is also the area that generates the strongest emotions throughout the region. The Valley is the only part of the pre-1947 state in which the majority of the population is seriously discontented with the current political configuration. At the same time, none of the other areas have any great desire to be ruled by the Muslims of the Valley.

❏ Jammu, with a Hindu majority but several Muslim-majority districts, is the home of the former ruling maharaja's family. Its population is about 4.5 million.

❏ Ladakh's two hundred thousand people are predominantly Tibetan Buddhist. There are some Shia Muslim areas as well.

The remaining two areas are today under Pakistani administration:

❏ "Azad (free) Kashmir," immediately adjacent to the Valley, has 3.1 million people, virtually 100 percent Muslim, and has ties both to Pakistani Punjab and to the Valley.

❏ The "Northern Areas" consists of a number of small principalities that had been tributary to the Maharaja of Kashmir, tucked away in valleys of this highly mountainous area. Its 1.1 million people are virtually all Muslim, but some are Shia or Ismaili, unlike the Sunni majority in the Valley, and several areas have their own language. It is isolated from the surrounding areas, and there is no road connecting it to Azad Kashmir.

Causes of the Kashmir Conflict

Kashmir was the most important part of British India whose fate after partition in 1947 was contested by the newly independent states of India and Pakistan. Under the procedures put in place by the departing British imperial power, India's princely states had to choose to accede to either

India or Pakistan. A princely state that did neither would in principle become independent, though this outcome was strongly discouraged. Problems arose in three states in which the ruler and the majority of the population were of different religions. Hyderabad and Junagadh, where Muslims ruled over predominantly Hindu populations in states surrounded by Indian territory, wound up joining India, albeit after an Indian show of force changed their rulers' initial inclinations.

In Kashmir the situation was reversed. A Hindu maharaja ruled over a Muslim majority population in an area contiguous to both India and Pakistan. In the fall of 1947, tribesmen entered the Valley of Kashmir from Pakistan following the outbreak of a rebellion in other Muslim-majority areas. This "spontaneous" incursion took place with the connivance of a Pakistani government that was determined that this large Muslim-majority state become part of Pakistan. The maharaja, still considering his options on accession, appealed to New Delhi for military aid, and Prime Minister Jawaharlal Nehru made military support conditional on Kashmir's accession to India. In October the maharaja signed the Instrument of Accession—an action whose technicalities are still contested on the Pakistan side—and the exchange of correspondence between him and the Indian government promised that the future of Kashmir would eventually be subjected to an "ascertainment of the will of the people."

The Indian troops fought to a stalemate with the tribal forces and Pakistani troops. The fighting, which began in October 1947, was confined to a relatively small area and was ended by a UN-arranged cease-fire fifteen months later. This first Kashmir war was in one sense an imperial legacy, fought to decide the main outstanding issue in the partition of India, but it was even then a war over two different concepts of the successor state, the competing nationalisms of Muslim Pakistan and secular India. The cease-fire line established then remains the Line of Control today, except for very minor changes of alignment. This line left the Valley of Kashmir entirely under Indian administration.

Pakistan's position was and remains that the state's final disposition must be settled by a plebiscite that offers voters the same two choices identified by the United Nations in resolutions of 1948 and 1949; that is, voters can opt for Kashmir becoming part of either India or Pakistan. In recent years, the Pakistani government has begun to give greater prominence to "the wishes of the Kashmiris," sparking speculation that Pakistan might at some point decide it could live with a three-option plebiscite: voters might be able to choose among Kashmir becoming part of India, becoming part of Pakistan, or attaining its own sovereign independence.

India's position is that the whole state—including the two parts now under Pakistani administration—belongs to India. Most observers believe that India could live with a solution that turned the Line of Control into a permanent boundary. The Indian constitution provided a special autonomous regime for Kashmir, but that autonomy has largely eroded. Indian spokespeople have given mixed signals about their willingness to negotiate some restored or new autonomy arrangement. India's stated policy is to persuade separatist leaders to join the Indian political process and accept Indian sovereignty, but in recent years Indian leaders have not been willing to offer much incentive for them to buy into autonomy. The development of an increasingly vocal and militant independence movement in Kashmir has vastly complicated the search for a settlement to an increasingly stubborn two-party dispute, by adding a third player, the Kashmiris, who have a sharply divided political lineup and weak leadership.

The Nature of the Dispute

Kashmir is only one part, albeit a central one, of a broader set of problems that have plagued India and Pakistan since they became independent. The larger India-Pakistan agenda also includes nuclear risk reduction as well as a grab bag of "normalization" issues (trade, visas, cultural exchange) and a dispute over territory at the very southern end of the long India-Pakistan border.

What makes Kashmir so central is that it has come to symbolize the two countries' identity dispute. For Pakistan, Kashmir represents the one Muslim-majority part of the South Asian subcontinent that did not become part of Pakistan, the "homeland for Muslims." For India, it is a symbol of the country's secular identity, and this symbolic significance has grown stronger with time. Moreover, many Indians fear that the loss of Kashmir would trigger massive anti-Muslim communal riots in India itself, where Muslims make up about 12 percent of the population.

Kashmir is also, of course, a territorial dispute, though since the 1970s those who have sought to address it have been less and less inclined to approach a solution by simply drawing lines on the map. The dispute has also become increasingly one over governance and self-government for Kashmiris. Since 1989, the dispute has also given rise to a bitter militancy, with increasing support from Pakistan and with a recurrent tendency to engage in terrorism.

The Parties to the Dispute

At the start, the parties to the dispute were India and Pakistan. To differing degrees, their dispute and the Kashmir problem in particular affected both countries' international postures. Obtaining U.S. help in its dispute with India was a major motivation in Pakistan's decision to join the U.S. Cold War alliance system—in spite of the fact that the U.S.-Pakistan agreements were explicitly directed against communist countries and not against India. India's international posture had a broader base, but Pakistan's membership in the Baghdad Pact, a U.S.-sponsored security arrangement designed to contain Soviet expansion in the Middle East, helped lead the USSR to endorse India's position on Kashmir, which in turn hardened the positions of both sides.

Since the current phase of the Kashmiri insurgency started in 1989, the Kashmiris have also been recognized as parties to the dispute. Largely because of India's rather cynical mismanagement of state-level politics in Kashmir, most Kashmiris under Indian administration—both political figures and the general population—have become deeply alienated from India. With one or two exceptions, state elections since the 1950s have been badly flawed, and recent ones have had very low turnout. India's security forces have a bad human rights record in dealing with militants and unarmed civilians. The alienation provided the backdrop for an independence movement and an insurgency to gather strength. The interplay between Kashmiri alienation from India and Pakistan's claims on the territory has largely driven the evolution of the Kashmir problem during this time. The interests of the Kashmiris and of Pakistan are not altogether congruent. Each fears being left out of an eventual settlement, generating a strong incentive for disruptive behavior in any two-sided peace initiative, that is, India-Pakistan or India–Indian Kashmiris.

But which Kashmiris? Among the Muslims of the Valley, the most politically vocal are pro-independence groups, which include both armed militants and political figures. But there are also pro-Pakistan groups, generally subsidized and sometimes armed from Pakistan and sometimes encouraged by Pakistan to undercut the pro-independence crowd. Also in the mix is the elected state government, a coalition of the Indian National Conference and a Kashmir-based political party. Since taking office in 2002, this government has sought to reach out to dissident groups and develop some measure of civility in the governance of the state. Its members have long since made their peace with India, and though it enjoys only limited support in the Valley, it represents a point of view that cannot simply be ignored in considering Kashmir's future.

Beyond the Valley, the Jammuites and Ladakhis are generally willing to remain under Indian rule but do not wish to be run by Valley Muslims in a state that would enjoy a greater degree of autonomy within India. On the Pakistan side, those who have led the state government under close Pakistani government tutelage value the perks they receive from Azad Kashmir's anomalous status as a separate political entity not constitutionally part of Pakistan but totally dominated by Islamabad. While various groups on the Pakistani side of the line have their own points of view, they show little interest in breaking away from Islamabad's rule. There are no political groups that effectively unite Kashmiris from all different parts of the state.

Obstacles to a Settlement

The principal obstacle to a settlement at the outset was the unwillingness of India or Pakistan to compromise on an issue both regard as fundamental to their national identity. In Pakistan it remains almost impossible to talk about any solution that leaves the map unchanged, because amid the devastating problems and insecurities that Pakistan is dealing with, dedication to the cause of Kashmir is one of the few things that most Pakistanis agree on.

Pakistan's internal weakness has thus become an additional obstacle, complicated by the power of the militant organizations within Pakistan. Since the 1980s, successive governments have allowed these organizations fairly free rein, largely because Islamabad depended on them to pursue its agenda in Afghanistan and Kashmir, under cover of semiplausible deniability. Following President Pervez Musharraf's September 2001 policy turnaround toward Afghanistan, his government has trod very gingerly in the Kashmir area. While it has periodically tried to restrict militants' operations across the Line of Control, there is little evidence that the infrastructure that supported Pakistan's interventionist policy in the Indian-controlled part of the state has been dismantled.

India's growing power and confidence have probably made it more willing to accept a solution that turns the present Line of Control into an international border. But its reluctance to consider any deviations from its standard practices in the governance of Kashmir has made it hard to take new initiatives. And in India's dealings with Pakistan, there is a kind of catch-22: a permanent change in Pakistani policy is probably impossible without a negotiated agreement with India; as long as there is violence, India will not negotiate, but Pakistan fears that without violence, India will conclude that there is no need to negotiate.

More recently, the absence of agreed-on Kashmiri leadership, even among the Muslims of the Valley, has become an important obstacle. Both India and Pakistan have systematically sought to prevent the rise of strong leaders in the state. They have found it easy to stoke disputes among the various Kashmiri politicians, thereby undercutting these politicians' efforts to build credible power bases that would enable them to challenge New Delhi and Islamabad.

The maneuverings before the September/October 2002 state elections illustrate how internal Kashmiri politics stifles creative initiatives. India wanted to persuade the principal dissident group, the All Parties Hurriyet Conference (APHC), to participate in the elections. However, India never offered the APHC the kind of conditions—a genuinely open political environment and foreign observers, for example—that could have made a difference in the group's long-standing reluctance to get involved in the Indian political system. Worse, all the second-ranking leaders and half of the top leadership of the APHC were arrested on flimsy charges in the few months before the elections. But the absence of agreed-on leadership led to a flurry of press speculation and backbiting among the leaders both in and out of the APHC. In the end, some of the APHC leaders called for a boycott of the polls, but a handful of independent candidates presented themselves anyway. The campaign was badly marred by violence, much of it directed against National Conference candidates by historically pro-Pakistan militants. The Indian security forces were accused of coercing Kashmiris to vote, although the number of instances of coercion was much lower than in the preceding election. Conduct at the polling booths was exemplary and a credit to the Indian election officials. But the net result of this mixed picture is that, while the election may have slightly shaken up the Kashmir political scene, it did not resolve the vexing question of who speaks for Kashmiris.

Although the coming to power in New Delhi in 2004 of a coalition led by the Indian National Congress could eventually have major consequences for Kashmir, the contests in that election for the state's six members in the national parliament did nothing to answer this basic question. Since control of the state government was not at issue, stakes were much lower than in the 2002 context. Despite serious acts of violence by insurgent forces, turnout was marginally higher than in 2002. But as in that earlier context, the numbers voting varied sharply from polling station to polling station. The APHC once again refused to participate. Most observers agree that the returns mostly reflected only local considerations.

Third-Party Involvement

Except for the earliest days of the dispute, when Britain played a coequal role, and a short time in the mid-1960s, when the Soviet Union took the lead, the United States has been the preeminent third party in official diplomatic efforts to resolve (or manage) the Kashmir issue. In the early years Washington exerted its influence through the United Nations, where it strongly lobbied for Security Council resolutions on Kashmir. In the early 1960s it offered the two sides a broad outline of a settlement formula. Especially after 1970, it urged India and Pakistan to deal directly with each other on the issue. It has also sought to mobilize other governments to persuade the Indians and the Pakistanis to move forward.

The Soviet Union made one brief effort to encourage a settlement. In January 1966, soon after the cease-fire that ended the second of India and Pakistan's wars over Kashmir, the Soviet government invited the leaders of India and Pakistan to Tashkent in an attempt to reach a more durable settlement. The United States supported this effort at Soviet peacemaking. The Soviet Union was trading on its long-standing close relations with India and its recently improved ties with Pakistan. Its credibility with the Pakistanis was no doubt enhanced by the fact that the United States had cut off arms supplies to both sides when the 1965 war started, an action that affected Pakistan far more severely than India. The Tashkent conference, however, simply restored the prewar status quo on the ground in Kashmir and failed to resolve Kashmir's future.

With this exception, no other country has played much of a peacemaking role in Kashmir. Among the major powers, Moscow (except in the mid-1960s) and Beijing have been too closely tied with one or the other of the rivals to be accepted as serious actors. The smaller South Asian countries have concluded that their interests are best served by keeping their heads down on the issue. Moreover, opposition from India, South Asia's preeminent power, to international involvement in Kashmir save under exceptional circumstances (e.g., actual hostilities) has inhibited outside countries from seeking a role. India's negative view of such outside "interference" has been heightened by its position as the status quo power in Kashmir. It holds the part of the state that really matters, the Kashmir Valley.

Washington's interests and objectives have changed over time. Its focus has moved from helping two friendly countries deal with a bilateral problem, to pursuing U.S. Cold War objectives, to preventing a nuclear war. Sometimes Washington has encouraged the contending parties to manage the problem so that over time it would go away (by the status quo eventually becoming a permanent solution acceptable to all concerned). At other times, when hostilities have broken out, Washington has tried to freeze the situation on the ground, hoping that once cooler heads prevail progress can be resumed. The Soviet Union's brief intervention was primarily an effort to increase its influence in South Asia, at the expense of China and, to a lesser degree, the United States.

The Early Years: The United Nations in the Lead

Kashmir first became a major subject for U.S. diplomacy when the government of Prime Minister Jawaharlal Nehru brought the issue to the United Nations Security Council in January 1948, less than five months after India and Pakistan won their independence. The Truman administration joined the British government as a prime mover in the Security Council's passage of the 1948 and 1949 resolutions referred to earlier, establishing a UN Commission for India and Pakistan (UNCIP). The resolutions called on the commission to work out specific arrangements that would set the stage for a plebiscite in which the Kashmiri people would decide which nation to join. UNCIP then brokered a cease-fire and passed nonbinding resolutions that laid out a formula for bringing about a settlement.

Despite strong backing from Washington, the commission failed to reach agreements with the Indian and Pakistan governments on how to deal with several contentious issues. These included the withdrawal of Pakistani forces from the state, the sizable reduction of the Indian military presence there, and the modalities for holding the plebiscite under a UN-appointed administrator. Over the next few years, a succession of UN negotiators who traveled to South Asia with U.S. encouragement also failed to break the deadlock. Washington recognized the UNCIP resolutions as the basis for a Kashmir settlement until the 1960s. Since then, it has at least implicitly regarded them as overtaken by events (and hence irrelevant) and has dodged the question of their continuing validity.

In making a major diplomatic effort to resolve the Kashmir problem during those early years, Washington was not moved by concern for any important U.S. interests in the state or elsewhere in South Asia. At that time, the United States paid little attention to the region. U.S. policymakers regarded it as an inconsequential sideshow compared with Europe and the Far East. They saw the Kashmir confrontation as a dispute between two countries with which the United States had friendly relations, typical of the regional problems the fledgling United Nations had been designed to resolve. The British, who worked closely with Washington, had greater South Asian concerns. Their interest in resolving the Kashmir issue was heightened by the fact that it was a dispute between two members of the Commonwealth, then a new institution on the world scene.

Although the Eisenhower administration briefly entertained the idea of a Kashmir settlement that did not involve a plebiscite and urged the two claimants to resolve the dispute bilaterally, it soon reverted to Truman's support of the formula spelled out in the UNCIP resolutions. The Nehru government had promised self-determination for the Kashmiri people when the state acceded to India, but it quickly became hostile to the UN plebiscite formula (probably because it had concluded that it would lose). This hostility was accompanied by increasing Indian suspicion that Washington favored Pakistan in the dispute. When the Eisenhower administration established a bilateral security relationship with Pakistan and enlisted it in two U.S.-promoted anticommunist pacts (CENTO and SEATO), India's concern heightened. Nehru charged that Pakistan's entry into the Western alliance system had brought the Cold War to the subcontinent and refused to discuss the plebiscite as a way to resolve the Kashmir issue. Soon afterward Moscow endorsed the Indian position. Its subsequent readiness to veto any Security Council resolution on Kashmir that India found objectionable meant that Cold War considerations had effectively ended any prospect that the United Nations could play a useful role in resolving the dispute. The Indians also rejected Eisenhower's efforts to tie Kashmir into a broader settlement of India-Pakistan problems. They were angered by mention of Kashmir in CENTO and SEATO communiqués and by another U.S. push to win support for a plebiscite in the United Nations. They saw these ineffectual moves, correctly, as further evidence of Cold War influence in leading the U.S. government to favor Pakistan on Kashmir.

U.S. Efforts in the 1960s, without the United Nations

The 1962 Sino-Indian border war over disputed territories in the Himalayas set the stage for another major Washington initiative to bring about a Kashmir solution, this time outside the UN framework. (The British were also involved in the initial stage of this effort but soon left it to the Americans.) The Kennedy administration saw the Chinese rout of the Indian army as an opportunity to persuade New Delhi to take a more forthcoming attitude toward a Kashmir settlement on terms acceptable to Pakistan. The administration reckoned that the Indians' concern about further Chinese moves would encourage them to seek better relations with Pakistan to avoid facing two hostile powers on India's borders. Washington thought that the improvement in its own ties with New Delhi resulting from its prompt supply of military assistance following the Chinese onslaught would make it possible for the United States to play the honest broker's role its pro-Pakistan policies on Kashmir had denied it earlier. Washington was significantly motivated by Cold War considerations. It believed that settlement of the Kashmir dispute could help make South Asia a bulwark against communism.

India-Pakistan talks held under strong U.S. pressure proved inconclusive. The two sides were far apart, and the unilateral Chinese withdrawal from Indian border areas China had seized reduced the pressure on New Delhi to make concessions to Pakistan. With bilateral talks stymied, Washington came up with some specific ideas of its own. One of these would have awarded part of the Kashmir Valley to Pakistan. In the end the talks failed. Neither side was willing to agree to an arrangement that left any part of the Valley in the other's hands, and the United States, recognizing that an agreement was beyond reach and frustrated with the sterility of the dialogue, allowed the talks to end. Summing up the experience, John Kenneth Galbraith, the U.S. ambassador to India, dryly remarked that the only thing the two sides could agree on was to denounce Washington's proposals. One interesting feature of the discussions, especially in light of the way the Kashmir issue has evolved since then, was that they focused so heavily on redrawing borders. The talks were also a strictly India-Pakistan affair: the Kashmiris did not participate in any way.

The failed 1962–63 negotiations proved the high-water mark in U.S. involvement in efforts to resolve the Kashmir dispute. Until the 1998 Indian and Pakistani nuclear tests and Pakistan's armed attack on the Kargil area of Indian-controlled Kashmir the following year again led U.S. policymakers to focus on the issue, Washington preferred to remain largely on the sidelines. It neither pushed for a settlement at international forums nor undertook any significant unilateral initiatives.

The 1965 India-Pakistan war over Kashmir significantly contributed to this hands-off attitude. Fought by both sides with U.S. arms that Washington had supplied for fighting potential communist aggressors, not each other, the war crystallized the feeling of many U.S. policymakers that the best approach to Washington's political and security relations with India and Pakistan was "a plague on both their houses," and on Kashmir as well. Indeed, so dismayed and disillusioned were they that, as noted, they welcomed Moscow's efforts to bring an end to the war, a position that opened the way to greater Soviet influence in the region.

After 1971: The Simla Agreement and Bilateralism

Following the 1971 India-Pakistan war over Bangladesh, the only armed conflict between the two countries not sparked by the Kashmir issue, Indian and Pakistani leaders pledged in the Simla Agreement to solve Kashmir and other problems bilaterally. The same document committed both sides to respect the Line of Control dividing their forces in the state and to refrain from the threat or the use of force in violation of that line.

It was reported that the two leaders had secretly agreed to make the Line of Control their international border.

Washington hailed the agreement, which gave the United States an unassailable, thoroughly respectable rationale for remaining on the sidelines. Unable to change the situation in Kashmir, it was quite prepared to let the contestants work out the problem by themselves. If, as seemed likely at the time and for years afterward, they chose to put the issue in cold storage and allow the status quo to become a de facto settlement, that would be fine with Washington. Successive U.S. administrations maintained this aloof position for the better part of two decades. Kashmir disappeared from the world's agenda. The Kashmiri people seemed to have become reconciled to their lot as Indian citizens.

The outbreak of insurgency in 1989 quickly returned Kashmir to Washington's radar screen. In the two preceding years, there had been growing indications that despite the relative quiet in the Kashmir Valley, or perhaps because of it, India had done little to create a better political relationship with the Kashmiris. The badly rigged state election in 1987 is often cited as an example of Delhi's continued cynical management of the state and of the role played by politicians close to the Indian government.

By the early 1990s the Pakistanis had become increasingly involved in what had initially been a home-brewed uprising, and U.S. worries grew about the implications of the insurgency for South Asian peace. Washington feared that this time an India-Pakistan war could develop nuclear dimensions. It was also disturbed by extensive human rights violations by Indian forces, including extrajudicial murder, rape, unaccounted disappearances, and routine torture of detainees. And it was troubled by the terrorist tactics favored by some of the insurgents, especially those with Islamic credentials.

Despite these concerns, Washington declined to seek a mediating role. It stuck to the line that "the best way to resolve the Kashmir dispute is through direct discussions between the governments of India and Pakistan as envisaged in the Simla Agreement." After the insurgency broke out, Washington added to this formulation the point that in their bilateral discussions the two governments should take into account the wishes of the Kashmiri people. It did not offer advice about how this should be done, however.

After the Bombs, Renewed U.S. Interest

The 1998 Indian and Pakistani nuclear tests greatly magnified concerns about Kashmir. By that time, Washington had considered both Pakistan and India to be nuclear-capable for a decade, and in 1990 it had cut off all aid to Pakistan because of its nuclear program. Preventing a chain of events that could lead to nuclear war was already well established as the top U.S. priority in South Asia, as had been demonstrated by Washington's active diplomacy during a war scare in May 1990. The nuclear tests brought into the open the danger that Kashmir might serve as a potential "nuclear flashpoint."

Washington's primary focus was on reviving and strengthening the system of nuclear-risk-reduction measures that India and Pakistan had begun to put in place in the late 1980s and early 1990s. The United States also urged the two countries to deal with the full range of their differences, including Kashmir, and enlisted the support of allied and other major countries to endorse its call for urgent action. Washington continued to insist, however, that it would not take a more direct role on Kashmir unless both sides agreed.

Pakistan welcomed this new highlighting of Kashmir and did what it could to encourage the "internationalization" of the issue. This has been its consistent position since the dispute first came to world attention. Pakistan regards the intervention of the international community as key to upsetting an unsatisfactory status quo that, as the less powerful claimant, it has not otherwise been able to change. The Indians, for their part, belittled the flashpoint argument. Their position was the mirror image of the Pakistanis'. As before, they believed that any attention by the world community to the issue would damage India's interests.

Both sides, it turned out, had failed to grasp the implications of the new nuclear environment. The tests strengthened the primacy Washington gave to the preservation of stability in South Asia and lessened the importance it attached to the equities of the Kashmir issue. For Washington and other members of the international community, the use of violence to change the status quo was now an unacceptable option.

This position became even clearer the following year, when President Bill Clinton pressured the Pakistanis to close out their cross-border operations in the Kargil area of Kashmir and withdraw behind the Line of Control. Clinton's intervention was the most direct high-level U.S.

involvement in the Kashmir issue since 1962. He followed up this action with some unvarnished talk to the Pakistanis during his brief visit to Islamabad in 2000. "This era," he told his Pakistani TV audience, "does not reward people who struggle in vain to redraw borders in blood."

September 11 and Its Aftermath

In December 2001, three months after Pakistani president Musharraf agreed to join the U.S. war on terrorism, militants from groups that operated freely in Pakistan attacked the Indian parliament. This assault on the center of India's government shocked India and the world, especially since it followed an even more murderous bombing in October 2001 at the State Assembly building in Srinagar, the capital of Kashmir and the political heart of the Indian-held Kashmir Valley. These events profoundly affected the way India, Pakistan, and the United States dealt with the Kashmir issue.

India reacted with a massive military buildup, the downgrading of its diplomatic relations with Pakistan, and the cutoff of all transportation links between the two. Interestingly, India was now using the potential nuclear danger to reinforce its insistence that Pakistan completely dismantle the infrastructure for its policy of low-intensity conflict in Kashmir before India would undertake any bilateral dialogue. "Flashpoint diplomacy" had previously been primarily a Pakistani enterprise. The enormity of the attack on the Indian parliament and this "coercive diplomacy" were remarkably successful in dissuading the international community from looking to India to make the first move to end what had become a highly dangerous confrontation.

Pakistan felt the brunt of international pressure, and Musharraf told the United States he would end his support for militancy in Kashmir. But the limitations of this promise soon became apparent, as the cycles of crises came closer together. A new surge of militant violence in Kashmir in May 2002 was followed by a more expansive promise to permanently cease operations across the Line of Control. Meanwhile, Pakistan called for talks with India, and India continued to argue that this was not possible until it was assured of a "permanent" end to Pakistani support for terrorism. And during the periods of intensified violence, both countries talked about their military strength in ways calculated to remind each other and the world that there were nuclear weapons in the background.

For the United States, the South Asian war scare was an unwelcome addition to the post–September 11 situation. The attack on the Indian parliament led the Bush administration to look at Kashmir largely as a terrorism problem, with India as the victim. The United States intervened energetically to tamp down the war scare, focusing chiefly on Pakistan. Between crises, it continued to work closely with both countries, building up its security and political relationship with India and placing great importance on Pakistan's cooperation in the increasingly demanding task of tracking down elements of al Qaeda and the ousted Afghan Taliban regime that had made their way into Pakistan. This led to a schizophrenia all too familiar to students of U.S.-Pakistan relations. It also may have led Pakistani leaders to conclude that if they calibrated things carefully, there was probably a level of Kashmir violence that the Americans would put up with.

The apparent effectiveness of its crisis management efforts led the U.S. government to consider taking on a more active diplomatic role aimed at promoting a peace process that could over time lead to a significant lessening of tensions and even to a de facto, if not a de jure, settlement of the dispute. The United States now enjoys excellent relations simultaneously with India and Pakistan, a situation unprecedented in the history of U.S. dealings with independent South Asia. Events in the first half of 2002 demonstrated how quickly an India-Pakistan crisis could arise—and how seriously it could distract the United States from the antiterrorism operations it was conducting. U.S. diplomacy through the summer of 2002 explored how an India-Pakistan dialogue could be reinstituted. Secretary of State Colin Powell and Deputy Secretary Richard Armitage visited the region and tried to lay the groundwork for a peace process. They became intimately familiar with the Kashmir issue in a way none of their predecessors could claim. But both the stubbornness of the dispute and, increasingly, the Bush administration's focus on Iraq and the 2004 U.S. presidential elections limited the administration's ability and willingness to sustain these efforts. By mid-2004, it seemed likely that Washington would play a more vigorous role in facilitating the India-Pakistan peace process only if dire developments such as a serious war scare compelled it to do so.

The nuclear dimension has made the Kashmir dispute more dangerous. On the one hand, it has convinced many in Pakistani army and leadership circles that they can safely pursue their policy of low-intensity conflict, since India will not risk a nuclear response by attacking Pakistan over provocations in Kashmir. This adds to the intractability of the conflict. On the other hand, the nuclearization of the subcontinent has forced a greater degree of international attention to be focused on the area. Moreover, it has greatly strengthened the international presumption that the map drawn by any settlement will need to roughly follow present borders. Ideally, these perceptions could open up opportunities for settlement that have been closed until now, but it still remains to be seen how their contradictory effects will balance out.

The global war on terrorism has had a similarly contradictory effect on the intractability of the Kashmir conflict. On the one hand, it has provided a context in which the United States has been more interested in pushing for a settlement, and India has been more willing to accept U.S. involvement. On the other hand, it has in some ways hardened the positions of both India and Pakistan. It provides a setting for Pakistan, if it so chooses, to carry on its support for militancy in the expectation that the United States will not want to push Pakistan to the wall over Kashmir while Afghanistan and Iraq are still unsettled. At the same time, it has given added weight to India's characterization of its dispute with Pakistan as simply a terrorism problem and could embolden those in India who will argue for preemptive action against Pakistan should the recently revived India-Pakistan peace process falter.

Local Efforts since 1998

The period since 1998 has also seen a number of initiatives that do not bear the fingerprints of the United States or of any other international actor. In early 1999 the Indian and Pakistani prime ministers met at Lahore, Pakistan, and signed pathbreaking agreements setting up procedures for talks (including on Kashmir) and pledging a serious effort at nuclear risk reduction. This initiative died in the fighting at Kargil a few months later and was disowned by the military government that took power in Pakistan in October 1999. During 2000 two Kashmir cease-fires, one initiated by a homegrown Kashmiri insurgent group and the other by the government of India, offered the greatest hope the region had seen in years. Unfortunately, the first cease-fire was a casualty of mutual suspicions and conflicting agendas between Kashmiris and Pakistan, econd never got the follow-up it needed from the government or India.

An India-Pakistan summit in Agra, India, in the summer of 2001 ended in highly publicized failure. This downturn was followed by a much more serious one when, following the attack on the Indian parliament referred to earlier, India deployed massive forces on the Line of Control and the international border. Pakistan followed suit. This dangerous eyeball-to-eyeball confrontation involving a million armed men lasted for a year and a half.

More recently, the two countries initiated yet another effort to improve relations. Meeting in Islamabad in January 2004, at a summit session of the South Asian Association for Regional Cooperation (SAARC), President Musharraf and Indian prime minister Atal Behari Vajpayee issued a joint statement in which they agreed to begin a "composite dialogue" leading to a peaceful settlement of all bilateral issues, including Kashmir. Musharraf reassured Vajpayee that he would not permit territory under Pakistani control to be used to support terrorism. The dialogue was scheduled to begin soon after completion of the Indian parliamentary elections in May 2004 but was subsequently delayed because of the change of government in New Delhi. The new Indian administration of Prime Minister Manmohan Singh has pledged to follow the road map its predecessor had developed. The extent to which it will be able and willing to do so is uncertain. Meanwhile, India and Pakistan have restored what passes for normal relations between them. In Kashmir, a cease-fire along the Line of Control begun in December 2003 was still in effect as of mid-2004, but considerable violence persists within the Indian-controlled portion of the state. And the peace of the region remains hostage to an accident or another serious incident.

These efforts were not third-party interventions, though many of them had energetic behind-the-scenes support from the United States and others. They demonstrated several important features of today's Kashmiri scene. First, despite the legacy of mutual suspicion, there is a constituency for peace—although there is still little constituency for the compromises peace will require. Second, any serious initiative nowadays needs to deal explicitly with the Kashmiris, and with the mutual suspicions between them and their ostensible supporters in Pakistan. Third, the drag of inertia on Indian and Pakistani policy is heavy indeed, and the likelihood of India and Pakistan reaching a breakthrough without at least discreet outside help is poor.

Track-Two Diplomacy

With Washington's encouragement, private U.S. organizations have often taken the lead in promoting unofficial dialogue, sometimes with official U.S. government funding. Typically, these track-two ventures involve U.S.-organized meetings between prominent and supposedly influential Indian and Pakistani private citizens, most of them retired military and civilian officials. Probably the longest-running has been the Neemrana dialogue, long sponsored by the Ford Foundation with U.S. government support. There have also been a number of similar dialogues sponsored by Indian and/or Pakistani newspapers or NGOs.

More recently, the Kashmir Study Group (KSG), founded in 1996 by Farooq Kathwari, a prominent Kashmiri-American businessman, has made a contribution to the debate. The group comprises well-regarded academics, retired diplomats, NGO leaders, and members of Congress, all long involved in South Asian affairs. It has achieved a reputation for nonpartisan objectivity that has earned it a hearing in New Delhi and Islamabad, and a measure of confidence among Kashmiri leaders.

Initially, the KSG sponsored a series of conferences and meetings involving Indian, Pakistani, and Kashmiri leaders. In 1999 it brought several retired Indian and Pakistani officials to the United States. Meeting quietly with KSG members, they developed a proposal recommending that a portion of the Kashmir state be reconstituted as one or two sovereign entities without an international personality. Under the proposal, the Line of Control would remain in place until it was altered by mutual agreement, and the "entities" would be largely demilitarized. The proposal was widely disseminated in attractive format and was the subject of discussion in both Pakistan and India.

These exercises in track-two diplomacy have developed greater rapport between old adversaries and have in some cases won the respect, or at least overcome the suspicions, of the Indian and Pakistani governments. They have also generated some novel and potentially useful ideas about managing and resolving the dispute. The experience of the KSG suggests that a well-organized and well-funded track-two effort that enjoys high-level access among the contenders can influence them to think about fresh options, even ideas that are well outside their normal policy framework. Participants in the Neemrana dialogue and the members of the KSG were both helped and hurt in their work by the widespread perception that they had close links to the U.S. government, which they had carefully kept informed of their efforts. The U.S. government ties gave their proposals greater weight but also aroused suspicions in India that the KSG, in particular, represented a new form of U.S. government interference.

Thus far, however, none of the track-two efforts have had any discernible impact on government policy in either India or Pakistan. Whatever insights they generated have not made the transition into government policy. Some critics hold that track two has too often been handicapped by the participation of retired figures who resisted change when they were in power and are at best hesitant converts to new thinking. In this view, it might make more sense to look beyond retired generals and former foreign secretaries to enlist active politicians and members of the business community. Track-two efforts to reach out to Kashmiri dissident political figures have probably served a useful purpose by increasing the dissidents' understanding of how the world regards their conflict and by revealing how the dissidents view outside intervention.

What Might a New Peace Process Look Like?

Both the history of Kashmir and the experience of other intractable conflicts suggest that finding a viable process is at least as important—and as difficult—as devising an appropriate solution. A complete discussion of the options for a potential Kashmir peace process is beyond the scope of this paper, but a few general principles emerge out of the foregoing discussion.

A peace process would need to proceed on at least two separate tracks: India-Pakistan and India-Kashmir. *India and Pakistan* would conduct their talks through issue-based working groups, so that each side's top priorities could at least in a formal sense be dealt with simultaneously. The *India-Kashmir* dialogue would address the relationship of the currently Indian-held parts of Kashmir with the Indian union. The dialogue would have to include substantial representation for dissidents and would have to be empowered to discuss a range of options for Kashmir's future that goes well beyond current Indian policy.

How and when these two dialogues might intersect would be a crucial question. India's hope of wrapping up an agreement with "its" Kashmiris and simply incorporating that in an India-Pakistan settlement is completely unrealistic. To prevent Pakistan from playing a spoiler's role, the India-Pakistan discussion of Kashmir would need to proceed at the same time as the India-Kashmir talks. The two tracks mentioned earlier might need to be supplemented by two more: between Kashmiris from the Valley and Pakistan, and between Kashmiris from both sides of the Line of Control. This would among other things help the Kashmiris talking with India to protect themselves against the charge that they are selling out.

Most important, the process would have to have persistent, vocal, and visible political support from the highest levels of both governments. Both governments would need to take an extremely strong stand against violence, even to the extent of cooperating in tracking down those using political violence in the Kashmir Valley.

Despite recent progress in restarting the peace process, the level of bitterness on all three sides of this dispute and the rut into which Indian and Pakistani policies have fallen suggest that a purely bilateral effort will not succeed. Besides the classic functions of a third party—cajoling the participants during difficult times, providing an outside perspective on both sides' political sensitivities, and discreetly feeding new ideas into the process—two additional functions could be important. The first would be to help the parties bring in proposals that could contribute to a stable settlement but might not fit neatly into the initial two-track format, such as unconventional ideas for partial sovereignty for Kashmir. The second would be to persuade India and Pakistan to begin putting in place, on a unilateral basis, building blocks for an eventual settlement. These could include, for example, sensors or other devices for making the Line of Control harder to cross or proposals for partial demilitarization.

Lessons Learned

The Kashmir conflict illustrates several problems that are common to more than one intractable conflict.

❏ *It is hard for a third party to intervene effectively when the disparity in power between the disputants is great.* In this case, India is both the status quo power and the more powerful, which gives it a strong bias against outside mediation.

❏ *"Allies" may be as big a problem as "enemies."* The partly overlapping and partly competing interests of Pakistan and the Kashmiris have made it excruciatingly difficult to develop a process in which one does not act as the spoiler. Indian initiatives toward the Kashmiris sparked Pakistani fears of being left out and inspired destructive behavior (e.g., during the November 2000 cease-fire); the reverse occurred when India made initiatives toward Pakistan (e.g., the India-Pakistan summit in July 2001). On the other hand, during periods when the Kashmiris were less unhappy, Pakistan's intervention did not have much effect. The lesson here is twofold: it is essential to engage with all those who have the potential to wreck an agreement, but the insiders may be more critical to progress than the outsiders.

❏ *There is no substitute for leadership.* The absence of clearly accepted Kashmiri leadership after 1982 has created a gap that has still not been filled and is compounded by the fragility of the Pakistani state.

Moreover, when there is a strong leader, his or her personal attachments may acquire larger-than-life importance, for good or ill. Prime Minister Jawaharlal Nehru's family attachment to Kashmir made much more difficult the kind of solution that otherwise might have been achievable during his long years in power in India, from 1947 to 1964. Conversely, Atal Behari Vajpayee's vision of a different India-Pakistan relationship, one he wanted to leave behind as his political legacy, seemed a powerful force for change before his defeat in the April–May 2004 Indian elections. Whether he could have sustained his initiative in the face of strongly anti-Pakistan Hindu nationalist hard-liners in his own Bharatiya Janata Party (BJP) will never be known. Now that the party is in the opposition, these hard-liners may well become more outspoken in denouncing any concessions to Pakistan. In Pakistan, the powerful pull of the traditional Pakistani army ethos on Musharraf similarly acts as a brake on progress. Most important, such negative attitudes in both countries make it unlikely that either government will take bold steps to prepare its people for compromise.

❑ *Peacemakers must mount a serious effort; dabbling is useless.* As long as the potential outside peacemakers have broader interests that could be jeopardized by their peacemaking efforts, they will intervene only if the consequences of inaction are extremely dangerous. Intractable conflicts tend to repel serious third-party efforts otherwise: they are too hard, the chances of success are too small, the list of failed efforts is too long. Eventually, peacemakers too conclude that they can live with the problem. Alternatively, in the absence of a serious leadership effort to produce results, they dabble, which is essentially useless.

❑ *Managing intractable problems will not necessarily make them easier to solve.* The alternative to trying to solve a problem like India-Pakistan relations is managing it. For many years, this looked like a good choice for U.S. policymakers. Even as India and Pakistan moved toward developing nuclear weapons, the rationale was that neither side wanted to stumble into a war, so that although neither had the political will to solve the problem, both had strong motivation to keep it below the boiling point. During most of the period since the early 1970s, managing the issue has been U.S. policy.

This raises two critical questions: first, do intractable conflicts moderate if they are simply managed below the boiling point for a number of years? This was the case for eighteen years after the Simla Agreement and even appeared to be the case in the mid-1990s. In retrospect, part of the answer is clear: unless something is done during this period of quiet to "ripen" the conflict, the passage of time alone will not make it easier to solve and may make it harder. India made no real progress in creating a different political dynamic between Delhi and Srinagar during the eighteen years after Simla; it had apparently concluded, wrongly, that there was no longer a problem that needed solving. As a result, the rise of the insurgency in the late 1980s produced a far worse situation than had prevailed before Simla, with the added dangers of nuclear explosions, the progressive weakening of the Pakistani state, the Kashmiri insurgency, and Pakistan's willingness to take unacceptable risks (as at Kargil).

Second, how can one tell when the balance has shifted and "management" becomes insufficient? We would argue that this has happened to the India-Pakistan problem. At a minimum, the dramatic events of September–December 2001 created a situation in which simply "putting the problem on ice" is insufficient and needs to be supplemented by a strategy for "ripening" the conflict. Fortunately, this development also coincides with what still appears to us to be a moment of opportunity for the United States. India's and Pakistan's decisions to make another try at peace talks is encouraging. But it remains to be seen whether the necessary leadership is there, both in the region and in this country.

13

"Intractable" Confrontation on the Korean Peninsula

A Contribution to Regional Stability?

Scott Snyder

THE KOREAN CONFRONTATION has been with us for more than five decades. A classic Cold War conflict not only survived but also transmuted itself in the post–Cold War world into the flashpoint for global concerns about nonproliferation in the 1990s, including a confrontation that in 1994 almost led to military escalation after four decades of "cold peace" through deterrence. The post–Cold War period gradually revealed that the balance of power on the Korean peninsula had shifted decisively in the direction of Seoul; North Korea, paradoxically, had become a failed economy in need of international humanitarian assistance but was not yet a "failed state." Although the Democratic People's Republic of Korea (DPRK) has taken on the characteristics of a failed state, its governing structure has somehow survived and has up to now remained in control, despite gradual signs of de-institutionalization and factional rivalry among branches of the bureaucracy and between the military, the party, and the government.[1] North Korea is increasingly dependent on external economic support from China, South Korea (or the Republic of Korea [ROK]), the United States, and the international community for its survival.

As we enter the "post–post–Cold War world," the conflict on the Korean peninsula has taken on new characteristics: North Korea is now one of the publicly identified key targets in the U.S. war on terror and was included in President George W. Bush's "axis of evil." Two radically different and competing ideological systems divided over half a century ago by the Cold War, an economically failed state and dysfunctional political system that remains in place and has weapons of mass destruction (WMD) proliferation and missile export capacity, North Korea as a member of the "axis of evil": the Korean confrontation, if nothing else, certainly seems intractable. Yet all these layers of confrontation, combined with heightened tensions related to the revelation of a covert North Korean highly enriched uranium (HEU) program in the fall of 2002 and North Korea's departure from the International Atomic Energy Agency (IAEA) and the Nuclear Nonproliferation Treaty (NPT) in early 2003, have led to the establishment of the first subregional dialogue, a six-party process hosted by the People's Republic of China (PRC), with Japan, the two Koreas, Russia, and the United States. This latest and most inclusive diplomatic effort to peacefully manage North Korea's nuclear weapons pursuits, which ultimately have their origins in the inter-Korean conflict, constitutes a potentially significant test of the roles of third parties in managing conflict on the Korean peninsula and may finally lead to the shaping of a new post–Korean conflict regional order in Northeast Asia.

For several decades, the Korean conflict has been a stable "cold peace." The interests of international actors are no longer overtly contradictory, and two Korean leaders (Kim Jong Il and former ROK president Kim Dae Jung) have met and shaken hands and no longer regard the threat of war as a serious possibility, despite the lack of movement to make the vision of Korean peace a reality on the ground. The confrontation endures, and if we examine the history of the Korean peninsula as a battleground among major powers, we will see that the existence of the confrontation itself ironically may contribute in its current form to regional stability in the same way that a divided Korea also reflected the Cold War balance among major powers, despite the fact that the status quo on the Korean peninsula is clearly unsustainable in the medium to long term.

As the balance of power on the Korean peninsula has shifted in favor of South Korea, the conflict has been thrown into relief, raising complicated policy dilemmas for Korea's neighbors. For major powers such as Japan, the People's Republic of China, Russia, and the United States, which have vital security interests tied to the Korean peninsula, the question of policy formation toward the peninsula is no longer simply about settling the current conflict or resolving the legacies of the past, but also about determining the future of North Korea, dealing with the global threat of WMD proliferation, and planning the future regional security order. How those neighboring states deal with North Korea may shape the opportunities for and limits of future regional cooperation. A central difficulty in pursuing inter-Korean reconciliation, and a possible partial explanation for the "intractability" of the Korean confrontation, is that these overlapping challenges have made both management of the Korean conflict and the possibility of a satisfactory resolution of it much more complex. Nonetheless, the fundamental challenge and objective remains clear: how to maintain a stable regional order and a nonnuclear Korean peninsula as part of a peaceful process that shifts the current focus from conflict management to a satisfactory resolution.

This chapter will provide a historical overview of key developments in the Korean confrontation to highlight characteristics of the conflict that have contributed to intractability. In particular, this chapter will examine the legacy of the Korean War, the initiation of inter-Korean dialogue in 1972, the end of the Cold War and the North Korean nuclear confrontation, and the impact of the inter-Korean summit on prospects for inter-Korean reconciliation. In each of these instances, special attention will be given to both international (third-party) and domestic factors and the extent to which the Korean conflict has been "impacted" (embedded in the concerns of major regional powers) versus the extent to which domestic factors may inhibit prospects for Korean reunification. The chapter will conclude with further analysis of the apparent stability derived from the continuation of the conflict, an assessment of the roles of third parties and the tools for overcoming inter-Korean confrontation, and a look at the Bush administration's view of North Korea in light of the second North Korean nuclear crisis.

Intractability and Its Origins: Legacy of the Korean War

Political scientists and historians of modern international relations have generally viewed the Korean conflict as a Cold War confrontation between Washington and Moscow, one of the early moves in a global chess game whereby local proxies tested intentions and sought to gain advantage as part of a system of bipolar contestation. By this line of reasoning, the fateful decision took place in the bowels of the Pentagon in the waning days of World War II, when Major Dean Rusk, then a member of the State-War-Navy Coordinating Committee, and his colleagues hurriedly pored over maps of Japan and Korea to determine a mutually acceptable temporary division of responsibility between the Soviet and U.S. armies for occupation of former Japanese territories in Korea at the 38th parallel. Although it could not be known at that time, the temporary division would become permanent, and Korea, historically a doormat for regional and global great-power rivalries, would become a victim at the vortex of a global superpower confrontation in Asia.

One lesson that can be drawn from declarations of Secretary of State Dean Acheson and General Douglas MacArthur before the outbreak of the Korean War that the Korean peninsula was outside the U.S. defense perimeter is that stating core policy interests runs the risk of ambiguity, which could lead to misinterpretation on the other side. The legacy of the Korean War and its indeterminate end through the signing of an armistice ending military hostilities in 1953 have contributed to the current anomalous state of unresolved, albeit essentially stable, confrontation. Thus, international actors were critical during the Cold War to the establishment and perpetuation of inter-Korean confrontation, a frozen conflict that was "impacted" by the conflicting interests of the surrounding major powers.

East Asian regional studies specialists and historians, while recognizing that the inter-Korean political context was shaped by the establishment of competing ideological systems during the Cold War, have argued that the deepening of confrontation and the establishment of the two Koreas immediately after the end of World War II were led by extraordinarily strong-willed Korean leaders, each of whom was determined to settle for nothing less than a unified Korean peninsula under his own authority. In this analysis, the preexisting divisions that had characterized faction-riven Korean independence efforts during the fight against Japanese colonial rule were personified by the two regimes in their struggle for supremacy in a postcolonial world. Kim Il Sung was a ragtag Korean nationalist guerrilla who had fought against Japanese colonial rule from Soviet-backed bases in northern China and the Soviet Far East, while Syngman Rhee was an exile in the United States who returned to take charge of the government in Seoul. Rhee's government relied heavily on partners who had previously collaborated inside Korea with the Japanese colonialists and who readily cooperated with the U.S. military authorities to assure their own positions within Korean society. Rhee and Kim had one thing in common: each intended to settle for nothing less than a reunified Korea under his own control. By 1948 the divisions were clear and Rhee and Kim established separate and competing Korean states with the approval of their respective backers in Washington and Moscow. Thus, the Korean conflict was not only a superpower conflict but also a civil conflict over differing visions of nationalism and ideology as the means by which to ensure the full recovery and survivability of a newly reconstituted Korean nation.

The character of the Korean conflict as both a civil and an international conflict (i.e., both interstate and intrastate) has posed serious obstacles to efforts to resolve it and has contributed to its intractability. Although the Cold War has ended, the inter-Korean confrontation has remained, at least partly owing to the existence of two competing governments that have defined their legitimacy and raison d'être in opposition to the other, quite apart from international considerations. Thus, the end of the Cold War offered an opportunity for inter-Korean reconciliation, but it could not erase the institutional and structural competition for legitimacy on the Korean peninsula that had characterized the national strategies and international diplomacy of the two Koreas through the Cold War.

The method by which the Korean War was prosecuted following North Korea's southward thrust, with a U.S.-led international force dispatched under UN auspices, and the freezing of the military stalemate under the terms of an armistice rather than a conclusive end have also contributed to the intractability of the Korean conflict. The Soviet decision to boycott the United Nations at the start of the Korean War allowed the United States to engineer the passage of a resolution that effectively made the United Nations a direct party to the conflict, in defense of South Korea against the surprise aggression of the North. The establishment of a command under UN auspices and the participation of more than sixteen countries under the UN flag have subsequently limited the possibilities for UN mediation. The United Nations as a party to the armistice (the ROK was not a signatory to the armistice) further institutionalized North Korean distrust of UN involvement, and it was clear that the envisioned 1954

Geneva Convention to resolve political aspects of the Korean confrontation would be a nonstarter. Although the decision by both Koreas to enter the United Nations separately in 1992 has mitigated this situation, as have UN efforts to respond to the DPRK's food crisis in the mid-1990s, the experience of having fought against a UN force still influences North Korea's perceptions of the United Nations as a party unfit to mediate between the two Koreas.

Post–Korean War: The Armistice and Third-Party Roles in Its Implementation

Following the signing of the armistice in 1953 until 1972, the primary responsibility for managing inter-Korean confrontation lay in the hands of the Military Armistice Commission (MAC), the body created under the armistice by which the DPRK and the UN Command were to resolve disputes over the implementation of the armistice. The members of the MAC were the parties on each side: the United Nations Command and the DPRK. The purpose of the MAC was to provide a mechanism through which it would be possible to negotiate and resolve disputes over the implementation of the agreement, but it quickly became a showpiece for continuing verbal confrontation and propaganda as a substitute for fighting.

Another mechanism provided as part of the Armistice Agreement was the Neutral Nations Supervisory Commission (NNSC), created in 1953. The NNSC was composed of four "neutral" parties, two of which were proposed by the DPRK (Czechoslovakia and Poland) and two by the UN side (Sweden and Switzerland). The NNSC had an independent investigatory capacity to deal with violations of the armistice or other issues referred to the NNSC by the two sides, but it did not have an independent role or mediating capacity. In practical terms, the NNSC came to have a facilitating and support function to clarify issues primarily related to repatriation in the event of accidental crossings. In the mid-1990s, following the UN decision to appoint a South Korean to head the MAC, a move to which the DPRK objected since the ROK technically is not a signatory to the armistice, the DPRK began to undermine the functioning roles of the NNSC, which also had a small monitoring and reporting presence at the Demilitarized Zone (DMZ), with the Czechs and the Poles located at a camp on the northern side and the Swedes and the

Swiss located at a camp on the southern side. With the dissolution of Czechoslovakia, the DPRK rejected the Czech Republic as a successor on the NNSC and literally cut off the lights and water to the northern NNSC camp in an effort to force the Poles out. This was part of a DPRK strategy to dismantle the armistice and force direct talks between the DPRK and the United States. The Swedish and Swiss representation on the NNSC remains and still plays a limited investigatory and interviewing role to verify intentions of northern defectors across the DMZ, but in fact the NNSC was never poised to play any third-party negotiating role in resolving the inter-Korean conflict.

The Establishment of Inter-Korean Dialogue and Third-Party Roles

Perhaps owing to the inherent mistrust resulting from centuries of experience as a small state surrounded by major powers, one of the striking characteristics of inter-Korean dialogue held intermittently since its initiation in 1972 has been the relative absence of third parties capable of gaining the trust of both Koreas as effective mediators. This was particularly the case during the Cold War, as the bipolar structure of global confrontation reinforced Korean divisions and inhibited opportunities for third-party roles. In addition, Korea's default strategy as a small nation surrounded by larger neighbors has been to play outsiders against one another. However, third-party institutions have been involved in inter-Korean communications and implementation of limited exchanges since the 1970s.

Shocked by President Richard Nixon's visit to China in 1972, North Korean president Kim Il Sung and South Korean president Park Chung Hee initiated secret talks through the Red Cross, resulting in the July 4, 1972, South-North Joint Communiqué. The communiqué laid out the three principles through which national reunification should be achieved: "[through] independent Korean efforts without being subject to external imposition or interference; through peaceful means, not through use of force against each other; and through pursuit of great national unity, transcending differences in ideas, ideologies, and systems." The initiation of an inter-Korean negotiation process was notable because after almost two decades of not talking, the two sides were able to agree on the Red Cross as a mechanism for pursuing unmediated dialogue.

In subsequent intermittent inter-Korean exchanges through the 1980s and 1990s, the North Korean and South Korean committees of the Red Cross became an important quasi-official channel through which dialogue and cooperation on specific inter-Korean matters could take place. The Red Cross has handled humanitarian deliveries of assistance from one side to the other since the 1980s, when the North volunteered to provide relief following serious flooding that affected South Korea. In the 1990s the Red Cross became a primary medium of exchange for the provision of South Korean rice and fertilizer to ease the North Korean famine. The Red Cross also functioned as an implementing mechanism for divided-family reunions for a brief period in the 1980s. It is now functioning as such on a more consistent basis since the June 2000 inter-Korean summit and declaration, under which reunions for a small number of divided families have taken place every two or three months.

The end of the Cold War and accompanying changes in the international structure surrounding the Korean peninsula provided an opportunity for new activity to decrease the level of tension between the two Koreas. With the end of the bipolar confrontational structure of international relations, it became possible for the two Koreas to pursue new relationships with countries formerly seen strictly as enemies. The end of the Cold War also widened possibilities for limited third-party roles in mediating the inter-Korean conflict. Through President Roh Tae Woo's *Nordpolitik* policy, launched in conjunction with South Korea's hosting of the 1988 Seoul Olympics, South Korea made contacts and eventually normalized its relationships with the PRC and Russia. North Korea also pursued normalization talks with Japan and initiated low-level dialogue with the United States in the early 1990s, including a single meeting in January 1992 in New York between Korean Workers' Party general secretary for international affairs Kim Yong Sun and Under Secretary of State for Political Affairs Arnold Kanter.

This meeting occurred in the aftermath of President George Bush's announcement that the United States would unilaterally withdraw nuclear weapons from foreign soil, an announcement that facilitated North Korea's entry into the IAEA and acceptance of IAEA inspections of North Korea's declared nuclear facilities. However, the emergence of concerns over North Korea's efforts to develop nuclear weapons removed any possibility of cross-recognition,[2] as North Korea failed to make progress toward diplomatic normalization with either Washington or Tokyo. The achievement of cross-recognition might have been an important step toward easing regional tensions and might have given North Korea greater confidence to participate in multilateral diplomacy on a number of subregional issues had the 1993–94 nuclear crisis not intervened.

After the end of the Cold War and the collapse of the Soviet Union, the two Koreas established a series of inter-Korean dialogue meetings to discuss various issues at the prime minister's level. The critical new element of the dialogue was that prime minister–level talks implied recognition of the legitimacy of the opposing government. The series of eight meetings took place from 1990 to 1992 and resulted in two agreements: the Agreement on Reconciliation, Nonaggression, Exchanges and Cooperation (the Basic Agreement), and the Joint Declaration on the Denuclearization of the Korean Peninsula. These agreements were both relatively forward-looking documents that spelled out mechanisms for managing inter-Korean exchanges and cooperation on political, economic, and security matters, including mutual inspections of nuclear facilities and pledges to forgo reprocessing of nuclear materials. However, after rising concern over the North Korean nuclear program, a spy ring case during the South Korean presidential election campaign of 1992, and North Korean protests over renewal of an annual U.S.-ROK joint military exercise called "Team Spirit," the establishment of the joint committee structure that would oversee exchanges and build confidence through the implementation of the agreements was suspended. The Basic Agreement and the Joint Declaration were negotiated without intermediaries. The lack of implementation of these agreements has been a constant sticking point between the two Koreas in the absence of trusted third parties who can play verification roles to ensure that each side is keeping its part of the agreement. North Korea in particular has been reticent to allow third-party involvement in formal verification mechanisms or to implement agreements reached (especially with South Korea).

The respective interests of the two Koreas had coincided to the extent that apparent "breakthroughs" were achieved, but neither the monitoring and verification mechanisms nor ultimately the support of the international community was sufficient. Rising U.S. concerns with North Korea's nuclear weapons production efforts came to overshadow the break-throughs and eventually caused North Korea to break off implementation of the inter-Korean agreements. A broadening sphere of inter-Korean interests was made possible by the reduction in tensions resulting from the end of the Cold War, but the emergence of a new set of concerns regarding North Korean nuclear weapons development intervened in the inter-Korean process and resulted in a protracted stalemate. U.S. and South Korean interests in the nuclear issue coincided with each other, and the promises embodied in the Joint Declaration on the Denuclearization of the Korean Peninsula were in particular an important step that reflected the interests of all parties—the major powers and the two Koreas. However, negotiations on the mechanism for implementing that agreement also foundered because of growing international concern during late 1992 and 1993 over apparent discrepancies in North Korea's reporting of nuclear materials and information the IAEA gathered during its inspection visits to North Korea.

Perhaps the most visible exception to the rule that outside intermediaries have not been accepted in the inter-Korean context came at the height of tensions over North Korea's nuclear program in 1994. The visit of former president Jimmy Carter, an intervention engineered at the invitation of Kim Il Sung, enabled leaders in both Pyongyang and Washington to pull back from the brink of an escalation that may well have culminated in renewed military hostilities. (A less visible intermediary was Billy Graham, who visited Pyongyang and brought with him messages from the first Bush administration and the Clinton administration in the early 1990s.) Former president Carter's role in averting a confrontation between the United States and the DPRK is well known and well documented, but perhaps the role he was able to play—despite strong skepticism in Seoul about his efforts—as the message bearer for Kim Il Sung to propose an inter-Korean summit with Kim Young Sam has received less attention. Although the summit did not occur because of Kim Il Sung's death on July 7, 1994, President Carter's role in getting inter-Korean dialogue back on track is notable; in fact, preparations for the unrealized summit between Kim Young Sam and Kim Il Sung proved to be a valuable foundation for subsequent negotiations between the two Koreas to prepare for the June 2000 summit between Kim Dae Jung and Kim Jong Il.

Other Third-Party Roles and Inter-Korean Reconciliation

This review of the intractability of the Korean conflict has revealed clearly how the international environment and neighboring major power interests have inhibited the inter-Korean reconciliation process throughout the Cold War. The character, historical experience, and psychology of Koreans on both sides have contributed to Korean reticence to engage third parties in the process. In fact, the one thing that Kim Il Sung and Park Chung Hee could agree on even at the height of the Cold War was that foreign interference should not be allowed to affect Korean reunification. The lack of third-party involvement, however, has also contributed to the stop-start nature of the inter-Korean dialogue process, which lurched forward sporadically and inefficiently before sputtering to a halt. The changing international context following the end of the Cold War is positively influencing prospects for inter-Korean relations, but more active international involvement may also be necessary for any inter-Korean reconciliation process to move forward.

The atmosphere of competition that had characterized the Korean peninsula's external environment during the Cold War had been replaced by the mid-1990s—following the North Korean nuclear crisis—with an essential convergence among the objectives of all the major power neighbors (China, Russia, Japan, and the United States) of the two Koreas. The three essential objectives were the prevention of war, the prevention of instability that might derive from the collapse of North Korea, and the prevention of nuclear proliferation on the Korean peninsula. The establishment of the Trilateral Coordination and Oversight Group (TCOG) by former defense secretary William Perry in 1999 as part of his assessment of U.S. policy toward the Korean peninsula and the reduction of friction in U.S.-PRC relations near the end of the Clinton administration were two external factors that helped to support prospects for a Korean-led inter-Korean reconciliation process. Thus, regional power confrontation that had previously appeared to prevent progress in inter-Korean dialogue and that had provided the two Koreas with the luxury of gamesmanship and competition for legitimacy during the Cold War had been replaced by a very different situation, in which North Korea desperately needed external inputs from its neighbors, including South Korea, to ensure regime survival.

One characteristic of post–Cold War dialogue efforts focused on the Korean peninsula has been the greater involvement of multilateral fora that have also facilitated inter-Korean contact. The Korean Peninsula Energy Development Organization (KEDO), a product of the U.S.-DPRK negotiations that yielded the Geneva Agreed Framework formula, which pledged to resolve North Korea's energy needs and to improve relations in return for North Korea's promise to give up its graphite-moderated nuclear program, contributed a great deal to the inter-Korean interaction and confidence building with North Korea, despite many difficulties along the way. KEDO provided an avenue for informal North-South contact between officials even at a time when there were no effective North-South dialogue channels during the Kim Young Sam administration in the mid-1990s. KEDO also provided a practical basis for envisioning other forms of multilateral dialogue with North Korea. The organization created a policy formation process for Japan, the ROK, and the United States, which requires coordination and consensus among members who might otherwise be split apart by DPRK tactical propensities to identify and take advantage of weaknesses or differences among negotiating counterparts. KEDO may also be seen as a necessary precursor to the North Korean decision to proceed practically and smoothly with the Hyundai project to develop Mount Kumgang. As such, it is an example of how U.S. and ROK efforts to engage North Korea in a confidence-building process are complementary to each other, rather than competitive with each other.

In the late 1990s the Four Party Talks, which included the two Koreas, the People's Republic of China, and the United States, was established as another potential vehicle for forwarding such a confidence-building process (this mechanism ultimately did not directly contribute to inter-Korean reconciliation). Also established in the late 1990s, the TCOG holds consultations among Japan, South Korea, and the United States. Although TCOG does not serve as a negotiating counterpart to North Korea, it has improved coordination of policy toward North Korea, preventing North Korea from playing allies against one another and enhancing the standing of South Korea in its bilateral negotiations with the North.

Inter-Korean Summit and Prospects for Inter-Korean Reconciliation

An important factor favorable to progress in inter-Korean dialogue and reconciliation was the 1998 inauguration of South Korean president Kim Dae Jung, who held a strong personal commitment to and a vision for inter-Korean reconciliation that were embodied in his Sunshine Policy toward North Korea. Even before his election, Kim Dae Jung made dialogue with North Korea his preoccupation. In his inaugural speech, rather than hew to the rhetoric of zero-sum confrontation, he laid out three principles designed to form a new policy toward North Korea based on hopes for cooperation. Kim Dae Jung asserted that South Korea would "never tolerate armed provocation of any kind," that the South had no intention of absorbing the North, and that his administration would "actively pursue reconciliation and cooperation between the South and the North."[3] He set aside the public declaration of any formulas for unification as an issue for future generations to resolve. His public articulation of a strategy was no longer couched in zero-sum terms but rather envisioned the "dismantling of the Cold War structure." Kim Dae Jung's initial articulation of his policy won qualified South Korean public approval but was greeted with silence and continued hostile actions from the North in the form of spy incursions and maritime violations of South Korea's Northern Limit Line (NLL), demonstrating that the North was initially strongly distrustful of Kim Dae Jung's reversal of long-standing South Korean policy toward the North. These incursions eventually led to a naval skirmish in the West Sea in June 1999, during which North Korean vessels were decisively defeated.

With the implementation of President Kim Dae Jung's Sunshine Policy, some South Korean nongovernmental actors began to play active third-party roles in promoting inter-Korean reconciliation. The pioneer in this regard was Hyundai Corporation chairman Chung Ju-young, a leading South Korean entrepreneur who sought to fulfill his dream of helping countrymen where he was born, in North Korea. Having made an initial trip to North Korea in 1989 under President Roh Tae Woo, Chung played a major role under President Kim Dae Jung in opening the way for the Mount Kumgang tourism project and the inter-Korean summit of 1998. Chung first met with Kim Jong Il in Pyongyang, after crossing the DMZ with up to a thousand cattle to deliver as a gift to Kim Jong Il and the North Korean people. Hyundai also financed and administered the Mount Kumgang tourism project, at a mountain range known for its extraordinary beauty (which happened to be located very close to Chung Ju-young's hometown), on an exclusive basis, paying hundreds of millions of dollars for exclusive rights. Some of those payments also paved the way for Kim Dae Jung to make a historic visit to Pyongyang in June 2000 and attend an inter-Korean summit meeting with Kim Jong Il. Although Chung Ju-young passed away in 2001 and Hyundai faced financial difficulties afterward, partly because of the payments to North Korea, Chung's third-party role proved to be decisive in bringing the number of inter-Korean exchanges to an unprecedented level. Likewise, under Kim Dae Jung's Sunshine Policy, South Korean NGOs began to enjoy direct relationships with North Korean counterparts. Government-to-government restrictions on such contacts lessened, and ROK government funding of certain NGOs increased to support inter-Korean cooperation efforts.

The June 2000 inter-Korean summit itself was a historic event in that it provided an opportunity for the leaders of North and South Korea to talk face-to-face for the first time on the key issues that concerned them, with no mediation or third-party involvement. North Korea's economic desperation and Kim Jong Il's consolidation of power were cited by President Kim Dae Jung as two reasons why the North finally responded through unofficial dialogue channels in late 1999 and accepted the idea of an inter-Korean summit in Pyongyang, plans for which were announced three days before South Korea's National Assembly elections in April 2000.[4] The two leaders had hours of discussion and on June 15 released a joint declaration that emphasized their independent efforts and commonalities in their proposals to achieve Korean reunification, agreed to allow family reunions and repatriation of long-term unconverted prisoners from the South, stressed the opportunity for "balanced development of the national economy" through continued exchanges in various fields, and pledged to continue their dialogue to ensure smooth implementation of the joint declaration. While Kim Dae Jung claimed to have discussed peace and security issues and declared following his visit that the summit would forestall another Korean war, security agreements were not a part of the Joint Declaration of June 15 and there has been no tangible change in the security situation since the summit.

A distinctive characteristic of the inter-Korean peace process is that unlike with the Irish and Middle East peace processes, in which the symbolic "handshake" between leaders of opposing sides represented the consolidation and institutionalization of the first phase of an already existing process, the "handshake" between Kim Dae Jung and Kim Jong Il came prior to the formal institutionalization of the process, thereby representing a symbolic hope of future reconciliation rather than the consolidation of work already accomplished. This fact underscores the fragility of the process, but it also suggests the positive role that political leadership on both sides of a dispute may play in the attempt to create a new vision or context in which interaction and negotiation may take place. It may also raise questions of continuity and consistency of leadership on both sides, as the process has subsequently become bogged down.

Practical cooperation at the working level, as the two governments grapple with the institutionalization of cooperation and concrete implementation of the June 15 Joint Declaration, is the critical litmus test for genuine progress. The North-South meeting of defense ministers held on Cheju Island in late September 2000 envisaged working-level cooperation between the two militaries to provide the necessary security support measures to carry out the reconnection of rail and highway links across the DMZ. After a long hiatus, military talks resumed in May 2004 and both sides agreed to establish a "hot line" for direct communication in June 2004. Working-level inter-Korean talks were also held to discuss building the infrastructure for economic cooperation, including investment guarantees and taxation, which are necessary if trade and investment between North and South Korea are to be sustained. The litmus test for operationalization of these agreements is most likely to come as part of the establishment of a South Korean industrial zone at the city of Kaesŏng, just a few kilometers north of the DMZ. Such progress has been very slow and has been made more difficult by the rise in tensions surrounding the second North Korean nuclear crisis, although signs of progress finally began to accumulate in 2004. If the Korean peace process is to truly become institutionalized and consolidated on a broad basis, these and other working-level meetings must become regularized, as the 1992 Basic Agreement envisaged.

The Inter-Korean Summit and Its Impact on South Korea's Domestic Politics

Given the propensity of past leaders to try to use "breakthroughs" in North Korean policy for their own domestic political purposes, the blockbuster announcement of the 2000 inter-Korean summit was automatically greeted with skepticism among many in South Korea, who saw policy toward North Korea primarily as a tool for pushing a hidden, progressive social agenda and for achieving political dominance by changing the rules of the game, or as a "magic bullet" that would gain the widespread support of the Korean people. Compounding this difficulty is the fact that the North prefers secrecy and unofficial dialogue as a means of pursuing diplomacy on the most sensitive issues, while transparency and full disclosure are necessary to gain domestic public support for such an important policy initiative in a democracy such as South Korea. If the timing of the announcement of the summit three days before South Korean National Assembly elections in April 2000 was designed to influence the National Assembly elections, it failed; the opposition Grand National Party performed better than expected and nearly captured a majority of seats in the election. To the extent that the inter-Korean summit brought success and international acclaim to Kim Dae Jung himself, it deepened public cynicism at home regarding Kim Dae Jung's motives in pursuing the Sunshine Policy.

If the process of reconciliation with North Korea represented by the inter-Korean summit marks the beginning of "the end of history," to borrow Francis Fukuyama's phrase describing the ideational and ideological impact of the end of the Cold War,[5] for Korean politics it also means the beginning of ideology as a factor in a national political debate heretofore constrained by anticommunism as a de facto prerequisite for participation in political dialogue. Moreover, domestic critics of Kim Dae Jung's summit meeting in Pyongyang saw the visit not as the "triumph of liberal democracy" that Fukuyama had posited but rather as an accommodation with communism and a willingness to compromise some of the hard-won democratic freedoms that South Korea itself had achieved only within the past generation.

Although the summit appeared to be a watershed that would bring about the end of inter-Korean confrontation, it has spawned the rise of a deep ideological division in Korean politics (a "South-South" divide) that had been hidden under the surface for many years as a result of South Korea's anticommunist ideology and authoritarian historical legacy. In fact, one effect of the summit was to infuse Korean factional politics with an ideological edge. Supporters and critics of the Sunshine Policy faced off against each other on policy toward North Korea and the future of Korea's democracy. Thus, a domestic political debate that has for decades been driven by personality and regionalism was infused with ideology just at the moment when in other parts of the world ideology is on the decline as a political force.[6] Ideological division has come to the surface most strongly in initial debates over whether the National Security Law[7] should be revised and in comments made by an opposition party lawmaker characterizing the Kim Dae Jung government as a wing of the North Korean Workers' Party. The prospect of rapprochement with North Korea under Kim Jong Il is truly revolutionary if one considers that the raison d'être of the ROK government, as embodied in the legal foundations of the state constitution, is anticommunist, and, strictly speaking, President Kim Dae Jung's visit to Pyongyang was a violation of the National Security Law.

These successes, which exceeded what almost all Koreans would have imagined possible at the beginning of 2000, have bred not political credit for Kim Dae Jung but rather higher expectations and the need to initiate more substantive projects that will both induce real change in North Korea and show clearly that North Korea no longer need be considered an adversary. North Korea's insatiable demands for assistance are likely to reveal clearly the limits of South Korean capacity to render humanitarian aid. Since South Korea is the largest and nearest available benefactor to North Korea, South Korean public opinion regarding the situation and prospects for change in the North will be the single critical variable that is likely in the long term to determine the level of economic assistance available to the North. To the extent that Kim Jong Il recognizes and responds to his need to maintain a positive image among the South Korean public in the future, the South is gradually developing a powerful lever for catalyzing change and eventually requiring further progress toward peaceful coexistence and the end of military confrontation on the Korean peninsula. (However, some critics worry that while the inter-Korean summit was designed to induce North Korea to change, it has been the South Korean political environment and public opinion toward North Korea that have been transformed in a direction that some feel promote North Korea's own aims.) If the second North Korean nuclear crisis can be successfully resolved, the development of inter-Korean exchanges will be the primary driver in the next phase of inter-Korean relations and will ultimately determine the pace, direction, and shape of progress toward peaceful coexistence and economic and political integration on the Korean peninsula.

The Second North Korean Nuclear Crisis and China's Mediating Role

The discovery in 2002 of a covert North Korean effort to develop highly enriched uranium (HEU) as a path to nuclear weapons in defiance of the spirit and the letter of the Geneva Agreed Framework has resulted in its unraveling and the development of a new nuclear crisis focused on North Korea's nuclear weapons procurement efforts. The second North Korean crisis has followed the same pattern of coercive diplomacy and crisis escalation between the United States and North Korea as that which developed during the first crisis, followed by attempts by third parties to mediate the crisis.

The PRC has emerged as an active mediator and host for the six-party talks in this second North Korean nuclear crisis. This is a departure from China's past doctrine of noninterference and peaceful coexistence, as the PRC has taken upon itself an active role in mediating a regional dispute for the first time. The PRC's activist role in this round is in sharp contrast to its relative passivity in the 1993–94 North Korean nuclear crisis. China's involvement may well reflect a new brand of diplomacy under a new Chinese leadership that feels more confident in its role as an emerging regional power and is more keenly aware of the potential risks that military conflict on its borders might hold for China's strategy of continued economic development as the basis for securing its long-term stability and prosperity.

The PRC has several motivations for becoming more active diplomatically in response to the escalation of tensions surrounding North Korea's nuclear program. First, the PRC determined that action would be necessary to maintain regional stability and avoid the specter of another

Iraq in its own backyard. Increasingly, the PRC's top priority has been maintaining an environment conducive to continued Chinese economic growth. Second, the "demonstration effect" of failed diplomacy at the United Nations that led to the U.S. military conflict with Iraq motivated China to intervene diplomatically as a means of avoiding the consequences of failed diplomacy with North Korea. Certainly, Beijing can ill afford the regional consequences of North Korea's nuclear program, including a likely chain reaction in which Japan, South Korea, and Taiwan may all consider possession of nuclear weapons necessary for their own self-defense. One fear among Chinese analysts is that a war on the Korean peninsula might also indirectly serve to strengthen U.S. dominance and complete a military "encirclement" strategy designed to isolate or weaken the PRC. Third, now that China has intervened to the extent that it has, its own prestige and direct national interests are on the line as it pursues a diplomatic solution rather than allowing the situation to escalate to the point of military confrontation, a scenario that would be highly detrimental to Chinese interests. So the stakes for China are high, but the decision to host the talks helps to cement China as an indispensable player in matters concerning the future of the Korean peninsula.

The other participants in the six-party dialogue will also play an important role in shaping the direction of the process as it unfolds. Their role is to provide intermediation to facilitate a deal and to provide isolation to either the United States or North Korea depending on their respective negotiating positions. Solidarity among the third-party participants against uncompromising positions of the United States and the DPRK will have an important influence on the direction of the negotiations.

The South Korean position is complex. Unlike with the first nuclear crisis, when Seoul was shut out, South Korea has its own stake in continuing inter-Korean economic exchange and cooperation, is a member of TCOG, and is participating as a full member of the six-party talks. Although South Korea is to a certain extent marginalized as nuclear tensions rise and the focus shifts to the U.S. and DPRK positions, South Korea has a certain measure of economic leverage with North Korea and possibly represents the lowest common denominator as Pyongyang tries to exploit differences among the participating parties in the dialogue.

Japan's position has hardened markedly with the public focus on the North Korean government's past involvement in the abduction of Japanese nationals to North Korea. The Japanese position is sufficiently tough that the North Koreans requested that Japan be excluded from future rounds of dialogue, and both Japanese and DPRK positions on bilateral issues have retrenched to the point that this bilateral channel is quite cool. Japan will support a tougher U.S. approach in the context of the TCOG efforts to coordinate policy among Japan, South Korea, and the United States.

Following an initial high-profile but relatively unsuccessful mediating effort by Russian deputy minister of foreign affairs Aleksandr Losyukov in January 2003, the Russians have been relatively quiet, barely making it into the room as plans for the dialogue developed in the summer of 2003. However, some analysts suggest that President Vladimir Putin's good personal relations with Kim Jong Il might be used effectively to induce North Korea's cooperation. As one of the five permanent members of the UN Security Council, Russia, along with China, will play a vital role in determining whether this issue goes to the Security Council.

Conclusion: The Bush Administration and the End of (Conflict with) North Korea

For decades, the Korean conflict has remained frozen with the consensus of the four major powers in favor of retaining an unsustainable status quo. The relative stability derived from Korea's division has been preferred to the uncertainty that would accompany the outcome of North Korea's collapse. Ultimately, North Korea faces either complete economic and political breakdown or radical reform. The second North Korean nuclear crisis adds a new twist to this assessment, as North Korean nuclear weapons may be seen by Pyongyang as the ultimate deterrent but at the same time are equally destabilizing for all of North Korea's neighbors. North Korea's challenge—and the regional response it has provoked—is mobilizing its own isolation as never before, with potentially dramatic implications for the future of the peninsula and the regional security order.

South Korea and the United States have dramatically shifted their respective positions toward North Korea in the decade since the mid-1990s. South Korea's containment policy toward North Korea has been transformed into one of active engagement and dialogue as a result of the implementation of Kim Dae Jung's Sunshine Policy. The U.S. willingness to seek a bilateral deal with North Korea through negotiations that prevailed in the Clinton administration has been replaced by skepticism among Bush administration officials, and the mood among specialists and policymakers in Washington is much more pessimistic about the viability of a negotiated settlement with North Korea. A strong sentiment within the divided Bush administration is that negotiations with North Korea bring recognition and affirmation of a despicable and illegitimate criminal regime. While there is a striking consensus among all of North Korea's neighbors on the unacceptability of North Korea's nuclear weapons development, there is also a striking divergence on prospects for a negotiated settlement. Chinese and South Korean policymakers expect a new deal, while Japanese and U.S. policymakers are considerably more skeptical.

The prospect of Korean rapprochement poses an interesting dilemma for the United States in the context of its role and presence in South Korea. The United States has made a significant investment over decades in its relationship with South Korea through the maintenance of a troop presence on the Korean peninsula. This has been an investment in the stability of the Korean peninsula and Northeast Asia. While it is not clear that Korean reconciliation would necessarily pose a threat to U.S. interests, it would change the configuration of regional stability in Northeast Asia in ways that would influence the fundamental calculus of each major player in the region. How to manage the costs of a "resolution" of the Korean standoff in ways that conform to U.S. interests will be a challenge, especially in managing the U.S.-ROK alliance while maintaining the U.S. role as a guarantor of regional stability. The fundamental goal of such a policy should be to ensure that the United States is perceived as neither irrelevant nor an obstacle to the process of Korean reconciliation and/ or reunification.

Thus far, the Bush administration's primary focus has been, not on diplomacy *with* North Korea, but on diplomacy *about* North Korea. First, diplomacy about North Korea has been the focus of the Bush administration's attempt to multilateralize the North Korean nuclear challenge, and it was a successful effort through August 2003. Second, the United States successfully brought all the major parties on board to endorse the "complete, verifiable, and irreversible" elimination of North Korea's nuclear program as a policy objective. Third, the United States was able to hold out for a six-party dialogue formula hosted in Beijing. However, since the focus of U.S. diplomacy has been about North Korea rather than with North Korea, there was no serious opportunity for bilateral U.S.-DPRK dialogue at the August meeting. In fact, the U.S. representative, Assistant Secretary of State James Kelly, was on such a short leash that he was barely authorized to speak to his North Korean counterpart and was unable to engage in any serious responses to North Korean questions about the U.S. position. At the same time, the United States has developed and pursued a multilateral initiative, the Proliferation Security Initiative (PSI), which thus far has been symbolic of a U.S. desire to take a more activist approach toward halting DPRK shipments of contraband such as drugs or illegal weapons shipments and to strengthen international prohibitions on the DPRK's missile exports.[8]

President Bush's statements during his stay in Seoul in February 2002 (and later moves to reconfigure the U.S. troop presence in South Korea) suggest that he recognizes the status quo is indeed unsustainable and that Korean reunification is inevitable and desirable. President Bush's speech at Dorasan train station made this quite clear and was striking in that the president's statements were the most forward leaning of any U.S. president or administration on the issue of Korean reunification and its inevitability.

China's greater activism and recognition of the profound risks to its national security posed by a nuclear North Korea and President Bush's vision of a unified Korea suggest that the international consensus in favor of the status quo may be unraveling. In the near future, there may be a new configuration on the Korean peninsula, in which the problem of North Korea is definitively resolved. Or a chain of events might be set off through which it may be possible to envision Korean reunification and a yet-to-be-determined realigned balance of power in Northeast Asia. President Bush's vision of a peaceful and democratic Korea that is no longer the last outpost of Cold War confrontation but rather is at the center of a peaceful and prosperous Northeast Asia is undeniably attractive and is nothing new: the question is whether all parties concerned can agree on how to get there. The prospect of dramatic change and an end of the confrontation on the Korean peninsula, with all of the consequences that it may entail, may be closer than ever. Of course, the past failures of all the parties involved to satisfactorily answer that fundamental question over five decades are what have made the Korean conflict so intractable.

Notes

1. The 1998 revision to the Constitution of the DPRK marginalized the role of the Central Party Committee and the Supreme People's Assembly in favor of the Central Defense Commission as the key governing institution. Unlike his father, Kim Jong Il has relied on the title of supreme commander and chairman of the Central Defense Commission as the governing authority, reflecting an increased influence for the Korean People's Army. Yet there are also contradictory signs that institutions of the bureaucracy are coming into conflict with one another, particularly over issues related to the control of economic resources. Despite an ostensibly strengthened role for the military, defector testimony of Hwang Jang Yop, the highest-level defector from North Korea and architect of North Korea's ideology of *juche* (self-reliance), and others suggests that real power lies in family relations with Kim Jong Il, rather than in high-ranking position within DPRK institutions.

2. "Cross-recognition" referred to the respective normalization of relations between the People's Republic of China and the USSR, on the one side, and the ROK, on the other side, in return for Japanese and U.S. recognition of the DPRK.

3. Nicholas D. Kristof, "South Korea's New President Appeals to North to End Decades of Division," *New York Times,* February 25, 1998, 8.

4. Author notes from meeting of President Kim Dae Jung with scholars at the Blue House, Seoul, May 2000.

5. Francis Fukuyama, *The End of History and the Last Man* (New York: Avon Books, 1992). Fukuyama presented his original argument in "The End of History," *National Interest* 19 (summer 1989): 3–18.

6. Korea's democratic consolidation and the transformation of terms of discourse in the South Korean political and social sphere are sharpening some fundamental, unresolved contradictions in policy toward North Korea. North Korea's future is a critical issue to be addressed as South Korea's new political leadership takes the mantle in designing its own policies toward the North. These issues are further discussed in Scott Snyder, "The End of History, the Rise of Ideology, and the Future of Democracy on the Korean Peninsula," *Journal of East Asian Studies* 3, no. 2 (May-August 2003): 199–224.

7. The ROK National Security Law outlaws unauthorized contact with North Koreans or praise of the North Korean system. It was misused for many years to repress democratic opposition to authoritarian rule.

8. The Proliferation Security Initiative was announced on May 31, 2003, by President Bush in Poland as an attempt to fight the illegal shipment of nuclear components across national borders. Under its auspices, a number of exercises and simulations have been held, and the membership is steadily growing from the initial eleven members who signed up in May 2003.

14

Intractability and the Israeli-Palestinian Conflict

Stephen Cohen

IS THE ISRAELI-PALESTINIAN CONFLICT a conflict that will never end? Or will it eventually burn itself out? Or is it a conflict that could be not only managed but also resolved through sustained, intense, and multifaceted third-party intervention, including mediation, supervised negotiation, economic and social planning and investment, muscular peacekeeping and monitoring, humanitarian aid, and self-organized indigenous facilitation and intervention? Alternatively, is it possible that the parties will themselves abandon their current conflict-maintenance strategies for a form of conflict—nonviolence—that would be much more amenable to conflict resolution?

Today, one of the major causes of the stalemate in the process toward peace is exactly that the history of this conflict is so long. The prolonged duration of the conflict has added a new dimension to its intractable nature. An entire generation has been raised knowing nothing else but a perpetual state of war with the "Other." The main parties and the international community have suffered through years, indeed almost one hundred years, of international attempts to intervene in the relationship between the indigenous population of Palestine, mostly Arab, and the emergent and now permanent Jewish populations of the same area organized through most of this period within the state of Israel. It is a characteristic of this conflict and its intractability over generations that intervention from the outside is coterminous with the existence of the conflict. The conflict itself is coterminous with the contemporary self-definitions of the identity of the two national movements and national entities to which the two parties adhere and to which they demonstrate great loyalty, above and beyond the capacity of these self-definitions to produce a situation of peaceful, long-term coexistence that allows for societal and economic development.

It is a characteristic of international intervention in the Israeli-Palestinian conflict that it has almost always been seen by the international intervener as (partly) an act of humanitarian assistance and is always perceived by one or both of the main parties as an unfriendly imposition of external will. It is a characteristic of this conflict that its story can be told, and is told, either as a narrative of one party or the other, as their national saga, or as a story of world history in which the local actors are only pawns in a much larger drama played by the major world powers—no matter who those powers might be at any given time.

It is no surprise, then, that some people always offer sophisticated arguments to the effect that the conflict is not yet or never will be ripe for solution. These arguments may or may not be true. I believe that they embody an unhelpfully deterministic view of an evolving human reality. More problematic than these arguments is the claim by some analysts that the lack of ripeness makes it futile for outsiders to try once again to resolve the conflict. Yet, all the time outsiders—or, more accurately, some non-indigenous parties to the conflict—continue to play powerful roles in sustaining one or both parties in the maintenance of the conflict.

Three Narratives of the Conflict

A comprehensive analysis of the protracted and intractable nature of this conflict should begin with the presentation of three historical accounts of the conflict. History here is defined not as a single, objective, and truthful account of events and their causal patterns but as parallel narratives or shared stories told by each people about their past, sometimes with important variants within each group. A critical issue in any conflict is how and what is taught with regard to history. Each side has its version of history, which most often denies the Other its version of history. In the Israeli-Palestinian conflict there are three main narratives: the Zionist narrative, the Palestinian/Arab narrative, and the general historical perceptions of the region.

According to the Zionist and now dominant Israeli narrative, the conflict stems from the persistent and consistent refusal of the Arabs to recognize the legitimacy and permanency of a Jewish national state in the midst of a predominantly Arab and mostly Muslim Middle East. In this Zionist/Israeli/Jewish nationalist narrative, the Jewish national movement creates a modern community as an act of rescue and an act of creative reconstruction of an ancient national, historical, geographical, and linguistic identity. It is the combination of the act of rescue of Eastern European Jews from a world that was rejecting and persecuting them and the creative force of national reconstruction by Jews from both Eastern Europe and the Arab and North African world that gives the movement its historical élan and justification. But it is the living community that the movement has produced that asserts its present claim to live in peace and without harassment whether or not one accepts the historical narrative. Moreover, the world community has in a number of guises over the past hundred years found this claim worthy of international support, first through the international arrangements of the post–World War I era and then through the actions of the United Nations after World War II.

In the dominant Arab and Palestinian narrative, the conflict is the story of the forceful displacement of the indigenous Arab population and the takeover of its land and settlement thereof by a colonial movement of mostly European Jews reinforced by imperial power and supported by Western technology and resources. In this narrative, it is the arrival on the land itself of the Jews from abroad and their subsequent acts of force (supported by successive imperial powers) that is the basic injustice, and it is the story of the indigenous people's refusal to be forced to accept that some or all of their aboriginal territory will be ceded to a foreign people that is the essence of the narrative and the heroic resistance. The story continues through the Israeli state's attempt to enforce, and the Palestinian attempt to resist, the aggressive and at times peaceful and prosperous cohesion of the settler state of Israel that emerges from this displacement of the indigenous community and its social structure. The state expresses itself eventually through the forcible and at times brutal military occupation of the remaining land of the indigenous people and the continual attempt to seize and hold their land through Israeli Jewish settlement.

The third narrative would begin with the military defeat by Western powers of the declining Ottoman Empire, conquered as almost a

consolation prize of a deplorably destructive European war. The lands of
the old empire continue to be a region of uncertain and unstable governance
and protracted underdevelopment. For reasons pertaining to geostrategy
and natural resources, it persists as a battleground for great-power influence
and is continually unstable because it lacks a clear, legitimate successor to
the Ottoman Empire. The region is also a hornet's nest of traditional cultural and ethnic rivalries, in which identities overlap and clash and boundaries are seen as borders drawn by imperial powers rather than natural
demarcations that coincide with national identity differentiation and consolidation. In that context, the emergence of Zionism and Israel becomes
the crucible of multiple conflicts in the region and multiple grievances
that feed upon one another and that produce recurring eruptions of violence. These eruptions tempt outside powers to try to control and dominate
the region for their own reasons, even though they claim to be helping to
calm the conflicts.

The narratives of national identity have also merged slowly into
narratives of victimization, oppression, and hate. Israelis and Palestinians
view themselves as the victim of each other as well as of the international
community. Both peoples want to believe that their narrative is the only
true one and can exist only if the other narrative, if not the other people,
disappears. Because each can understand itself to be the victim of history,
and can point to much evidence of that victimization, both historical and
contemporary, each can justify any and almost all actions toward the other.
The rounds of violence that continue yearly and sometimes daily are perpetuated by this self-understanding. The zero-sum game of victimhood is
a critical part of the problem of intractability. The violent actions on both
sides have led many Israelis and Palestinians to feel deprived not only of
quiet but also of dignity, but neither is able to see or is willing to acknowledge through official representative institutions and accounts that the
same is true for the other—that both sides feel this way.

The complexity created by these three competing but parallel narratives is compounded by the fact that each narrative is itself contested by
its own people; there is in each case a continuing internal battle between
rival perspectives and political elements who see different futures for the
national narrative. Some elements emphasize the need to continue the conflict until there is a clear winner or loser; others press for eventual compromise, if not reconciliation. The refusal of the third parties to acknowledge

that conflicting narratives of the future are present not only between the two parties but also within the each party, and even within third parties, makes mediation and intervention more difficult still.

The conflict must be understood and managed not only as a conflict between the parties but also as a conflict within the parties about opposing sources of national legitimacy and competing emphases within the narrative of national identity.

Religion as a Further Dimension of Conflict

The Israeli-Palestinian and Arab-Israeli conflict in its regional and more general form has additional layers of complexity that cannot be ignored, though they are exceedingly difficult to handle. This conflict is not only a strategic, national, and intercommunal conflict but also a conflict among myths, myths that have deep resonance in the cultures of monotheism. The conflict's intractability is exacerbated by the subtext of religion-based historical perceptions, theological or quasi-theological judgments, and aspersions and popular myths cast about the relationship among Judaism, Christianity, and Islam. This level of the conflict cannot be dismissed or papered over by piously declaring the brotherhood of man and humankind or by invoking the all-important but much violated belief that we are all creatures of one God. The most terrible violations of basic humanity are practiced and justified in the name of the One God.

The parties compete not only for the crown of victimhood but also for the place of primacy at the right hand of God. Who is the greatest victim of human perfidy and who is closest to God's truth? An unusual kind of moral intervention, as well as very energetic and powerful third-party facilitation, is required to supplant moral absolutism and to replace it with a perspective in which a life-affirming peaceful agreement is regarded as morally significant and the Other is accepted as human and morally legitimate. To accomplish this will require, above all, moral and political leadership from within the parties to transcend the prevailing myths and to create a larger myth of a shared destiny for the coming generations. Thus, the conflict resolution process has to be sensitive to and engage the cultures and civilizations of these peoples so that internal divisions do not undermine any reconciliation process and any process of getting each side to accept the legitimacy of the other. The danger faced within the conflict resolution struggle is that one or both sides will contain a powerful sub-group that sees the whole of reconciliation as a sacrilegious abomination. Such a group and its perceptions can derail efforts to move toward a fair-minded agreement that promises a brighter future to both groups.

Most attempts at conflict resolution and even conflict management in the region have tried to avoid completely the religious dimension, except for the occasional attempt to face the problem of Jerusalem, which represents the most palpable example of the religious dimension. However, the individuals and institutions that enjoy religious legitimacy on each side probably need to be recruited to help encourage conflict resolution, the humanization of the enemy, and respect for the enemy's religious commitments and beliefs. They must feel that their place can be one of honor in such a reconciliation, not that they are going to be swept away as the detritus of traditional history.

The Three Levels of Conflict

An often-overlooked characteristic of this conflict is that it exists on multiple levels, all of which must be engaged in order to break the stalemate. These levels serve to intensify and complicate the conflict. Each level is known and discussed in isolation, but it is the knowledge of how these three levels affect one another that will help move the parties toward a solution.

The most basic is the local level, at which the focus is on the relationship between Israelis and Palestinians on the ground, the intercommunal conflict. In today's environment, that relationship is embodied in the personal narratives of occupation, terrorism, and economic disaster. The local level is entrenched in concerns of national identity, in the experience and sense of victimhood, and in political and educational cultures that over the course of generations have perpetuated the conflict.

At a second level, the Israeli-Palestinian conflict is greatly influenced by the larger relationships between the Arab world and Israel. The larger Arab world has been intimately involved in the saga of the control of Palestine since the end of World War I, when issues of the succession to Ottoman rule were being argued, and more so since the end of the 1930s, when the British were too alienated from Palestinian leaders to invite them to take part in consultations in London and instead invited other Arab leaders to listen and to speak. This pattern of Arab involvement followed in war and peace has made the conflict a part of Arab state history and society and brought the Arab world into the narrative in many ways. It is only with the cooperation, encouragement, and participation of major Arab governments and wider Arab public opinion that the communal conflict can be solved. We have veered over the decades from the error of imagining that we can solve the problem over the heads of the Palestinians with the Arabs alone, to the parallel error of imagining that the Palestinians can reach historic compromises without the strong backing and help of key Arab governments and the acceptance of key Arab public opinion. We need the simultaneous involvement of both levels.

Moreover, Israel is most likely to reach a peace agreement with the Palestinians if it believes that such an agreement will end the entire Arab-Israeli conflict and not leave combustible issues unresolved and likely to reignite the conflict in the future. The same principle of working on multiple levels simultaneously is true also of key conflict issues. For instance, the refugee issue cannot be resolved without Jordanian, Lebanese, and Syrian consent, as well as Palestinian and Israeli political will. Water rights are another Israeli-Palestinian issue that is also deeply important for Jordan, Lebanon, and Syria. The question of water resources will also involve Turkey—which is the repository of most of the region's water—and the international community—which will be required to provide the resources and some of the technical and mediation expertise to work out the complex relationships between supply of water, price of water, and use of water.

The third level involves the international community. Since at least the end of World War I, when Britain and France divided up the Middle East, much of which had been conquered by force of British arms, the international community has played a role in the affairs of the region. Whether as colonial powers or third-party interlocutors, many other countries have had an important hand in the region. But it is not simply states that have a role in the international arena. Various constituencies have a political and even economic effect on the conflict, among them the American Jewish community and the European Arab community, as well as nongovernmental organizations and international organizations. The Balfour Declaration, which for many purposes can be seen as the diplomatic declaration of this war, makes reference to a participant who, though much ignored, is essential to conflict resolution. The Balfour Declaration talks not only about the Jewish homeland and the British intention to assist in its creation, and not only about the awkwardly described "non-Jewish inhabitants" and their rights, but also about those Jews who do not become a part of the Zionist enterprise. Any facilitator who refuses to deal with the non-Israeli Jewish dimension of the conflict is bound to fail. Throughout the history of this conflict, the interaction between modern Jewish identity within the homeland and Jewish identity outside the homeland has been an essential force multiplier for Israel. This conflict has always blurred the boundaries between state actors and nonstate actors in international relations. Conflict resolution will never succeed if it ignores the nonstate actors, Jewish or Arab.

Thus, the conflict resolution process will have to face up to the role of the Jews abroad, whether those in America or those who left Arab countries to reside in Europe and elsewhere and who have their own claims and grievances. Conflict resolution will have to deal with the export of Middle Eastern Christians to the West and to Latin America, which makes the solution of such problems as Jerusalem and Lebanon more complicated and less tractable. The Arabs now living within Israel are another constituency that plays a role in shaping the Israeli-Palestinian conflict; the future status of Arab Israelis is a major concern for both sides when contemplating the long-term consequences of a two-state solution and whether it can be permanent and stable.

The core of the conflict's intractability lies in repeated attempts by third parties to intervene on one or other of the conflict's three levels without having a firm analytic hold on other levels. For example, during the fifteen years from the mid-1980s to the outbreak of the second intifada, there was an attempt by the United States, Israel, and the Palestine Liberation Organization (PLO) to focus on the key bilateral intercommunal conflict of Palestinians and Israelis and to break down the resistance in each party to an officially sanctioned negotiation, without prior conditions, between the PLO and the Israeli government. This effort was successful —for a while. It was aided by the decline of the Soviet Union in the 1980s and by the growth of U.S. hegemony just before and just after the fall of the Soviet Union. Initially, it was simplified by the shattering of the united Arab front that occurred as a result of Anwar el-Sadat's decision to make peace with Israel and Saddam Hussein's decision to invade Kuwait. Subsequently, however, the fragmentation of the Arab political system made it difficult to achieve broad support within the Arab world for the Oslo experiment, when issues of permanent status came to the fore and when Palestinian leadership split into nationalist Fateh and Islamic groups such as Hamas, which were appealing to some Arab conservatives.

With the reconfiguration of international politics in this period of European assertiveness, and with the emergence of the extremist anti-American challenge from Osama bin Laden and his ilk, the Arab system is being forced to, and wants to, reemerge as a player in the regional interstate conflict to encourage a rapid settlement between Israel and the Palestinians. Meanwhile, the United States, while still the predominant power, is not alone in its concern with conflict in the Middle East. The Quartet structure—which brings together the United Nations, the European Union, Russia, and the United States—has yet to prove itself effective, but it demonstrates changing tendencies in the international level of the conflict that could balance the American role to a certain extent.

Thus, these other levels, the second level—interstate (Arab states and Israel)—and the third level—the international level—have to be fully brought to bear in an affirmative way. They can provide some leverage that they did not have in the 1990s. The inter-Arab level was the least well handled in the days of the Clinton administration but is more in play today than ever, even though Arab state power is very compromised and divided as a result of the Iraq conflict and the ineffective coordination among the key powers of Syria, Egypt, and Saudi Arabia in making their Beirut Summit initiative an effective instrument of international diplomatic influence.

However, the Palestinian intragroup conflict is raging again, and within Israel the school of thought that sees no solution, only a continued struggle, is dominant. Fateh and the Palestinian Authority, even the PLO itself, have lost their vaunted role as the sole legitimate representative of the Palestinian people due to the growing influence of Hamas and the stalemate over control of the Palestinian Authority, which suffered as Arafat lost full control of the movement and which has shown an increasing inability to make decisions. What had once been the assertion of Palestinian independence of decision has deteriorated into a Palestinian right to indecision. On the Israeli side, the settler movement has shown an ability to impose a veto on Israeli government peace efforts by its insistence on the priority of settlements over all other Israeli security and national interests.

Methods of Conflict as Part of Intractability

The century of murderous conflict between the indigenous population of
Palestine and the Jewish people and their national movement cannot be
ended by a series of cease-fires. Measures that attempt to stop these two
peoples from employing their preferred methods of struggle while leaving
their basic demands and national aspirations uncertain of achievement are
bound to fail in the future as they have so often in the past. The two sides
will inevitably revert to their traditional methods, either because they are
ordered to do so by their leaders or because the pressure from the streets
to do so is irresistible. The belief in retaliation and revenge has become a
solemn obligation in both narratives, more important than the strategic
logic or rational effectiveness of the approach.

For the Palestinians as an indigenous people, the methods of struggle have been, and continue to be, the use of their bodies and their words,
expressing their anger and their refusal of the Jewish national presence.
This is their unending resistance to the Jewish national movement, which
is more technologically advanced, better organized, better funded, and better linked to the flow of international power, but whose will to prevail is
matched by the Palestinian will to resist.

For the Israeli Jews as successors to the Zionist movement, the
method of struggle has always been a threefold combination: superior
power (to guarantee in perpetuity the present balance of power); settlement of the land (to threaten the Palestinians with physical displacement
and replacement); and linkage to the dominant power of the day (to ensure
diplomatic ascendancy and prevent international efforts to forcibly change
the balance of local power).

Given these preferred and by now traditional strategies, every action
of Israel intended to end terrorism is perceived by all Palestinians as an
act to deepen Israel's occupation and perpetuate its control. Every Palestinian attempt to resist occupation is for Israelis an act of terrorism. Instead
of separating terror from Palestinian society, Israel, in seeking to uproot
terrorism, has effectively sought to uproot Palestinian society, even though
a majority of Israelis would much prefer a peaceful solution in which both
sides could live in their own states. Support for terrorism has become very
widespread in Palestinian society, as Palestinians perceive no other credible way to attain their freedom, even though the majority would prefer

nonmilitary leadership that is competent to lead them to independence and into a life without confrontation.

At this stage, only an authoritative third party can disentangle Israel's war against terrorism from Israel's war to maintain occupation, as perceived by Palestinians. Only a third party can disentangle the Palestinians' war against occupation from the Palestinians' war to destroy Israeli statehood, as perceived by more and more Israelis. Only a third party can separate the development of Palestinian civil society from the dismantling of the Palestinian infrastructure of terrorism. Only a third party can facilitate the emergence of a peaceful new Palestinian leadership that is not made up of the captains of violence. A dramatic act of peaceful transformation, undertaken at the invitation of the parties, is urgently required.

Third parties often imagine the transformation of Palestinian resistance from violence to nonviolent civil resistance. The problem is not a Palestinian addiction to violence; rather, the problem is that effective nonviolent civil resistance requires a high level of mutual trust within the confronting society, trust that all members of society will act in unison, therefore bringing more pressure to bear on the dominant society than it can withstand. Attaining this level of internal trust is the primary challenge for a confronting society, and it usually requires the emergence of a leadership that enjoys full public confidence and firmly believes in the efficacy of militant nonviolent resistance.

The success of nonviolent resistance also requires Palestinians to come to believe that the dominant society, Israel, will not be able to engage for long in the wholesale slaughter of peaceful civil resisters without paying a high price in terms of its international reputation and support and without experiencing unacceptable levels of dissension within Israel. Sections of Israeli society have objected strongly to the occupation and have shown an ability to mobilize public opposition to government policy. Such opposition led, for example, to the Israeli decision to withdraw from Lebanon. Somehow, the Palestinians have failed to appreciate that this division within Israeli society would likely make nonviolent militant action an effective method for attaining their goals. The deaf ear that the Palestinians turn toward Israeli opposition to the occupation convinces many Israelis that Palestinian goals must not be limited to a two-state solution, because that end could be achieved by nonviolent resistance. For Palestinians, the problem is more basic: they believe that the ideology of the settlers and their supporters will prevail in Israel and that support for the suppression of the Palestinian resistance by military force will always trump any civil objections within Israel.

These fine judgments about the deeper dynamics of the two societies are important for third parties to understand: What will bring about change in the dynamics of the conflict? Is Palestinian violence equalizing the balance of power between the dominant Israelis and the very determined Palestinians, or is it perpetuating the conflict? Is there a way of inculcating different rules and mechanisms for fighting each other that would be less self-destructive and less discouraging of mediation efforts by third parties? Can third parties be convinced that they would not become targets themselves if they intervened with a physical presence? Is there a way to engage wider elements of the two societies in the peacemaking process, or must it remain a process of secretive negotiation between a few men and a very few women?

Since so much of the problem of continued violence is related to the low level of trust within and between societies, secrecy should be used sparingly, not wholesale, as the modality of conflict resolution. Too much secrecy reinforces the divisions within each society as to who owns the society and who is peripheral. Great attention must be paid not only to making progress in the negotiations but also to ensuring that different factions of society are not forgotten in the design of the future that is being negotiated by others.

Is this conflict by now so bound by violence and repression that it will require the application of a superior external force to stop the parties from the repetitive compulsion of violence and repression? There is a growing belief among observers of the conflict who see the need for moving more quickly to a Palestinian state living in peace with Israel that muscular third-party intervention is what the parties need, because they are themselves unable to break the violent habits of generations, even though they no longer believe that violence will be decisive.

The Israeli-Palestinian conflict has become intractable because of the political culture that it has fostered over the course of generations and that is inculcated not only by each side's media but also by its educational system. The hope for those seeking peace is that new generations will come to the conclusion that inflicting maximum pain on the other side also means maximum pain for one's own side; such a realization would make them consider approaches that might end the conflict and still achieve national goals through negotiation or nonviolence and/or through encouraging forceful third-party intervention. Bringing about this sort of change in political culture will require a multifaceted campaign involving exchange programs, the media, and a wide variety of educational initiatives.

Conclusion

The intractability of the Israeli-Palestinian conflict stems from (1) the multilevel nature of the conflict; (2) the prolonged duration of the conflict, which has also permitted the conflict to penetrate the political culture of the peoples of the region to the extent that to become an Israeli or Palestinian or, albeit to a lesser extent, to become an Arab or a Jew is to be inculcated in a conflict-maintenance national narrative of the conflict; and (3) the persistent failure in successive resolution attempts to recognize one or other dimension of the conflict, including the intraparty dimensions.

World War I was never truly ended in the lands of the Ottoman Empire. The simultaneous collapse of the Hapsburg Empire and the empire of the czars brought Jewish history and Arab history into a fatal common destiny. The exhausted British and French Empires never created a fully legitimate successor to the Ottoman Empire, and the successor states never fully reconciled their ambitions to the limited territory they could claim and the limited power they could wield. The United States, which has chosen to overthrow Saddam Hussein and which has been forced by Osama bin Laden to deeply involve itself in the future of the Arab and Muslim world, has become the successor power to whom has fallen the task of resolving the unfinished business of World War I. The problems of Israel, Jordan, Lebanon, Palestine, and Syria form one of the two main strands of that unfinished business (the other strand concerns the future of Iraq, Iran, Saudi Arabia, and the emirates of the Gulf). If the intractability of the conflict has been a product of its complexity and its longevity, now those two factors provide a window of historic opportunity. At all three levels of the conflict—intercommunal, regional, and international—these problems have become simultaneously urgent in all their dimensions. The longevity of the conflict is exhausting and debilitating societies on both sides, and a reluctant but palpable willingness to end the strife is beginning to emerge. The challenge of third-party leadership is to ensure that this unresolved legacy of World War I does not have to be dealt with as it was in Europe, with a still more devastating conflict.

15

Beyond Resolution?

The Palestinian-Israeli Conflict

Shibley Telhami

MY OBJECTIVE IN THIS CHAPTER is to make three central points that may help explain the difficulty in overcoming the Palestinian-Israeli conflict and to look at the requirements of successful peacemaking efforts. In making these points, I will argue that the conflict is now in a phase of increasing intractability, even as opportunities for a peaceful settlement remain.

First, it is necessary to understand the way each side has come to frame the conflict, and to analyze the narratives that each side holds about the conflict and how and why these narratives change over time. Narratives are essential to understanding how each party interprets events; they affect the perceived options available to the parties and limit their views of the possibilities. It is clear that these narratives have played a significant role in shaping the attitudes toward peacemaking since the creation of Israel in 1948.

Second, I will address the strategic calculations behind the difficulty in breaking out of cycles of violence that entrap the parties in a tit-for-tat reaction. The norm of reciprocity takes hold over time, reinforcing the kind of violence cycle that engaged the parties after the collapse of the Camp David negotiations in July 2000. Research suggests that, even where power is unequal between the parties and where both sides are losing, learning to cooperate does not necessarily lead them to break out of a seemingly self-defeating cycle of violence.[1]

Third, I will address the role of third parties in breaking the dead-lock. Here I will specifically address the role of the United States in try-ing to break the Israeli-Palestinian cycle of violence and to mediate a peace agreement.

The Framing of the Conflict

It is difficult to understand or interpret what has occurred in the Palestinian-Israeli conflict and the Arab-Israeli conflict without first understanding the prevailing paradigms that each side holds. These paradigms affect the identity of individuals and communities, in both the long and short terms. If one examines the evolution of the Palestinian-Israeli conflict between 1948 and the Oslo Accords of 1993, one can argue that these narratives have changed dramatically and that without this change the possibilities that emerged with the Oslo Accords would not have otherwise done so.

In the history of Palestinian nationalism, the year 1974 is critical. That was the year the Arab states recognized the Palestine Liberation Organization (PLO) as the sole legitimate representative of the Palestin-ian people. In that recognition there was a profound change, not only in Arab politics, but also in the norms of sovereignty in the region and in the increasing focus on states as the central units of politics in the region above and beyond all else. The notion of a Palestinian nation separate from other Arab nations was thus normalized.

After the Palestinian dispersion in 1948, the Palestinian narrative of the *nakba* (catastrophe) was initially one of conflict over the issues of jus-tice and the right of Palestinians to return to their original homes in what had become the state of Israel. The conflict with Israel was necessarily de-fined in zero-sum terms. It was impossible to reconcile the Palestinian issue, focused on the full return of refugees, with Israel as a Jewish state. The refugee problem as such was seen as an issue of justice, and the right of refugees to return was seen as the absolute core of the Palestinian prob-lem. The problem was much less about political identity or about a right to national self-determination.

That was the narrative that carried the Palestinians through much of the first decade of the conflict, until the late 1950s, when Egyptian presi-dent Gamal Abdel Nasser essentially redefined the narrative. With Nasser's framing of the question as an issue of Arab nationalism, not Palestinian nationalism, the Palestinian issue became part of a broader transnational Arab movement. The promise of support from Egypt, the Arab world's largest and most powerful state, greatly appealed to Palestinians, who had watched as Arab governments paid only lip service to their cause after the war of 1948. The Palestinians thus linked themselves to the broader Arab national movement, which also did not accept Israel and framed the conflict with it in zero-sum terms. The prospects for justice, as Palestinians saw it, were simultaneously tied to prospects of pan-Arabism and incompatible with the notion of Israel as a Jewish state. There was no space for territorial compromise that would divide the land between Jews and Arabs.

The possibility for a settlement of the Palestinian-Israeli conflict that would allow territorial compromise opened up only after the Palestinians redefined their struggle as primarily a nationalist Palestinian struggle, which did not occur until the 1970s. Certainly a number of factors led to this evolution, especially the 1967 war, which not only brought the West Bank and Gaza, in addition to the Sinai and the Golan Heights, under Israeli control, but also ended the Palestinians' hope that Nasser's pan-Arabism could deliver justice for them.

At the Arab summit in Rabat, Morocco, in 1974—following the perceived success of the Arab armies in the 1973 war—the Arab states collectively and unanimously agreed that the PLO, and only the PLO, represented the Palestinians. In essence, this decision helped establish what was already in practice: the norm of statism in the Middle East and of conceiving the Palestinian struggle as fitting into a world of states in the Middle East. The Arabs not only accepted that the Palestinians represented themselves but also were saying to the Palestinians that Arab states would look after their own interests first. This Rabat decision must be seen as a prelude to Egypt's striking its own bilateral deal with Israel, which it could not have done without this changed view of Arab politics, of nationalism, and of the role of states in the region. Palestinian justice was a core issue of pan-Arabism, and Palestinian nationalism became a necessary step for normalizing statism in the Arab world. In fact, the relative power of transnational movements in the Arab world has been very much a function of the perceived prospects of a settlement of the Palestinian problem in terms that are compatible or incompatible with each movement.

The 1970s ushered in a dominant nationalist paradigm that overshadowed all else. By nationalist paradigm I mean that the core of the struggle became the establishment of a Palestinian state to represent Palestinian nationalism in a world of states, which the Palestinians had come to grips with after two decades of assuming otherwise, and which incorporated a tacit acceptance of Israel by virtue of accepting the system of states. To the extent that Palestinian statehood became a priority, it superseded the "right-of-return" issue. There was now a possible territorial compromise to accommodate the notion of Israel as a Jewish state and a Palestinian state existing side by side. Without that change in the Palestinian paradigm, it is impossible to conceive that there would have been a chance for compromise—and thus for serious negotiations to end the conflict. In this regard, it is clear that the negotiations always had an implicit, if unstated, understanding that the final settlement of the refugee problem would not jeopardize the notion of Israel as a Jewish state.

It is interesting to look at the changes that have occurred in Israel, putting aside for the moment the important demographic shifts that have taken place in Israel over the decades to consider the two competing ideological trends. On the one hand, there was the more liberal and modest Zionist vision represented by the left wing of the Labor Party, which saw the need first and foremost for a Jewish state that would represent Jewish nationalism without necessarily thinking of the Jewish state in grand historical terms or associating itself directly with the possible conquering of territory beyond what was needed for Israeli security as a contemporary Jewish state, even if the limits of what was possible would be constantly tested. On the other hand, there was another kind of Zionism that was much more ambitious in its vision, that did incorporate the notion that the West Bank was part of Israel. The latter paradigm was represented roughly by Likud, which had been on the defensive in the early years of the state and in fact did not accommodate a compromise on the Palestinian issue. By the time the Palestinians developed a narrative of their own that was accommodating the possibility of a Jewish state in the mid-1970s, Israel had gone through a different shift when Menachem Begin and Likud rose to power. There was a different kind of vision, irreconcilable even with the nationalist Palestinian vision that implicitly accepted a two-state solution. As Palestinians moved closer to possible territorial compromise, the governing ideology in Israel moved in the other direction. It is therefore not a coincidence that the Oslo Accords emerged when a new Labor government was elected again and the PLO had been accepted internationally as representing the Palestinians. The change in each side's narrative is thus critical in explaining the possibilities for negotiations and eventual agreement.

The question is, why and how do narratives change? Much of the answer can be found by examining two factors: the prevailing assessment of the prospects of competing options, and the unpredictable factor of leadership. One can argue that the Palestinians became more realistic over time as they faced the fact that the Middle Eastern world was made of self-interested states, that pan-Arabism was an idea but not really a reality, that Israel was there to stay. All of this was very much influenced and accelerated by the Arab defeat in the 1967 war. Similarly, on the Israeli side, the first Palestinian uprising, the intifada that began in 1987, changed the Israeli public perception that controlling the West Bank could come on the cheap. But one should not underestimate the role of leadership. One can look back at so many different junctures in this conflict when the paradigm itself was affected significantly, if not changed, by single acts of leadership. And the same set of events can recommend completely different responses to different leaders. It is doubtful, for example, that a Likud leader would have been willing to accept the PLO in 1993 and sign an agreement similar to the Oslo Accords.

Regardless of the cause of their change, the national narratives are essential for opening up the negotiating space for compromise. These narratives can change in the opposite direction by closing the available negotiating space. This was precisely the outcome when the Palestinian-Israeli negotiations collapsed in July 2000 and the second intifada subsequently emerged. The most devastating impact of the collapse goes beyond the obvious and tragic cycle of death and violence that followed—which itself is difficult to overcome, especially given the inevitable mistrust that builds with every blow. The biggest danger may be the evolution of each side's narrative away from possible compromise.

The breakdown of the negotiations may have ushered in a paradigmatic shift that is once again redefining the way each side views the conflict, with the conflict increasingly being seen as an ethno-religious struggle instead of a nationalist conflict. The creeping of religious and ethnic terms of reference into the discourse about the conflict became noticeable after the failure of the Camp David negotiations, in part because of the focus on Jerusalem, and in part because the opposition movement on the

Palestinian side happened to be mostly Islamists employing religious terms of reference. These dynamics combined to profoundly change the discourse in both polities. If this new paradigm takes hold, negotiations become more difficult, as it is hard to envision any negotiating space if the conflict is seen to be largely over religious issues or ethnic purity. Such transformation, if permitted to take full hold, could preclude a peaceful settlement in this generation.

Prevailing narratives are important not only for the long-term view of history but also in explaining public attitudes in the short term. The most interesting thing about the failure of Camp David may be the speed of the psychological transformation on both sides. Palestinians and Israelis have gone from the strong hope that prevailed in the spring of 2000 that the conflict was about to end, even if it may have taken another two or three rounds of negotiations, to the horrible violence that followed and to the increasing loss of faith in even the possibility of peace. How can this be explained?

One way to understand this change is to recognize first and foremost that each side had a completely different narrative about what happened at Camp David. The two sides came into Camp David with different views of the negotiations and the terms of reference. The language of competition during the negotiations, before the negotiations, and after the negotiations was telling. The Palestinians, for example, thought they had the right to all of the West Bank and Gaza. In their narrative, they had already given up 78 percent of Palestine, which is now Israel. So every inch they concede from the West Bank and Gaza, every settlement they concede for inclusion in Israel, is something that they "give," something that they are conceding to the Israelis. The Israelis thought that because they control the West Bank and Gaza, every inch they are "giving" to the Palestinians is a concession. Even when one talks about the Palestinians keeping only 60 or 90 percent of the territories, which to them meant ceding to Israel the rest, the Israeli view was that they were "giving" the Palestinians 60 percent, or 80 percent, or 90 percent. So the language of giving and taking was completely different during the negotiations—depending on how each side defined the status quo ante and their own narrative of events. But more important, after the failure of Camp David, there emerged completely different narratives of what led to the collapse of the negotiations. The dominant Israeli narrative was pervasive across Israeli society, far beyond former Israeli prime minister Ehud Barak and his allies, including most of the left and the right in Israel, moderates and hard-liners alike. Their basic story was this: Prime Minister Barak offered the Palestinians the most that an Israeli prime minister could offer, maybe even more, including a contiguous viable Palestinian state on more than 90 percent of the West Bank and Gaza and control of Arab East Jerusalem. Yasir Arafat simply rejected the offer, in large part because he wanted to extract more concessions from Israel through violence or because he would never accept anything less than the destruction of Israel as a Jewish state. Arafat's rejection of the Camp David offer, coupled with the rise of the second intifada, was seen by most Israelis as a rejection of any negotiated settlement. The most optimistic Israeli view saw this rejection merely as Arafat's personal position, which could not be changed, and placed all hope on his demise from the scene. Here I am speaking of the prevailing popular Israeli narrative, not necessarily what Israeli government officials believed or sought as a matter of policy. It is difficult, regardless of this paradigm, to imagine that the Likud government of Ariel Sharon would have accepted a settlement similar to what was discussed at Camp David, or that it sought to maximize the chance of such a settlement in its policies. But the point here is that the Israeli public narrative about the collapse of the negotiations gave the Sharon government considerable freedoms, whatever its agenda.

The Palestinian narrative of failure was considerably different but equally pervasive across society. This was their story: the Palestinian negotiators had made more concessions than they felt was possible, with Arafat conceding that two-thirds of the Jewish settlers would come under Israeli sovereignty, out of the West Bank; Arafat accepted Israeli sovereignty over the Jewish quarter of Jerusalem, the Western Wall, and the Jewish neighborhoods of Jerusalem, which were occupied by Israel in the 1967 war; the Palestinian negotiators accepted the idea that their state of Palestine would be demilitarized; they accepted Israeli observation locations in the West Bank and Gaza, to accommodate Israeli security needs. In exchange, the Palestinian story goes, Barak offered a noncontiguous truncated state without sufficient control over East Jerusalem and the Hiram al-Sharif mosque—the sort of deal that no Palestinian leader could or should accept. Palestinians, in fact, saw the negotiations at Camp David as constituting only one round to be followed by others. Their view was

that Barak was intent on imposing a solution and thus framed the negotiations as a "take-it-or-leave-it" offer, which, if not accepted, would leave
him no alternative but to unleash his overwhelming forces in the West Bank
and Gaza. Their view was also that Barak fully believed that the Palestinians were so weak that they had little choice but to accept his dictate. In
that regard, many Palestinians, including those who had opposed violent
methods in the past, saw the intifada as an equalizing force, as a strategic
asset to show the Israelis that they were not as helpless as the Israelis
thought. Such became the prevailing paradigm on the Palestinian side.

In the end, each side had profoundly different views of events and the
intentions of the other. Holding these views was bound to change each
side's calculations and interpretation of events. Holding these views also
made it very difficult for each side to mobilize a constituency that could
effectively press for a different option than the one being pursued. Even
those few moderates who did not accept the prevailing narratives found it
impossible to swim against the overwhelming tide.

The Normalization of Revenge

Narratives aside, violence often creates it own dynamics. Here I will address
the strategic calculations of the parties once they are trapped in a cycle of
violence, of action and reaction. In some of the international relations literature there is a notion that, over time, international actors learn to cooperate if they keep doing the same thing over and over again and see that
they are worse off every time they do it. In such circumstances, when conflict is obviously a lose-lose proposition, they may eventually evolve toward
cooperation through learning. This is at least the theory that has gained
credence in the past couple of decades in international relations, that it is
possible that cooperation evolves over time even though the parties may
be trapped in the short term in a conflict in which they think they may be
better off engaging in violence than not.

I published a study with three colleagues (Joshua Goldstein, Jon
Pevehouse, and Deborah Gerner) that looked at conflict and cooperation in the Middle East over a twenty-year period (1979–97).[2] We examined daily data to see how each party reacted to the other party's actions.
We found two things: first, that reciprocity becomes the norm as people
increasingly behave in a tit-for-tat fashion. Over time such behavior

intensifies and becomes normalized. Second, despite the fact that they were worse off behaving in a revengeful fashion, cooperation did not necessarily result from learning that violence did not pay. Why?

A first answer is domestic politics. When there is an attack on one side, public opinion demands action. People do not accept the idea that they are helpless. They do not accept the idea that they have to sit back. Even if retaliation does not pay, domestic political conditions always create pressure to take some action, including action that does not work—even when the public may realize that it will not work. Revenge is often an end in itself.

Second, there is an insidious belief on each side that not acting is worse than acting: that if one does not respond, the other side will interpret the lack of action as weakness, and that the nonacting side will therefore be the target of more violence. So even though they know that acting does not solve the problem, people often feel that they are better off by acting than by not acting. This is the type of explanation that one hears from parties in conflict in general and that has certainly been expressed by both Israelis and Palestinians.

Third, each side tends to "learn" from the wrong examples in history to rationalize its predisposition to respond in kind. For example, Palestinians say, "Violence worked in Lebanon—the Hezbollah guerrillas were able to force Israel out. Therefore, we can do the same." The obvious differences between the two situations do not prevent people from seeing such parallels. Similarly, many Israelis try to draw parallels between their actions in the Palestinian areas and the seemingly successful U.S. military campaign in Afghanistan, as if the situations are comparable. These rationalizations are driven by the first two tendencies that I have suggested.

It is instructive to compare Israel's situation in Lebanon with the Palestinian-Israeli struggle in the West Bank and Gaza. Such a comparison helps illuminate two central points: why Israel's superior power is unlikely to enable it to dictate terms of agreement, and why the Palestinians will not in turn be able to compel full Israeli withdrawal from the occupied territories through violence.

Military strategists have long understood that one central issue in the outcome of any conflict is motivation, both one's own and the adversary's. The extent to which a cause is seen as more or less "legitimate" internationally affects the degree of parties' motivation. Military power is obviously central to the outcome, but in the long term the importance of motivation balances the importance of military power. As a stronger party's will to fight or accept even limited casualties decreases, the will of its weaker opponent increases and its threshold of pain rises. In this regard, the contrast between Israel's experience in Lebanon on the one hand and its confrontations with Palestinians on the other is telling.

Israel withdrew from Lebanon in 1999 after years of occupation. Although the lesson learned by some in the region was that guerrilla warfare works against Israel because of the perception that Israel was militarily defeated by the Lebanese Hezbollah group, the outcome was in large part a function of each party's motivation. Militarily, Israel possessed overwhelming power as compared with Hezbollah, the Lebanese state, and its domineering neighbor, Syria. Hezbollah forces numbered in the hundreds and had limited equipment. Israel not only had decisive military advantages but also inflicted considerably more pain on Hezbollah and on Lebanon (and sometimes on Syrian forces) than was inflicted on it. Because of Israeli actions, Lebanon faced the problems of tens of thousands of refugees, hundreds of casualties, and the serious undermining of its economy through methods such as the destruction of power stations that paralyzed its capital, Beirut. In contrast, Israel's economy was minimally damaged by its presence in southern Lebanon, and the number of casualties it sustained (a few dozen a year) was small by the measures of warfare. Israel could have afforded to continue its presence, and many within Israel's military establishment did not want to pull out of Lebanon without a peace agreement.

However, in the end Israel did withdraw without such an agreement. Hezbollah members and others in the region interpreted this result as a military victory that could be replicated in the Palestinian areas. Their interpretation was erroneous and unfortunate. Israel's withdrawal and Hezbollah's success simply cannot be understood by the power equation alone, or by the usual measures of winning or losing a war. At issue was each side's motivation. More important, the degree of motivation was a function of two factors that are not directly related to power: the extent to which the conflict was seen by each side as vitally important to its existence and the extent to which the cause was perceived as legitimate in international eyes.

The fact that Israel occupied Lebanese lands and operated from them was seen by most Lebanese, including those who opposed Hezbollah, as a threat to their sovereignty that superseded any divisions among Lebanese citizens. The fact that there was no imminent threat to Israel's existence from Lebanon and that the Hezbollah guerrillas largely focused their operations against Israeli troops on Lebanese soil raised questions in the minds of the Israeli public about the need to stay in Lebanon and about the justification of even the smallest number of Israeli casualties. Had Hezbollah framed its objectives in terms of eradicating Israel rather than liberating Lebanon, and had it sent suicide bombers to kill Israeli civilians, Israel's motivation would have been significantly different. At a minimum, motivation affects each side's threshold of pain and its will to exercise power. To achieve independence, Lebanon could endure immense pain; for no obvious vital interests, Israel could endure little. This issue of motivation is also affected by outside notions of the legitimacy of each side's cause: the sense that Lebanon's drive to seek independence was in harmony with the principles of sovereignty that most people around the world accept generated more international sympathy for Lebanon than for Israel, which in turn reinforced the determination of the Lebanese.

The Palestinian-Israeli confrontation in the West Bank and Gaza has been of a different nature. Here, too, Israel has had overwhelming power superiority. The Palestinians have even more motivation than the Lebanese because they have no state at all and are under occupation. Their threshold of pain has thus been very high because the issue is ultimately about existence. For Israel, three issues make the question of motivation significantly different than in Lebanon. First, the proximity of the West Bank to the heart of Israel makes the outcome much more important. Second, a significant portion of the Israeli population has always wanted to claim the West Bank as part of Israel. Third, the suicide bombings targeting civilians inside Israel have made the issue of the West Bank and Gaza more important because the threat is more immediate. As a consequence, even though the Palestinians have inflicted many more casualties on Israel than Hezbollah has, Israeli motivation has increased rather than diminished. Thus, the balance of motivation on the Israeli-Palestinian front fuels the conflict even more than the actual distribution of military power and reduces the chance that the conflict can be won through Palestinian attacks or through Israel's military superiority. Israel can inflict far more pain on the Palestinians than it suffers, but that is not the same as winning or achieving peace.

The dynamics of the cycle of violence are thus reinforcing and do not on their own lead to the "learning" that propels parties toward cooperation. They also exacerbate the deep psychological fears of parties: for Palestinians, the sense of helplessness and humiliation, and for Israelis, a deep sense of insecurity. These psychological predispositions are central to understanding the conflict and to contemplating a diplomatic process to end it.

To most Arabs, especially Palestinians, Israel is all too powerful: it has repeatedly defeated combined Arab armies; it continues to occupy Arab lands after thirty-five years; it acts freely regarding the Palestinians under occupation; it is backed by the sole remaining superpower, the United States; and it fields one of the most powerful armies in the world with the only nuclear weapons in the Middle East. It is able to withstand international pressure, including UN resolutions, without altering its basic policies. For the Palestinians in particular, especially those under occupation, Israel dominates their daily lives, their economic prospects, their mobility, and their future. They are often at the mercy of the seemingly arbitrary decisions of local military officers. The depth of these feelings of helplessness is not sufficiently appreciated by Israelis, who are trapped by their own pain.

Similarly, the Arab sense of Israeli power has prevented most Arabs from coming to grips with the extent to which Israelis feel profoundly insecure. Many Arabs believe that the issue of security is a mere instrument of Israeli foreign policy intended to gain international sympathy for aggressive measures. Although some Israeli leaders and politicians do use this issue to their advantage, there is a real, pervasive sense of insecurity among Israelis. In the same way that Arabs have a narrative of victimization because of the way their history unfolded during the twentieth century, Israelis, and many Jews more broadly, have a collective consciousness that is inevitably characterized by insecurity: the horror of the Holocaust has much to do with it, but the history of Israel, seen through Israeli eyes, is also a factor. Regardless of its military and political successes, Israel remains a small, demographically vulnerable state. Whereas Arabs can recover from defeats over time, Israel cannot afford a single defeat. Although Israelis have made peace with Egypt and Jordan, they fear deep down that Arabs have not really accepted their presence in the region. This psychology is a central factor in rapid shifts to the right in Israel after events that exacerbate the sense of insecurity. Like the psychology in the Arab world that lends itself to exploitation by ambitious politicians, the Israeli psychology of insecurity is fertile ground for ambitious politicians.

The conclusion to be drawn from this discussion is that cooperation is not likely to emerge strictly from the dynamics of the conflict itself, such as exhaustion or learning. That is not to say that these factors do not create opportunities or that some moments of conflict are not more sensitive to diplomatic intervention than others. But each such opportunity even more often is exploited by those who seek to maintain the conflict.

Conflicts do end, and even in the case of the Arab-Israeli conflict there were episodes of success. What explains these cases? There are usually three factors that lead to cooperative strategies.

One factor is a major change in the distribution of power that causes a shift in the parties' priorities. For example, a consequence of the 1991 Persian Gulf War was a major shift in regional priorities and in the actors' perceptions of power and interests. Although such changes do occur, one cannot plan a political solution based on such unpredictable developments. The second factor is unusually bold leadership. When one looks at what occurred in both the Egyptian-Israeli relationship and the Oslo Accords, whether one likes them or not, they were breakthroughs. One will find that it is impossible to explain them without explaining acts of bold leadership. One can look at the strategic shifts that preceded the breakthroughs and say there were circumstances that necessitated some change in policy, but there is no real reason for one to think that the change had to be cooperative. In almost all cases, leaders can adopt completely different strategies, and more often than not, they adopt noncooperative strategies in similar situations. But bold leadership is rare and sometimes also dangerous for the state or for the leaders. Yitzhak Rabin and Anwar el-Sadat paid with their lives.

The third way toward cooperation is through third-party diplomatic intervention, to which I will now turn.

The Role of Third Parties

Although it is theoretically possible to contemplate roles for a number of international actors, such as the European Union and the United Nations, in mediating the Israeli-Palestinian conflict, only the United States has the ability to succeed, in large part because it can provide both the assurance and the lever with Israel and has more influence with Arab states and the Palestinians than any other international actor. If one looks at the history of the breakthroughs in the Middle East, one can make an argument that in both the Camp David negotiations with Egypt and the Oslo Accords, the people in the region made the first moves. Clearly bold leadership preceded the role that the United States had to play in these cases. And the United States capitalized on opportunities that were opened up. Although U.S. politicians interpreted the situation as being ripe, it is clear that had they not acted, the prospects for success for the parties themselves would have been very limited.

A number of points must be made about the U.S. role in mediating Palestinian-Israeli peace. First, while the United States has more influence with both parties than any other state, and thus has much leverage to use in its mediating effort, it cannot impose the terms of a solution on the parties. Neither party would accept terms that did not meet their minimal requirements, and even the Palestinians, who are considerably weaker than the Israelis, were able to reject what was on the table during the Camp David negotiations of 2000 despite strong presidential involvement from Bill Clinton. Second, because of the psychology of Israeli insecurity and Palestinian humiliation, any efforts that would be seen to increase the insecurity or humiliation of one side or the other would only exacerbate the problem. In that regard, U.S. leverage is most helpful for assurance, even more than for threat.

Third, the United States has more than a moral interest in mediating the Arab-Israeli conflict broadly, and the Palestinian-Israeli conflict in particular. On the one hand, the United States is committed to the security and well-being of Israel and provides significant military and economic support to that state. On the other hand, it has important interests in Arab and Muslim countries. It is clear that the Palestinian-Israeli conflict remains the prism through which many Arabs and Muslims see and judge the United States. This conclusion has been confirmed by surveys I have conducted in the Arab world that show that most Arabs rank the Palestinian issue the highest in their priorities and that they shape their attitudes toward the United States on the basis of American policies, not American values. When the Palestinian-Israeli conflict is intense, and the United States is not seen to be doing enough to stop the violence, most

Arabs blame U.S. foreign policy. A good example is reflected in the U.S. State Department's own public opinion surveys. In the spring of 2000, when the prospects for Palestinian-Israeli negotiations were encouraging, more than 60 percent of those surveyed in the United Arab Emirates and Saudi Arabia showed confidence in the United States. After the collapse of negotiations and the emergence of the second intifada in the fall of 2000, confidence in the United States dropped dramatically and continued dropping to the 30s by the spring of 2001. The decline continued even further after the tragedy of 9/11. As long as the Palestinian-Israeli conflict continues, the United States will continue to face difficult trade-offs in its policy toward the Middle East broadly.

Fourth, the American public perceives Arab-Israeli peace to be important to U.S. interests. Surprisingly, roughly two-thirds of Americans want U.S. foreign policy to be evenhanded, and 60 percent believe that it is not now evenhanded. Despite the war on terrorism and the increasing absence of differentiation between cases of terrorism in the public discourse, only about 17 percent of Americans in four surveys conducted in 2002 and 2003 believed that Israel's war with the Palestinians is part of the war on terrorism and similar to the U.S. war with al Qaeda.[3] Most Americans saw it as a nationalist struggle over land. This suggests that the American public has a better understanding of the issues of the conflict and has views on these issues that would permit a president to place Middle East mediation higher on the U.S. list of priorities.

The problem for U.S. leaders is this: while public opinion in the United States could be rallied behind an effective mediation effort, there is no built-in political incentive for a president to expend leverage both domestically and internationally to tackle the Arab-Israeli issue. In fact, conventional wisdom among U.S. politicians is quite the opposite—that it is a thankless job with a high political cost. Even President Jimmy Carter, who successfully mediated a peace treaty between Egypt and Israel, continues to believe that his loss in the following presidential election was in part because of his Middle East policy. In short, while the public would broadly support an effort once it was mounted by a president, most Americans do not care deeply enough about this issue to propel it to the top of presidential priorities.

In the end, two factors are central in determining the degree of presidential involvement in mediating Arab-Israeli peace: an international

crisis that results in a widely shared public perception that the lack of
intervention jeopardizes important U.S. interests (as happened, for example,
following the 1973 Arab-Israeli war) and the personal inclination of a U.S.
president, especially if there is a perceived new opportunity for peacemaking, as happened with Carter's response to Sadat's visit to Jerusalem in
1977, and as in Clinton's response to the secretly negotiated Oslo Accords
in 1993.

Once presidents decide to make the issue a higher priority, they can
succeed only if they build a domestic constituency that supports their
strategy, as the effort requires expending resources both abroad and at
home. It requires building coalitions in Congress and among U.S. groups
that care deeply about the Middle East, such as Jewish-American and
Arab-American organizations. Given that the U.S. agenda is almost
always full of other important issues, such as the economy and international crises, it would take unusual circumstances to propel the United
States to play the sort of role that is required to bring an end to decades
of conflict between Israel and the Palestinians, and between Israel and the
Arabs more broadly.

For these reasons, the outlook is gloomy. The chances of assembling
the required elements for success appear remote. But while pessimism
about the prospect of a lasting Israeli-Palestinian peace agreement seems
a safe bet, it is good to remember that such factors as leadership are almost
always unexpected and unpredictable. Few expected the Egyptian-Israeli
breakthrough in the late 1970s or the reconciliation between Israel and
the Palestine Liberation Organization in the early 1990s. Peace remains
possible, but if it happens, it will be for reasons that most of us cannot
foresee at the moment.

Notes

1. Joshua S. Goldstein, Jon C. Pevehouse, Deborah J. Gerner, and Shibley
Telhami, "Reciprocity, Triangularity, and Cooperation in the Middle East, 1979–97,"
Journal of Conflict Resolution 45, no. 5 (October 2001): 594–620.

2. Ibid. The arguments in this section are based on those presented in my
book, *The Stakes: America and the Middle East* (Boulder, Colo.: Westview Press, 2003).

3. See Steven Kull and Shibley Telhami, "Public, Leaders a Poll Apart," *Los
Angeles Times,* May 26, 2002.

When Endless Conflicts End

16

Conclusion

From Intractable to Tractable— the Outlook and Implications for Third Parties

Chester A. Crocker,
Fen Osler Hampson,
and Pamela Aall

BY THEIR VERY NATURE, intractable conflicts are hard to manage and even harder to resolve. They have multiple sources and are propelled by a range of factors—including greed, self-interest, security dilemmas, and bad neighbors (or bad neighborhoods)—that have little to do with the "original" causes of the conflict. This book, however, does not accept the conclusion commonly drawn from looking at this evidence that some regions or societies are doomed to endless conflict. The theoretical discussions in this volume vary widely in their approach and focus, but they also share a common feature in their rigorous effort to understand how intractability occurs and the circumstances in which it appears to ebb and flow. As the contributors to this volume argue, intractability is not fixed or immutable. It is contingent on the circumstances and conditions that trigger or prolong it.

The task of third parties—whether they be great powers, international organizations, small states, or nongovernmental organizations—is to understand and isolate those factors that make a conflict "intractable," to create and exploit fluid moments of tractability, and to apply best practices so as to avoid making matters worse. The case chapters in the volume also underscore the importance of understanding the specific historical, cultural, and political context in which a conflict arises, develops, and continues. It is in the interplay of these variables that intractability is brewed. By the same token, when something changes in the mixture this same interplay explains why a conflict moves from the intractable column toward settlement and an end to violence.

Closer examination suggests that the triggers permitting forward movement in a stalled peace process may often be the flip side of the factors that produced the initial intractability. A conflict impacted in its surrounding geopolitical environment, such as Cambodia or Mozambique, may yield to diplomatic ministrations once the surrounding context shifts. This should not surprise us. After all, we know from Roy Licklider's review of the quantitative literature on contemporary international conflict that wars that last beyond a few years are the exception rather than the rule. Wars of long duration (especially in recent years) tend to be resolved through negotiation rather than outright victory by one side. In a sense, therefore, we may be justified in suggesting that when a conflict moves from the intractable to the tractable column, it is "falling into place," escaping from the conditions that fueled and sustained it.

The case chapters in the volume clearly illustrate this logic, enabling us to talk about the things that must change in order for the conflict to wind down. In some cases the critical keys are at the level of party leadership: some leaders appear to live off "their" conflict, and their removal or containment becomes the sine qua non of forward movement. A new prime minister in Sri Lanka opened the door to hopeful developments in the Norwegian-led peace talks that began in 2002 between the government and the Tamil insurgency known as the Liberation Tigers of Tamil Eelam (LTTE). More recently, however, a top-level political struggle between the prime minister and the president in 2003–4 produced the sort of ethnic outbidding among Sinhalese faction leaders that effectively poisoned the negotiations, at least in the short term. The chances that negotiations can resume while these feuding politicians use the conflict as part of their political arsenals are very slim.

The killing by government forces of long-standing "struggle" leader Jonas Savimbi in 2002 in Angola brought that decades-long armed conflict to an end, as Paul Hare's chapter records. In this case, military victory by one of two autocratic rivals ended the era of intractability and opened the door to at least the possibility of a political opening and reconciliation. As both Shibley Telhami and Stephen Cohen note, leadership succession or change has also marked some of the major watersheds in the Middle East peace negotiations over many years, at times opening the door to forward movement and at times closing it. In South Africa Nelson Mandela's unique statesmanship coupled with a leadership change from P. W. Botha to F. W. de Klerk in 1989 led to a dramatic breakthrough in relations between the white minority government and the African National Congress leadership, leading to the transition of power in 1994.

The implication of this picture is that third parties should give intense scrutiny to the role of leadership—its presence, its absence, changes in its quality, and how to foster the emergence of leaders who can lead their societies out of the conflict trap.

Other cases demonstrate the central importance of the external, geopolitical context in which conflicts become intractable. Some become impacted to such a degree that only a fundamental strategic shift will enable them to break free. Cambodia escaped its trauma only when Southeast Asia experienced a geopolitical realignment at the end of the Cold War. The Korean standoff, which Scott Snyder discusses in detail, may ultimately come to an end when the major powers of East Asia find sufficient common ground to hammer out a basis for settlement of this long-frozen conflict. South Africa's negotiated internal transition would have been far less likely in the absence of the immediately preceding regional settlements of Angola, Mozambique, and Namibia. As Stephen Morrison and Alex de Waal argue, progress toward settlement of the Sudanese civil war clearly owed something to the changed international environment created by the war on terrorism after September 11, 2001, and Khartoum's desire to find ways of getting along with Washington and London. And it would be difficult to imagine the still-incomplete Northern Irish peace process moving as far as it has without the impact of actions and pressures emanating from London, Dublin, Washington, and Brussels. Third parties engaged in peacemaking in intractable conflicts must keep a sharp eye on the ways in which local, regional, and global influences interact to create new opportunities for negotiation and marshal their best arguments and inducements accordingly.

Intractability can also be influenced by discontinuities at the societal and state levels that alter the calculations of the conflict parties and may create moments of opportunity for external actors. In the Cyprus case these actors have taken advantage of trends toward integration in the eastern Mediterranean, the process of EU enlargement, and recent developments in Turkish politics to break the logjam. This gave fresh leverage to the mediation effort led by the United Nations and backed by the United States and the European Union until the UN plan was voted down by the Greek community in the spring of 2004. In Sudan the emergence of a dynamic petroleum industry has altered the calculations of both Khartoum's leaders and the Southern Sudanese leadership of the Sudan People's Liberation Movement (SPLM), raising the stakes in the war while also underscoring the limits to what the rebel movement can achieve on the battlefield. As Howard and Teresita Schaffer underscore in their assessment of the conflict over Kashmir, the new post-9/11 geopolitical climate has combined with intense pressures within Pakistan and a clear sense of opportunity in Delhi to create a fresh opportunity to break open the stalemate. But geopolitical and regional pressures can also cut the other way. As Cynthia Arnson and Teresa Whitfield argue, the decades-long agony in Colombia has seemingly been reinforced by developments transforming a sociopolitical class conflict into a struggle over turf and illicit revenue streams. This will change only when Colombian leaders can untangle the knots of this many-sided war and contain its spread by persuading armed factions to come to the table.

These illustrations are not predictions that the end of intractability is at hand. As some hard cases edge closer to resolution, other candidates stand in the wings. Fresh geopolitical and societal shifts could spawn fresh occurrences. For instance, the age of terrorism made the world aware that failed and failing states have the capacity to engender conflict and to create permissive environments in which terrorist cells can flourish and recruit. These conflicts can also spread ominously across national borders into entire subregions. Certain types of leaders and militarized factions thrive in circumstances of state collapse, creating awesome challenges for the major powers and leading security institutions. Such scenarios suggest that the term "third parties" will need in the coming period to be understood in the broadest sense as "agents of conflict management and transformation" as well as "mediators and sponsors of peace processes."

The Limits of Third-Party Assistance

In the discussions of intractability in this volume and in the United States Institute of Peace's experts group on intractable conflicts, some important lessons emerge about how third parties can help intractable conflicts come to an end. The first lesson is that conflict management, which usually involves freezing the conflict through a negotiated and durable cease-fire and the subsequent long-term deployment of outside forces, may be the best option among bad alternatives. In Cyprus and the Balkans conflict management has helped quell the violence and allowed time and changing circumstances to moderate political passions so that new forms of political accommodation can develop. As Louis Kriesberg argues, however, this process is not necessarily linear, because violence can erupt again unless a capable third-party peacemaker simultaneously supports an ongoing negotiating process and demonstrates a real commitment to achieving a negotiated result. Intractable conflicts do not necessarily subside if they are simply managed below the boil for some years. After the Simla agreement, the conflict in Kashmir was managed—in the sense that there was little direct fighting—for eighteen years and yet violent conflict broke out again in mid-1990s. Unless something is done during quiet times to ripen a conflict, the passage of time alone will not make the conflict easier to solve and may make resolution harder as new issues, agendas, grievances, and levels of bitterness set in.

A second lesson is that partiality or mediator bias is an effective or desirable trait only if the mediator is willing to exercise its leverage by delivering that party to the negotiating table. The "bias-sometimes-helps" thesis is an important and widely understood element in the international mediation literature.[1] But the proposition rests on the core assumption that bias helps only if the third party enjoys some freedom of maneuver during the actual negotiation process. In many intractable disputes, the third party faces very strong internal domestic political pressure—from groups that are allied, or see themselves as allied, to the parties in the conflict— which constricts its own negotiating options. Biased mediation can be effective if the mediator can deliver the side toward which it is biased by coaxing or forcing it to make concessions at the negotiating table.

In many of the cases in this volume, mediator bias has proved to be more of a handicap than a source of leverage because domestic pressures severely restrict the flexibility of the mediator. As I. William Zartman observes, over the years the United States and other third parties have been biased toward one side in a number of conflicts—Afghanistan, Angola, Colombia, Korea, the Middle East, Northern Ireland, and Sudan— but have not been in a position to deliver the relevant party (or parties) in a negotiation because of mobilized domestic political constituencies. If a third party is committed to making sure that one side prevails, rather than trying to find common ground between the parties to the dispute, then the conflict parties are not going to get any real help. These mobilized domestic constituencies may serve to feed the conflict's intractability at certain junctures in its life history and may serve to put pressure on the parties to reach some sort of resolution at other junctures. Sudan offers an interesting example of both. For many years, a number of U.S. and European church groups threw their support to the Christian and animist South and effectively barred or constrained official communication with Khartoum. But when the United States decided finally to engage, these same groups gave the U.S.-led effort some added leverage through their support of the president's envoy, former senator John Danforth.

The pressure of domestic politics on the foreign policy choices and bargaining strategies of the mediator is clearly an important feature of intractable conflicts and their management. As the chapters by Stephen Cohen and Shibley Telhami illustrate, the Israeli-Palestinian conflict is rife with what Robert Putnam calls "two-level" negotiation games, not just within the key parties to the conflict but also within the domestic arena of the third-party mediator—in other words, the United States. The United States has been a party to this conflict from the very outset. And the historical U.S. role as mediator in this conflict highlights the many complex issues related to the coherence and priorities of the third party. Recent administrations have found themselves increasingly torn by crosscutting domestic and foreign political pressures.

This raises the interesting if rather sensitive subject of the suitability of large, unruly, open democratic systems to play a primary mediating role in places where there are diaspora or political linkages that outweigh or counterbalance the centrist effort to mediate in the so-called national interest. It is also true that in other intractable conflict cases—for instance, Cyprus, Northern Ireland, and Sudan—serving administrations have been very conscious of the impact of their intermediary efforts on relations with particular domestic constituencies. The presence or absence of such domestic pressures may also help to explain why countries—Norway, for example—that do not have large immigrant populations or diaspora communities may enjoy certain comparative advantages in playing intermediary roles, especially when less intrusive kinds of bargaining strategies are warranted.

A third lesson is that poor or weak statecraft by third-party interveners has the potential to exacerbate the problem and further deepen an intractable conflict. To the extent that some intractable conflicts are not of high priority for some mediators (and the countries they represent), a tepid or halfhearted negotiated intervention may be only marginally better than none. An example is the U.S. response to the conflict in Sudan in the 1980s and 1990s. During this time, U.S. interest in Sudan was derivative of other policies, for instance, the efforts to move forward the Israeli-Palestinian peace process or to deal with international terrorism. The conflicts that were wracking Sudan at the time received limited attention from U.S. policymakers—although they did receive attention from some mobilized domestic groups—and as a consequence, relatively little value was placed on putting pressure on the parties to negotiate seriously.

Competing agendas among different mediators who step into a conflict can also pose serious problems and compromise negotiations, as Steven Burg points out in his case study of international mediation in the Balkans. In the 1991–95 period the weak performance of a series of Western mediators—which was reflected in their own internal divisions and vested interests—as well as their separate agendas and the mixed and confused messages they conveyed to the warring parties, ultimately compromised their own proposals and mediation effectiveness.

Mediation Strategies and Tactics in Intractable Conflicts

Louis Kriesberg and Jacob Bercovitch argue in their chapters in this volume that mediated interventions must be attuned to the specific dynamics or phases of intractable conflicts. During the course of an intractable conflict, the nature of the conflict may change in terms of the level of violence, the willingness of affected constituencies to seek a negotiated way out of the conflict, the degree to which perceptions are hardened (or immutable), the degree to which "external" regional or global players are engaged in the conflict, and the level of weariness of the affected populace with continued violence. Given these changing conditions, different bargaining and negotiation strategies may be called for at different phases or stages of these conflicts. For instance, if an intractable conflict is escalating and shows dangers of spilling over its traditional boundaries, third-party intervention may focus on controlling the conflict or preventing further escalation. These mediated interventions may be diplomatic or they may include some coercive elements, such as use or threat of sanctions or military deployment, to persuade or push parties to de-escalate. In these circumstances, as Louis Kriesberg also notes, global norms, such as those regarding human rights and genocide, can affect third-party propensities to intervene with military means as a prelude to formal mediation. If, on the other hand, a conflict has entered a stage of exhaustion, when parties have lost their will to fight but cannot seem to move to negotiations, the mediator may take a more facilitative approach to peacemaking, passing messages between the parties and/or providing a neutral forum where the parties can meet.

Charles King's analysis of the various intractable conflicts in Transcaucasia illuminates a paradox of many intractable conflicts: one of the reasons why parties are wedded to conflict is that they gain from it. Mediators and third parties have to recognize that there are powerful individual and group incentives to keep an intractable conflict going, and one of the central challenges is not only to wean the parties from their "addiction" to violence but also to change incentive structures so the parties see that there are real, concrete gains to be realized by ending violence.

At the same time, we must recognize that intractable conflicts are not just battles of interest, but also battles of wills, beliefs, values, religion, and needs. These are critical psychological elements of intractable conflict that cannot be left unattended or ignored by third parties. Various unofficial intermediaries, discussed in Diana Chigas's chapter, have played a key role in addressing the "subjective" dimensions of the conflicts, including such issues as identity, survival, and the demonization of the other side. Informal dialogue and communication that deal with deep-rooted fears and perceptions are often key to changing attitudes and the hostile images warring parties have of each other. The solution lies in what Harold Saunders has called a process and pattern of "circum-negotiation"—working in the wider community to supplement and reinforce so-called track-one diplomacy by creating a supportive political climate and constituency for peacemaking.[2]

Effective mediation in intractable cases is also about good strategy. It is important that potential mediators maintain a watching brief over the conflict and get ready to engage should a window of opportunity emerge as a result of leadership changes, an escalation in the level of violence that fundamentally alters public perceptions and discredits the "warring" status quo, or a change in regional or global power balances that signals to the warring parties that various external actors recognize they have a changing stake or set of interests in the conflict. This watching brief should include a constant calculation of the costs—to the mediator (and his or her supporting institution) as well as the parties—of action and inaction.

It often takes a special kind of leadership to leap through the windows of opportunity that emerge in these kinds of situations. As William Zartman argues in his chapter, there is no automaticity to this process. The tectonic plates of the global (or regional) geopolitical system may shift, but leadership and strong intermediary skills are nonetheless required to move the peace process in the right direction. One role for third parties, as both Louis Kriesberg and Diana Chigas argue, is to mentor new leaders and foster the emergence of new elites that are more open to the idea of negotiated settlement. This new leadership may be even more necessary to the implementation stage, as it is very rare that a "struggle politician" can make the transition from military leader to advocate of reconciliation.

At the same time, mediators must continue to work with the existing leadership, helping it come to terms with the enormous personal, political, and social risks that moving toward peace entails. Ending intractable conflicts demands a quantum leap in terms of leadership requirements, both for the warring parties and for the mediator. Here it is important that a wide range of outside institutions support the mediation process. Tangible support in the form of incentives to the parties to settle—for instance, promises of trade, aid, and other material resources—is very helpful in these circumstances. But the kind of support that is critical to the process is intangible—expressions of confidence in the mediator, absence of dissenting voices from the mediator's home institution, unified international support for keeping the process moving forward.

Good mediation strategy also has to be complemented by effective mediation tactics. When a negotiation process has gone stale or reached a dead end, mediators may have to change their negotiating tactics. In these circumstances, mediators typically have to secure new sources of leverage over the parties or change the perceptions about the costs and benefits of those who have become too comfortable with the status quo. They sometimes have to reframe issues and create (or identify) new options for parties who are stuck in a rut.

Intractable conflicts suffer from negotiation roadblocks and discredited solutions. A salient solution to the conflict may no longer be available if it has already been tried on the parties one or more times and has become discredited because of its failure to help parties reach a negotiated settlement. Here the challenge for the mediator is not so much of trying to invent something new as it is to resurrect discredited formulas and/or to keep them alive for the time when the parties are serious about getting back to the negotiating table. The challenge, in other words, may be less about the parameters for designing the eventual settlement than about how to get there; as one working group participant put it in describing the Israeli-Palestinian conflict, most people understand the need "to go from A to Z, but no one knows how to get from A to B."

Finally, intractable conflicts require a special level of unity of effort among mediators and others who seek to intervene. As many of the chapters in this volume have shown, coordination among third-party efforts is a serious issue, as is the relationship between the mediator and other outside parties. Unless different mediators are working from a common script, the parties to the conflict will invariably try to play different mediators against one another as well as engage in various kinds of forum shopping.

But garnering support among third parties is very important, as is the effort to widen the circle of supporters beyond the institutions immediately engaged. The Angolan and Colombian examples also underscore the importance of various "friends" to the peace process who can provide leverage and also use their special relationship with the parties to move a negotiation process forward. In a very different way, the leading third-party actors in the Balkans conflicts have, over time, worked assiduously to broaden their base and leverage the involvement of other major institutions and states in managing the issues. Such groups can also help place conflicts on the international radar screen (in the case of conflicts that have been orphaned by the international community) and ensure that they are the focus of credible, serious third-party action. This has certainly been the case with British, Norwegian, and various regional initiatives in the conflict in Sudan.

Conclusion

Intractable conflicts are hard to mediate, as Jacob Bercovitch reminds us in his chapter. But because they are hard, persistent, embedded, and enduring does not mean that they are impossible to deal with and resistant to any and all kinds of negotiated solutions. In most cases the best possible solution is a "management" solution that contains the conflict and ideally reduces the level of tension and violence. But as the chapters in this book also show, management is ultimately neither an effective long-term solution nor necessarily a stable one, unless it is accompanied by third-party efforts to change attitudes, foster and promote dialogue, and exploit windows of opportunity when they emerge. William Zartman has observed that freezing is better than boiling in the world of intractable conflict. But this project also recognized that the patient—be it Cyprus, East and West Germany, or Korea—cannot indefinitely be left in a state of suspended animation. At some point, third parties must raise the temperature and revive the patient by moving the conflict (and the parties) toward a firmer, and more durable, set of negotiated commitments. A more conscious understanding of good medical practice in the treatment of intractable conflicts will help more patients survive the experience. And as we understand better the dynamics of intractability, we may be able to help shorten the duration of the disease, and in fact prevent the conflict from moving to the intractable stage in the first place. Intractable conflicts produce a huge amount of destruction, waste, pain, and despair in the affected societies. They exact a toll—sometimes very large—in human lives. They rob youth of their future and adults of their past. They destabilize their neighborhoods and sometimes spread pathogens—in the form of terrorists—far beyond their immediate surroundings. Intractability is a dangerous disease, and finding ways to prevent it from developing would make an inestimable contribution to the health and stability of the whole international system.

Notes

1. Saadia Touval and I. William Zartman, eds., *International Mediation in Theory and Practice* (Boulder, Colo.: Westview Press, 1985); Saadia Touval and I. William Zartman, "International Mediation in the Post–Cold War Era," in *Turbulent Peace: The Challenges of Managing International Conflict,* ed. Chester A. Crocker, Fen Osler Hampson, and Pamela Aall (Washington, D.C.: United States Institute of Peace Press, 2001), 427–444; Saadia Touval, *The Peace Brokers: Mediators in the Arab-Israeli Conflict, 1948–1979* (Princeton, N.J.: Princeton University Press, 1982); and Saadia Touval, "Coercive Mediation on the Road to Dayton," *International Negotiation* 1, no. 3 (1996): 547–570.

2. Harold H. Saunders et al., "Interactive Conflict Resolution: A View for Policy Makers on Making and Building Peace," in *International Conflict Resolution after the Cold War,* ed. Paul C. Stern and Daniel Druckman (Washington, D.C.: National Academy Press, 2000), 251–293.

Index

Page numbers in italics indicate charts or tables.

abeyant intractable conflict, 11–12, *13*, 119, 120
Abidjan Protocol, 220
Abkhazia conflict, *276*, 280
  economic issues, 273
  ethnic hatred in, 270
  exports, 273
  IDPs in, 273, 279
  international relief agencies in, 287
  Russia in, 281, 283
  UN in, 288
  See also Georgia
Abu-Nimer, Mohammed, 150
Abuja talks (1992–93), 162
Accord of San Andrés (1996), 88
Acheson, Dean, 322
active intractable conflict, 10–11, *13*
Acuerdo de Santa Fe de Ralito, 236–237
Addis Ababa Agreement, 162
Afghanistan
  as buffer state, 57–58
  U.S. military campaign in, 365
Africa
  intractable conflicts in, 3, 22
  regional diplomacy in Angola crisis, 216–217, 226
  See also individual countries
African National Congress (ANC), 71, 145, 146, 209

African Union, 181
  See also Organization of African Unity (OAU)
Agra summit, 312
agrarian reform, 238
Agreement on Reconciliation, Non-aggression, Exchanges and Cooperation (Basic Agreement), 327–328, 333
al Qaeda, 310, 371
Albanians, in Macedonia and Kosovo, 189, 192–193, 194, 201
All Parties Hurriyet Conference (APHC), 301–302
Alvor Agreement, 212–214
ANC. *See* African National Congress (ANC)
Angola conflict
  Eastern Revolt, 212
  effect of Cold War on, 210
  elections in, 54, 218–219, 228
  embedded relationships in, 62
  ethnicity in, 210–211
  financing of, 211
  independence struggle, 209–210
  liberation movements in, 209–211, 212
  national reconciliation in, 216
  peacemaking
    Abidjan Protocol, 220
    African initiatives, 216–217
    Bicesse Accords, 20, 62, 217–220, 226, 227, 228, 229

Angola conflict *(cont.)*
  Cold War and regional diplo-
      macy, 214–216
  continuity, 229–230
  funding peacekeeping opera-
      tions, 229
  Government of National Unity
      and Reconciliation, 222
  Joint Political-Military Com-
      mission, 219, 222
  liberation and Alvor Agreement,
      212–214
  Lusaka Protocol, 20, 220–223,
      226–227, 228, 229–230
  mediation tactics and strategy,
      228–229
  mediators, 226–228
  role of individual in, 224–225,
      384
  Savimbi's death, 223–224, 376
  symmetrical military balance,
      225
  Troika in, 218, 219, 221, 224,
      227
  post–Cold War period, 210–211
  protraction in, 49–50
  Rapid Intervention Police, 219
Angola Verification Mission
    (UNAVEM II), 218–219
Annan, Kofi, 59, 251
Annan Plan (Cyprus), 147
Anstee, Margaret, 218, 220
ANUC. *See* National Association of
    Peasant Users (ANUC)
APHC. *See* All Parties Hurriyet Con-
    ference (APHC)
Arab community in Europe, and
    Israeli-Palestinian conflict, 349
Arab countries
  Israel's relations with, 348
  nationalism of, 358–359
  and Palestinian struggle, 345,
      348–349, 351, 370–371

  PLO recognized by, 358
  view of Israel, 368–369
  view of U.S., 370–371
Arab-Israeli war (1973), 372
Arab League, 173
Arafat, Yasir, 20, 141, 363
Ardzinba, Vladislav, 272
Armenia
  in Nagorno-Karabakh conflict,
      281, 284–285, 287
  relations with Georgia, 280
  Russian troops in, 282
Armenian genocide, 272
Armitage, Richard, 310
arms embargoes, 89
Asmara Declaration (1995), 167
AUC. *See* United Self-Defense Forces
    of Colombia (AUC)
"axis of evil," 320
Azar, Edward, 100
Azerbaijan
  Armenians in, 272
  ethnic issues, 279
  IDPs in, 286
  Minsk Group in, 284–285
  need for end to conflict deadlock,
      289
  Russian actions against, 282
  separatist zone in, 273
  as weak state, 272–273
  See also Nagorno-Karabakh conflict

Baghdad Pact, 299
Balfour Declaration, 349–350
Balkan conflict
  competing solutions in, 53–54
  conflict management in, 379
  embedded relationships in, 56
  International Conference on the
      Former Yugoslavia, 197–198,
      199–200
  irredentas in, 189–190
  justifying mythology in, 49

Balkan conflict *(cont.)*
  mediation of, 194–204, 381
  protraction in, 48
  See also specific states; Yugoslavia
Barak, Ehud, 20, 363
Barco, Virgilio, 246
Bashir, Omer al, 52, 164, 165
Basic Agreement. *See* Agreement on
    Reconciliation, Nonaggression . . .
Beirut Summit (Israeli-Palestinian
    conflict), 351
Betancur, Belisario, 246
Beye, Alouine Blondin, 221
Bicesse Accords, 20, 62, 217–220,
    226, 227, 228, 229
  "Triple Zero" provision, 218
bicommunal rapprochement, 146
Bicommunal Trainers Group, 146–147
bin Laden, Osama, 4, 351, 355
Bishkek Protocol, 284
"blood" diamonds, for financing civil
    wars, 8, 38, 51, 60, 211, 223,
    225–226
Bosnia, 183
  central institutions in, 200
  coercive diplomacy in, 199–200, 204
  Dayton negotiations, 200
  economic development in, 187
  election of 1990, 191
  ethnic nationalist conflicts in,
    195–200
  European Community Conference
    on Yugoslavia and, 197
  intergroup violence in, 185
  irredenta in, 189–190
  multiple actors, competing inter-
    ests, 203
  partition proposals, 198–199, 201
  third-party mediation in, 8,
    197–199, 204
  Vance-Owen Plan for, 198,
    205–206
Botha, P. W., 377

Boutros-Ghali, Boutros, 219
buffer states, in intractable conflicts,
    57–58, 61
Burton, John, 134
Burundi conflict, 136, 177
Bush, George H. W., administration
    of, in Korean conflict, 328
Bush, George W., administration of
  and "axis of evil," 320
  in Kashmir conflict, 310
  in Korean conflict, 338–340
  in Sudan, 178
  unilateral withdrawal of nuclear
    weapons from foreign soil, 326

Camargo, Alberto Lleras, 238
Cambodia
  geopolitics in, 377
  resource control in civil war, 38
Camp David accords, 61, 357,
    361–362, 363, 370
Carter, Jimmy
  administration of, 141
  Middle East policy as president,
    371, 372
  in North Korea, 328
  as unofficial mediator, 131–132,
    137, 138
Castaño, Carlos, 232, 242, 244–245
Catholic Church, in Colombian
    conflict, 232, 234
CENTO pact, 304, 305
Chad, 174, 180, 181
Chechen conflicts, 270
Chipenda, Daniel, 212
Chung Ju-young, 331–332
civil wars. *See* intrastate wars
Clark Amendment, 214, 215
Clerides, Glafcos, 56
Clinton, Bill, administration of
  in Colombian conflict, 250, 253
  in Israeli-Palestinian conflict, 20,
    351, 370, 372

Clinton, Bill, administration of *(cont.)*
  in Kashmir conflict, 308–309
  in Korean conflict, 328, 329–330
CMG. *See* Conflict Management
  Group (CMG)
CNR. *See* Commission on National
  Reconciliation (CNR)
coalitions across conflict lines, 146
coercive diplomacy, 199–200, 204
Cold War
  effect of on Korean conflict, 320,
    326, 327, 329, 331
  as Great Intractable, 56
collaboration problems, in intractable
  conflicts, 53
Colombian conflict
  1991 Constitution, 246
  Acuerdo de Santa Fe de Ralito,
    236–237
  agrarian reform, 238, 258
  causes of, 231–232, 237–243
    social conflict, 237–238
    struggle for land, 238–239
    urban-rural divide, 239
  Colombia as buffer state, 58
  colonization of frontier territories,
    238–239
  counterterrorist operations, 235
  democratic security policy, 236
  despeje in, 233, 234, 252, 255
  drug trafficking, 232, 240–243,
    244, 245, 250, 253, 259–260
  human rights issues, 245–246
  intractability, 9, 231–232, 239–243,
    258–259
  kidnappings in, 252, 253
  La Violencia, 237–238
  "Law 002," 252
  lessons learned, 258–261
  National Association of Peasant
    Users (ANUC), 238
  National Front, 238
  obstacles to settlement, 243–249

    duration and lack of state
      response, 245–246
    fragmentation, 243–244
    government negotiations with
      insurgents, 246–248
    involvement of outside actors,
      248–249
    negotiation fatigue, 247
  paramilitaries and guerrilla groups
    in, 232, 238, 240–241
    AUC, 232–233, 236–237, 240,
      241, 244–245, 257
    ELN, 232, 233, 236, 237, 243,
      252, 253, 254, 255–256
    EPL, 246
    FARC, 232, 233–236, 237, 241,
      242, 243–244, 246–248, 250,
      252, 254, 256–257, 259
    M-19, 239, 246, 247
  Pastrana peace process, 232,
    233–237, 247, 252
  Patriotic Union (UP), 246–247
  professionalization of military, 259
  protraction in, 48, 49–50
  third parties in, 232, 249–257,
    260–261
    European countries, 253–254
    groups of friends, 254–255, 384
    OAS, 257
    Plan Colombia, 248, 250, 251,
      253
    ripeness, 249–250
    UN, 250–252, 254–255
    U.S., 249
  urban terrorism, 247–248
  War of the Thousand Days, 237
Commission on National Reconciliation (CNR), 144
communal separation, 14, 79–80, 100
communication, positive, in
  intractable conflicts, 142
communication-facilitation mediation
  strategies, 113, 115

Community of Sant'Egidio, 130–131, 137

concessions, in intractable conflicts, 89

conciliatory gestures, 91

Conference on Security and Cooperation in Europe (CSCE), 62

confidence-building measures, 80

conflict
  abeyant intractable, 11–12, *13*
  active intractable, 10–11, *13*
  coalitions across, 146
  existential, 50–51, 53, 124, 196
  institutionalization of, 7, 90–91, 125, 144–147
  interstate and intrastate, 10, *13*
  orphaned, 22, *26–27*
  See also interstate wars; intractability; intrastate wars

conflict management, 35, 104, *105*, 106, 379

Conflict Management Group (CMG), 132–133, 140, 145

conflict norms, 125

conflict resolution
  after violence, 35
  training for, 132, 133
  See also mediation

Conflict Resolution Program (Carter Center), 131

context, in intractable conflicts, 56, 107–110

cooperation, in intractable conflicts, 365, 369

Corrigan, Mairead, 73

Council of Ministers of Water Affairs of the Nile Basin States, 80–81

coup-based civil war, 38–39

Croatia, 183
  in Bosnian conflict, 199
  conflict resolution by force, 199
  conflict with Serbia, 196
  early history, 185
  economic development in, 187

ethnic nationalism in, 189
EU involvement in, 195–196
nationalism in, 184–185, 186
recognition of, 196
Serb minority in, 191
third-party mediation in, 204

Croatian Democratic Union (HDZ), 191

Crocker, Chester, 59, 61–62, 215

Cuba
  in Angola conflict, 210, 213, 214, 217
  in Colombia conflict, 236, 254, 256

Curle, Adam, 130

Cutileiro, Jose, 197

Cyprus conflict
  as abeyant intractable conflict, 12
  conflict management in, 379
  Cyprus as buffer, 58
  embedded relationships in, 56, 62
  European Union plan, 55, 62, 147, 378
  external actors in, 378
  Green Line, 141
  one-sided blockage in, 52
  protraction in, 48, 49
  resistance to settlement of, 9
  social network–building in, 147–148, 148–149
  subsidiarity in, 23
  third-party mediation in, 138–139, 144, 146–147, 378

Czechoslovakia, in Korean conflict, 324–325

Dakar Conference, 146
Danforth, John, 380
Darfur conflict, 162, 174, 179–182
Dartmouth Conference Regional Conflicts Task Force, 135, 144
Dayton negotiations, 200
de Klerk, Frederik Willem, 75, 78, 377
de Soto, Alvaro, 59

deadlock, as preferred status in conflicts,
    278–281, 288–290
Declaration of Principles on Interim
    Self-Government Arrange-
    ments, 74
delivery dilemma, in intractable con-
    flict, 19–20
democratic institutions, as preventive
    technique against intractability,
    84
Democratic League of Kosovo (LDK),
    192, 201, 202, 203
Democratic People's Republic of Korea
    (DPRK)
    Carter's visit, 328
    entry into IAEA, 27
    external economic support for, 319,
        329–330, 335
    as failed economy, 319, 320
    fear of North Korean nuclear capa-
        bility, 337
    in Four Party Talks, 330
    Japan normalization, 326
    manipulation of crises by, 52
    Mount Kumgang tourism project,
        331–332
    nuclear testing and inspections, 131,
        326–328, 329–330, 336–338
    as target of U.S. antiterrorism cam-
        paign, 319–320
    third-party verification in, 327
    See also Korean conflict
democratic states, civil wars in, 40–41
democratization, 169, 187, 190–191
Denktaş Rauf, 56
despeje, in Colombia conflict, 233
Diamond, Louise, 127, 137
diasporas
    effect of on mediation, 380
    involvement in conflicts, 282
Dinka Nuer reconciliation, 136
diplomacy, types of
    multitrack, 137

track-one, 127–128
track-one-and-a-half, 129,
    130–133, 140, 143–144
track-three, 135–137, 144–145
track-two, 127, 133–135, 141–145
directive mediation strategies, 113, 115
disengagement, pattern of, 23
domestic politics, as factor in intrac-
    tability, 7–8, 380
dos Santos, José Eduardo, 52,
    216–217, 218, 224
double game. See two-level game
DPRK. See Democratic People's
    Republic of Korea (DPRK)
drug trafficking, as source of war
    financing, 38, 51, 60, 232,
    240–243, 244, 245, 250, 253,
    259–260

Eagleburger, Lawrence, 50
East Timor conflict, 146
Eastern Kosovo Stabilization Pro-
    gram, 148
Eastern Revolt (Angola), 212
Educational Agreement for Kosovo,
    130–131, 138
Egeland, Jan, 251–253, 254, 256
Egypt
    Camp David negotiations, 61, 357,
        361–362, 363, 370
    Israel relations, 72–73, 350, 369
    in Israeli-Palestinian conflict, 351,
        358–359
    in Sudan conflict, 172
Eisenhower administration, in Kash-
    mir conflict, 304–305
El Salvador, civil war in, 59
Eliasson, Jan, 139
ELN. See National Liberation Army
    (ELN)
embedded relationships, in intractable
    conflicts, 56–57, 61–62, 124
enduring rivalries, 36, 37, 40, 42

EPL. *See* Popular Liberation Army
(EPL)
equilibrium, in intractable conflicts,
172
Eritrea, in Sudan conflict, 165, 166,
167, 177
Eritrean People's Liberation Front, 168
Ethiopia, in Sudan conflict, 165, 167,
168, 174, 177
ethnic nationalism, in intractable conflicts, 14, 184, 187–188, 191–
193, 270
Eurasian conflicts
competing solutions in, 53–54
cost/benefit ratio of nonimplementation of agreements, 285, 382
deadlock usefulness in, 278–281,
288–290
ethnic hatred in, 270
external mediators in, 284–288
IDPs in, 271
inculcation of loyalty and identity
among citizens, 280–281
intractability in, 269–271
legitimacy problem in, 290–291
links between corrupt governments
and separatist regions, 278–279
protraction in, 48, 270
relationship between citizens and
governments, 286
Russia factor in, 281–283
seen as new state formation, 272
state weakness as central issue,
269–270
statehood claims inadvertently
bolstered, 286–287
See also specific conflicts
Europe, intractable conflicts in, 4
European Community Conference on
Yugoslavia, 194, 197
European Union
in Balkan conflict, 194, 195–196
Cyprus plan, 56, 62, 147, 378

in Israeli-Palestinian conflict, 351
in Sudan conflict, 165, 178, 181
exploratory overtures, 91
external actors, in intractable conflicts,
39–40, 41–42, 56, 73, 82–83,
90–91, 94, 212, 232, 248–249,
377–378
See also third parties
external factors, in intractable conflicts,
81–82, 89
EZLN. *See* Zapatista National Liberation Army (EZLN)

facilitated joint brainstorming, 133,
145
faction-traction problems, 18–19
FARC. *See* Revolutionary Armed
Forces of Colombia (FARC)
Fashoda Agreement (1997), 169
Fateh, 351
Fisher, Ronald, 134
FNLA. *See* Frente de Libertação de
Moçambique (FNLA)
Folberg, Jay, 106–107
Ford Foundation, 313
Four Party Talks (Korean conflict),
330
4-S stalemate, 52, 53
Fox, Vicente, 88
France
in Colombian conflict, 254
in Middle East, 349, 355
Frelimo (Mozambique), 209
Frente de Libertação de Moçambique
(FNLA), 209, 210, 212,
213–214
"frozen" conflicts, 33, 119, 120, 322,
338
Fukuyama, Francis, 334

Gaitán, Jorge Eliécer, 237–238
Galbraith, John Kenneth, 306
Gambari, Ibrahim, 59

Garang, John, 52, 58, 165, 166, 167, 171, 176
Gaviria, César, 246, 257
Gaza, 359, 362–363, 365–366, 367–368
General Agreement (Inter-Tajik Dialogue), 144
Geneva Agreed Framework (Korean conflict), 330
geopolitics, as factor in intractable conflicts, 6, 14–15, 55–58, 377
Georgia
    ethnic issues in, 272, 280
    IDPs in, 279, 286
    links between corrupt government and separatist region, 278–279
    need for end to conflict deadlock, 289
    OSCE in, 288
    relations with Armenia, 280
    Russia troops in, 282, 283
    separatist zone in, 273
    UNOMIG in, 284
    U.S. train-and-equip program in, 290
    as weak state, 272–273
    See also Abkhazia conflict; South Ossetia conflict
Georgia-South Ossetia Dialogue Project, 133, 144
Germany, in Colombian conflict, 253
Gerner, Deborah, 364
Goldstein, Joshua, 364
Good Friday Agreement, 148
Gorbachev, Mikhail, 78, 284
Graham, Billy, 328
Great Britain. See United Kingdom
Great Lakes crisis, 22
Green Line (Cyprus), 141
grudge culture, 51

Hamas, 351
Harvard Study Group, 144

HDZ. See Croatian Democratic Union (HDZ)
Helsinki Final Act, 62
Hezbollah, 365, 366–367
Hobsbawn, Eric, 238
Hodges, Tony, 220, 224–225
Holbrooke, Richard, 56, 203
hurting stalemate, 196, 259
Hussein, Saddam
    invasion of Kuwait, 350
    overthrow of, 355
Hyundai Corporation, 331–332

IAEA. See International Atomic Energy Agency (IAEA)
ICFY. See International Conference on the Former Yugoslavia (ICFY)
identity
    common, in intractability, 50–51, 84–85
    salience of, 70
    zero-sum notion of as factor in intractability, 7, 53, 60, 151–152
IDPs. See internally displaced persons (IDPs)
IGAD. See Inter-Governmental Authority on Development (IGAD)
IGOs. See international organizations (IGOs)
India
    accession of princely states, 296–297
    Agra summit, 312
    China relations, 305–306
    elections in, 316
    human rights violations by troops, 307
    in Kashmir conflict, 297, 298, 301–302, 304–305, 307, 308, 309, 311–312, 314–315
    nuclear testing in, 308

India *(cont.)*
    Pakistani militants' attacks on, 309,
        312
    partition of, 296–297
    Simla Agreement, 306–307, 379
    Sino-Indian border war, 305
    wars with Pakistan, 295, 306
India-Pakistan war (1965), 306
India-Pakistan war (1971), 295
Indian National Conference, 300, 301
Indian National Congress, 302
individuals, mediation by, 111, *112*,
    224–225
Institutional Revolutionary Party
    (PRI), 88
institutionalization of conflict, 74,
    90–91, 125, 144–147
insurmountable risks, 20–21
Inter-Governmental Authority on
    Development (IGAD), 162,
    165, 167, 170, 175–179
    Declaration of Principles, 170–
        171, 177
    Partners' Forum, 179
inter-Korean summit (1998), 331–332
inter-Korean summit (2000), 326,
    328, 332–333, 334–336
Inter-Tajik Dialogue, 135, 141, 144
    General Agreement, 144
    social networks created by, 148
interactive problem-solving workshop,
    134
intermediaries, 92–93
    See also external actors, in intrac-
        table conflicts; third parties
internal characteristics, of parties in
    intractable conflicts, 109–110
internal instability, as cause of
    intractability, 6
internally displaced persons (IDPs),
    271, 273, 286
International Atomic Energy Agency
    (IAEA), 131, 320, 327, 328

International Camp for Conflict Reso-
    lution, 136
International Conference on the
    Former Yugoslavia (ICFY),
    197–198, 199–200
international organizations (IGOs),
    83
    mediation by, 111, 113
    in prevention of intractability, 86,
        89
    in sustaining transformation, 93
interstate wars, 10, *13*
    of attrition, 11
    as "comfort zone," 6–7
    enduring rivalries and, 36, 37
    factors associated with length and
        duration, 41, 42, 269
    intractable, 36–37
    societal characteristics contributing
        to, 77–78
    See also intrastate wars; violence
intervention
    external, 82–83, 90–91
    unofficial, 151–154
        building social networks,
            147–149
        consultation, 132–133
        creation of changed attitudes,
            139–141
        direct mediation and concilia-
            tion, 130–132
        impact of, 137–149
        improvement in communica-
            tions, relationships, trust,
            141–147
        institutionalization and,
            144–147
        limitations of, 149–151
        role of, 128–129
        track-three diplomacy, 135–137
        track-two diplomacy, 127,
            133–135
        typology of, 128–129, *129*

intervention *(cont.)*
    versus official, 126–128
    See also mediation; third parties
intractability
    buffer states and, 57–58, 61
    causes and factors, 5–6, 12–15,
        16–17, 24–25, *26–27*, 28, 375
        avarice and profiteering, 7–8
        civil wars, 6
        communal or ethnic cleavages,
          14
        domestic politics, 7–8, 380
        double games, 6
        failure of earlier peacemaking
          efforts, 8, 9
        failure to accept mediation, 8–9
        geography and geopolitics, 6,
          14–15, *27*, 55–58, 377
        lack of serious third-party inter-
          vention, 15
        leadership lack of accountability,
          12–13, 376–377
        polarized identity, 7
        stasis, 6
        weak or divided decision-making
          structures, 14, 169–170,
          269–270
    defined, 4–5, 33–34, 65, 66–68,
        99–101
    embedded relationships and,
        56–57, 61–62, 124
    as equilibrium option, 288–290
    exceptionality of, 37
    "happy intractables," 289
    institutionalization of, 7, 87–89,
        90–91, 125, 144–147
    management of, 104, 106, 317–318
    mediator bias in, 57, 60–61,
        379–380
    method of conflict as part of,
        352–355
    nature of conflict and, 124
    negotiation challenges, 15

    delivery issues, 19–20
    discredited salient solutions, 20,
        60, 384
    faction-traction problems, 18–19
    incurable default risks, 20–21
    two-level games, 18
"Other, the" as issue, 50–51,
    139–141, 343, 344, 347
outsider influence on, 39–40,
    41–42, 212
phases of, 68–69
    de-escalation and transforma-
        tion phase, 74–75
    eruption phase, 70–71
    escalation phase, 71–72
    external factors and actors,
        81–83
    failed-peacemaking-efforts
        phase, 72–74
    institutionalization phase, 74
    internal factors affecting, 77–79
    relational factors affecting,
        79–81
    termination and recovery phase,
        75–76
preventive policies, 58–62, 84,
    84–85, 86–87
process, 48
    identities, 50–51
    profitability, 51–52, 60, 79, 124
    protraction, 48–50, 59
    ripeness, 10, 22, 52–53, 59–60,
        123–124, 138, 139,
        249–250, 379
    solutions, 53–55, 205
psychological elements in, 382
regional distribution of conflicts,
    103
resistance to settlement, 9
self-reinforcing escalatory tactics
    in, 125
spectrum of, 12–15, *13*
transformation of, 91–94, 376

intractability *(cont.)*
  types of
    abeyant intractable conflicts,
      11–12, *13*
    active intractable conflicts,
      10–11, *13*
    interstate and intrastate conflicts,
      10, *13*
  vested interest in, 100, 376–377, 382
  of war, 36–37
  See also conflict; mediation; third
    parties
intrastate wars, 10, *13*
  coup-based, 38–39
  in democratic regimes, 40–41
  effect of in international neigh-
    borhood, 39
  factors associated with length and
    duration, 41, 42
  as intractable conflicts, 6
  outside intervention in, 39–40,
    41–42, 212
  patterns in, 36, 37
  peripheral, 38–39
  rebel financing of, 38–39
  secessionist goals in, 41
  security dilemma in, 40
  settlement in, 34–35, 39
  See also interstate wars
Iraq, invasion of Kuwait, 350
irredentas, in Balkan conflict,
  189–190, 191
Islam, radical movement in Sudan,
  164, 166
Israel
  Arab-Israeli war (1973), 372
  Arab view of, 368–369
  Arabs in, 350
  Balfour Declaration, 349–350
  Egypt relations, 72–72, 350, 369
  insecurity of, 368–369
  Jewish identity inside and outside
    of, 350

Labor Party in, 360
in Lebanon, 365–367
Likud in, 360, 361
settler movement in, 351
view of Israeli-Palestinian conflict,
  345, 352, 353, 360–363
Zionism in, 345, 352, 360–361
Israeli-Palestinian conflict, 343–344,
  353
  action versus nonaction, 365
  as active intractable conflict, 11,
    354–355
  and Arab-Israeli conflict, 349
  Beirut Summit, 351
  as bilateral intercommunal conflict,
    350–351
  Camp David accords, 61, 357, 360,
    361–362, 363
  Declaration of Principles, 74
  delivery dilemma in, 19–20
  domestic politics in, 365, 377, 380
  effect of European Arab commu-
    nity on, 349
  effect of Jewish community in
    America on, 349
  embedded relationships in, 61–62
  as ethno-religious struggle,
    361–362
  framing of, 358–364
  intifadas in, 350, 361
  justifying mythology in, 49
  leadership issues, 377
  learning from the wrong example,
    365
  levels of conflict, 355
    Arab world's relations with
      Israel, 348–349, 351
    international community,
      349–350, 351
    local level, 348
  method of conflict as part of
    intractability, 352–355
  mutual trust issues, 353–354

Israeli-Palestinian conflict *(cont.)*
  narratives of the conflict, 344, 346–
    347, 361–364
    Arab/Palestinian view, 345,
      358–360, 363–364
    instability following defeat of
      Ottoman Empire, 345–346
    Zionist (dominant Israeli) view,
      345, 360–361
  negative political culture fostered
    by, 354–355
  Oslo negotiations, 19, 52–53, 54,
    55, 134, 145, 351, 360–361,
    369, 370, 372
  Palestinian nationalism in, 358,
    359–360
  power shifts in, 369
  protraction in, 48, 49–50, 343–344
  Quartet structure in, 351
  Rabat summit, 359
  reciprocity in, 357
  religion as dimension of conflict,
    347–348
  revenge normalized, 364–369
  right-of-return issue in, 360
  rights to West Bank and Gaza,
    362–363, 367–368
  salient solution in, 54, 55
  "security for territory" in, 55
  self-definitions of national move-
    ments in, 343–344
  Six-Day War (1967), 359
  third-party mediation in, 138–139,
    144, 343–344, 350–351, 353,
    354, 355, 369–372
  victimization beliefs in, 346, 347
  World War I effect on, 355
Istanbul summit (1999), 282, 283, 287
Izetbegovic, Alija, 191

Janjawiid militia, 180
Japan, in Korean conflict, 320–321,
    326, 329, 330, 337–338

Jewish community in America, and
  Israeli-Palestinian conflict, 349,
  350
JLEI. *See* Joint Libyan and Egyptian
  Initiative (JLEI)
Joint Declaration (2000 inter-Korean
  summit), 333
Joint Declaration on the Denucleari-
  zation of the Korean Peninsula
  (1992), 327–328, 333
Joint Libyan and Egyptian Initiative
  (JLEI), 167, 170, 176, 177, 179
Joint Political-Military Commission
  (Angola), 219
Justice and Equity Movement
  (Sudan), 180

Kanter, Arnold, 3326
Karadzic, Radovan, 191
Kashmir conflict, 6, 81–82, 295
  acceptance of mediation in, 8–9
  accession of princely states,
    296–297
  All Parties Hurriyet Conference
    (APHC), 301–302
  causes, 296–298
  cease-fires in, 311–312, 316
  competing solutions in, 53–54
  embedded relationships in, 56–57
  geography and ethnicity, 295–296
  geopolitics in, 378
  Kashmir as buffer state, 57–58
  Kashmir Study Group, 133–134,
    143–144, 313–314
  lessons learned, 315–318
  Line of Control in, 54, 297, 298,
    306–307, 308, 312, 313
  local mediation efforts, 311–313
  militant violence in, 309
  nature of dispute, 298–299
  Neemrana dialogue, 313–314
  new peace process for, 314–315
  nuclear dimension, 309–311

obstacles to settlement, 200–202
one-sided blockage in, 52
parties to, 299–300
resistance to settlement, 9
Simla Agreement, 217, 306–307,
317, 379
state elections, 299, 300, 301–302
third-party involvement, 302–303,
315–316
antiterrorism concerns, 309–311
Simla Agreement and bilateral-
ism, 306–307, 379
UN, 303–305
U.S., 305–306, 308–309
track-two diplomacy in, 313–314
Kashmir Study Group (KSG),
133–134, 143–144, 313–314
Kathwari, Farooq, 313
Kaye, Dalia, 149
KEDO. See Korean Peninsula Energy
Development Organization
(KEDO)
Kelly, James, 340
Kelman, Herbert, 134, 144, 145–146
Kennedy administration, in Kashmir
conflict, 305–306
Kenya, in Sudan conflict, 165
Kenyatta, Jomo, 213
Khartoum Agreement (1997), 167,
169
Khmer Rouge, 38
Kim Dae Jung, 320, 328, 331, 332,
335
Sunshine Policy, 331–333, 335,
338–339
Kim Il Sung, 131, 322, 323, 325, 328,
329
Kim Jong Il, 320, 331–332, 335, 338
Kim Yong Sun, 326
Kim Young Sam, 328, 330
KLA. See Kosovo Liberation Army
(KLA)
Kocharian, Robert, 272

Korean conflict, 319–321
Agreement on Reconciliation,
Nonaggression, Exchanges and
Cooperation (Basic Agree-
ment), 327–328, 333
Demilitarized Zone (DMZ),
324–325
dialogue in, 325–328
economic cooperation and infrastructure, 333
essential objectives of settlement,
329–330
Four Party Talks, 330
as frozen conflict, 320
Geneva Agreed Framework, 330
geopolitics and, 377
"handshake" timing in, 333
institutionalization of cooperation
and implementation, 333
inter-Korean summit (1998),
331–332
inter-Korean summit (2000), 326,
328, 332–333, 334–336
Joint Declaration (2000), 333
Joint Declaration on the Denuclearization of the Korean
Peninsula, 327–328
Korea as buffer state, 58
Korean Peninsula Energy Development Organization
(KEDO), 330
Korean War and intractability,
321–324
Military Armistice Commission
(MAC), 324
Mount Kumgang tourism project,
331–332
multilateral involvement in, 330
Neutral Nations Supervisory Commission (NNSC), 324–325
Nordpolitik process, 326
nuclear proliferation during,
326–328, 329–330, 336–338

Korean conflict *(cont.)*
  one-sided blockage in, 52
  post–Korean War, 324–325
  Proliferation Security Initiative
    (PSI), 340
  protraction in, 48, 49
  reconciliation in, 329–330,
    331–333, 334
  reunification as goal, 325, 329, 340
  salient solution in, 54
  South Korean NGOs in, 331–332
  South-North Joint Communiqué,
    325
  subregional dialogue in, 320, 327
  Sunshine Policy, 331–333, 335,
    338–339
  as superpower conflict and civil
    conflict, 323
  third parties in, 320, 324–328,
    329–330, 332
  Trilateral Coordination and Over-
    sight Group (TCOG), 329, 330
Korean Peninsula Energy Development
  Organization (KEDO), 330
Korean War, 321–324
Kosovo conflict, 130–131, 137, 138,
    183, 186, 194
  Eastern Kosovo Stabilization Pro-
    gram, 148
  economic development level, 187
  ethnic nationalism in, 189, 194,
    196, 201
  outcome of, 201–204
  political organizations in, 192, 201
  Rambouillet negotiations, 203
  third-party mediation in, 204, 205
Kosovo Liberation Army (KLA),
    201–203
KSG. *See* Kashmir Study Group
  (KSG)
Kuanda, Kenneth, 217
Kucan, Milan, 193
Kuwait, invasion of by Iraq, 350

La Violencia (Colombia), 237–238
Labor Party (Israel), 360
Latin America, 4
"Law 002" (Colombia), 252
LDK. *See* Democratic League of
  Kosovo (LDK)
leadership
  absence of, 316
  "bad," 124, 376–377
  delivery of constituency by,
    19–20
  lack of accountability of,
    12–13
Lebanon
  Hezbollah in, 365, 366–367
  Israel in, 365–367
legitimacy problem, in Eurasian
  conflicts, 290–291
LeMoyne, James, 234, 254, 256
Liberation Tigers of Tamil Eelam
  (LTTE), 376
Likud (Israel), 360, 361
Line of Control (Kashmir conflict),
    54, 297, 298, 306–307, 308,
    312, 313
Lippman, Walter, 37
Losyukov, Aleksandr, 338
LTTE. *See* Liberation Tigers of Tamil
  Eelam (LTTE)
Lusaka peace process, 20, 59, 62,
    220–223, 226–227, 228,
    229–230
  Memorandum of Understanding,
    224

M-19 (Colombia), 239, 246, 247
MacArthur, Douglas, 322
Macedonia, 183
  economic development in, 187
  ethnic nationalism in, 189,
    192–193, 194
  political parties and elections in,
    192

Machakos Protocol (2002), 163, 165,
    171, 179
Madrid peace process, 62
Mahdi, Sadiq el, 176
Malaysia, conflict in, 85
Mandela, Nelson, 71, 177, 377
Mbeki, Thabo, 146
McDonald, John, 127
mediation
    behavioral factors, 110–116
    contextual factors, 107
        intensity, costs, fatalities,
            109
        internal characteristics of parties,
            109–110
        issues, 108
        systemic features, 108
    defined, 107
    by individuals, 111, *112*
    initiation of, *114*
    institutional support for, 383
    by international organizations, 111,
        113
    in intractable conflicts, 92, 101,
        102, 104, 106–107, 317,
        381–384
    leverage in, 177–178
    mediator behavior, 113
    mediator bias, in intractable
        conflicts, 57, 60–61, 177–178,
        379–380
    negotiation cadres, 145
    outcomes, *118*
    by regional organizations, 111
    strategies, 113, 114–115, *117*,
        381–384
    timing, 109
    tradecraft, 22, *26–27*, 124,
        150–151, 179, 381
    See also external actors, in intrac-
        table conflicts; intervention;
        third parties
Mercy Corps, 148

Mexico
    Chiapas conflict, 87–88
    in Colombia conflict, 253
    Indigenous Rights Law, 88
    political parties, 87–88
Middle East
    Arab view of U.S. in, 370–371
    Britain and France in, 349
    Christians moved out of, 350
    conflict and cooperation in,
        364–365
    See also Israeli-Palestinian conflict;
        specific countries
military action, in intractable conflicts,
    51, 100
Military Armistice Commission
    (MAC), 324
Milosevic, Slobodan, 52, 56, 191, 193,
    201, 202, 203
Minsk Group, 284–285
Mirghani, Mohamed Osman al, 176
Mitchell, Chris, 106
Mobuto Sese Seko, 216–217
Moi, Daniel arap, 165
Moldova
    during Soviet period, 278
    elections in, 291
    ethnic issues, 279–280
    government responsiveness to
        conflict, 286
    industry in, 278
    links between corrupt government
        and separatist region, 278–279
    need for end to deadlock, 289
    OSCE mission in, 284, 287, 288
    Russian troops in, 282–283
    separatist zone in, 273
    steel dumping by, 278
    as weak state, 272–273
    See also Transnistria conflict
Montville, Joseph, 127
Moore, Charles, 106
Mozambique, 130, 137, 209

MPLA. *See* Popular Movement for
   the Liberation of Angola
   (MPLA)
Mugabe, Robert, 209
multitrack diplomacy, 137
Musharraf, Pervez, 300–301, 312, 316

Nagorno-Karabakh conflict, *274*
   Armenia in, 281
   autonomous status for Karabakh, 54
   economic issues, 273
   ethnic issues in, 270, 279
   institutions of statehood in, 287
   Karabakh as buffer state, 58
   mediation in, 284–285
   Minsk Group, 284–285
   need for end to deadlock, 289
   Russia in, 281
   state weakness in, 273
   UN in, 288
Naivasha talks (Sudan), 171, 179, 182
Nakuru Declaration, 213
Namibia, 209, 215
Namibian-Angolan conflict, 59
Nasser, Gamal Abdel, 72, 358–359
National Association of Peasant Users
   (ANUC), 238
National Democratic Alliance
   (NDA), 167, 169, 170, 176
National Front (Colombia), 238
National Liberation Army (ELN),
   232, 233, 236, 237, 243, 252,
   253, 254, 255–256
National Party (South Africa), 145, 146
National Union for the Total Inde-
   pendence of Angola (UNITA),
   216, 217, 225
   after Portuguese transfer of power,
      213–214
   after Savimbi's death, 211, 223–224
   as anticommunist force, 210
   base of, 209
   direct talks held with, 218

financing of, 211, 223
in Joint Political-Military Com-
   mission, 219
as liberation movement, 212
in peacemaking process (Lusaka
   Protocol), 220–223, 228–229
in post–Cold War period, 210–211
South African support of, 214–215
U.S. support of, 210, 216, 226
See also Angola conflict
Nazarbaev, Nursultan, 284
NDA. *See* National Democratic
   Alliance (NDA)
Neemrana dialogue, 313, 314
Nehru, Jawaharlal, 297, 303, 304, 316
Netanyahu, Benjamin, 19–20
Neto, Agostinho, 213
Neutral Nations Supervisory Com-
   mission (NNSC), 324–325
New Sudan Council of Churches, 136
NGOs. *See* nongovernmental organi-
   zations (NGOs)
Nigerian conflict (1967–70), 130
Nile Basin Initiative, 80–81, 85
Nile Waters Agreement, 173
Nimeiri, Jaafar, 52, 54
Nixon, Richard, visit to China, 325
Nkomo, Joshua, 209
NLL. *See* Northern Limit Line (NLL)
NNSC. *See* Neutral Nations Supervi-
   sory Commission (NNSC)
nongovernmental organizations
   (NGOs), 83, 86–87, 89
   accountability of, 126
   in conflict mediation, 136, 138–139
   in Kashmir conflict, 313–314
   in sustaining transformation, 93
   See also specific NGOs
"Nordic mafia," 253
Nordpolitik process (Korean conflict),
   326
North Korea. *See* Democratic People's
   Republic of Korea (DPRK)

Northern Ireland conflict, 81
  community relations work, 148
  eruption phase of, 70
  failed-peacemaking-efforts phase, 73
  geopolitical context, 377
  Good Friday Agreement, 148
  third-party mediation in, 138
Northern Limit Line (NLL), 331
Norway
  in Colombian conflict, 254
  in Sudan conflict, 164, 165, 176,
    178, 384
Norwegian Refugee Council (NRC),
  133, 140
NRC. *See* Norwegian Refugee Council
  (NRC)
Nuclear Nonproliferation Treaty
  (NPT), 20
nuclear proliferation
  in India, 308
  in North Korea, 131, 326–328,
    329–330, 336–338
  in Pakistan, 308
Nyerere, Julius, 177

OAS. *See* Organization of American
  States (OAS)
OAU. *See* Organization of African
  Unity (OAU)
oil, as source of conflict financing,
  211, 225–226
Organization for Security and Coop-
  eration in Europe (OSCE),
  62, 86
  in Eurasian conflicts, 270, 283,
    284, 287, 288
  high commissioner on national
    minorities (HCNM), 86
  Istanbul summit, 282, 283, 287
  Minsk Group, 283–285
Organization of African Unity
  (OAU), 212–213, 214.
  See also African Union

Organization of American States
  (OAS), 249, 257
orphaned conflicts, 22, *26–27*
Oslo negotiations, 19, 52–53, 54, 55,
  134, 145, 351, 360–361, 369,
  370, 372
"Other, the," concept of in conflicts,
  50–51, 139–141, 343, 344, 347
Ottoman Empire, 272, 345–346,
  348, 355
outside actors, in intractable conflicts,
  39–40, 41–42, 212, 232,
  248–249
Owen, David, 197, 198, 206

Pakistan
  Agra summit, 312
  cooperation with U.S. on al Qaeda,
    310
  in Kashmir conflict, 297–298, 299,
    307, 308–309, 311–312, 314–
    315, 316
  militant organizations in, 300–301,
    309, 310, 311, 312
  nuclear testing in, 308
  Simla Agreement, 306–307
  wars with India, 295, 306
Palestine
  Arab world's involvement in
    struggle over, 348–349
  intragroup conflict in, 351
  nakba (1948), 358–359
  nationalism in, 358, 359–360
  nonviolent civil resistance con-
    nected to trust issues, 353
  occupation of, 352–353
  PLO recognized as legitimate
    representative, 358
  rights to West Bank and Gaza,
    362, 367–368
  self-determination as issue,
    358–359
  terrorism in, 352–353

Palestine *(cont.)*
    view of Israeli-Palestinian conflict,
        345, 358–360, 363–364
    See also Israeli-Palestinian conflict
Palestine Liberation Organization
    (PLO), 141–142, 350, 351, 358,
    359, 361, 372
Palestinian Authority, 74, 351
Pan African Congress, 71
Parfait, Daniel, 234
Park Chung Hee, 325, 329
Party of Democratic Action (SDA),
    191
Pastrana, Andrés, 231, 233–237, 247,
    248, 254
Patriotic Union (UP), 246–247
Paulo, Lukamba "Gato," 224
People-to-People process (Sudan), 136
People's Republic of China (PRC), 319
    India relations, 305–306
    in Korean conflict, 320, 329,
        336–337, 340
    Nixon's visit to, 325
    Sino-Indian border war, 305
Perry, William, 329
Persian Gulf War, 369
Pevehouse, Jon, 364
Plan Colombia, 248, 250, 251, 253
PLO. *See* Palestine Liberation Orga-
    nization (PLO)
political leaders, in intractable conflicts,
    6, 51–52, 78, 81
Popular Liberation Army (EPL), 246
Popular Movement for the Liberation
    of Angola (MPLA), 209, 210,
    211, 212, 213, 214, 218
Portugal
    in Angola, 209, 212, 213–214, 218,
        226, 227
    "Revolution of Carnations" in, 213
poverty, role of in intractable con-
    flicts, 6
Powell, Colin, 310

PRC. *See* People's Republic of China
    (PRC)
PRI. *See* Institutional Revolutionary
    Party (PRI)
Prisoner's Dilemma, 53
procedural-formulative mediation
    strategies, 113, 115
profitability and profiteering, in
    intractable conflicts, 6, 7–8,
    51–52, 60, 79, 124
Proliferation Security Initiative (PSI),
    340
protraction, in intractable conflict,
    48–50, 59, 343–344
PSI. *See* Proliferation Security Initiative
    (PSI)
Public Committee for Promoting
    Democratic Processes, 148
public peace process, 134–135, 143
Putin, Vladimir, 288, 338

Quartet structure, in Israeli-Palestinian
    conflict, 351

Rabat summit (1974), 359
Rabin, Yitzhak, 19
Radical Party (Serbia), 191–192
Radio Macedonia, 148
Rambouillet negotiations (Kosovo),
    203
Randle, Robert, 108
Rapid Intervention Police (Angola),
    219
reciprocity, in intractable conflicts,
    364–365
recognition (as independent state), as
    issue in negotiations, 194, 196,
    205, 286–287
reconciliation, in transformation of
    intractable conflicts, 93
Red Cross, in Korean conflict,
    325–326
Redman, Charles, 56

reentry problem, 150
regional diplomacy, in Angola, 214–216
regional interests, in intractable conflicts, 172–173
regional organizations, mediation by, 111, *112*
relational factors, in intractable conflicts, 79–81
religion, in intractable conflicts, 347–348, 361–362
Republic of Korea (ROK), 319
  1988 Olympics in, 326
  active engagement with North Korea, 338–339
  balance of power shifting toward, 320
  elections in, 327, 332, 334
  in Four Party Talks, 330
  in KEDO, 330
  National Security Law, 335
  NGOs from, 331–332
  Nordpolitik policy, 326
  Northern Limit Line (NLL), 331
  "South-South" divide in politics, 334–335
  Sunshine Policy, 331–333, 335, 338–339
  See also Korean conflict
"resource curse" in civil wars, 38, 51, 225–226, 259–260
Restrepo, Luis Carlos, 232
revenge, in intractable conflicts, 364–369
"Revolution of Carnations," 213
Revolutionary Armed Forces of Colombia (FARC), 232, 237, 240, 242, 243–244, 246–248, 250
  engagement in peace process, 233–236, 252, 256–257, 259
  group of friends constituted by, 254
  kidnapping by, 253

Law 002, 252
  See also Colombian conflict
Rhee, Syngman, 322–323
Ricardo, Víctor G., 252
"ripeness," in intractable conflicts, 10, 22, 52–53, 59–60, 123–124, 138, 139, 249–250, 379
Roberto, Holden, 212, 213
Roh Tae Woo, 326, 331
ROK. *See* Republic of Korea (ROK)
Romania, in Transnistria conflict, 272
Rugova, Ibrahim, 192, 201
Rusk, Dean, 322
Russia
  in Angola conflict, 215, 226
  Bishkek Protocol, 284
  de facto recognition of separatist states, 287–288
  as factor in Eurasian conflicts, 270, 271, 281–283, 284
  in Israeli-Palestinian conflict, 351
  in Korean conflict, 320–321, 329, 338
  See also Soviet Union (USSR)

SAARC. *See* South Asian Association for Regional Cooperation (SAARC)
Sadat, Anwar el-, 72, 73, 350, 372
salient solutions
  competing, in intractable conflicts, 53–55, 60
  discrediting of, 8, 20, 54, 384
Samper, Ernesto, 250, 253
sanctions, 89
Sant'Egidio. *See* Community of Sant'Egidio
Sassou-Nguesso, Denis, 216
Saunders, Harold, 134, 143
Savimbi, Jonas, 52, 54, 210, 211, 212, 213, 219–220, 376
SDA. *See* Party of Democratic Action (SDA)

SDS. *See* Serb Democratic Party (SDS)
Search for Common Ground, 136,
      148
SEATO pact, 304, 305
secessionist goals, in civil wars, 41
security dilemma, 40, 188–189
Seeds of Peace, 136
self-determination, as issue in intrac-
      table conflicts, 167, 187–188,
      190, 194, 271–272, 304, 358–359
self-reinforcing escalatory tactics, 125
September 11, 2001, terrorist attacks,
      4, 81
      See also terrorism, war on
Serb Democratic Party (SDS), 191
Serbia
      conflict with Croatia, 196
      ethnic minorities in, 192
      nationalism in, 184–185
      political parties and elections in,
        191–192
Seselj, Vojislav, 191
settlement
      definition of, 33–34
      negotiated, 34–35, 39–40
      postsettlement institutions
        included in, 40
Sharpeville demonstration (South
      Africa), 71
Shevardnadze, Eduard, 278
Simla Agreement (Kashmir conflict),
      217, 306–307, 317, 379
Singer, J. David, 36
Singh, Manmohan, 312
Sino-Indian border war, 305
Six-Day War (1967), 359
Slovenia, 183
      economic development in, 187
      negotiated conflict solution in,
        194–195
      secession of, 193
Smirnov, Igor, 272
social networks, creation of, 147–149

Socialist Party (Serbia), 191
solutions
      mediator-proposed, 205
      polarization of in intractable con-
        flicts, 53–55
      salient, 8, 20, 53–55, 54, 60, 384
South Africa
      in Angola conflict, 210, 214, 216,
        217
      apartheid struggle in, 71, 377
      geopolitics as factor in internal
        conflict, 377
      political parties in, 209
      third-party mediation in, 138–139,
        145, 146
South Asian Association for Regional
      Cooperation (SAARC), 312
South Korea. *See* Republic of Korea
      (ROK)
South-North Joint Communiqué
      (Korean conflict), 325
South Ossetia conflict, 132–133,
      277, 280
      community-building projects, 148
      economic issues, 273
      ethnic hatred in, 270
      geography as government's asset,
        273, 278
      Georgia–South Ossetia Dialogue
        Project, 133, 144
      history of recorded in texts, 280–281
      illegal trade with Russia, 278
      outflow of IDPs, 173
      Russia in, 281, 283, 284
      third-party mediation in, 151
      track-one-and-a-half diplomacy
        in, 140
      See also Georgia
South West Africa People's Organiza-
      tion (SWAPO), 209, 210
Soviet Union (USSR)
      in Angola conflict, 210, 213, 216,
        217–218, 226, 227

Soviet Union (USSR) *(cont.)*
  boycott of UN, 323
  collapse of, 327
  ethnic sovereignty and self-
      determination in, 187–188,
      271–272
  in Eurasian conflicts, 270,
      271–272, 281–283
  expansion in Middle East, 299
  in Kashmir conflict, 302–303,
      305, 306
  in Korean conflict, 322–323
  See also Russia
Spain, in Colombian conflict, 253, 254
SPLM/SPLA. *See* Sudan People's
      Liberation Movement/Army
      (SPLM/SPLA)
spoilers, 149
Sri Lanka, conflict in, 78, 376
stalemate
  4-S, 52, 53
  hurting, 196
Stalin, Joseph, 185
"stamina war," 11
state weakness, intractability and,
      169–170, 258–259, 269–270
statehood. *See* recognition (as inde-
      pendent state)
Stoltenberg, Thorvald, 198
strategic impaction, 23–24, *26–27*
subsidiarity, 23, *26–27*
Sudan conflict
  Abuja talks (1992–93), 162
  Amendment 14 to Constitution,
      167
  Asmara Declaration (1995), 167
  background and history, 161–166
  Darfur conflict, 162, 179–182
  Dinka Nuer reconciliation, 136
  external actors in, 379
  external factors, 172–175, 377
  faction-traction problems in,
      18–19

  government (GoS) as antagonist,
      163, 166, 167, 169, 171, 176,
      177, 179–180
  humanitarian relief in, 174, 180
  identities in, 50
  IGAD in, 162, 167, 175, 176–177,
      178, 179
  internal factors, 166–172
  Janjawiid militia, 180
  JLEI in, 167, 170, 176
  Justice and Equity Movement,
      179–180
  justifying mythology in, 49
  Khartoum Agreement, 167
  literature of accord in, 166, 178
  Machakos protocol (2002), 163,
      165, 171
  mediation in
    culture and principles of nego-
        tiation, 178
    extent of, 174–175
    leverage and impartiality,
        176–178
    mediator bias, 380
    regional initiatives, 384
    structure of, 176–177
    tradecraft, 178–179, 381
  Naivasha agreement, 171, 179, 182
  NDA in, 167, 169, 176
  oil in, 168, 378
  one-sided blockage in, 52
  protraction in, 48, 49–50
  radical Islamists in, 164, 166, 167
  as regionally destabilizing factor, 173
  salient solution in, 54
  self-determination as issue in, 167
  SPLA as antagonist, 162, 163, 166,
      168, 169, 171–172, 176, 177,
      178, 180
  Sudan as buffer state, 57, 58
  terrorism and, 174
  track-three diplomacy in, 136
  Umma Party, 170

Sudan Liberation Army, 180
Sudan Peace Act, 168, 178
Sudan People's Liberation Movement/
    Army (SPLM/SPLA), 162, 163,
    164, 165, 166, 168, 169, 171–
    172, 176, 177, 178, 180, 378
Sunshine Policy (Korean conflict),
    331–333, 335, 338–339
Support Group of the Peace Process
    in Colombia, 253
SWAPO. *See* South West Africa Peo-
    ple's Organization (SWAPO)
Sweden, in Korean conflict, 324–325
Switzerland
    in Colombian conflict, 254
    in Korean conflict, 324–325
    in Sudan conflict, 165, 178
Syria
    in Israeli-Lebanese conflict, 366
    in Israeli-Palestinian conflict, 351
systemic features, in intractable con-
    flicts, 108

Taha, Ali Osman Mohammed, 166
Tajikistan Centre for Citizenship
    Education, 148
Taylor, Alison, 106–107
TCOG. *See* Trilateral Coordination
    and Oversight Group (TCOG)
terrorism
    in Israeli-Palestinian conflict,
        352–353
    war on, 81, 82, 174, 175, 235, 290,
        309–311, 371, 377
third parties
    coordination among, 384
    limits on, 379–381
    mediation by, 21, 113, *114*,
        123–126, 302–311, 375–376
        Angola conflict, 226–228
        Balkans, 204–206
        Colombian conflict, 249–257,
            260–261

Eurasian conflicts, *274–277*,
    284–288
Israeli-Palestinian conflict,
    138–139, 144, 343–344,
    347–348, 350–351, 353,
    354, 355, 369–372
Kashmir conflict, 302–311
Korean conflict, 325–330,
    336–340
Sudan conflict, 174–179
official, 127
operations of in intractable con-
    flicts, 21–24, *26–27*, 315–316
orphaned conflicts, 22, *26–27*
strategic impaction, 23–24, *26–27*
subsidiarity, 23, *26–27*
unavailability of in intractable con-
    flicts, 15
See also external actors, in intrac-
    table conflicts; intervention;
    mediation
Tito, Josip, 185, 186
Touval, Saadia, 113
track-one-and-a-half diplomacy, *129*,
    130–133, 140
track-one diplomacy, 127–128, 150
track-three diplomacy, 135–137,
    144–145
track-two diplomacy, 91, 133–135,
    141–144, 144–145, 313–314
tradecraft, poor, 22, *26–27*, 124,
    150–151, 179, 381
Transnistria conflict, *275*
    central government responsiveness
        to, 286
    economic issues, 278
    ethnic hatred in, 270
    fear of unification with Romania,
        272
    need for end to deadlock, 289
    as "net exporter" to Moldova, 278
    OSCE negotiations in, 287
    Russia in, 281, 283, 284

Trilateral Coordination and Oversight Group (TCOG), 329, 330, 337
"Triple Zero" provision (Bicesse Accords), 218
Troika (Angola), 218, 219, 221, 224, 227
Tudjman, Franjo, 52, 56, 191
Turabi, Hassan al, 164
Turkey
    Armenian genocide, 272
    as guarantor in Eurasian conflicts, 288
two-level game, in mediation, 8, 15–18

Uganda, in Sudan conflict, 165, 167, 168, 177
Ukraine, as guarantor in Eurasian conflicts, 288
UNITA. *See* National Union for the Total Independence of Angola (UNITA)
United Kingdom
    in Israeli-Palestinian conflict, 348, 349–350, 355
    in Kashmir conflict, 302
    in Sudan conflict, 164, 165, 176, 384
United National Independence Party (Zambia), 209
United Nations
    administration of Kosovo, 203
    in Angola conflict, 215, 218–219, 220–221, 221–223, 224, 226–227, 228–230
    Annan Plan, 147
    in Bosnian conflict, 197–198
    in Colombian conflict, 248–249, 250–252, 254–255
    in Cyprus conflict, 377
    in Eurasian conflicts, 270, 288
    in Kashmir conflict, 297, 302, 303–305
    in Korean War, 323–324

    mediation by, 111, *112*, 120
    in Nagorno-Karabakh conflict, 284
    Resolution 242 (Middle East conflict), 55
    in Sudan, 181
    UNAVEM II (Angola Verification Mission), 218–219
    UNCIP (UN Commission for India and Pakistan), 303–304
    UNESCO, 93–94
    UNOMIG (UN Observer Mission in Georgia), 284
United Self-Defense Forces of Colombia (AUC), 232–233, 236–237, 240, 241, 244–245, 257
United States
    in Afghanistan, 365
    in Angola conflict, 210, 214, 215–216, 220, 226, 227–228
    in Bosnian conflict, 199–200
    in Colombian conflict, 235, 248, 249, 250, 258
    in Cyprus conflict, 378
    in Eurasian conflicts, 270, 287, 290
    and Iraq war, 355
    in Israeli-Palestinian conflict, 350–351, 355, 368, 369–372, 380
    in Kashmir conflict, 299, 302–303, 304, 307, 310, 311, 312, 314, 318
    in Korean conflict, 320–321, 328, 329–330, 337, 338–340
    in Kosovo conflict, 202
    as mediator, 57
    nuclear concerns in Pakistan and India, 308
    PLO and, 141–142
    in Sudan conflict, 162, 164, 168, 174–175, 176, 178, 181, 380
    war on terrorism, 81, 82, 174, 175, 235
United States Institute of Peace, 4–5, 93

unofficial intermediation. *See* inter-
    vention, unofficial
UP. *See* Patriotic Union (UP)
Uribe Vélez, Álvaro, 231, 232,
    235–236, 245, 248, 258
USSR. *See* Soviet Union (USSR)

Vajpayee, Atal Behari, 312, 316
van der Stoel, Max, 86
Vance, Cyrus, 196, 197, 206
Vance-Owen plan, 198, 205–206
Vance Plan, 196
Venezuela, in Colombian conflict, 256
vested interest, in intractable conflicts,
    100
victimization, as narrative of conflict,
    346, 347
violence
    effect of on conflict resolution, 35
    intergroup, 185
    level and persistence of in
        intractable conflicts, 10–11,
        33–34, 100, 109, 119
    as transformative experience, 269

weapons of mass destruction
    (WMD), 320
West Bank, 359, 362–363, 365–366,
    367–368
Williams, Betty, 73
World Peace Foundation, 144
World War I, effect of on Israeli-
    Palestinian conflict, 355

Yeltsin, Boris, 284
Yemen, alliance with Sudan, 174

Yu-summits (Yugoslavia), 193
Yugoslavia
    communist regime in, 185–186
    devolution in, 186
    dissolution of, 183–184
        conflict dynamics, 184–188
        intractability in, 188–193
        mediation, 194–204
        "security dilemma" in, 188–189
    economic disparities in, 186–187,
        190
    elections in, 190–193
    ethnic nationalism in, 184, 187,
        188, 191–193
    International Conference on the
        Former Yugoslavia, 197–198,
        199–200
    relegitimation in, 185–186, 190
    Yu-summits, 193
    See also individual successor states

Zambia, 209, 217
Zapatista National Liberation Army
    (EZLN), 87–88
Zartman, I. William, 113
zero-sum problems, 7, 53, 60,
    151–152, 189–190, 193, 194,
    331, 346
Zimbabwe, 209–210
Zimbabwe African National Union,
    209
Zimbabwe African People's Union,
    209–210
Zionism, in Israeli-Palestinian con-
    flict, 345, 346, 352, 360–361

United States Institute of Peace

The United States Institute of Peace is an independent, nonpartisan federal institution created by Congress to promote the prevention, management, and peaceful resolution of international conflicts. Established in 1984, the Institute meets its congressional mandate through an array of programs, including research grants, fellowships, professional training, education programs from high school through graduate school, conferences and workshops, library services, and publications. The Institute's Board of Directors is appointed by the President of the United States and confirmed by the Senate.

Grasping the Nettle

This book is set in Adobe Caslon; the display typefaces are ITC Symbol BT and Futura. Marie Marr Jackson designed the book's cover; Mike Chase designed the interior. Helene Y. Redmond made up the pages. The text was copyedited by David Sweet and proofread by Karen Stough. The index was prepared by Sonsie Conroy. The book's editor was Nigel Quinney.